Becoming a Teacher Who Writes

Frameworks for Writing

Series Editor: Martha C. Pennington, Birkbeck University of London and University of Reading

The series offers books focused on writing and the teaching and learning of writing in educational and real-life contexts. The hallmark of the series is the application of approaches and techniques to writing and the teaching of writing that go beyond those of English literature to draw on and integrate writing with other disciplines, areas of knowledge, and contexts of everyday life. The series entertains proposals for textbooks as well as books for teachers, teacher educators, parents, and the general public. The list includes teacher reference books and student textbooks focused on innovative pedagogy aiming to prepare teachers and students for the challenges of the twenty-first century.

Published:

Academic Writing Step by Step: A Research-based Approach
Christopher N Candlin, Peter Crompton and Basil Hatim

Arting and Writing to Transform Education: An Integrated Approach for Culturally and Ecologically Responsive Pedagogy
Meleanna Aluli Meyer, Mikilani Hayes Maeshiro, and Anna Yoshie Sumida

Creativity and Discovery in the University Writing Class: A Teacher's Guide
Edited by Alice Chik, Tracey Costley, and Martha C. Pennington

Creativity and Writing Pedagogy: Linking Creative Writers, Researchers, and Teachers
Edited by Harriet Levin Millan and Martha C. Pennington

Digital L2 Writing Literacies: Directions for Classroom Practice
Ana Oskoz and Idoia Elola

English Composition Teacher's Guidebook: How to Survive (and Even Thrive) as an Adjunct or Part-time Instructor
Tom Mulder

Essential Knowledge and Skills for Essay Writing: A Practical Guide for ESL and EFL Undergraduates
Neil Evan Jon Anthony Bowen

Exploring College Writing: Reading, Writing, and Researching across the Curriculum
Dan Melzer

Investigative Creative Writing: Teaching and Practice
Mark Spitzer

Reflective Writing for Language Teachers
Thomas S. C. Farrell

Tend Your Garden: Nurturing Motivation in Young Adolescent Writers
Mary Anna Kruch

The "Backwards" Research Guide for Writers: Using Your Life for Reflection, Connection, and Inspiration
Sonya Huber

The College Writing Toolkit: Tried and Tested Ideas for Teaching College Writing
Edited by Martha C. Pennington and Pauline Burton

Understanding the Paragraph and Paragraphing
Iain McGee

Writing Better Essays: A Rhetorical Guide to Writing and Revision (Second International Edition)
David L. Rogers

Writing Poetry through the Eyes of Science: A Teacher's Guide to Scientific Literacy and Poetic Response
Nancy S. Gorrell, with Erin Colfax

Writing the Pandemic: An Instructor's Reflections on a New Era in Education
Tom Mulder

Becoming a Teacher Who Writes

Let Teaching Be Your Writing Muse

Nancy S. Gorrell

UNIVERSITY OF TORONTO PRESS
Toronto Buffalo London

Published by University of Toronto Press in 2024
Toronto Buffalo London
utorontopress.com
Printed in Canada

ISBN 978-1-4875-6656-2 (cloth)
ISBN 978-1-4875-6657-9 (paper)
ISBN 978-1-4875-6659-3 (EPUB)
ISBN 978-1-4875-6658-6 (PDF)

Publication cataloguing information available from Library and Archives Canada.

Cover credit: Illustration by Michael Kravit; William E. Sauro/The New York Times/Redux
Cover image: Nancy Gorrell in the creative writing classroom at Morristown High School.

We wish to acknowledge the land on which the University of Toronto Press operates. This land is the traditional territory of the Wendat, the Anishnaabeg, the Haudenosaunee, the Métis, and the Mississaugas of the Credit First Nation.

University of Toronto Press acknowledges the financial support of the Government of Canada, the Canada Council for the Arts, and the Ontario Arts Council, an agency of the Government of Ontario, for its publishing activities.

Canada Council for the Arts | Conseil des Arts du Canada

ONTARIO ARTS COUNCIL
CONSEIL DES ARTS DE L'ONTARIO
an Ontario government agency
un organisme du gouvernement de l'Ontario

Funded by the Government of Canada | Financé par le gouvernement du Canada | Canada

FSC www.fsc.org
MIX
Paper | Supporting responsible forestry
FSC® C016245

To my English and creative writing students
too numerous to name
you know who you are.
Together we walked the path of becoming.
Forever in my heart
never forgotten.
To you I owe the joy and the gift of gratitude.

And to my husband Joe,
light of my life.
For over a half century we walked together
the path of becoming.
To you I owe children
Sara Kate and Elizabeth Marie
and grandchildren Eli, Levi, and Ari
and extended family from countries and continents,
And most of all, eternal love.

Contents

Acknowledgements ix

Series Editor's Preface xvii

PRELIMINARIES 1

Prologue: The Grasshopper in the Window Or What Keeps Me Teaching 3

Foreword: Musings Upon a 10th Muse *Mark Gutkowski* 8

Introduction: Becoming a Teacher Who Writes 11

SECTION ONE: THE TEACHER SELF 29

1 Works in Progress 31

2 It Takes Creativity and Windows 47

3 It Takes Courage and Heart 69

4 Knowing Where You've Come From: Writing Memories 81

5 Discarding Baggage: Reframing Myths 99

6 Knowing Where You're Going: The American High School 119

7 Knowing Your Students: Times of Transition and Transformation 142

8 Knowing the Creatively "Gifted" Student 158

9 Balancing Freedom and Structure: The Paradox of Boundaries 177

10 Breaking Boundaries Within Your Discipline 195

SECTION TWO: THE WRITER SELF 215

11 Discovering the Creative Writer Within 217

12 Discovering the Poet Within 233

13 Discovering the Professional Writer Within 245

14 Discovering the Power of Audience 265

15 Discovering the Creative Process 280

SECTION THREE: THE TEACHER-WRITER SELF 305

16 Discovering the Teacher-Writer Within 307

17 Writing About Your Students and Your Discipline 328

SECTION FOUR: THE TEACHER-ARTIST SELF 345

18 Discovering the Teacher-Artist Within 347

Epilogue: "The Students in the Window" 383

Conclusion 397

Afterword: On Musings 411

Notes on Contributors 413

References 417

APPENDICES 431

Appendix A: Poetry Watch and Hawk Watch Resources (Chapter 2) 433

Appendix B: "The Weight of Nothing," by Amy Uyematsu (Chapters 3 and 8) 437

Author Index 440

Subject Index 444

Acknowledgments

I wish to thank all my colleagues, past and present, in Morristown High School's English Department who helped me walk my path of becoming a teacher who writes. Particular thanks are due to Jennifer Furphey, Joyce Levenson, and Mary Grow, whose stories entered my path and are recalled in this book, and to other colleagues whose enduring friendship and wisdom sustained years of collaboration – Vicky Willson, Marily O'Connor, and Karen Rush. Special thanks to my supervisor, Frank Leloia, who allowed me to let teaching be my muse.

I wish to thank Erin Colfax, my colleague, science partner in Morristown High School's Science Academy, and kindred spirit. Together we walked the path of becoming teachers who write science poetry. Together we wrote a book on science poetry (*Writing Poetry Through the Eyes of Science: A Teacher's Guide to Scientific Literacy and Poetic Response*, Equinox, 2012). Together we will continue to work to influence a new generation of teachers and students to see poetry through the eyes of science.

I also wish to thank Erin Colfax for introducing me to Jayne Mackta, founder of Curious Young Writers (cYw) and Curious Science Writers (cSw). Thank you, Jayne, for your extensive interview outlining the long history and evolution of the initiative from 2010 to the present day. And thank you, Jayne and Erin, for your long involvement with the only independent program in the United States addressing the critical need of combating scientific illiteracy on the high school level. I am most grateful to both of you for contributing your knowledge and wisdom to this book.

I wish to thank Jennifer Furphey, my English Department colleague at Morristown High School, for teaching a creative writing exercise of mine to her creative writing classes during the pandemic. I want to thank each of the students who participated in the "Inside Looking Out/Outside Looking In" exercise producing the pandemic poems in the Epilogue titled "The Students in the Window": Colleen Lavin, Kasey Lynch, Alexandra Lysiak, Jocelyn Andrade Mancia, Haven McGuinn, Amarie Orbeta, Ella Pfahler, Shane Quinn, Jordan Robinson, Shivani Vel, and Mary Wisloff. I am forever grateful to Jennifer Furphey for her enthusiastic support and partnership.

I wish to thank Mark Gutkowski, colleague and friend, for contributing the Forward to this book and his boundless enthusiasm for teaching, learning, and innovative education. Mark, you continue to be an inspiration to the profession and to me personally. I was so fortunate to teach with you for over a decade. Avenues is equally fortunate to have your leadership now.

I wish to thank Steven N. Handel, my science mentor and advisor, neighbor, and lifelong friend, for contributing to this book not only his scientific wisdom, but also his creative, artful, and personal writing – especially as editor of *Ecological Restoration*, with his unforgettable "A Seed Op-Ed" published in that journal (University of Wisconsin Press, 2011), and his childhood memories, "Beginning at the End," published in *The Sound of the Woodpecker Bill: New York City* (Humboldt Books, 2019). Your artful writing touched my heart.

I wish to thank Barbara Nadolny, biology teacher at Morristown High School, whose Hawk Watching Project launched my creative writing "Poetry Watch" lesson. The "Hawk Watch" project inspired generations of students to go outside and write on location. Barbara contributed her hawk watching pedagogy to this book.

I wish to thank Arthur J. Stewart, scientist, science educator, and science poet, who has become a mentor, advisor, and dear friend to me – all through email correspondence. Our mutual love of teaching, science, the earth and its waters, and poetry made us a likely match, and I will forever treasure his generosity in sharing the wealth of his poetry, articles, and his co-edited science education textbook, *Converting STEM into STEAM Programs* (Springer, 2019). You have my utmost gratitude for your personal and professional wisdom and contributions to this book.

I wish to thank Amy Uyematsu, math teacher and lifelong poet for contributing her vast knowledge of teaching, mathematics, Asian-American identity, Zen mastery, and math poetry to this book. Ever since we became acquainted through email correspondence in 2012, we have become coast to coast friends. I am forever grateful for Amy's wisdom, the complexity and enlightenment of her poetry, and her enduring friendship. I am eternally grateful for all of the poems, commentary, and email correspondences Amy contributed to this book. Amy Uyematsu's poetry is the light this world needs.

I wish to thank Stefanie DeFronzo (Class of 2020), student contributor, who agreed as a senior biochemistry and molecular biology major at Drew University to contribute writing exercises to this book. Our writing sessions together became a pure pleasure, as Stefanie enjoyed the "escape" from the lab into creative writing and I enjoyed teaching creative writing to an eager science student. Thank you, Stefanie, for all your artful contributions.

I wish to thank Ben Nelms and Leila Christenbury, past editors of *English Journal*, for mentoring my professional writing in my formative years. I would also like to thank Karin Dahl for engaging me to write "A Teacher's Story of Renewal" for *Teacher as Writer: Entering the Professional Conversation* (National Council of Teachers of English, 1992). Those experiences confirmed to me I was a writer. I am forever grateful.

Thanks to both the *English Journal* and the National Council of Teachers of English for giving permission for me to reprint in this book work of mine which they first published.

I also wish to thank Equinox Publishing Ltd, for granting permission to reprint student science poetry from my first book, *Writing Poetry through the Eyes of Science: Scientific Literacy and Poetic Response* (2012), co-authored with my science partner, Erin Colfax.

Lastly, I wish to thank my editor, advisor, and mentor Martha C. Pennington for her enduring faith in me as an author, her patience to allow me to let this book unfold over an inordinate period of time, and her encouragement to allow me to update the book and see it through the pandemic and beyond. This has been an uncertain and difficult time for all. I thank Martha for her meticulous editing, her thoughtful comments, her unbounding enthusiasm, and her support for creativity in all its forms.

In addition, permission to reprint the following works is gratefully acknowledged:

Brookman Harris, Randi (1997) "Muse Soup." *Tricorn Literary Magazine*, 32: 9. Morristown, NJ: Morristown High School. Reprinted by permission of Randi Brookman Harris.

Busch, Debbie (1990) "Christmas (Portland Oregon, 1969)." Qtd in Gorrell, Nancy (1990) Taking off the mask: Teaching the recurring image in poetry writing. *English Journal*, 79 (7): 29. Reprinted by permission from *English Journal*.

Davis, Alex (2012) "The Second Law of Thermodynamics." Qtd in Gorrell Nancy S. with Erin Colfax *Writing Poetry through the Eyes of Science: Scientific Literacy and Poetic Response*, 145. Sheffield, UK and Oakville, CT: Equinox Ltd. Reprinted by permission from Equinox Publishing Ltd.

DeFronzo, Stefanie (2021) "Annemarie Hohensee." First published in this volume by permission from Stefanie DeFronzo.

Fortier, Nicole (2004) "The Morristown Cycle." *Tricorn Literary Magazine*, 39: 8. Morristown, NJ: Morristown High School.

Gorman, Sheila (1990) "Untitled." Qtd in Gorrell, Nancy (1990) Taking off the mask: Teaching the recurring image in poetry writing. *English Journal*, 79 (7): 29. Reprinted by permission from *English Journal*.

Gorrell, Nancy (1989) "Kindergarten Creation." *The Rockford Review*, 8: 62. Rockford, IL: Rockford Writers' Guild. Reprinted by permission from *The Rockford Review*.

Gorrell, Nancy (1989) Let found poetry help your students find poetry. *English Journal*, 78 (2): 30–34. Reprinted by permission from *English Journal*.

Gorrell, Nancy (1990) "Blueberry Pie." *English Journal*, 79 (8): 88. Reprinted by permission from *English Journal*.

Gorrell, Nancy (1990) Taking off the mask: Teaching the recurring image in poetry writing. *English Journal*, 79 (7): 27–29. Reprinted by permission from *English Journal*.

Gorrell, Nancy (1992) A teacher's story of renewal. In Dahl, Karin (ed.) *Teacher as Writer: Entering the Professional Conversation*, 19–33. Urbana, IL: National Council of Teachers of English. Reprinted by permission from National Council of Teachers of English.

Gorrell, Nancy (1992) "Dear Dolphin." In Dunning, Stephen and Stafford, William (eds.) *Getting the Knack: 20 Poetry Writing Exercises*, 32. Urbana, IL: National Council of Teachers of English. Reprinted by permission from National Council of Teachers of English.

Gorrell, Nancy (1992) "To See." In Dunning, Stephen and Stafford, William (eds.) *Getting the Knack: 20 Poetry Writing Exercises*, 130. Urbana, IL: National Council of Teachers of English. Reprinted by permission from National Council of Teachers of English.

Gorrell, Nancy (1993) Publishing the poetry chapbook: Defining a public self. *English Journal*, 82 (2): 42–46. Reprinted by permission from *English Journal*.

Gorrell, Nancy (1993) "Grandma Came Down." *Footwork: Paterson Literary Review*, 23: 114. Paterson, NJ: Passaic County Community College. Reprinted by permission from Nancy S. Gorrell.

Gorrell, Nancy (1993) "The River." *Footwork: Paterson Literary Review*, 23: 115. Paterson, NJ: Passaic County Community College. Reprinted by permission from Nancy S. Gorrell.

Gorrell, Nancy (1997) One person's opinion: What keeps me teaching. *English Journal*, 86 (5): 18–19. Reprinted with modifications by permission from *English Journal*.

Gorrell, Nancy (1997) "Sometimes Poems Come." One person's opinion: What keeps me teaching. *English Journal*, 86 (5): 18–19. Reprinted by permission from *English Journal*.

Gorrell, Nancy (2000) Teaching empathy through ecphrastic poetry: Entering a curriculum of peace. *English Journal*, 89 (5): 32–41. Reprinted by permission from *English Journal*.

Handel, Steven N. (2011) A seed op-ed. *Ecological Restoration*, 29 (4): 320–321. Copyright 2011 by the Board of Regents of the University of Wisconsin system. Reprinted by permission from the University of Wisconsin Press.

Handel, Steven N. (2019) Birnam Woods, moving closer, shadows our work. *Ecological Restoration*, 37 (1): 1–2. Copyright 2019 by the Board of Regents of the University of Wisconsin system. Reprinted by permission from the University of Wisconsin Press.

Handel, Steven N. (2019) Beginning at the end. In Rovaldi, Antonio and Benedetto, Francesca *The Sound of the Woodpecker Bill: New York City*, 522–527. Milan: Humboldt Books. Reprinted by permission from Humboldt Books.

Kim, Michelle (2004) Idiocy? What's love got to do with it. *Tricorn Literary Magazine*, 39: 26. Morristown, NJ: Morristown Public High School.

Kingsporn, Geoff. "Veteran." Qtd in Gorrell, Nancy (1989) Let found poetry help your students find poetry. *English Journal*, 78 (2): 34. Reprinted by permission from *English Journal*.

Pitt, David (2012a) "O Asymptote." Qtd in Gorrell, Nancy S. with Eric Colfax *Writing Poetry through the Eyes of Science: Scientific Literacy and Poetic Response*, 297. Sheffield, UK and Oakville, CT: Equinox Ltd. Reprinted by permission from Equinox Publishing Ltd.

Pitt, David (2012b) "Redwood." Qtd in Gorrell, Nancy S. with Eric Colfax *Writing Poetry through the Eyes of Science: Scientific Literacy and Poetic Response*, 273. Sheffield, UK and Oakville, CT: Equinox Ltd. Reprinted by permission from Equinox Publishing Ltd.

Rosenberg, Elise (1997) "Poetry on a Plane." *Tricorn Literary Magazine*, 32: 8–9. Morristown, NJ: Morristown High School.

Rothman, Marni (1990) "30 Second Memory." Qtd in Gorrell, Nancy (1990) Taking off the mask: Teaching the recurring image in poetry writing.

English Journal, 79 (7): 29. Reprinted by permission from *English Journal*.

Schwartz, Anne (2012) "Us." Qtd in Gorrell Nancy S. with Erin Colfax *Writing Poetry through the Eyes of Science: Scientific Literacy and Poetic Response*, 385. Sheffield, UK and Oakville, CT: Reprinted by permission from Equinox Publishing Ltd.

Stewart, Arthur J. (1999) "Learning": On the need for poetry by scientists. *Bulletin of the Ecological Society of America*, 80 (2): 133. Reprinted by permission from Arthur J. Stewart.

Stewart, Arthur J. (2003) "Weavers Needle." *Rough Ascensions and Other Poems of Science*, 10. Knoxville, TN: Celtic Cat. Reprinted by permission from Arthur J. Stewart.

Stewart, Arthur J (2005) "Rat Dissection." *Bushido: The Virtues of Rei and Makoto*, 80. Knoxville, TN: Celtic Cat Publishing. Reprinted by permission from Arthur J. Stewart.

Stewart, Arthur J. (2010) "Getting it Right." *Circle, Turtle, Ashes*, 91. Knoxville, TN: Celtic Cat Publishing. Reprinted by permission from Arthur J. Stewart.

Stewart, Arthur J. (2010) "Ladoga Lake and Nyos." *Circle, Turtle, Ashes*, 39–41. Knoxville, TN: Celtic Cat Publishing. Reprinted by permission from Arthur J. Stewart.

Stewart, Arthur J. (2010) "Limnology Quiz." *Circle, Turtle, Ashes*, 37. Knoxville, TN: Celtic Cat Publishing. Reprinted by permission from Arthur J. Stewart.

Stewart, Arthur J. (2010) "Professor Thermocline." *Circle, Turtle, Ashes*, 36. Knoxville, TN: Celtic Cat Publishing. Reprinted by permission from Arthur J. Stewart.

Stewart, Arthur J. (2017) "Edges." *Elements of Chance*, 51. Knoxville, TN: Celtic Cat Publishing. Reprinted by permission from Arthur J. Stewart.

Stewart, Arthur J. (2021) "Pathway." *The Hallelujah Series and Other Poems*, 3. Nashville, TN: Periploi Press. Reprinted by permission from Arthur J. Stewart.

Uyematsu, Amy (1998) "Florentino Diaz." *Nights of Fire, Nights of Rain*, 6. Brownsville, OR: Story Line Press. Reprinted by permission from Amy Uyematsu.

Uyematsu, Amy (2005) "Desert Camouflage." *Stone, Bow, Prayer*, 50. Port Townsend, WA: Copper Canyon Press. Reprinted by permission from Amy Uyematsu.

Uyematsu, Amy (2005) "Simple Division." *Stone, Bow, Prayer*, 49. Port Townsend, WA: Copper Canyon Press. Reprinted by permission from Amy Uyematsu.

Uyematsu, Amy (2005) "The Invention of Mathematics." *Stone, Bow, Prayer*, 30–33. Port Townsend, WA: Copper Canyon Press. Reprinted by permission from Amy Uyematsu.

Uyematsu, Amy (2005) "The Weight of Nothing." *Stone, Bow, Prayer*, 72–74. Port Townsend, WA: Copper Canyon Press. Reprinted by permission from Amy Uyematsu.

Uyematsu, Amy (2005) "When Geometry Gets Mixed Up with God and the Alphabet." *Stone, Bow, Prayer*, 27–29. Port Townsend, WA: Copper Canyon Press. Reprinted by permission from Amy Uyematsu.

Uyematsu, Amy (2016) "A Handful of Knowing." *Basic Vocabulary*, 65–66. Pasadena, CA: Red Hen Press. Reprinted by permission from Amy Uyematsu.

Uyematsu, Amy (2016) "Dipping into Infinity." *Basic Vocabulary*, 90–92. Pasadena, CA: Red Hen Press. Reprinted by permission from Amy Uyematsu.

Uyematsu, Amy (2016) "Juan's Numbers." *Basic Vocabulary*, 32–33. Pasadena, CA: Red Hen Press. Reprinted by permission from Amy Uyematsu.

Uyematsu, Amy (2016) "On Poets." *Basic Vocabulary*, 76. Pasadena, CA: Red Hen Press. Reprinted by permission from Amy Uyematsu.

Uyematsu, Amy (2016) "This Thing Called Infinity." *Basic Vocabulary*, 102. Pasadena, CA: Red Hen Press. Reprinted by permission from Amy Uyematsu.

—Nancy S. Gorrell
Bridgewater, New Jersey
April 2024

Series Editor's Preface

In this eminently readable and useful volume, Nancy Gorrell leads educators into her own decades-long journey of becoming a teacher who writes and who nurtures students and colleagues as writers and co-learners. The second of Gorrell's teacher-oriented books in the Frameworks for Writing series, *Becoming a Teacher Who Writes: Let Teaching Be Your Writing Muse* richly documents the chronology of that journey, from novice English teacher to writer, published author, and teacher mentor, showing teachers of English and other subjects how they can follow a similar path and laying out the value and benefits of doing so.

The chronology moves through the author's evolution as a creative writer, a teacher-writer, and then a teacher-artist, all the while writing and learning with her students in English classes and reaching out to students and teachers across the curriculum. The book is intended to help teachers develop competence and confidence in themselves as writers as they also help to develop that same competence and confidence in their students. It is based on the propositions that all people are innately creative, that teaching and learning are creative acts of becoming through self-learning and self-discovery, and that creativity and literacy are fundamental to all disciplines.

Becoming a Teacher Who Writes serves as both an inspirational account of Gorrell's personal story of becoming and as a guidebook for teachers to reflect on and create their own analogous story of becoming. Chapters describe the stages in Gorrell's evolution and encourage teachers to learn from her example in their own development as teachers and writers. Each chapter includes an illustrative teaching story or poem and the author's reflections on her evolving journey, along with model student writing intended to both instruct and inspire readers and their students in their own writing. It also contains reflective exercises for teachers to work through and teaching activities that they can use in their classes. An additional feature of the book is its attention to writing across the curriculum and its inclusion of interdisciplinary models and applications. The book incorporates the work of the author as well as that of her many collaborators, including a number of interdisciplinary contributors and former students.

I am delighted to include this outstanding teacher reference book in my Frameworks for Writing series, and I highly recommend it to all teachers of English as well as to teachers in other subjects who wish to gain more knowledge about how they can incorporate writing in their classes. I can also recommend it as an inspirational read for anyone about the influential life and career of an enthusiastic and talented English teacher and creative writer.

—Martha C. Pennington
Series Editor, Frameworks for Writing

PRELIMINARIES

Prologue

The Grasshopper in the Window Or What Keeps Me Teaching

In my 25th year of teaching, magic came into the classroom in the form of a grasshopper. It was early September, the seventh period of the day. The students were fresh with the sense of wonder the beginning of a new year brings; the day was warm and sunny, the air a balmy velvet still reminiscent of summer, and the window was open. I was standing in front of a creative writing elective class, introducing an opening writing lesson on observation.

"How do writers get ideas for writing?" I asked, and just then I noticed a grasshopper resting on the floor near my foot. Without saying a word, I bent over and captured the magnificent creature in my two hands.

"By observing the world around them," I continued, rising with the grasshopper springing against my tightly clenched palms. I waited, waited for the darkness within my hands to quiet the grasshopper's confusion. At that moment, few students seem to notice. Then, I extended my arms for all to see that I was grasping something. Next, I slowly opened my hands, and, as if on cue, there rested the grasshopper, poised regally on my outstretched palm.

I do not know what possessed me, but I heard myself say, "How far do you think he will jump?" Suddenly, as if on command, he did just that, springing from one student's shoulder to another student's desk, and then finally, landing on the floor. Evan, without saying a word, picked up the grasshopper and placed him gently on the window sill. The grasshopper stood there, gazing at us with an indescribable air of composure, and for one moment, nothing breathed in that classroom, not even the wind. Then the breeze beckoned, and the grasshopper was gone, almost as quickly as he came.

My students, surprised and amused, looked to me to continue the "lesson." I found myself handing Jim a dictionary and asking him to look up *grasshopper*. As he read to the class the scientific definition, I recalled Paul Fleischman's poem for two voices, "Grasshoppers" and wordlessly reached for the book, *Joyful Noise* (Fleischman, 1988), in my resource cabinet.

"Kate," I said, motioning for her to join me in front of the room, "let's look at grasshoppers another way." As we read together Fleischman's poem, "Grasshoppers," our two voices alternating, blending, and bouncing to the spirit of the word, the bell rang. Brandyn came over to me as the class was exiting, and with a look of amazement said, "Mrs. Gorrell, how did you do that?"

"Why Brandyn, whatever do you mean?" I replied.

"How did you make the grasshopper come?" he asked with all sincerity.

"I didn't make the grasshopper come," I said, quite taken by surprise.

"But, the poem?" he mused, "You read the poem."

The faith our students place in our power to control what happens within those four sacred walls never ceases to amaze and inspire me. Although Brandyn was seventeen years of age, he still was able to see the world with childlike awe. I took another leap of faith and said to him, as he exited the room, "Why Brandyn, don't you know? That's how poems come!"

That evening, I reveled in the joy of teaching, and in particular, the joy of teaching a spontaneous lesson. What more could I offer my students about the powers of observation than that magic moment, when all eyes were fixed in unison on one small creature and not a "creature stirred!" Not all classes can be a sheer joy. But when that magic happens, it should be recognized and savored.

That evening, I wrote the following poem, dedicated to my creative writing class.

Sometimes Poems Come
by Nancy Gorrell

sometimes poems come
like the grasshopper
poised on the floor
in front of the class
that Friday afternoon,
7th period. I cupped
the pulse of life in my hands
felt the skip-hop-pop
rub heavy against the skin
of darkness, on again, off again
the class hushed as I said,
"let's see how far he will jump,"
and I opened my hand
so all could see him
still, in a sea of light.
he must have wondered
how he got there,
hot with the last rays
of summer sun and then,
he skip-hop-popped
to Scott-Jim-Evan,
landing in the rocky
haven of crumpled paper
on the hard floor below
while the class flapped,
fluttered and stuttered,
he found himself once more
at the open window sill
and all was still, if only
for the moment, and then
he was gone
the lesson swooned.

Jim read from the dictionary
"what is a grasshopper?"
and I unearthed a poem,
"grasshoppers" from the cabinet
of my heart and together,
Kate and I skip-hop-popped
through a choral reading
of the grassy, hopper terrain—
and the bell rang, when a student
asked "how did you do that?"

Sometimes poems come
that way, like the grasshopper.

(Gorrell, 1997b)

The following day, as I read the poem to my students, I knew they had grasped the "lesson." All that I hoped to accomplish in those early days of creative writing flew into my classroom on the wings of a grasshopper. Ever since, I have been looking, waiting, and hoping for other teachable moments, and of course, they appeared throughout the year, though I had not always in the past been so aware of their presence and power.

What keeps me teaching after 25 years? Students like Brandyn, Kate, and Evan, and most certainly, open windows.

Postscript

The above anecdote, "The Grasshopper in the Window or What Keeps Me Teaching," a slightly revised version of "One Person's Opinion: What Keeps Me Teaching," originally published in *English Journal* (Gorrell, 1997a), shows us the faith that our students place in us as teachers. They believe we can teach; we have to believe they can write. Much of what has happened in our high schools in the last decades impedes, stifles, and sometimes destroys this faith. You teachers know what I mean; you hear it at department meetings and in public forums: "They can't write; look at these test scores."

Why This Book?

This book hopes to restore teachers' faith in students' creativity and ability to voice. But this is not possible unless teachers discover and reclaim the creativity and voice within themselves. For teachers who are reading my book, this can happen if you *let teaching be your writing muse.* It happened to me, and it can happen to you. Open the windows of your classroom, literally and figuratively, and begin *becoming* a *teacher who writes*.

Prologue References

Fleischman, Paul (1988) *Joyful Noise*. New York, NY: Harper & Row.

Gorrell, Nancy (1997a) One person's opinion: What keeps me teaching. *English Journal*, 86 (5): 18–19. https://doi.org/10.2307/820437

Gorrell, Nancy (1997b) "Sometimes Poems Come." One person's opinion: What keeps me teaching. *English Journal*, 86 (5): 18–19. https://doi.org/10.2307/820437

Foreword

Musings Upon a 10th Muse

Mark Gutkowski, Global Academic Dean, Avenues: The World School

The Muses

While the number and the functions of the Muses may have varied over time, it is the poet Hesiod (c. 700 BCE) in his *Theogeny* who will create the tradition that fixes their number at nine. They are goddesses in the strictest sense, the daughters of Zeus and Mnemosyne, to be revered and worshipped for the artistic gifts and feats of memory that they bestow upon humans. Poets and writers across millennia will begin their works with the utterances of their names: *Calliope*, *Clio*, *Erato*, *Euterpe*, *Melpomene*, *Polyhymnia*, *Terpsichore*, *Thalia, and Urania.*

Muse, *Mouseion*, Museum

In this day and age, the Muses' names mean little to us. However, it is important to remember that they were designated goddesses by the ancient Greeks and, as such, were worthy of formal worship. Devotees even built temples for them, called *mouseion,* across the ancient world. Beyond their function as a place of worship for a particular Muse, these *mouseion* – as with most temples at that time – acted as storehouses for votive offerings and included valuable objects, which would have been dedicated to that specific goddess. Imagine some of these dedicated objects on display inside the temple and be tempted by an ancient precursor to our modern museums. Muse – *mouseion* – museum. Yet, these votive offerings would not have been open to public view. In fact, devotees would have been barred entry to the temple by priests and guards in order to keep those objects safe. This means that any formal acts of worship by commoners would have taken place *outside* of the temple, where an altar would have been located for these public ceremonies.

Museum of Alexandria: A Place of Teaching and Learning

But something radical happens in Alexandria during the 3rd century BCE, something so miraculous that it will forever change how the world interprets and worships the Muses: Ptolemy I Soter creates that ancient wonder of the world, the Museum of Alexandria, commonly known as the *Library of Alexandria*. This Museum will remain a religious center with a head priest leading the management of the institution, as we learn from Strabo's *Geography* (17.I.8). So it is a temple of sorts, but the function of this *mouseion* has shifted to a place of *learning*, which includes a world-famous library with a wondrous collection of scrolls, as well as a research institution for teaching and learning. Those little *mouseion* have been transformed into a unique place in the world that invites visitors *within* its walls, where the goddesses are worshipped through the activity of learning. The power that the Museum of Alexandria will hold over the world is unquestionable, and its very existence will influence the form of universities and places of learning to our current day.

The 10th Muse: Teaching and Learning

Although the museum of Alexandria is widely accepted as a *mouseion* for all nine Muses, much as the Roman Pantheon was a catch-all temple for the major gods of the ancient Italians, we miss something vital about the human experience if we neglect to acknowledge the common thread that unites the Muses and their disparate functions. We might look to Mnemosyne, the goddess of memory and matriarch of the Muses, as that connecting thread. But her function as a goddess of remembering alone doesn't adequately capture the magnificence of the endeavors that were taking place in the Library of Alexandria. Memory only gets us so far.

When Nancy Gorrell posits the existence of a tenth muse, one of teaching and learning that inspires us to consider both our practice and also our classrooms as worthy of any epic, comedy, or history ever written, her argument has considerable leverage. In briefly examining this transformation of the *mouseion* from a religious center to a somewhat more secular place of learning, we must remember that *what* was happening in those meeting halls and lecture rooms at the Museum of Alexandria was, in some tangible way, under the purview of a muse.

We might ask why the ancients took this muse for granted, having never given her a name or an identity. Perhaps her presence was so obvious to them that they required no name for her, or perhaps hers was the shared *heart of the muses* themselves, the singular beat of their disparate passions: *Learning*.

Those of us who have spent our careers in education can tell you that the classroom is a world unto itself, a world of endless human potential and inspiration, of accidents and occasions. Truly, these are spaces that require contemplation and action.

Your muse exists. Now, it is time for you to stop being negligent of your duties: To formally establish a connection with this goddess, to celebrate the small moments of humanity that exist in the classroom, to begin to recognize – in a deeper way – the spiritual connection between the practice of teaching and of learning, to capture those moments in words and to share them with the world. So open your laptops, teachers, and offer your words. Your muse has been patient, but the time has come to revere her power.

Introduction

Becoming a Teacher Who Writes

TO TEACH IS TO LEARN

A Teaching Poem Meant for Sharing
by Lone Wolf

to teach is to learn
to learn is to be
to be is to sing the earth's song
and walk in the path
to become whole people
let us touch, let us listen
let us be a gift to the other
let our gifts and our spirits ride
in our hearts and minds
and give us the strength
to complete the great circle
do not be afraid to be
differences teach
do not be afraid to sing
your heart's song
to the earth with honor and love
walk gently
sing loudly
teach

(Lone Wolf, 1976)

The Story Behind the Poem

I first heard a reading of "to teach is to learn" in 1991 by Lynn Manning at a convocation of New Jersey Teachers of the Year. When I requested a copy, Lynn graciously shared with me not only the poem, but the story behind it. Her grandfather, an Apache shaman, wrote the untitled, unsigned, and unpublished poem as a gift for her. Since he had "gone to the mountain," she told me that using his name would be disrespectful. Therefore, she signed the poem, Lone Wolf (1976). The poem she said is "meant for sharing."[1]

By Way of a Definition: On Becoming

I never knew how to write. Even after completing a graduate degree and a Master's thesis, I never felt I could write, let alone teach others to write. Creative? Not me. A writer? Unthinkable. And yet, searching for that first job out of graduate school, I found myself teaching English to middle school students at a small private day school in Head of the Harbor, New York. What happened next serves as the subject of this book: the muse of teaching transformed me from teacher, to writer, to teacher-writer, and ultimately, to teacher-artist. For me there was a paradigm shift from being a teacher of writing to becoming a teacher-writer and then a teacher-artist. That shift involved taking on the identity of writer as a lifelong process, and it involved forging a path of becoming. Whether you teach writing or any other subject, you can be transformed by the process of becoming a teacher who writes.

"To teach is to learn, to learn is to be." "To be…" you couldn't find a more complex or profound two-letter word in the English language.

This book is grounded in the belief that we are all creative and we are all becoming, students and teachers alike. In this regard, I view my students' writings as *works in progress*. I view my own writings as works in progress. What's more, I view my students and myself as works in progress, as we learn together to "walk in the path" of becoming teachers and learners who write.

This Book is for All Teachers

If you are reading this book, you are most likely a teacher in a secondary school, perhaps, like me, an English or creative writing teacher. But you may also be a teacher in a middle school teaching language arts, or a teacher in college teaching composition or basic writing. As a reader of this book, you have an interest in writing and perhaps want to develop yourself more as a teacher who writes. You know that writing is integral to all disciplines for expressing what one knows, for communicating formal knowledge, and for facilitating critical, analytic, reflective, and creative thinking. You may not know how to integrate writing practice into your own teaching, but you value writing and want to use it more in your subject or discipline. You may have been told that every teacher needs to be a writer, or every teacher should be a writing teacher because every discipline relies on reading and writing literacy, but you have not yet adopted the identity of writer yourself. You know you are a teacher, but you are not as certain about being a writer or teaching writing.

If you value writing personally for its creative and expressive skills, this book will guide you. If you value writing professionally, this book will guide you to enter the discourse of your discipline. Most importantly, if you value teaching and feel excited at the thought of bridging bridges, this book will guide you to become a teacher-artist, seizing the teachable moment, teaching the spontaneous lesson, and building bridges between the arts and sciences. How is this possible?

This Book Resolves the Obstacles of Time, Self-Doubt, and Baggage

If you are wondering how to integrate writing into your personal and professional teaching life, this book can serve as your guide.

For it addresses the obstacles preventing teachers from walking the path of their own becoming: *time*, *self-doubt*, and *baggage*. In regard to *time,* this book says let teaching be your writing muse. You can then use some of your teaching time to write with your students, for your students, and to your students in the writing component of your classes, workshops, and laboratories as well as outside doing fieldwork. You can write models of instruction for your students based on your discipline and lessons while you teach them to write. In regard to *self-doubt*, this book encourages you to believe that as a teacher and a human being you are innately creative and are a work in progress. In order to start the process of becoming a writer, all you have to do is agree to let teaching be your writing muse. In doing so, ideas for writing and reflections in the form of poems, stories, and professional writing can blossom from the rich soil of your daily teaching life. In regard to *baggage* that you may be carrying, knowingly or unknowingly, this book says it is time to face that baggage, recognize it, and discard it. In discarding baggage you have been carrying, you free yourself to touch the joy that is the heart and art of your teaching and your discipline.

But where do you begin? Wherever you are – that place, that moment, that classroom, that workshop, that laboratory, or the field outside – becomes your entry point. *And you begin right now*. For in reading this book and following its guidance, you will be teaching yourself and teaching your students as you create your own path and their individual paths of becoming. If you are a veteran teacher, a newcomer beginning your career, or a teacher returning to post-pandemic teaching, this book is for you. It will guide you in becoming a teacher who writes while you teach your students to write in English class or in any other subject or discipline.

This Book is for All Teachers Who Never Believed They Could Write

This book is designed especially for teachers who are interested in writing but have never believed they could write, and therefore feel tentative about addressing writing within their discipline. Perhaps you have come to the profession with no formal training or personal experience in the art and craft of writing. Perhaps you are an English teacher who sees yourself primarily as a teacher of literature, not composition or creative writing. Perhaps you have only experienced academic writing and formula-driven writing instruction. Perhaps you love literature so much you cannot imagine writing your own poems or stories. Perhaps you are a teacher whose education reflects the division of the arts and sciences in the academy, and as a result, you never had the chance to discover the writer in you. Perhaps you question your own creativity. Whatever your starting point, this book says to you, *trust the process*. It will work, if only you let teaching be your writing muse. How do I know? Because when I began teaching, I never believed I could write either.

My Personal Path

I could not have come to the teaching profession at a more exciting time; nor could I have come more ill-prepared, with no education courses, no teaching experience, and no certification – not required for teaching in private or independent schools. The year was 1970. It was the day and age of the "student-centered classroom" – interactive lessons, hands-on activities, and process writing were the catch words and practices of the day. While process writing projects blossomed coast to coast to teach English teachers how to teach writing, I found myself facing middle school students without a single notion of how to teach English, let alone how to teach writing. So I did what all untrained teachers do: I went to my colleagues. Carl, the resident English teacher at Harbor Country Day School, showed me his plan book. It had lessons written down from September through June. "This is what we do," he said. It took all of five minutes for him to tell me: "Vocab. on Monday, grammar on Tuesday, and Friday, the weekly comp." After seeing Carl's plan book, I felt desperate.

I called up an English graduate student I knew and said, "Help! How do I teach English?" I'll never forget her response because to this day, I know it was her words that guided me on my path. She said, "Oh, you're teaching English? Well then, you're really going to have to teach them to write." She gave me the names of pioneers in the field: James Moffett, Ken Macrorie, Peter Elbow, and Kenneth Koch. So I read; I read about teaching writing, and then I practiced teaching writing to my students. "To teach is to learn…, to learn is to be…." The result? I fell in love with teaching writing to middle school students, especially creative writing, and I soon became my own student. I had found my path.

In the two years I taught English at Harbor Country Day School, I came to the realizations I would carry with me for the rest of my life. These realizations form the core beliefs of this book.

Core Beliefs of This Book

- *We are all innately creative, possessing limitless gifts of creative potential.*
- *The act of becoming is a creative act of self-learning and self-discovery.*
- *Teaching writing at its heart is a creative, joyful act of becoming.*
- *Nothing is more exciting than creating with a group of students who are becoming while you are becoming.*
- *Writing is best taught in a workshop*[2] *where students and teachers alike are co-learners, forming a community of writers and learners.*
- *Literature is best taught in a community of readers practiced in responding to literature in kind, that is, using the literature read as models for creative and imaginative response.*
- *Creativity and literacy are fundamental to all disciplines.*
- *Creativity and literacy build bridges uniting teachers and disciplines.*
- *Creative writing is an interdisciplinary tool for writing across the curriculum.*

Two years later, I walked into the halls of my alma mater, Morristown High School, a large, diverse public school in Morristown, New Jersey. With little to guide me but my newfound love of teaching writing, I began walking the path of my *becoming a teacher who writes while teaching my students to write*. I was thus leading them down the same path I was going along myself. At the time, I still had never written a poem, story, article, speech, or essay for myself, my students, or the profession. And yet, I, like so many other literature teachers, was faced with the daunting task of teaching writing. Gradually, I started to write with my students, for my students, and to my students.

In 1974, I wrote the curriculum for the first Creative Writing I and II elective program at Morristown High. I would teach that elective program for the next three decades along with sections of Honors English III and composition electives. I became the literary magazine advisor, encouraging all students in the high school to submit their writings for publication. I organized poetry readings and festivals to encourage students to act like professional writers, sharing their work with various audiences, entering writing contests, and seeking publication.

After a decade of teaching writing, my students began to question me: "Ms. Gorrell, why haven't you published any writing?" They began to urge me to submit my poems and stories to literary reviews and journals. In 1987, at the suggestion of a colleague, I began to write about my teaching and my students. Two years later, my first professional publication in the *English Journal* finally confirmed for me that I was a writer. At the same time, my first poem, "Kindergarten Creation," was published in *The Rockford Review*. It was not until I published the poem that I felt I could take on the identity of writer.

What I Learned: Teaching is My Muse

Walking the path for over three decades of teaching writing, I learned that teaching is my muse. What that means is that I see teaching not only as a method for my students and classroom, but as a way of knowing the world and of defining and expressing my evolving, inner self. For me, teaching is my life. It's the means for weaving the connections of my selfhood – the teacher in me, the writer in me, the teacher-writer in me, and ultimately, the teacher-artist in me.

WHY THIS BOOK?

The question arises: Why is my story or any story of a high school English teacher becoming a writer worthy of attention? The answer has much to do with what makes a creative teacher and what keeps us teaching, and that I believe is joy – joy as the creative expression of one's inner being. If you have never written personally for yourself, or creatively for your students, or professionally for your colleagues, the aim of this book is to guide you in the process of *becoming a teacher who writes*. If you have written poems, stories, and essays for yourself, but never for your students, the aim of this book is to inspire you to begin modeling and sharing that writing with your students. If you are already a teacher who writes, the aim of this book is to illustrate for you how to make your teaching life and your writing life one joyful act. Ultimately, the aim of this book is to encourage you to discover the heart and art of your teaching, your subject, and your profession. (You may wish to preview Chapter 16 on the joy of teaching.)

The Dilemma English Teachers Face

English teachers continue to face an unresolved dilemma. That dilemma stems from the well-accepted premise that teachers of English should be teachers of writing, and that all teachers of writing should be writers themselves. Although most would agree with these premises, far too few high school English teachers see themselves as writers. The large majority see themselves primarily as teachers of literature and secondarily as teachers of the academic essay written in response to that literature. This should come as no surprise since high school teachers are products of the academy that has historically privileged the teaching of literature over the teaching of writing and composition. English teachers who think they cannot write, or who think they have to be writers to teach writing, will inevitably avoid teaching writing in all its rhetorical forms. But if they do not begin teaching writing, they most certainly will never become writers themselves and thus more authentic teachers of literature and writing in their classrooms.

Herein lies the English teacher's dilemma: *How do teachers who are not writers begin teaching writing if they think they have to be writers in the first place*? This book suggests a simple answer. That answer rests in the knowledge that teachers do not have to be writers to begin teaching writing; becoming a writer is a life-long process that will evolve if teachers *let teaching be their writing muse*. Emphasizing that it's never too late to begin, this book holds as its primary aim the transformation of the personal and professional life of the teacher – from teacher, to writer, to teacher-writer, and finally to teacher-artist.

The Dilemma Other Subject Teachers Face

For teachers outside of English departments who must cope with writing in their disciplines, the dilemma is the same, and equally challenging. If science and mathematics teachers think they cannot write, how are they going to teach their students to write in their disciplines? How are they going to be able to teach not only discipline-related writing, but "writing-to-learn" strategies within their disciplines, a concept formulated by Janet Emig in her groundbreaking article, "Writing as a Mode of Learning (Emig, 1977)"?

Most importantly, how are they going to be able to teach in the spirit of Writing Across the Curriculum (WAC), a movement founded in the 1970s that evolved into Creative Writing Across the Curriculum (CWAC) and spawned *The WAC Journal*. For half a century, this movement has been in the forefront of helping to improve the writing skills of all students. The movement operates on three principles:

- *Writing is completely intertwined with learning.*
- *Students need a wide variety of types of writing – formal, informal, creative, personal, exploratory, informational, analytical, and academic.*
- *Students in different majors need explicit, guided instruction on how to write in the various genres of their fields.*

(Peary, 2015: 198)

In English and creative writing classes, writing across the curriculum also looms large, as students need to learn writing skills that are transferable to their other classes. Recent scholarship such as Alexandria Peary's "The Pedagogy of Creative Writing Across the Curriculum" confirms the vital role that creative writing can play "as an invaluable transferable skill" (Peary, 2015: 196) that can improve students' writing and related skills of critical thinking and reading.

A SOLUTION FOR THE DILEMMA ALL TEACHERS FACE

> *Creative writing carries enormous potential as an interdisciplinary pedagogy and can improve the learning environment of the twenty-first-century university.*
>
> – Alexandria Peary, "The Pedagogy of Creative Writing Across the Curriculum" (Peary, 2015: 195)

Unifying Fundamentals: Creativity and Literacy

This book provides a solution to the dilemma all teachers face. Because at its core, this book addresses two of the underlying fundamentals that unite all teachers and all disciplines: *creativity* and *literacy*. If you value creativity and want to see more of it in your discipline, your classroom, and our educational system as a whole, then this book is for you. If you value literacy, that is, reading and writing, then this book is for you. And if you value learning, co-learning with your students, and are a lifetime learner yourself, this book is for you. Most importantly, if you value interdisciplinary collaborations, projects, and partnerships, this book is for you.

Although my teaching story is one of a high school English and creative writing teacher, in 2006 I co-taught English with a science colleague in Morristown High School's Science Academy. The interdisciplinary co-teaching opened my eyes to a little-known genre – science poetry – and made me realize how over three decades my teaching of creative writing had been unknowingly informed by my untapped love of science. The result was my first book, *Writing Poetry through the Eyes of Science*, with Erin Colfax, my science co-teacher (Gorrell with Colfax, 2012). As a consequence of the Science Academy experience and the many across-the-curriculum projects my students and I have engaged in, this book includes poetry, creative writing, journal articles, and creative writing from teachers, professors, scientists, and mathematicians across the curriculum.

THIS BOOK IS INTERDISCIPLINARY

Meet My Interdisciplinary Contributors

- **Mark Gutkowski** *Global Academic Dean, Avenues: The World School, New York City*
  Mark, a colleague and Latin teacher from Morristown High School contributes the Forward to this book. I first met Mark over 30 years ago when he walked through the doors of the English Department. Although he began by teaching English, that was short-lived. Mark became the celebrated Latin department. We collaborated with our Latin and creative writing students in writing poetry. I'd work with his Latin students reacting to their poems. Mark and I also collaborated in teacher

writing workshops and faculty diversity training. We share a lifetime love of teaching, learning, and creativity.

- **Dr. Steven N. Handel**, *Plant Ecologist and Landscape Designer*
  Steven has been a long-time friend, neighbor, trusted advisor, and contributor to my first book, *Writing Poetry through the Eyes of Science*, in which he describes his love of botany, trees in particular, and park design, one of his major professional endeavors besides teaching and mentoring graduate students. Steven contributes to this book selections from his creative editorial writing, his commentaries, and his more recent memoir writing.
- **Dr. Arthur J. Stewart,** *Aquatic Ecologist and Ecotoxicologist*
  Arthur and I met through email interviews after the publication of my first book in 2012. As a science poet, he shared with me his passion for science poetry, for science, and for across-the-curriculum education. Ever since then, we have become colleagues and friends, sharing our latest publications, projects, mutual passions, and educational visions. Arthur contributes his science poetry, commentaries, and a journal article excerpt to this book.
- **Amy Uyematsu**, *High School Mathematics Teacher and Poet*
  I have Amazon's "Frequently bought together" suggestion to thank for introducing me to Amy, a *sansei* or third-generation Japanese-American, poet. When I saw her collection, *Stone Bow Prayer*, matched online with my book, *Writing Poetry through the Eyes of Science*, I bought it immediately, read it, and contacted her. Amy became, through email correspondences, my West Coast poetic muse, colleague, and ultimately, friend. She contributes to this book much of her teaching life and life story through her multi-layered and diverse subject poetry, and her term paper, written for the first Asian American Studies class offered at UCLA: "The Emergence of Yellow Power in America."

- **Stefanie DeFronzo** (Class of 2020), *Biochemistry and Molecular Biology Major*, *Drew University*
  I recruited Stefanie DeFronzo in 2019 to participate in my book project. I was interested in having more interdisciplinary student writing models. Stefanie and I met in a coffee shop near the Drew University campus. At the time she was taking a writing workshop for descendants of Holocaust survivors. Stefanie was committed to her career as a scientist, but was eager to do more writing. After I explained the book project, she was excited to participate. Despite her incredibly busy schedule, she said, "Just send me the prompts, and I'll do them!" As a biology major, Stefanie contributes to the book's "Interdisciplinary Applications" with her poetry, commentaries, and reflections.

HOW TO READ THIS BOOK: INTERACTIVELY

The Story of Your Becoming

Although part of this book is my story of becoming an English and creative writing teacher, the unwritten part of this book is the story of your becoming as well. In that spirit, I ask you to do more than read this book. I ask you to read with an open mind, an open heart, and an open journal in your hand, pausing at the end of chapters to reflect and respond as you walk the path of your many selves.

About the Term *Journal*

For the purpose of this book, the term *journal* will broadly refer to whatever writing tool or mode you prefer – pencil, pen, notebook, writer's manual, iPad, tablet or field manual. Writing does not care how you do it, writing just cares that you do it.

Overview of the Book: Evolving Identities of the Teacher

This book is divided into four Sections based on the evolving identities of the teacher.

> **Section One:** ***The Teacher Self***, walks you through the path of becoming a teacher who writes.
> **Section Two**: ***The Writer Self***, walks you through the path of becoming a writer both personally and professionally.
> **Section Three**: ***The Teacher-Writer Self***, walks you through the path of making your writing life and your teaching life one.
> **Section Four:** ***The Teacher-Artist Self***, walks you through the path of making your teaching life and your writing life one creative act.

Becoming a Teacher who Writes offers an interactive and interdisciplinary approach. Each chapter presents a teaching story or poem, followed by commentary for the teacher, as well as practical and model lessons for students. Each chapter concludes with "Interdisciplinary Applications" providing writing models and activities for students and teachers. The book includes models of student writing from the author's creative writing and English classes along with models from science and math students of all levels and abilities. Chapter discussions refer to basic students, reluctant writers, and gifted student writers as well.

Key Chapter Contents

A Teaching Story or Teaching Poem

- To illustrate for you the chapter's lesson. I hope you will be inspired to try the chapter's lesson and adapt it in some way to your teaching and subject.

What I Learned: Author's Commentary

- To relate what I have learned in "walking the path" of my becoming. I hope you will be inspired by my story to walk in some way your own path from teacher to ultimately, teacher-artist.

For Your Teacher Journal: Reflecting and Responding

- To take a moment for reflection and responding as you read or teach with your students. I hope you will be inspired to become a co-learner with your students as you walk your path to become a writer and a teacher-writer.

Model Student Writing

- To provide student models that inspire your students to respond in kind. I hope student models will also be instructive for you in your teaching as a teacher-writer.

For Your Students: Writing Prompts

- To provide specific writing prompts for your students based on the chapter's lesson.

Interdisciplinary Applications

- To provide for all students and teachers writing models from an interdisciplinary contributor. I hope you will be inspired by the essays, poetry, and memoirs of the major contributors.

Model Interdisciplinary Articles, Poems, or Memoirs

- To provide an interdisciplinary model for you to teach to your students or to adapt to your particular subject. I hope the model will inspire you to write your own model, or to adapt the model in some way to your subject or discipline.

*****

Ultimately, this book is a beginning, the beginning of you walking your path.

All you have to do is. . .
walk gently,
sing loudly,
and teach,

and of course,
write.

Introduction Notes

1 During my service as New Jersey State Teacher of the Year (1991–1992) I shared the poem with teachers in every school, convention, and public forum where I was invited to speak. The poem, timely and timeless, resonates now as powerfully as it did then. I share "to teach is to learn" with you, the reader, so you may share it with your colleagues and students.

2 I use the term *workshop* broadly to mean a group of students sharing writing in a non-judgmental, appreciative method. I am not specifically referencing the Iowa Writer's Workshop pedagogy. Historically, this term applies to the pioneering Iowa Writer's Workshop, a model pedagogy formulated whereby undergraduate or graduate students submit pieces of writing for criticism by fellow students and a master writer, usually one of fame or a professor. When I began writing the curriculum in 1974 for the first creative writing elective course in my high school, I was unaware of this specific model. Instead of *workshop*, I used the terms *sharing* and *sharing circle* for voicing student writing in progress, a pedagogy more affirming for beginning writers and more conducive to process writing.

I also prefer to use the term *feedback* (giving and receiving) when teaching the revision process rather than talking about *workshopping* a piece of writing, which is a specific way of giving feedback. Readers should note that by the late 20th century, the Iowa Writer's Workshop pedagogy has come under considerable criticism and debate within the academy and is presently questioned by scholars, researchers, and creative writing studies (for discussion, see Harper, 2017; Mayers, 2015).

Introduction References

Emig, Janet (1977) Writing as a mode of learning. *College Composition and Communication*, 28 (2): 122–128. https://doi.org/10.2307/356095

Gorrell, Nancy S. with Erin Colfax (2012) *Writing Poetry through the Eyes of Science: Scientific Literacy and Poetic Response*. Sheffield, UK, and Oakville, CT: Equinox.

Harper, Graeme (2017) The unworkshop. In Clark, Michael Dean, Hergenrader, Trent and Rein, Joseph (eds.) *Creative Writing Innovations: Breaking Boundaries in the Classroom*, 21–31. London, UK: Bloomsbury.

Mayers, Tim (2015) Creative writing and process pedagogy. In Peary, Alexandria and Hunley, Tom C. (eds.) *Creative Writing Pedagogies for the Twenty-First Century*, 30–51. Carbondale, IL: Southern Illinois University Press.

Peary, Alexandria (2015) The pedagogy of creative writing across the curriculum. In Peary, Alexandria and Hunley, Tom C. (eds.) *Creative Writing Pedagogies for the Twenty-First Century*, 195. Carbondale, IL: Southern Illinois University Press.

SECTION ONE: THE TEACHER SELF

Chapter 1
Works in Progress

You must tell yourself that you're a writer. A work in progress, but a writer.

– Pat Conroy, *My Losing Season*
(Conroy, 2003: 144)

PART ONE: A TEACHING STORY

The Greatest Pep Talk

Pat Conroy in his memoir, *My Losing Season*, recalls the "greatest pep talk" he ever heard (Conroy, 2003: 144). It came not from his basketball coach at the Citadel Academy but from his English teacher, John Doyle. Doyle tries to encourage Pat by telling him he must think of himself as a writer. Pat protests that he's not. He can't make his writing sound like what he wants. Doyle continues the pep talk by telling Pat that his writing is getting better. He should not compare himself to the masters like Fitzgerald or Hemingway, but think instead, of himself as *work in progress.* He tells Pat that calling himself a writer is an essential first step that all writers must take. It's hard and takes courage.

> "Now this is the hard part for all writers, Mr. Conroy, but it is necessary. You must think of yourself as a writer."
>
> "I'm not good enough yet, Colonel Doyle."

> "No, you're not. But you're getting better. You're doing the hard work. But you must tell yourself that you're a writer. *A work in progress*, but a writer. Can you tell me that?"
>
> "Not yet, Colonel. I can't make a sentence sound like I want it to.
>
> "That will come [...]. But [you] have to take the first step. That is the first revolutionary act a writer has to make. It takes courage. But it's necessary, Mr. Conroy."
>
> (Conroy, 2003: 144)

This moment of epiphany for Pat Conroy had all the elements of dream teaching: a brilliant, talented student burning to become a writer; a passionate teacher, burning to impart the wisdom of his discipline; and lastly, the magic of the moment ripe for rebirth. But the epiphany would never have happened if it were not for one other essential ingredient, the ingredient of a teacher's faith in his student. Conroy recalls John Doyle carried an "unshakeable faith that I'd one day write novels" (p. 145).

Not many of us in our careers as teachers will have the joy of teaching a Pat Conroy. Nevertheless, in over three decades of teaching writing, I have felt the joy of John Doyle in my classroom. Such teaching enters my classroom with students from all walks of life by having "unshakeable faith." The lessons of Colonel Doyle prevail whether the student is a yearning to be like Pat Conroy or a voiceless soul waiting to hear itself.

PART TWO: WE ARE ALL WORKS IN PROGRESS

A Most Unlikely Creative Writing Class

> *We need to reevaluate the assumption that only a chosen few are capable of creative writing or creative thinking.*
>
> – Joseph Moxley, "Tearing Down the Walls: Engaging the Imagination"
>
> (Moxley, 1989: 28)

I offer another example of dream teaching in the world of reality, that is, the world of Morristown High School, a large, diverse public school in northern New Jersey. It began in late October when my supervisor approached me: "Nancy" he said, "we have a problem. Joyce is teaching the senior High School Proficiency Test (HSPT) class, and it's too large. You're free during third period. We'd like to split the class and have you teach the other half." My supervisor's request struck a note of trepidation within me. Although I had taught most levels of English, I had never before taught the HSPT students. The class consisted of 30 seniors who had failed the test twice. The stakes were high: if they did not pass, they would not graduate. They would become 5th year seniors, remediated again just to pass the test. In fact, Joyce's class included three 5th year seniors.

Although my heart went out to the students, I knew I could not teach them to pass the HSPT test by simply giving them more of the same endless remediation through standardized tests. But my supervisor had made the request, and I wanted to help.

"Frank," I said, "I have a thought. I'd like to teach these students creative writing. They've just had it up to here (I motioned to my chin) with HSPT writing exercises. Let me teach them something new. Although I didn't express it to my supervisor, I was digging deeply into beliefs central to all my teaching and the teaching of writing:

- *To teach requires an "unshakeable faith" that every student possesses an innate ability to learn.*
- *To teach creativity requires an "unshakeable faith" that every student possesses a creative soul waiting to find its place of expression.*
- *To teach creative writing requires an "unshakeable faith" that every student possesses an inner voice waiting to hear itself.*
- *To teach a creative writing class requires an "unshakeable faith" that the class will provide a community where the creative soul will find its place.*

Yes, faith, translated as belief, is the root of all great teaching. I knew I must believe that these students, limited as they may seem to themselves and others, were like all of us, works in progress. They were creative; they were writers; they just needed a teacher to believe in them, and they needed a teacher to tell them so. Colonel Doyle was right; I knew it because I had been teaching creative writing by recognizing my students from day one as writers, teaching them as writers, respecting them as writers and honoring every piece of writing they produced. And as works in progress, even "these" students could take the first step and call themselves writers, if only they had a chance. Couldn't they?

My supervisor looked aghast at my suggestion. Then he smiled, "You're going to teach poetry to those kids?" The subtext in his words implied volumes. Most of the students were boys, and my supervisor harbored the belief that boys didn't take creative writing. In addition, these were students defined by the school as illiterate, ranking at the very bottom of their class. Was it possible?

"Yes," I said with all the conviction I could muster. So it was decided that each and every day, Joyce would teach the students the required HSPT exercises; once they successfully completed Joyce's work, they would be released to come to my classroom for creative writing instruction. Joyce was to be the stick; I was to be the carrot.

The first day, I waited about 20 minutes into the period. Then, a group of about 12 students slowly appeared at my door. Heads down, shoulders bent, they slunk into their seats, filling the back rows first. Some talked, others gazed out the window with vacant eyes. One stretched out in his seat, head back, arms resting on the desk behind, bearing a lifetime of attitude on his shoulders. I knew I had to do something different to bring this group together in some semblance of a class. I took out my only trump cards, the cards known as "truth, honesty, and respect." Then I said, "Some people think you're not smart enough to be writers. Some people think you can't write at all. But I know better. I'm a teacher, but I'm also a writer too. I know writers when I see them. I know all of you are creative; and if you are creative, you can be writers. I want to spend time with you sharing with you what I know about *real* writing, not writing for the test, not writing what everyone else wants you to say, but writing for yourself, writing what you want to say." The class turned quiet. I turned my back and wrote on the board, "real writing." Then I swung around. "Yes, real writing. That's what we're going to do. We're going to get real."

At that moment I realized my supervisor was standing in the hallway, observing the silent, rapped attention in my room. As he walked away, I took out Nikki Giovanni's poem, "Cotton Candy on a Rainy Day (Giovanni, 1978).[1] I asked, "How many of you have ever felt lonely? How many of you have ever felt so bad you just couldn't put it in words?" Hands went up; a sign of recognition even from Mr. Attitude. "Real writing is making us feel the feelings of the writer; and we can only do that by writing what our feelings are *really* like, just to us, no one else." I read aloud Giovanni's poem. Then I asked, "What is your loneliness like? Write only one line. Just one. Not more."

Paradox: ask for less and you will get more. Then when a student goes beyond the one line, you can be amazed. "Wow, you wrote all that!" The students were all writing, they were taking the prompt seriously, and they seemed engaged. But what were they writing? I walked around, praising, encouraging, urging them to continue. After about five minutes, I asked for volunteers to share one line or more. Some said they were still working; they weren't ready.

"Good," I said, "you're still writing. What you're writing is a work in progress. You keep writing while we hear the others. Now, who has a work in progress we can hear?" A shy girl raised her hand tentatively and read, "Loneliness is like when my boyfriend doesn't call." A few students smiled, but I could see they were taking it seriously.

"Good," I affirmed again, "that's so lonely. Let's hear another work in progress. Who has one? Sonia in the back raised her hand and read, "Loneliness is like a bird without a song."

"Wow, that's so lonely too!"

"She writes poetry" a boy in the class called out "and so does Jamal." I looked at Jamal and smiled. He smiled too, and there was softness in his eyes. I could tell he really did write poetry and that it meant something to him. Jamal by the way was Mr. Attitude.

"We all can write poetry," I replied. Then, to my surprise, a meek boy in the back raised his hand and began to read with seriousness, "Loneliness is like sitting on the toilet taking a dump all by yourself." Remarkably, no one in the class laughed. Somehow, they recognized the truth of that human loneliness.

"That's *really* lonely," I said. "That's a great work in progress." And so those students became my students, and on Day One we decided as a class to be writers. Each student would write a book of poems. If they wrote ten, they would get an "A." If they wrote eight or nine, they would get a "B+," and so forth. I told everyone I wanted to give them all "A" grades in creative writing, and Joyce agreed to average the creative writing grades with her own grades. Caveat: If creative writing is to have value within a grading system, it has to count.[2] These students had not seen "A" grades in a long time. But the grades were clearly not why they were writing. They were writing because they wanted to have someone believe in them. They were starving for praise; they were starving for self-affirmation; they were starving for a sense of identity; and they were starving for a place for their creative souls.

What I Learned: The Power of "Real" Writing

The experiment was a success. Each day, students were eager to get out of Joyce's class and into creative writing. My colleague saw high motivation when it came to completing the HSPT exercises, and most importantly, we all saw a marked improvement in the students' work. I too had the pleasure of bearing witness to the growth of the students as writers. Each day, they would enter my class, take out their journals, and begin to freewrite. The swell of their rising pride was almost palpable. At the end of the semester, all of the students produced short poetry collections and all received grades of A's or B's. They took their poetry writing seriously, and the poems they wrote out laboriously in long hand in our class came from their "real" selves.

Their poems were works in progress. And like their poems, the students were works in progress, too. The beauty of this works-in-progress paradigm shift is that it enables students to throw off the shackles of negativity, self-criticism, and self-doubt that judgment, perfectionism, and competition foster replacing them with the affirming freedoms of experimentation, play, and joy, all vital components of creativity. My students had taken the first, courageous step. They recognized themselves as writers, they acted like writers, and they produced writing worthy of being heard. It was writing so real, so respected that we not only created self-made books, but we ended the semester with an evening reading when the students read their poems to family, friends, and the school community.

Teaching that HSPT creative writing class proved to my then supervisor the power of "real" or authentic writing. For what else could explain the fact that all those students passed the HSPT test that year and proudly walked in their graduation ceremony? But equally important, it validated the value of teaching creative writing as a bridge to facilitate and to improve all kinds of writing. Once my students found the writer inside themselves, once they began to hear their own inner voices, transformation occurred on multiple and portable levels.

Teaching for this transformation is at the heart of this book. It can happen to your students; it can happen to yourself, if only you realize we are all works in progress letting teaching be your muse.

Can Creative Writing Improve Student Attitudes Towards Writing?

My anecdotal observations of my "most unlikely creative writing class" answer this question with a resounding "yes." Creative writing can transform student attitudes towards writing from defeatism and negativity, to positivity, achievement, and joy. The experiment in this chapter worked. Without question, some credit is due to my co-teacher, Joyce, who taught the students skills to pass the state test. How much my students' newfound confidence and positive attitudes affected the outcome of the test is unknowable, and thus impossible to measure. The proof remains in the result. These failing students had remediation before and still had not passed the test multiple times. The problem was not the over-tested students. The problem was the pedagogy that relegated such basic students to remedial English classes devoid of authentic and creative writing experiences.

Teachers of basic writing students in the academy also have experienced similar observations. Martha Pennington, editor of the series in which this volume appears, has taught basic writing classes on the university level for many years. On the first day of every class, she always surveyed her students' attitudes towards writing. Pennington notes that entering students included "few if any English or writing majors" and that more than 80% taking the required writing classes demonstrated "low confidence" as writers, "negative attitudes" towards writing, and "low motivation" to write (Pennington, 2015: 89). She confirms this profile as a typical one for a class of students in a college writing program (Pennington, 2021, personal communication).

After developing and employing a pedagogy centered on creativity and discovery, Pennington confirms the transformation of her students' attitudes from "negative to positive" as reported in their end-of-course survey (p. 89). In "Writing Creativity and Discovery: Process and Pedagogy," Pennington outlines detailed pedagogical recommendations confirming a pedagogy for teaching creative writing on the university level that this book supports for secondary level creative writing as well. Among the recommendations, the most important one is the first step: "motivating the writing process and getting sufficient buy-in and attachment to a topic to drive the whole process from beginning to end, to make it truly a process of discovery (Pennington, 2015: 81).

Further confirmation of the efficacy of this chapter's pedagogy for basic students can be found in Clyde Moneyhun's "A Basic Writing Teacher Teaches Creative Writing" (Moneyhun, 2015). Although Moneyhun teaches basic students on the university level, his creative writing pedagogy for such writers supports the pedagogy of this chapter, He notes that the "ineffectiveness of a grammar-based curriculum has been thoroughly documented by scholars" (p. 223). Moneyhun describes basic writing and basic writers as follows:

> Since basic writing is most often characterized by writing that is riddled with errors, and basic writers as people who habitually make errors, basic writing pedagogy can be focused on the identification and remediation of errors. Basic writing classes may focus heavily, if not primarily, on grammar.
>
> (pp. 222–223)

Whether such students are in high school or the academy, they are typically remediated with an error correction and reduction approach that limits their creativity, voice, and self-confidence as writers.

For Your Teacher Journal: Works in Progress

The "Cotton Candy on a Rainy Day" creative writing prompt is particularly useful as an opening for teachers in both arts and sciences when writing across the curriculum is the focus. Use this as a vehicle for a first day ice-breaker or first week introduction to your discipline and the concepts of creativity, literacy, and works in progress which unite all of the disciplines.

Reflecting: Works in Progress

1. Do you see yourself as a work in progress?
2. Do you see your students as works in progress?
3. Does your discipline foster the concept of works in progress?

4. How may this concept better inform your teaching and writing life?
5. What path do you envision or imagine you are now on?
6. Or, what path would you like to follow?
7. Do you see the writing prompts below informing your discipline?
8. Do you see connections in terms of teaching creativity and literacy across the disciplines?

Responding: Writing Prompts

1. Write your own journal entry or prose piece inspired by your reading of Nikki Giovanni's poem, "Cotton Candy on a Rainy Day." Form does not matter. Think about your writing as a work in progress. Put it aside for one week. Then go back to it. Reflect. What does it reveal to you about your writing as a work in progress?
2. Write something new from your journal entry. Start with your favorite word or line and then write more. Form doesn't matter. Continue writing.
3. Two weeks later, if so moved, write a poem, prose poem or prose piece from your works in progress.
4. If inspired, write your own poem or prose piece "On Loneliness."

For Your Students: "Cotton Candy on a Rainy Day" Writing Prompt

Teacher Instructions

1. Read to your students Giovanni's "Cotton Candy on a Rainy Day," or have your students view Giovanni's reading on: www.youtube.com (May 30, 2015).
2. Follow the writing lesson model above. Ask your students to write what their loneliness is like using comparisons from Giovanni's poem as examples.

3. Encourage your students to write quickly and freely, telling them that their poems are works in progress.
4. When students are finished, ask them to share one or more lines from their works in progress.
5. Either at the end of class or the next day, create a sharing circle. Ask for volunteers to share their works in progress. Then, share your work in progress with the class based on Giovanni's poem. Use your first draft or notes to show your students your first attempt.
6. Encourage discussion regarding students' works in progress, and your own writing if this is or is not your first poem. The objective here is to establish a writerly conversation, a sense of emerging community within the class.
7. Model praise and approval for all works in progress. Establish the sharing circle in your class as a place for listening, hearing, giving attention, and affirming creativity and the creative process that unites all disciplines.

PART THREE: INTERDISCIPLINARY APPLICATIONS

Relate the core teaching of this chapter through the lens of your discipline. For example, complex, important, and original creations require development over time allowing for reflection, discovery, and collaboration. When does an artistic, literary, or scientific discovery or creation become a finished product? When the art is hung? The book published? The rocket launched? I'm reminded of a line of poetry that my uncle crossed out and rewrote in my presence when he handed me a signed volume of his earliest poetic collection, *The Wrong Angel*. Similarly, scientists and mathematicians know that their discoveries and products need corroboration, proof or disproof even after trials, testing, and publication; in that sense, all creative and scientific advances are in essence works in progress.

Model Student Poem: "The Mind's Eye" by Stefanie DeFronzo, Biochemistry and Molecular Biology Major, Drew University

The Mind's Eye
by Stefanie DeFronzo

I wonder how much darkness pupils need
to completely eclipse the irises…
I lay on my back trying to grasp onto
that small strand of moonlight leaking in my bedroom
like the drop of milk that drips down the carton
accidentally
every time you pour some into your cereal.

My toes crinkle and my fingers brush my cheek
as I twist from side
to back
to side
trying to find
comfort.

My mind races my heart
to the finish line of sleep.
Reminiscent of the minutes spent
standing under the shower head
or sitting on the toilet
reflecting on the mysteries of life.
I stare at the black hole on top of me,
contemplating my reflection
and trying to find the best angle
of the sun.

My eyes are wide open
as I lie in my bed
thinking about you
and all of the mistakes I hold on to.

I always try to shut my eyes before the rain comes.
But an umbrella is easy to forget
and no one wears their heart on their raincoat.

Stefanie's Reflection on "The Mind's Eye"

I first wrote this poem on July 29, 2019 and then came back to it in December after reading Giovanni's "Cotton Candy on a Rainy Day." I was immediately reminded of the fragments I scrype (my new word, combining scribble and type) into my Notes app. Fortunately, I didn't have to dig deep when I found my notes, unnamed, but perfectly describing a personal instance of loneliness: a girl and her thoughts. I read them over, changed some of the phrasing, and gave the poem a name. I usually don't struggle with naming my poems, but I still don't know how I feel about this one. Maybe I'll come back to it in a week.

Model Contributor Poem: "Pathway" by Arthur J. Stewart, Aquatic Ecologist and Ecotoxicologist

Pathway
by Arthur J. Stewart

Years ago when I first
readied myself to set out
into the world I had a vivid dream

about ploughing a field,
with red soil on one side and white soil
on the other. The plough
was rough and made of wood and it cast
red soil onto the white soil, and white soil
onto the red soil and for years that image held,
sometimes cloudy and sometimes clear.

I worked thereafter
to make it so: mixing
science and poetry, two strong modes
of creativity, two ways

for understanding the world.

Hallelujah, I say,
Looking forward, living the dream
or dreaming
while living—
when I have filled
that which I can fill,
it is done.

It is over.

(Stewart, 2021)

For Your Students: Interdisciplinary Applications

Teacher Instructions

1. After reading to your students Arthur J. Stewart's poem, "Pathway," ask them if they think science and poetry go together. Discuss: Can one be a scientist and a poet, too? Stewart, an ecologist and science poet, has done just that pursuing both arts and science with equal passion and dedication. Stewart has written by his own account seven books of "science-flavored poems for scientists" and a poetry chapbook, *Uncoils a Snake* (Stewart, 2021). (You can reference Stewart's scientific writings and poetry for your students in Chapters 4, 9, 14, 16, and 17.)
2. Discuss: Can one be a mathematician and a poet, too? Amy Uyematsu, high school mathematics teacher and poet, has done just that. Pursuing poetry writing while teaching math for over three decades, she has published five books of poetry. Uyematsu writes math poetry about her students and with her algebra and geometry students as well. (You can reference her math-related and teaching poems as well as her personal poetry for your students in Chapters 3, 7, 8, and 17.)
3. Discuss with your students, discipline-related writing which is relevant for your course and subject. What types of writing

do scientists or mathematicians do in research and for the profession? Identify with your students the intersection of the writing process in your discipline as well as types and genres of writing within your discipline.

4. After reading Arthur J. Stewart's poem "Pathway," ask students to write a poem or prose piece about the "path" they envision they are walking now or will walk in the future. Ask them if it is related in any way to a discipline they prefer or the one they are learning with you. You may wish to reference Chapter 18 for an instructional definition of science poetry as a genre, or consult this author's previous Equinox book, *Writing Poetry through the Eyes of Science: Scientific Literacy and Poetic Response* (Gorrell with Colfax, 2012), for further pedagogies.

Chapter 1 Notes

1 To hear Nikki Giovanni reading "Cotton Candy on a Rainy Day," go to www.youtube.com for May 30, 2015.

2 A Note on grading for the HSPT students: I use a contract/portfolio grading system for all my creative writing classes (see Chapter 6). In this system student writings do not receive individual grades on their writings. Such grading would be antithetical to works in progress, the pedagogy that writing is in a continual process of reflection, revision, and discovery. However, within a graded institutional setting that nearly all schools impose, a final grade must be given at the end of the course. Therefore, I used a contract grading system based on the satisfactory completion of required writing assignments: e.g., for the HSPT students, 10 poems for an "A."

Chapter 1 References

Conroy, Pat (2003) *My Losing Season*. New York, NY: Bantam Dell Random House.

Giovanni, Nikki (1978) "Cotton Candy on a Rainy Day." *Poems by Nikki Giovanni*, 21–23. New York, NY: William Morrow.

Gorrell, Nancy S. with Erin Colfax (2012) *Writing Poetry through the Eyes of Science: Scientific Literacy and Poetic Response*. Sheffield, UK and Oakville, CT: Equinox.

Moneyhun, Clyde (2015) A basic writing teacher teaches creative writing. In Peary, Alexandria and Hunley, Tom (eds.) *Creative Writing Pedagogies for the Twenty-First Century*, 221–242. Carbondale, IL: Southern Illinois University Press.

Pennington, Martha C. (2015) Writing creativity and discovery: Process and pedagogy. In Chik, Alice, Costley, Tracey and Pennington, Martha C. (eds.) *Creativity and Discovery in the University Writing Class*, 61–92. Sheffield, UK and Oakville, CT: Equinox.

Stewart, Arthur J. (2021) "Pathway." *The Hallelujah Series and Other Poems*, 3. Nashville, TN: Periploi Press.

Stewart, Arthur J. (2021) *Uncoils a Snake*. Nashville, TN: Periploi Press.

Chapter 2

It Takes Creativity and Windows

We express our being by creating. Creativity is a necessary sequel to being.

– Rollo May, *The Courage to Create*
(May, 1975: 8)

PART ONE: ON CLASSROOM WINDOWS

A Teaching Story

When I was a child, my grandfather, a high school principal, enjoyed teaching me difficult words. One that I particularly remember was *education*. He would look at me and say, "Do you know what education is? It comes from the Latin, *educere*, meaning to bring forth." And then he would smile. When I think of my grandfather, the first great teacher in my life, I think of education. And when I think of education in the sense of *educere*, I think of my fourth grade classroom and my teacher, Miss Aussiker. In that classroom, we sat in five straight rows of rigid wooden desks, the kind with holes in the upper right-hand corner for our ink wells, each desk permanently fixed to the floor. Every day we sat there, facing the blackboard, and only the blackboard, and the heads of the students in front of us. Then, one day in early fall, Miss Aussiker said, "Stand up at the sides of your desks." I remember being excited. Where were we going? "Now" she said, "I want you to face the window." We all turned in unison and looked outside, up at the top of the mountain. "Do you see the tower?" We had to search to see it because most of it was covered by fall foliage. "Every day you come into this classroom," Miss Aussiker said, "I want you to watch that tower; you'll see it change." And then we sat down.

It was a simple moment, I doubt it was even in Miss Aussiker's lesson plan book, but it was a moment which affected me so profoundly, I have carried it with me all my life. Miss Aussiker had opened up a window: somehow, she knew how I felt sitting in those rows; and suddenly I realized there was a world out there – a world of beauty and transience which Miss Aussiker had brought to me, and I loved her for it. All that year I watched the tower from my classroom window, and then, one Saturday in late spring, I had an impulse. I wanted to go to the tower. I packed a snack, told my mother I was going on a hike, and set out. I had no idea how to get there, but I knew if I walked in the general direction of the tower, I would somehow find my way there. Hours later, when I reached the top of the mountain and touched the tower which loomed over me several stories high, I knew I had learned something.

At nine years of age, I did not have the words to describe how I felt as I turned, looked down, and saw my school and the window which began it all. I only knew that I had changed, and this change had come to me by way of one teacher, Miss Aussiker, who revealed to me a part of myself – an inner truth.

Education, in the truest sense changes the learner. Facts inform, skills develop technique, and in all deference to Miss Aussiker, I did also look at the blackboard that year, because I do remember learning long division. But, more importantly, inner truths transform. My grandfather's words: *educere,* "education" in Latin, meaning to bring forth. I teach to transform the mind and hearts of my students.

Another Classroom Window: Teaching the Spontaneous Lesson

Twenty-one years later, in the same town, in the same school system, I sat behind a desk in another classroom. But this time it was my creative writing classroom, and the school was Morristown High. The desks were not fixed in rows, but rather formed an inviting circle. I sat at a desk within the circle among my students. We were not facing the windows that lined one wall of the room, nor were we facing the blackboard which lined the other wall. We were facing each other, and the students were asking me, "Mrs. Gorrell, can we go outside? Please! I didn't know what they were talking about, so I walked up to the windows which faced the back of our school. There, I gazed upon the scene. It was a magnificent fall day: the air crisp, the sky sunny and blue, and the mountain ranges beyond the football field seemed to burst with color. In the center, on the 50-yard line was Barbara Nadolny, a biology colleague. She was surrounded by her class, binoculars in hand, and they all seemed to be looking at the sky. "What are they doing?" I asked my class. "Oh," my students shouted, "They're watching for hawks! Can we go outside, too?"

The young teacher in me hesitated for a moment. After all, I did not yet have tenure. *Going outside? Was that permissible? What about my lesson plan?* But the creativity bursting in me knew I had to do something. I had to seize the teachable moment. My students were biting at the bit to go outside. If I taught the planned lesson, everyone would be disappointed, and I certainly did not want to teach a lesson to a group of discouraged students. If only I could harness that energy into a creative channel, just maybe. I gazed at Picasso's words on the poster in my classroom: *The important thing is to create. Nothing else matters. Creation is all.*

I found myself saying, "We can't just go outside and do nothing! Ms. Nadolny's students are watching for hawks." Then the "aha moment" struck. "I know," I said, answering my own question.

"We'll watch for poems!" My students laughed as the excitement in the classroom rose. And so the idea of "poetry watching" was born. That particular creative writing class helped me create the spontaneous lesson we would later name "Poetry Watch." I immediately set up rules and guidelines:

- *Take your journal with you.*
- *Separate from the other students.*
- *Do not talk or interact with anyone.*
- *Walk in silence and observe with all your senses.*
- *Find a place you like; sit there and take notes.*
- *Write down what you see, hear, smell, taste, and touch.*
- *Focus on one thing or one object: observe, sense and describe.*
- *Watch for a poem.*
- *When you find one, write it.*

My students quickly gathered their gear, asked no questions, and were lined at the door before I could get my notebook and pencil. "To avoid Ms. Nadolny's class, we are going to the front of the school," I said. "We will be there for 25 minutes. Then I want you to return to class to share your results. Now go watch for poems!" The excitement in the classroom was palpable. Outside, like soldiers on command, my students walked in silence, separated on sidewalks, grass, and steps, and sat in private locations, observing, sensing, and writing. I had no idea what they were about to produce; but inspired by the beautiful day, empowered by the permission to take risks, and energized by the fun of doing something different, they discovered startling poems.

And what did I do, watching them, watch for poems? I found myself watching for poems, too. I wrote in my journal the following poem in note form:

Poetry Watch
by Nancy Gorrell

I watch
my students watch
for poems
"watch out!"
someone says,
the principal might
watch us watching
I wait and watch. . .
the house across the street
a mélange of junk
a no trespassing sign
an open fence latch
I watch myself smile
while three chipmunks
scamper across the lawn –
father, mother, son –
the name on the doorpost
Nutt, a cosmic joke?
The Nutt house
watches
the school
watch
while I
watch
for more
poems.

When we returned to class, my students were eager to exchange their poems in our sharing circle.[1] Marni reads: *just sitting. . . the ground cold. . . the air warm. . . the sun new. . . sparkling light. . . on curls and black shoe. . . rays penetrating library windows. . . absorbed by red geraniums. . . outside, a paper cartwheels. . . with orange leaves. . . on the lawn. . . but no one chases. . . they just sit. . . school work is insignificant. . . under a clear blue sky.* Others eagerly joined in. At the end, I share my work in progress. I do not believe it is a good poem, but I share it anyway because modeling the process is more important than producing a perfect product. My students laugh. Some nod in recognition; they had noticed the name "Nutt" too. Others are surprised and eager to go outside once again to see "Nutt" for themselves. Before the bell rings, I announce that they should take their notes, reread them, and write a draft of something new – a poem or prose poem. Marni's first draft from her notes, titled "On the School Steps," can be found in Appendix A.

What I Learned: Planning for Spontaneity

That evening I reveled in the joy of teaching the spontaneous lesson. I realized how perfectly the "Poetry Watch" fit into what we were learning. I had always introduced creative writing class with a unit on observation and sensory notetaking; going outside and writing on location was an activity I previously assigned for homework. From that moment on, I decided to "plan" for spontaneity. No longer did I assign the activity or choose the moment for my students. I knew it would be much more inspiring if the students chose it for themselves. And I knew I could always count on my students to do just that – the sunny glow of a crisp fall day, the sudden burst of downy flake – "Can we go outside?" I can hear them asking even now.

A Word on Windows

The significance of windows, both actual and metaphorical, is central to this book and to a "Windows" pedagogy that incorporates the notions of openness and receptivity, two attitudes fundamental to creativity and creative teaching. Teachers who practice a "windows" pedagogy are open to the moment and receptive to their students. They can therefore more readily teach the spontaneous lesson, seizing valuable "teachable moments." Openness and receptivity also lead to discovery and creativity through playfulness and chance, essential mindsets for creative writing and creative teaching. The "window" metaphor can be applied directly to the act of writing creatively, and especially to writing poetry: poetry can be viewed as itself a window on creativity.

PART TWO: CREATIVITY, CREATIVE TEACHING, AND CREATIVE WRITING

Creativity

Up to this point, I have been using the terms *creative* and related words rather freely – *creativity*, *creative teaching*, and *creative writing.* We can go no further in our path of becoming without a more rigorous understanding of these terms. *Creativity* denotes the process of "making, of bringing into being." I teach my students it is the process of building – taking isolated or separate elements and bringing them together to form a new whole, something else, or something decidedly different. That definition works for my students. It's concrete and empowering. For in this sense of *creativity*, are we not all in possession of an infinite capacity to create?

Many authorities would agree. Early in the 20th century, Dorothea Brande, in *Becoming a Writer*, affirms the vast creativity in us all:

> Its resources at the feeblest are fuller than you can ever exhaust. No human being is so poor as to have no trace of genius; none so great that he comes within infinity of using his own inheritance to the full. What we need is not to add to that natural endowment, but to learn to use it.
>
> (Brande, 1934/1981: 157–158)

Almost a half century later, John Gardner, in the foreword to the 1981 edition of Brande's book, concurs: "Genius is as common place as old shoes. Everybody has it, some more than others, perhaps; but that hardly matters, since no one can hope to use up more than a very small portion of his or her native gift" (Gardner, 1981: 12–13).

By the end of the 20th century, Csikszentmihalyi's (1996) seminal study, *Creativity: Flow and the Psychology of Discovery and Invention*, advances our understanding of "some more than others," in all its complexity. His theory that creativity "is a *process* by which a symbolic domain in the culture is changed," considers those change agents, like Einstein and Picasso, as possessing "creativity with a capital C" (p. 27). But what of the "others?" Scholars in the field have distinguished between "Large C" creativity, possessed by a few, and the "small c," "everyday" creativity, possessed by all human beings (Lasky, 2014; Pennington, 2014).

In the 21st century, Sky Marsen furthers our understanding of creativity in written discourse. She posits that creativity in writing may be viewed on a continuum with "more original combinations on one end (*high-level creativity*) and more conventional combinations on the other (*low-level creativity*)" (Marsen, 2014: 91; emphasis in the original). This makes pedagogical sense and provides a paradigm shift for teachers and students of writing across the curriculum. As Marsen affirms: "Thus, a scholarly text can have a high level of creativity [...], and a fictional text can have low level creativity" (p. 91). Her main tenet, "that creativity is associated with [...] the new and unfamiliar, and exists in written discourse across genres, bridging the fiction/nonfiction dichotomy" (p. 91), encourages creativity in the academic essay, discipline-related writing, and all rhetorical modes. (For example, see the creativity in Steven Handel's scientific editorials in Chapters 10 and 13.)

Sociologist Richard Swedberg's "'*How do I know what I think till I see what I say*' An aphorism and its implications for creative theorizing" (Swedberg, 2020) brings us full circle. In concert with Brande, Gardner, and Noam Chomsky (Chomsky, 1966) Swedberg endorses a new term for the vast, innate creativity attributed to the human species – *species-specific creativity* (Swedberg, 2020: 14). He explains:

> The real mystery, according to this line of thought, is to be found in what every human being can do: to think and to speak. These are two wonders: how the brain is constructed in such a way with its 85 billion neurons that you can think, and how you can speak by blowing some air through your throat while you move your lips and tap with your tongue. What is involved here may be called *species-specific creativity*; and it may well be this type of creativity that ultimately accounts for the inexhaustible wealth of art, literature, and science.
>
> (p. 14)

Creative Teaching: Three Elements of the Creative Act

Authorities agree that as human beings, we all possess the innate potential to create. In further defining creativity, Rollo May emphasizes that creativity "can be seen only in the act. If we were purists, we would not speak of a 'creative person,' but only of '*a creative act*'" (May, 1975: 43; emphasis in the original). In this regard, all teaching that involves the transformation of isolated and separate students into a community of learners, all teaching that involves collaborative learning among students and teachers alike, all teaching that involves the "opening of windows" is, as a consequence, a creative act.

May identifies three elements in the creative act. Each of these elements is essential in framing the lessons for creative teaching.

The first element is the *encounter*. There must be specific engagement with the "thing" to be built or created. In the case of the hawk watch lesson, the students "encountered" through their "watch" for a poem, the environment. Then they gathered isolated data and based on their visions, created something new – their individual poems.

The second element May (1975: 43) identifies is the *intensity* of the encounter. He describes it this way: "*Absorption, being caught up in, wholly involved*, and so on, are used commonly to describe the state of the artist or scientist when creating or even the child at play" (May, 1975: 44; emphasis in the original). May goes on to say: "Genuine creativity is characterized by an intensity of awareness, a heightened consciousness" that the artist [...] feels not as anxiety or fear, but as joy (pp. 44–45). In our Poetry Watch lesson, I could certainly observe the encounter, the intensity, and the absorption of my students. Clearly, a creative act had occurred.

The third element essential to the creative act answers the question: What is this intense encounter *with?* May (1975) believes this encounter is always a process of doing: "specifically, a process interrelating the person with his or her world" (p. 50). By *world* May does not just mean the immediate environment, but rather the totality of one's culture and existence.

Here's where we as creative teachers help facilitate *originality*. In the intense encounter, each student sees a different poem, watches a different poem in action, and in doing so, expresses a different vision. One of the ever-present joys of the sharing circle is working within a common boundary or space, yet at the same time, producing such different visions, interpretations, and written products. As Lone Wolf said: "*differences teach*" (recall the poem by Lone Wolf in the Introduction). The point of sharing is to notice, validate, and honor those differences, in other words, honor originality. I am forever asking my students, "Who has written something different?"

Defining the Act of Creation: *Flow*

In sum, May (1975) offers us a working definition of the act of creation: "an encounter of the intensively conscious human being with his or her world" (p. 50). At the end of the 20th century, Csikszentmihalyi would name this intensity of awareness in the act of creation, *flow*. In *Creativity: Flow and the Psychology of Discovery and Invention,* he describes this "optimal experience" as an almost "automatic, effortless, yet highly focused state of consciousness" (Csikszentmihalyi, 1996: 110). In the *flow* of creativity, the individual loses sense of time as self-consciousness, distraction, and fear of failure disappear. They are replaced by an intense sense of awareness, focus, and joy.

I use the term *flow* in my teaching to inspire my students to write freely, with intensity and focused awareness. We do warm-up exercises to "get into flow." If the bell rings, the students understand my grief because our "flow" is broken. When we come back to class the next day, I can say with their immediate understanding, "Ok. Now we have to get back into flow." As a creative act, teaching means "getting into flow." I always know I am in flow when the period is over, and I feel it has just begun. I know my students are in flow when they say, "Oh, the period is over, already?"

Creative Writing: The Conundrum

The term *creative writing* itself presents a conundrum in the academy. Few seem to like the term. Jacqueline Berke in *Twenty Questions for the Writer* explains: "The term 'creative writing' should not be limited, as it often is, to poetry, short stories and novels. *All* writing is creative when the writer forges out of his or her raw material a new whole: a poem, an expository article, an essay" (Berke, 1972/1981: 12). Joseph Moxley, in *Creative Writing in America: Theory and Pedagogy* agrees that "all writing carries the seeds of creativity: when our images and concepts develop, combine and connect and take shape in the form of words, writers discover and construct their meaning" (Moxley, 1989: 26). Quoting

David Smith, he concurs that the term *creative writing* "when applied solely to fiction, drama or poetry is largely a misnomer" (p. 26). (Note Steven Handel's creative strategies for writing scientific essays, reviewed in Chapters 10, 11, and 13.)

Despite the acknowledgement that "every act of writing is creative," the term *creative writing* has prevailed in the academy and in high schools, reflecting the persistent division within the discipline between composition and creative writing teachers, programs, and departments. The term *creative writing* may appear to some to be a misnomer; but practically speaking, the term remains at the center of the conundrum in which composition studies and composition teachers are privileged over creative writing studies and faculty (Mayers, 2015: 30–31). This privileging or division in the field of English is at the center of the present movement in the academy to formulate creative writing studies.[2]

What I Learned: It Takes Creativity and Windows

Poetically speaking, I learned in those early days of teaching that I must open the windows of my classroom, from without and from within. If I could do it, I know you can do it too. You can do it through the opening of your eyes, your heart, and mind. You can do it through your risk taking, through your willingness to listen to your students, and through your willingness to teach the spontaneous lesson. In doing so, you will discover the joy of teaching as a creative act. You will actualize the *creative* teacher within.

For Your Teacher Journal: Creativity and Windows

Reflecting: On Creativity

1. Do you believe you are creative? If so, how do you express it? If not, why not? What obstacles impede you?
2. Recall a time when you experienced creativity. How old were you? Where were you? What did you create?
3. As a student, did you ever experience teaching as a creative act? Who was that teacher? How did that teacher affect you?

4. Have you ever experienced teaching as a creative act in your own classroom?
5. In or out of school, have you ever felt creative *flow*?

Responding: Writing Prompts

1. Did you have a Miss Aussiker in your life? If so, write about that teacher's impact on you in a poem, prose poem, or memoir.
2. Have you ever experienced creative *flow*? If so, write about the experience, describe it, how it felt, step by step, in a poem, prose poem, or memoir.
3. Have you ever witnessed a creative act? Describe its impact upon you in a poem, prose poem, or memoir.

For Your Students: "Gift of Windows" Prompt

The "gift of windows" writing prompt is a powerful introductory tool for any subject course. It encourages students to use their creativity and personal voice to recall and describe a vivid observation. Students may write in either poetry or prose poetry (paragraph form) as a work in progress (see Chapter 1). This writing exercise serves as an ideal "window" for getting to know your students within the first week of school.

Teacher Instructions

1. Tell your students that they must keep their eyes closed and must choose a visual perspective: either "inside looking out" or "outside looking in."
2. Wait until all students have chosen a stance and a "window" before you begin reading the writing prompt instructions to them.
3. Ask (by show of hands) if everyone has visualized a window.
4. Then ask, "Are you outside looking in? Or inside looking out?
5. Next tell students to open their eyes and write for a preliminary title either *Outside Looking In*, or *Inside Looking Out*.

6. Have students close their eyes and proceed with the "Gift of Windows Writing" prompt below.

Student Writing Prompt: "Gift of Windows"

1. Close your eyes. Imagine a window in your past that has some significance for you. Picture that window. See it clear in your mind's eye.
2. Picture yourself there. Are you *inside the window looking out?* Or are you *outside the window looking in?*
3. Keeping your eyes closed, take a clear visual perspective. Observe closely what you see, either inside looking out or outside looking in. When you are certain you have seen "all" clearly, open your eyes and jot down notes in your journal. It can be a phrase or a few lines.
4. Close your eyes again. Then imagine opening the window slightly. What do you *hear*? Open your eyes, jot down notes again in your journal. A phrase or a few lines.
5. Close your eyes again. Then imagine opening the window slightly more. What do you *smell*? What do you imagine *tasting*? When you are ready, open your eyes and jot down notes.
6. Close your eyes again. Imagine opening the window so that you can touch something on the other side. How does it *feel*? Open your eyes and jot down a few phrases or lines.
7. Close your eyes again. Imagine opening the window all the way. What do you see, hear, smell on the other side of your window?
8. When you are finished, reread your notes.
9. Write a poem or prose poem (paragraph form) on your "window." Think of this as a work in progress.
10. After students have written for a few minutes, ask: "What would your life be like without your window?"

Model Student Poem: "Inside Looking Out" by Elise Rosenberg, Creative Writing

Inside Looking Out

Windows

Inside looking out
a large old beech tree branches and reaches for what seems
like miles, but it's

only my backyard.
the rain pit-patters against its hands, its leaves,
and the honeyed smell of spring dew touches my nose,
seducing my mind to the tree's trunk.
its bark is cold and wet
rough and bumpy
a dripping jigsaw puzzle,
allowing only a single drop to please my tongue
with sweet sap.

I fear that my childhood would be lost
and my love of nature forgotten
if I never found the tree's embrace
or gazed at it
from my window.

Additional Model Student Window Poetry and Prose

Creative writing students, past and present, intrigued by the "Inside looking out/Outside looking In," prompt frequently write authentic poetry and prose that matters to them. Elise Rosenberg was so inspired she wrote several window poems. You may wish to read "Grandpa" in Chapter 14 and "Poetry on a Plane" in this book's Conclusion. Ella Pfahler, a 2021 creative writing student from Morristown High School, recalls a childhood memory in "A Window in Time," contrasting the "windy city" of Chicago to the present pandemic and the "calamity of life" (see Chapter 11).

PART THREE: INTERDISCIPLINARY APPLICATIONS

> *Creative writing carries enormous potential as an interdisciplinary pedagogy and can improve the learning environment of the 21st century university.*
>
> – Alexandria Peary, "The Pedagogy of Creative Writing Across the Curriculum,"
> (Peary, 2015: 195)

To face the conundrum, this book offers the building of bridges between the arts and the sciences through an inclusive creative writing pedagogy. Creativity, literacy, and writing unite all disciplines. The question we should be asking is: *How do we best teach these interdisciplinary unifiers – creativity, literacy, and writing in the 21st century?*

One answer is Writing Across the Curriculum (WAC), the interdisciplinary educational movement begun in the 1970s, and more recently, Creative Writing Across the Curriculum (CWAC). In "The Pedagogy of Creative Writing Across the Curriculum," Alexandria Peary confirms that "creative writing-based writing across the curriculum helps individual faculty from different disciplines increase and improve the writing assigned in their courses specifically through the genres associated with creative writing – not expository or persuasive (Peary, 2015:195). Another answer is the interdisciplinary literacy tool, *science poetry*. Consider "Blank Page" by Arthur J. Stewart, science poet.

Model Contributor Poem: "Blank Page" by Arthur J. Stewart, Aquatic Ecologist and Ecotoxicologist

Blank Page
by Arthur J. Stewart

I stare first at the blank page, then out the window
where drops of water hang
from the down-pointing

tips of the dogwood leaves, bending
blades of grass, delicate tips

of totality. It seems
everything is wet and on the move from one place
to another. Global warming has caused
the hydrological cycle to speed up.
Now water moves

faster from the oceans to the air
and it comes down harder and more sporadically,
here and there with a vengeance
but oddly the soil is drying faster now, too—
so the dry places are getting drier, wet places
are getting wetter and here

I am, doing nothing, just
writing, staring.

(Stewart, 2021)

Commentary on Far More than "Nothing"

In the first two lines of his poem, Stewart stares down at the "blank page" and then "out the window" where drops of "water hang," effortlessly merging the two passions and preoccupations of the moment and his life – poetry and science, and in particular, his specialty, aquatic ecology. This poem moves from the personal micro-moments of "drops," and "blades," and "tips" to the macro "totality" of global climate change, only to end where Stewart began, "writing, staring" with one ironic twist: "I am, doing nothing, just." Here, he reasserts himself, "I am" but faults himself for "doing nothing." Nothing could be further from the truth. For one, the poem itself is an example of creativity when the words begin to flow like water, one off the other. Quite appropriate for an aquatic ecologist. Then, like water, everything in the poem "is wet and on the move." "Faster from the oceans to the air," we are facing the problem of global warming. This poem from the heart protests climate change offering words that speak louder than they first seem coming from a scientist who has spent his entire career studying water. Like the "blank page," there are no easy answers. Stewart may be overwhelmed by the vastness of the problem, but readers know he has done far more than "nothing, just writing and staring."

For Your Students: Creativity and Windows

Reflecting on "Blank Page"

Teacher Instructions

1. Read "Blank Page" to your students.
2. Ask students to identify the science they see in the poem. What scientific issues? Terms?
3. Ask students to identify the poetry they see in the poem.
4. Ask them what the poet is "seeing" through his window.
5. Is he just staring and doing nothing?

Responding: Writing Prompt

Teacher Instructions

The "Gift of Windows" writing prompt is applicable for all students as long as the students have an understanding of the following concepts from this chapter: *creative, creative act, creativity*. You may want to teach prior to giving your students these writing prompts that creativity is the foundation of the arts and humanities as well as the scientific and mathematic domains, such as creating a STEM (science, technology, engineering, and mathematics) or STEAM (science, technology, engineering, arts, and mathematics) project; achieving an artistic, scientific, mathematic, collaborative, or interdisciplinary creation, product, or invention.

1. Use the "Gift of Windows" writing prompt instructions in Part Two.
2. For science and math students: suggest the "windows" of microscopes, telescopes, lens, magnification, optical illusions, geometrical perspectives and relationships.

Postscript: On Hawk Watching and Project Based Learning (PBL)

For readers wondering what Barbara Nadolny's students were actually up to on the football field that day, please note, I was curious too. After my students' spontaneous "poetry watch," I questioned my colleague. Barbara was most excited to share her entire lesson. She called it "The Ultimate Watch." Unfortunately, I had no knowledge at the time of science poetry, the subject of my previous book in this series (Gorrell, 2012), or we would have had a collaborative project in the making. Instead, my colleague gave me her hawk watching resource folder. In it was a *New York Times* article by Pete Dunne, "In the Natural State," describing a statewide High School Hawk Watch program funded by the Geraldine R. Dodge foundation of Morristown. According to Dunne (1989):

> The program's most telling attribute is its authenticity. The research the students conduct is real, not erudition, not simulated. The data on the number and types of hawks that migrate over their school each day are primary data [...] and students from all over the state piece together a picture of hawk migration.
>
> (p. 33)

Morristown High School was one of a number of New Jersey high schools involved in hawk watching, an example of project-based learning (PBL), a movement influenced by Dewey's (1938) philosophy of experiential learning.[3]

At the time of the hawk watch, I had no formal knowledge of project-based learning as a pedagogy or movement. For interested teachers, Appendix A offers a description of Barbara Nadolny's hawk watch project and resources. (See Chapter 18, "Youth Birding Alaska YBA 2020," for a 21st century bird watching project.)

Chapter 2 Notes

1 A note on the term *sharing circle*: I credit Peter Elbow's *Writing without Teachers* (Elbow, 1973/1998) for helping me develop the early pedagogy

that has sustained my practice. The term *sharing* is his, the term *sharing circle* is mine, as far as I know. They both reflect the philosophy of teaching early-stage writing in a community of safe space, a supportive atmosphere with no response other than appreciation for hearing what each student wrote. Such listening and voicing, individual and communal, facilitates reflection, process writing, and confidence building. The sharing circle is not to be confused with the term *workshop* or *workshopping* a piece of writing, which involves critiquing or giving and receiving feedback on one's writing.

2 Teachers interested in the current academic debate within the field of English should first consult Tim Mayers' "Creative Writing and Process Pedagogy" (Mayers, 2015) for historical overview of the conundrum and dilemma. For contemporary discussions of the development of a creative writing pedagogy, you might start with these two works: *Creative Writing Pedagogies for the Twenty-First Century* (Peary and Hunley, 2015) and *Creativity and Discovery in the University Writing Class: A Teacher's Guide* (Chik, Costley, and Pennington, 2015).

3 PBL is an instructional strategy in which project work is central – not peripheral – to the learning process. In such projects, students assume much responsibility and control over their own learning. The PBL lesson plan directs the activities of the students, rather than the activities of the teacher" (Ubben, 2019: 68). PBL has been given many different names over the years, such as *experiential learning, inquiry-based learning, problem-based learning, and challenge-based learning*. All of these forms of learning involve individual or group activities seeking solutions to shared tasks or problems. Today, PBL is advancing science and arts education in STEAM movements to solve the complex issues Arthur J. Stewart and colleagues call the "wicked problems" – *global climate change, social injustice, and pandemic diseases.* The term, *wicked problems*, first introduced by Horst Rittel and Melvin Webber in the early 1970's (Rittel and Webber, 1973) remains as prophetic then as it is in the 21st century.

Chapter 2 References

Brande, Dorothea (1934/1981) *Becoming a Writer*. New York, NY: Tarcher/Putnam. Originally published by Harcourt, Brace.

Berke, Jacqueline (1972/1981) *Twenty Questions for the Writer* (3rd edition). New York, NY: Harcourt Brace Jovanovich.

Chomsky, Noam (1966) *Cartesian Linguistics: A Chapter in the History of Rationalist Thought*. New York, NY: Harper & Row.

Csikszentmihalyi, Mihaly (1996) *Creativity: Flow and the Psychology of Discovery and Invention*. New York, NY: Harper Perennial.

Dewey, John (1938) *Experience and Education*. New York, NY: MacMillan.

Dunne, Pete (November 5, 1989) In the natural state. *New York Times*. https://www.nytimes.com/1989/04/30/nyregion/in-the-natural-state.html

Elbow, Peter (1973/1998) *Writing without Teachers* (2nd edition). New York, NY and UK, Oxford: Oxford University Press.

Gardner, John (1981) Forward. In Dorothea Brande, *Becoming a Writer*, 11–18. New York, NY: Tarcher/Putnam.

Lasky, Dorothea (2014) Examining 'small c' creativity in the writing classroom. In Millan, Harriet Levin and Pennington, Martha C. (eds.) *Creativity and Writing Pedagogy: Linking Creative Writers, Researchers, and Teachers*, 117–136. Sheffield, UK and Bristol, CT: Equinox.

Marsen, Sky (2014) Detecting the creative in written discourse. In Millan, Harriet Levin and Pennington, Martha C. (eds.) *Creativity and Writing Pedagogy: Linking Creative Writers, Researchers, and Teachers*, 89–118. Sheffield, UK and Bristol, CT: Equinox.

Mayers, Tim (2015) Creative writing and process pedagogy. In Peary, Alexandria and Hunley, Tom C. (eds.) *Creative Writing Pedagogies for the Twenty-First Century*, 30–51. Carbondale: Southern Illinois University Press.

May, Rollo (1975) *The Courage to Create*. New York, NY: W.W. Norton.

Moxley, Joseph (1989) *Creative Writing in America*. Urbana, IL: National Council of Teachers of English.

Peary, Alexandria (2015) The pedagogy of creative writing across the curriculum. In Peary, Alexandria and Hunley, Tom C. (eds.) *Creative Writing Pedagogies for Twenty-First Century*, 194–220. Carbondale, IL: Southern Illinois University Press.

Peary, Alexandria and Hunley, Tom (eds.) *Creative Writing Pedagogies for the Twenty-First Century*. Carbondale, IL: Southern Illinois University Press.

Pennington, Martha C. (2015) Writing creativity and discovery: Process and pedagogy. In Chik, Alice, Costley, Tracey and Pennington, Martha C. (eds.) *Creativity and Discovery in the University Writing Class*, 61–92. Sheffield, UK and Oakville, CT: Equinox.

Rittel, Horst W. and Webber, Melvin M. (1973) Dilemmas in a general theory of planning. *Policy Sciences*, 4 (2): 155–169. https://www.cc.gatech.edu/fac/ellendo/rittel/rittel-dilemma.pdf. https://doi.org/10.1007/BF01405730

Stewart, Arthur J. (2021) "Blank Page." *Hallelujah Series and Other Poems*, 62. Nashville, TN: Periploi Press.

Swedberg, Richard (2020) '*How do I know what I think till I see what I say*?' An aphorism and its implications for creative theorizing. *Distinktion: Journal of Social Theory*, 21 (1): 1–18. https://doi.org/10.1080/1600910X.2019.1630846

Ubben, Gary (2019) How to structure project-based learning to meet STEAM objectives. In Stewart, Arthur J., Mueller, Michael and Tippins, Deborah (eds.) *Converting STEM into STEAM Programs: Methods and Examples from and for Education*, 85–100. Cham, Switzerland: Springer.

Chapter 3

It Takes Courage and Heart

In human beings, courage is necessary to make being and becoming possible.

– Rollo May, *The Courage to Create*
(May, 1975: 13)

PART ONE: THE COURAGE TO TEACH

When it comes to writing, we as teachers are not very different from our students. We bring to the classroom ourselves, shouldering all of the attitudes and experiences we have gleaned from our education as English students in primarily academic, literature-centered environments. For many of us, those experiences have not always been nurturing. Some English teachers do not think they are good writers, let alone good poets or storytellers. It takes courage to teach writing, and there are many reasons why.

A Teaching Story: The Courage to Teach

When one of my colleagues, an experienced high school mathematics teacher was assigned to teach AP calculus, she revealed to me her hesitancy. I was surprised by her concern. She was a veteran mathematics teacher held in high regard by faculty and students alike. Nevertheless, she took an additional calculus course over that summer "just to be sure." She was also known among her peers as always "the most prepared," never teaching a class without solving every problem. After she began teaching AP calculus, I asked her how the course was going.

She replied, "I've never been so stressed. I can barely keep up. I'm on the same chapter as the kids. I'm preparing the night before each class. Last week, I was observed during a lesson, and I just went home and cried." I was shocked by her reply.

I'm sure your observation was great (she nodded), and what's so wrong about learning with your students? In creative writing, I don't always know what they're going to do or say; I have a plan, but I often teach from what they write in the moment."

"Oh" she said looking at me puzzled. "I could never do that; that's English." And she laughed.

We, as teachers do not always give ourselves enough credit. It takes courage to teach a subject for which there is no one right answer, and we cannot anticipate all of the questions that may arise. It takes courage to teach a subject like creative writing in which the lesson is dependent upon student responses that may or may not be instructive. It takes even more courage to teach a subject in which you and your students "walk on the path" *together* to learn a discipline. Lastly, it takes courage to teach a subject that requires multiple roles of the teacher – reader, writer, mentor, coach, evaluator, and ultimately, co-learner and fellow human being.

What is Courage? Heart, Passion, and Commitment

> *Courage, after all, is a matter of heart, and hearts do their work one beat at a time.*
>
> – Julia Cameron, *The Artist's Way: A Spiritual Path to Higher Creativity*
> (Cameron, 1992: 201)

The word *courage* comes from the same stem as the French word *coeur* meaning "heart." When we teach with courage, we are teaching with "heart." That means we are teaching from our inner most being our selfhood. Rollo May confirms: "In human beings, courage is necessary to make being and becoming possible" (May, 1975: 13). That is one of the reasons why teaching is such a courageous act, for teaching with heart, passion, and commitment means you teach authentically from somewhere in the innermost landscape of yourself. Doing so, may make yourself vulnerable – vulnerable to being wrong, vulnerable to being human in front of your students.

We all know teachers who want to be always right, expert authorities – in other words, *perfect.* But teaching is not the art of perfection. Rather, it is much more the art of being *human*. It takes courage to teach any subject when you know you cannot be perfect.

The Paradox of Courage: Conviction and Doubt

May points out the inherent paradox of courage: "We must be fully committed, but we must also be aware at the same time that we might possibly be wrong (May, 1975: 20). For May, this dialectic relationship between conviction and doubt is a positive characteristic of the "highest type of courage" (p. 20). "To believe fully and at the same moment to have doubts is not at all a contradiction. It presupposes a greater respect for truth, an awareness that truth always goes beyond anything that can be said or done at a given moment" (p. 21).

Parker Palmer, in the *Courage to Teach* (Palmer, 1998) sheds light on the courage to teach any subject when teacher and student are co-learners exploring, discovering and experiencing a subject and its relationship to the landscapes of self and the world. Such teaching requires *heart*, best defined by Palmer "as the place where *intellect, emotion*, *spirit* and *will* converge in the human self" (p. 11). His point that good teachers are able "to weave a complex web of connections among themselves, their subjects, and their students, and that these connections are held more in their hearts rather than in their methods or techniques encourages us as teachers to seek not only the "courage to teach" but the "courage to create" classroom environments that support such teaching (p. 11).

PART TWO: CREATIVE COURAGE AND MORAL COURAGE

Creative Courage: The Heart of Our Teaching

Among all types of courage May identifies *creative courage*, the discovering of new forms upon which a new society can be built, as the most important. Why? Because "if you do not express your own original ideas, if you do not listen to your own being," you will have betrayed not only yourself, but the community as a whole (May, 1975: 12–13). Although creative courage may seem overwhelming to individual teachers who have not yet realized their creative souls, May "heartens" us by stressing that those creations do not have to be monumental. All creations, however small, are creative acts of courage. "Whatever sphere we may be in, there is a profound joy in the realization that we are helping to form the structure of a new world. This is creative courage, however minor or fortuitous our creations may be" (May, 1975: 35).

In this sense, teaching becomes one of the most creative and courageous of acts. In the heart of our teaching, do we not transform students? Do we not transfer culture? Do we not in this process "help to form the structure of a *new* world?" Then why are not teachers more confident in their own creative powers? Why do we not recognize the value of our intellect, emotion, spirit and will, the heart of our creative courage?

My Grandfather's Wisdom: Not Perfect?

When I was a child as young as five, my grandfather started the tradition of quizzing me on every visit. You might think of this as testing, but I thought it was fun. On one visit he would teach me a new word, proverb, or state capital. On his next visit, he would quiz me. I'll never forget the joy on his face when I would give the right answer. That's where his wisdom would come in. Sometimes grandpa would be wrong. He made intentional mistakes. *Grandpa, not perfect*? His expression was always so serious. But one day he said, "The capital of New Jersey is Newark." I knew he was wrong, and shouted, "No, Trenton!" He just beamed with laughter. Another time when I said I could not remember one more proverb, he answered in kind, "Just try. Remember…*if at first you don't succeed, try, try, again!*"

What I Learned: Discarding the Tyranny of Perfection

> *If you're not prepared to be wrong, you'll never come up with anything original.*
>
> – Sir Ken Robinson, "Do Schools Kill Creativity?" (Robinson, 2006)

I believe my grandfather somehow gave me the courage to create. Although his wisdom took me a lifetime to truly appreciate, I have slowly learned the value of discarding the tyranny of *perfection* and its close companion, the tyranny of *absolute authority*. Sharing my nascent poetry and creative writings with my classes, knowing that they may be instructive but not intrinsically worthy, took courage. But I could see that my students valued my efforts. They also learned from my process and struggle to write. I was no longer the absolute authority; I was a co-learner, a partner in an art form, learning by trial and error. In the end, it gave me far more authority in the classroom than any other perfect role I could have played. My students came to regard me and respect me as a fellow writer and human being. In the process, they sought my comments and reactions to their work, inside and outside of class. For how can a creation – a work in progress – be perfect or wrong?

Reflecting upon my own creative courage, I know it was not easy to begin. I remember that sinking feeling in my stomach the first time I was wrong in front of a class. Now, thanks to my grandfather's wisdom, I relish such moments. It gives me the opportunity to smile, just like him, and praise the student for noticing the error and correcting me. Sometimes it gives me a teachable moment. My mistake might just be the opportunity to further clarify an ambiguity. I love to note, "We are both correct. And thank you for pointing out another way of looking at the text or poem." *Becoming* asks us to discard the weighty baggage of perfectionism, replacing it instead with the mindset of *works in progress* and the *role of co-learner*.

It Takes Moral Courage

Related to creative courage and the courage to teach is, above all else, *moral courage*. To teach or write in moments affecting one's heritage or humanity takes moral courage, especially when taking a stand or protesting injustice is involved.

Amy Uyematsu, high school mathematics teacher, explains: "My grandparents and parents were forced into Manzanar and Gila concentration camps" the former in California, and the latter in Arizona (Uyematsu, 2019). Writing as a *sansei*, a third-generation Japanese American, she shows the moral courage to bear witness in her math poem, "Simple Division," and the creative courage to write about the injustice of her grandfather's internment in Gila. When I asked Amy if she ever shared "Simple Division" with her math students, she replied:

> I'm guessing I wrote "Simple Division" in the late 90s or early 2000s. All five of my books contain poems about Japanese American 'camp' experiences. I never taught this short poem or shared it with my math classes.
>
> (Uyematsu, 2019)

Model Contributor Poems: "Desert Camouflage" and "Simple Division" by Amy Uyematsu, High School Mathematics Teacher

Desert Camouflage
For Jiro Morita
by Amy Uyematsu

Grandpa was good at persuading the others
after the official evacuation orders.

Detained at Tulare Assembly Center,
he was the voice of reason among his angry friends,
raising everyone's spirits
when he started the morning exercise class.

Some issei said Grandpa couldn't be trusted –
after all, hadn't he volunteered
to fight in World War I?
And why did he speak better English
or brag that he was already a U.S. citizen
when the government denounced them as aliens?

At Gila, when nobody was willing
to make camouflage netting the military needed,
only Grandpa could talk them into it.
How many American soldiers would ever suspect
the netting protecting them was sewn by issei
whose faces could never be camouflaged?
(Uyematsu, 2005a)

Simple Division
by Amy Uyematsu

My history echoes
from small diameters –

120,000 issei and nisei
divided among 7 states

equals 10 barbed-wire
desert prison camps.

(Uyematsu, 2005b)

For Your Teacher Journal: It Takes Courage

Reflecting: On Courage

1. Recall a time in your life when you experienced courage.

2. Recall a time in your life when you observed a courageous act? Where were you? What happened? How did it affect you?
3. Recall a time in your life when you experienced creative courage.
4. Recall a time in your life when you observed or witnessed an act of moral courage. How did it affect you?
5. Recall a time in your life when you experienced moral courage.

Responding: Writing Prompts

1. Describe in detail an act of courage you experienced. Where were you? How did it affect you? Then write a poem, prose poem, or prose piece, "On an Act of Courage."
2. Describe in detail an act of courage or creative courage you observed. Where were you? How did it affect you? Then write a poem, prose poem, or prose piece, "On Courage or Creative Courage."
3. After reading Amy Uyematsu's poem dedicated to her grandfather, write a poem, prose poem, prose piece, or letter to someone you regard as having moral courage.
4. Write a poem, prose poem, prose piece, letter, or memoir about "bearing witness" or the courage to bear witness. This could be about moral courage you observed or experienced.

PART THREE: INTERDISCIPLINARY APPLICATIONS

The first person that enters my mind when I think of courage is my grandmother, Hanna, who passed away in May of 2017. She survived the Holocaust in Essen, Germany by going into hiding and assuming a different name. I often write to not only recall and record my memories of her, but to tell her amazing story. She is my hero.

– Stefanie DeFronzo, Reflection on "Annemarie Hohensee"

The writing models and prompts in Part One may be assigned to all students as long as students have an understanding of the concepts of "courage," "creative courage," and "moral courage" as they apply to this chapter. If not, before students across the disciplines respond, you may want to teach that courage may include breakthrough scientific, mathematical, artistic, or athletic tasks, discoveries, or inventions. For example: first-time creations, performing an original experiment; composing a new score; achieving a scientific discovery; creating a collaborative STEM or STEAM project. Other examples may include protesting injustice (moral courage), conscientious objection, standing up for "the other" as well as rescuing or saving those in need (more commonly termed *bravery*).

Model Student Poem: "Annemarie Hohensee" by Stefanie DeFronzo, Biochemistry and Molecular Biology Major, Drew University

Annemarie Hohensee
by Stefanie DeFronzo

The name that made her free.
I always thought,
had I met her then,
what would she say to me?
How did she act?
How did she live, one soul inside another?
And do I now think of her
as a person completely other
than my Grandmother
of a different name
and perhaps a different being?
Is this girl that she once knew
inside the woman I'm seeing?
How did she feel?
How did she let
herself be someone she was not?

In that time did she let herself
be someone she forgot?
To hide her truth
and expose another
does she now forget?
And am I to think this girl
a person I've never met?
How can I ignore, how can I push
away the thought of meeting
the girl that kept my Grandmother's life
when her true heart wasn't beating?
I remember in awe
in pain
in hope
this girl that is now just a name.
And I think of her
as the woman I've met
for her soul remained always the same.

(DeFronzo, 2021)

For Your Teacher Journal

Reflecting: On Courage

1. Recall a time in your life when you experienced or observed *courage* or a courageous act by a colleague within your discipline.
2. Recall a time in your life when you observed a colleague from another discipline performing a courageous act? Where were you? What happened? How did it affect you?
3. Recall a time in your life when you experienced or observed *creative courage* by a colleague within your discipline or within another discipline.
4. Recall a time in your life when you witnessed an act of moral courage affecting your discipline or a colleague's discipline. How did it affect you?

Responding: Writing Prompts

1. Write a poem, prose poem, letter, or memoir “On Observing an Interdisciplinary Act of Courage.”
2. Write a poem, prose poem, letter, or memoir “On Observing an Interdisciplinary Act of Creative Courage.”
3. After reading Amy Uyematsu’s poem dedicated to her grandfather, write a poem, prose poem, prose piece, or letter to someone you regard as having moral courage.
4. Write a poem, prose poem, prose piece, letter or memoir about “bearing witness” or the courage to bear witness. This could be about moral courage you observed or experienced.

On the Courage to Teach: A Poem by Amy Uyematsu

The Weight of Nothing, Part IV
by Amy Uyematsu

To end with nothing, is something
Suvan Geer

IV
Without my friend Nothing
on the page, I’d never have to write
another poem. but Nothing waits
here, waving me on, inviting me
to rap and rant, pray, sing, testify
what is, was, could, and always will be.
I greet all that’s coming,
Contained as sheer breath
into word, born
to crave and engrave the emptiness
that Nothing can’t stop giving.

(Uyematsu, 2005c)

Commentary on "Nothing"

Amy Uyematsu's poem speaks to the creative courage that exists in the face of "Nothing" – that it is always something "that can't stop giving," but giving what? For her, that space – that "emptiness" – is "to crave and engrave" – a courageous challenge. Uyematsu brings this chapter full circle, reminding us that the courage to wrestle the possibility of making something out of *Nothing* – the poetic blank page – is ultimately, the *courage to teach.* (See Appendix B for the complete poem.)

Chapter 3 References

Cameron, Julia (1992) *The Artist's Way: A Spiritual Path to Higher Creativity*. New York, NY: Penguin/Putnam.

DeFronzo, Stefanie (2021). "Annemarie Hohensee." Copyright Stefanie DeFronzo.

May, Rollo (1975) *The Courage to Create*. New York, NY: W.W. Norton.

Palmer, Parker (1998) *The Courage to Teach*. San Francisco, CA: Jossey-Bass.

Robinson, Sir Ken (June 26, 2006) Do schools kill creativity? https://www.ted.com/talks/sir_ken_robinson_do_schools_kill_creativity

Uyematsu, Amy (2005a) "Desert Camouflage." *Stone, Bow, Prayer*, 50. Port Townsend, WA: Copper Canyon Press.

Uyematsu, Amy (2005b) "Simple Division." *Stone, Bow, Prayer*, 49. Port Townsend, WA: Copper Canyon Press.

Uyematsu, Amy (2005c) "The Weight of Nothing, Part IV" *Stone, Bow, Prayer*, 74. Port Townsend, WA: Copper Canyon Press.

Uyematsu, Amy (2016) "On Poets." *Basic Vocabulary*, 76. Pasadena, CA: Red Hen Press.

Uyematsu, Amy (August 6, 2019) Email correspondence with Nancy S. Gorrell.

Chapter 4

Knowing Where You've Come From: Writing Memories

Every child is an artist. The problem is how to remain an artist once we grow up.

– Attributed to Pablo Picasso; qtd by Sir Ken Robinson, "Do Schools Kill Creativity?" (Robinson, 2006)

PART ONE: A TEACHING POEM

Kindergarten Creation
by Nancy Gorrell

The mountainous easel
stood before me
a vast matted grey sky.
Below,
mouths of mayonnaise jars beckoned
cavernous reds and bubbling blue whirlpools.
Deep within, forests of black timber
sprouted tall peaks,
dug roots in the red/blue
brushed heavy and expectant.

"Now" said a cloudless voice,
and my hands knew and flew
with full expanse of wings
and landed nearly wounded
on the peaks of each black shaft.
And one hand gripped
the viscous red and the other clung
for life to the blue of possibility
and the earth quaked,
and the white world was no more.

And it was good
(or so I thought)
But the teacher,
shards of glass in her voice
spoke "No!"
And the floor,
quicksand sinking leaden feet,
and my heart,
rushing a thousand beats,
and the easel,
rivers of red/blue
dripped, dropped—
And I wondered,
how long I could live
on the precipice of purple.

(Gorrell, 1989)

What I Learned: On the "Precipice of Purple"

I loved colors and painting. Everything in the poem is true, literally. Red and blue make purple. Teachers say "no." What I did not know at the time: I would never take an art or painting course in high school, college, or adult life. I didn't touch a paint brush until my 70th birthday when an artist friend inspired me. I oil paint now for my own creative pleasure.

PART TWO: WRITING MEMORIES

Elementary Creations

When I was in kindergarten in the early 1950s, I had a teacher named Miss Geary. I have only one vivid memory from that year, and it concerned my inability to color and paint within the lines. I loved to paint. You got to stand on a plastic sheet in front of a tall easel. You had on a pretty apron to prevent any stains. And there were enormous brushes set in mayonnaise jars of primary colors. My mother recalls how Miss Geary called her up to say that I needed to work on "staying within the lines." I suspect that applied not only to painting, but to penmanship as well. I always got "needs improvement" in penmanship. I remember the fat lead pencils without erasers. We printed on soft, lined, yellow paper, the kind that tore easily. When we did get erasers, they were big, lumpy, and separate – not the small kinds of erasers attached on the ends of pencils. On the yellow paper they made ugly, irreversible smudges. I usually ended up with a hole in my paper. I don't think I saw white paper until second grade. White paper was very special. It meant you were perfect and could write something without making any mistakes, which of course wasn't true. I was always nervous about writing, that is, moving from the yellow to the white that the teacher sometimes said was "copying over." I can't remember what would happen if you made a mistake on the white paper. I guess you would have to just ask for another piece of paper, definitely an embarrassment.

In first grade I had a teacher with snow white hair. She was soft spoken and my mother said she loved my story about the two pigs that got married. I have no memory of that story, but apparently, Miss Dempsey was very amused. In second grade we began to learn to write faster. *Cursive* was what they called it. I'll never forget the black and white penmanship charts that framed the blackboards of my elementary classrooms; the slant, the curlicue of cursive was artful to me. One day Miss Gillen said, "We are going to write in ink tomorrow. Please bring with you a pen and a bottle of ink." My mother took me to an exclusive stationary store, called the Exclusive Shoppe, to buy my first Esterbrook fountain pen. I'll never forget my excitement at choosing my own color ink. There were three choices: black, blue, and something in between. I think I chose something in between. The next day we were instructed in the art of dipping into the ink well, opening the little lever, allowing the ink to gently rise in the pen, closing the lever, removing the pen from the well, dipping the dripping pen into the paper towel on our desks, and then, printing our names on the lined paper. I don't think I got beyond "Nan" when the ink ran out, and I had to repeat the procedure.

I don't remember anything I actually wrote in all of my primary school experience. But I do remember the "tools of my trade." As a child, writing to me had more to do with the mechanics of the process than the substance of the words. And that was undoubtedly because my primary education was just that – limited to primary colors. I grew up in the age of conformity – the 1950s when teaching meant primarily the 3 R's. The rainbow of colors of the felt pens and fluorescent highlighters would be for another generation. Oh, what I would have given for those pen sets in graduated rainbow colors of every hue! My schooling was creatively barren. I do not remember a story, a poem or a personal essay I wrote until I entered high school.

High School Creations

Freshman year I had my first male English teacher, Mr. Haber. Fresh out of private school teaching, Mr. Haber believed in the discipline of the weekly "comp." The "comp" was a 250-word essay on a given topic; the topics were all foreign to me, and I remember "writing" beginning with the dictionary. There I would go to find the "meaning" of my topic, and then I would spend endless time trying to literally fill up my paper to complete the 250 words. Ironically, it was within the colorless strictures of the assigned "comp" mode of teaching that I had my first taste of creative writing. To this day, I thank Mr. Haber for assigning "free choice" for topics. Yet with freedom of choice, I do not remember a sudden swelling of imagination. Instead, there was even more dread. What was I going to write about? My mother came to the rescue. "Why don't you write about your Uncle Stanley," she said. My uncle was at the time a poet, and I was in awe of his stature, 6'4," as well as his persona.

"How do I do that?" I puzzled. I had never before written anything personal and certainly not anything personal for school.

"Why don't you just describe your memories of him, how he looks and makes you feel." *Describe*. It was a word I had never before conceptualized. Then I "saw" a picture of my uncle in my mind, and I started writing my first lines: *He picked me up and raised me high up onto his shoulders. I was on top of the world, holding his curly black hair.* Suddenly the writing felt real and I loved it. I do not remember what else I wrote, but I do remember Mr. Haber liked my "comp." I got my first "A" on a writing assignment. Unfortunately, that first attempt at creative writing was my last in high school. I do not remember writing creatively again until I became a freshman in college, and that too was a short-lived experience.

College Creations

My college writing memories are framed essentially in blue – blue books filled to the brim, lecture halls of students bent over blue books, professors handing back blue books, and me discarding blue books after I received my grades. These memories framed in blue fade in the background compared to what seemed to matter more to me at the time. As an entering freshman at the University of Wisconsin in 1964, I did not place out of English Composition 101, a required course. The placement test, heavy on grammar, was not my strength. In reality, I had no interest in the subject of English. I turned to politics, history and political science; poetry, literature, and writing seemed like indulgent pastimes. Then, in the spring of my freshman year, events turned to the personal. I contracted a bad case of mononucleosis and was confined to the hospital infirmary. At the time, I was in the middle of Freshman Composition 101. Little did I know that completing the work bedside would not satisfy the English Department's strict attendance rule of no more than three absences from class. I received no credit in the course and was advised instead to take a correspondence course over the summer to satisfy the requirement.

As a result, that summer I began my one and only formal writing course. It was a strange experience. I had no idea what to expect from the faceless teacher I never met. I only knew that each week he mailed me an assignment, which turned out to my surprise, to be a creative writing assignment. Each week I had to complete the assignment immediately so that he could correct it and mail me back the next one. Together, "we" had to complete ten mailed assignments. I remember being more worried about the mailing than the writing. There was no reading, no instruction, no guidance, and essentially no teaching. When I got my first assignment back, there was a little comment written at the end – something like, "You have a vivid imagination" or "Interesting idea." That was it.

In retrospect, the experience taught me more about writing than all of the English classes I took in college put together. Writing for a faceless, non-judgmental teacher seemed strange but then became liberating. For the first time I experienced writing for myself, without caring what anyone else thought. Under the pressure of the United States mail, I quickly overcame writer's block by realizing it didn't matter what I wrote: I just had to write. And I did. By the end of the summer, I was amazed at my own fluency and productivity. I may not have written well, but I wrote and wrote. I remember distinctly writing a long war story, something so foreign from my experience as to be comical. Yet the faceless teacher liked it. When the summer was over, I received a "B" in my writing course.

What I Learned: Defining the Writing Teacher I Hope to Be

My writing memories reveal to me the creatively barren existence I had in the institution known as "school" from kindergarten to college. "Kindergarten Creation," which opens this chapter, reveals to me the pain I felt in elementary school living on the "precipice of purple." I was always on edge afraid of angering the teacher, wanting to please, yet sensing that pleasing would require controlling my creative impulses. And so I did. For all those years, I was a model, conforming student.

These experiences directly affected what kind of teacher I became. I knew I never wanted to teach writing to my students the way I was taught. I wanted to instill creativity, excitement, and passion. Because of the stifling of my own creative spirit, I have always had a special place in my heart for the creative student – the nonconformist, the closet writer or artist wanting to do it differently. Unlike Mrs. Geary, I find myself saying "Yes" each time a student asks, "Mrs. Gorrell, can I do it this way?" Knowing where I have come from, informs my teaching, and guides me in defining the writing teacher I hope to be.

Defining the Writing Teacher You Hope to Be

> *Clearly, I could not teach the way I had been taught.*
> – Wendy Bishop, "Afterword – Colors of a Different Horse: On Learning to Like Teaching Creative Writing" (Bishop, 1994: 286)

What are your writing memories? Have you experienced a teacher who was able to "bring forth" the creative writer in you? Have you experienced a teacher who had faith in your abilities and nurtured your creativity? Have you experienced a writing mentor whose teaching was transformative? Have you encountered the teaching you would want to emulate? In other words, have you experienced education in the most fundamental sense? Or, have you experienced *mis-education*; teachers that caused you to doubt yourself, your creativity, and ability as a writer?

Unfortunately, too many teachers of English and writing have experienced miseducation themselves when it comes to writing. Wendy Bishop, in the Afterword to *Colors of a Different Horse: Rethinking Creative Writing Theory and Pedagogy* (Bishop and Ostrom, 1994), recalls her own mis-education in the academy. She believes she is not alone in that mis-education:

> I have talked to others about teaching creative writing who feel as I do. We were in creative writing classrooms a lot, but didn't feel supported there. Some of us were simply muddling along trying to right the wrongs we felt were done to us by our own previous teachers. Some of us had internalized a destructive self-doubt: that it wasn't just teaching that our poet or fiction teachers distained, maybe it really was us, the young aspiring writers in their classes.
>
> (Bishop, 1994: 280)

As Bishop concludes in the Afterword, "Clearly, I could not teach the way I had been taught" (p. 286).

Part of walking the path is knowing where you've come from. Knowing where you've come from will guide you in knowing what kind of teacher you hope to be and hope to become. Whether you have experienced education or mis-education is not the point. How you define yourself in terms of that education is the point. *To teach is to learn, to learn is to* be: trust the process, trust the path that you walk on, trust that together, with your students, you will become the teacher you hope to be.

For Your Teacher Journal: "Writing Memories"

Reflecting: Education or Mis-Education?

1. What are your writing memories? Reflect upon your own writing experiences. What were your elementary, high school and college creations?

2. What do your writing memories reveal to you about your education? How do you think your experiences affect your thoughts and feelings about writing?
3. Were your writing or English class memories one of education or mis-education? Reflect and evaluate.
4. How do you think your experiences affect the teacher you hope to be or become or presently are?

Responding: Writing Prompts

1. Write your own elementary creations, high school creations and/or college creations based on your memories.
2. After reading the teaching poem, "Kindergarten Creation," write your own poem or prose poem about your own kindergarten or elementary creations or writing experiences.
3. Write an entry in your journal exploring your writing memories in terms of education or mis-education.

For Your Students: Writing Memories

Instructions for Students

1. What are your writing memories? Reflect upon your experiences with writing throughout your schooling. What were your elementary and high school creations? Describe and record your memories.
2. What do your writing memories reveal to you about your attitudes, feelings and experiences with writing? Reflect and evaluate.

PART THREE: INTERDISCIPLINARY APPLICATIONS

Writing Memories Across the Disciplines: Education or Mis-Education?

Asking students to reflect and respond about their writing memories throughout their elementary and high school years is a valuable introductory lesson for any discipline. It opens "windows" not only about writing skills, but about interdisciplinary attitudes, knowledge, and education. I know this having used this chapter's exercise with all my English and Science Academy classes at Morristown High School. In Bishop's words, that is how I have worked to become the teacher I hope to be.

Consider the following writing memories from Stefanie DeFronzo, senior at Drew University and Arthur J. Stewart, aquatic ecologist and ecotoxicologist. Both explore their writing memories and mis-education across the disciplines of English and science.

Model Student Response: "My Poetry Book" by Stefanie DeFronzo, Biochemistry and Molecular Biology Major

My Poetry Book
by Stefanie DeFronzo

I started with a blank, white, hardcover book full of a third grader's fluffy poetry and somehow ended up in college, remembering the words passionately placed in that book. Growing up on Dr. Seuss, my love for rhyme and reason expanded with acquired knowledge and curiosity. Through my classroom (and bedroom floor), my interest and affinity for writing has bloomed into a book cover full of green, blue, and purple flowers. . .

Stefanie's Elementary Creations

It was a hot and sticky afternoon in Mrs. Snyder's third grade class. The fans were blowing onto the red-faced and droopy-eyed students who were writing quietly into blank, hardcover books at their desks. Each book was decorated with a student's design and "My Poetry Book" printed, scripted, or scribbled on the front cover. Each day, Mrs. Snyder would talk to the class about a different type of poetry, and we would then later write (or attempt) our very own piece. As odes, sonnets, and haikus filled the pages of our books, some students became disturbed, disinterested, or ready to go home, while others became appreciative of this unique form of art and communication.

Even after our poetry unit had concluded, our books closed and brought home, I continued this new art consistently. I could whip up a poem or a small paragraph with ease at my parents' request after an interesting event. Before I knew it, I was out of school and into summer, sitting with pen and pad in hand at the Rensselaer Polytechnic Institute's poetry camp. For one week we occupied various locations, both grassy and air conditioned, and spilled our senses onto pages. Most times we were creating our own work, but sometimes we partnered up and got to exude double the creative energy. One particular partner poem that sticks out in my memory is an "Ode to Doughnuts"; it was undoubtedly one written just before lunch. Not only did the camp nurture my newfound love for poetry, it helped me learn the importance of creative expression and communication.

Stefanie's Middle and High School Creations

All throughout my middle and high school career, poetry continued to be a background skill that allowed me to convey ideas both cleverly and concisely. I wasn't one to turn history papers into haikus, but if a writing piece didn't limit me to a certain genre, my scheming mind leaped to rhyme.

Stefanie's College Creations

When I got to college, I didn't immediately think about writing, as my high school AP and college-level credits carried over to satisfy Drew University's requirements. However, the Honors English and AP English classes I took in high school had a structure that basically negated creativity. The way we were taught the one interpretation of each novel, short story, or poem seemed painfully one-sided. Since I didn't always come up with the one "correct" meaning behind the work, I was left thinking that I might not be as good a writer as I had thought I was in elementary and middle school.

Except for coursework essays and assignments, my first two years at Drew I didn't write. Although I did well in the first-year Drew seminar class that was designed to aid in the transition from high school to college writing, the honors colloquium I also took in my first year defeated my confidence with its infamous

250-word essays. Not only is it enormously difficult to write a well-organized thought and response in 250 words, the harsh grading of the professors made me once again question my abilities. What was so right or wrong about my own thoughts and my own words? How did my creativity deserve a "B+" and not an "A"?

The first time I elected to write creatively college was in my third year when I received an email about a writing workshop for second generation Holocaust survivors, hosted by Drew University's Center for Holocaust and Genocide Studies. Although I was grandchild of a Holocaust survivor, a third generation, I emailed the organizer, and the next thing I knew I was sitting in a room with twenty other people, writing about the stories of our families. It was an amazing experience that I am beyond grateful to have been able to be a part of, and out of it came a series of poems that I was truly proud of and a rekindled confidence to write.

The spring of that same year, I decided to sign up for a poetry course. I thought that it would be a change from writing lab reports and short answers on chemistry problem sets. Scientific writing to most people is a completely different skill set than creative writing. To me, this is completely wrong. Different disciplines have different formalities, but the framework on which you write in each should be the same. Each piece of writing has its own characters and plot, but in poetry, science, or otherwise, everyone wants to tell a story.

The poetry course I took was a civic-based service course in which the seven or so students enrolled wrote poetry together on campus, then traveled to Morristown Neighborhood House's afterschool program to teach workshops to the students there. This was an eye-opening experience. I always find myself learning from my younger counterparts, as the amount of fearlessness and imagination they have is unmatched and untainted. Interpretation inhibits but imagination ignites.

Commentary on Stefanie DeFronzo's Writing Memories

Stefanie's writing memories reveal both education and miseducation, creativity seized and lost in 21st century education. Her elementary memories reflect the schooling of a child captivated by a creative teacher at a young age. Her "Poetry Book" project in third grade sustained her love of poetry, enabling her to continue this new art form on her own outside of school. As a child, she attended a poetry camp, which helped nurture her newfound love for poetry.

So motivated, one would think Stefanie would have pursued "the importance of creative expression and communication" throughout her middle and high school years. Not so. Instead "poetry continued to be a background skill," something sought but not taught. Her honors and AP English classes in high school "negated creativity." Her New York State high school did not offer a creative writing elective program. In college as a first-year biochemistry major, Stefanie's honors colloquium "defeated" her confidence with its "infamous 250-word essays" that limited her reflective thinking and creativity.

Stefanie was not able to bridge the divide until her junior year at Drew University when, as a third-generation descendant, she took a Holocaust writing workshop that rekindled her "confidence to write," and then her first formal poetry writing course which she describes as "an eye-opener."

Stefanie's writing memories confirm what I had been hearing from my creative writing students for decades: that the last time they wrote poetry or wrote creatively was in elementary school. (See Chapter 6 for a similar observation from Mark Hess.) Stefanie's memories also confirm the difficulties multi-talented science and arts students face when they want to pursue both disciplines during their school careers.

Despite the widespread call in the academy for the development of a creative writing pedagogy that casts a wide net of creative writing strategies across the curriculum, Stefanie's writing memories attest to the persistence of the lack of creativity and creative writing experiences in her high school and early university education.[1]

Model Contributor Poem: "Weaver's Needle" by Arthur J. Stewart, Aquatic Ecologist and Ecotoxicologist

Weaver's Needle
by Arthur J. Stewart

Do not dangle your participles or split infinitives,
my wild-haired high-school English teacher said.
She could build sentences from the cool dry breeze
that worked the walls of the ragged canyons

deep in the Superstition Mountains, where even now
the red sun dips behind the Weaver's Needle.
Do not, she said,
use words you do not know.

Never circle a clean center with fuzz.
Her voice, we said,
quivered like the call of a thin coyote,
adding nearly nothing to the morning air.

Now my skin tingles, my ear strains
for the last trembling note of her. She leans
forward in my memory: her gold wire-rim glasses rest
precariously on the narrow bridge of her nose.

She's serious; she puts her stare
hard to each of us, trying to teach us
something fundamental.
We sit, dolts, hopeless even by our own accounting.

One of us might become something useful—
somehow, someday, by accident or luck
or divine intervention. She hesitates,
building a web of love in her mind as we sit,

our thoughtless little heads bowed
in acquiescence, incapable of learning

but appreciative of her attempt to teach us
things she thought had value.

After class that day we filed out
silent, one after another, ragamuffin whipped.
But in the school's locker-lined hall
we soon gathered the strength of youth again:

safe in that brick canyon
with familiar metal echoes,
we lined up three deep and howled
like coyotes.

(Stewart, 2003)

Commentary on Being "Ragamuffin Whipped"

Stewart's memories of high school writing came from his teacher, a "weaver of grammar, words and sentences" whose instruction negated creativity and risk-taking: "Do not use words you do not know." The heyday of this pedagogy, modeled from Harvard's first-year required composition course, dominated the first half of the 20th century attempting to improve entering students' writing skills through a strict grammarian approach (Mayers, 2015: 31–32). The fact that students' writing did not improve, nevertheless did not quell the advocates of this approach of their enthusiasm: "She's serious…trying to teach us." Despite his "ragamuffin whipped" mis-education, Stewart's innate creativity enabled him to walk the path of becoming both a scientist and a poet of seven books of poetry and a chapbook, *Uncoils a Snake*.

For Your Teacher Journal: Writing Memories

Reflecting: Education or Mis-Education?

1. What are your writing memories? Reflect upon your own writing experiences. What were your elementary, high school and college creations?

2. What do your writing memories reveal to you about your education? How do you think your experiences affect your thoughts and feelings about writing?
3. Were your writing or English class memories one of education or mis-education? Were you "ragamuffin whipped" like Arthur Stewart? Reflect and evaluate.
4. Did you ever have a teacher like the one in "Weaver's Needle?" Was that teacher an English teacher, science, math teacher, or teacher in another subject? Reflect and evaluate.
5. How do you think your experiences affect the teacher you hope to be, or become, or presently are?

Responding: Writing Prompts

1. Write your own elementary creations, high school creations, and/or college creations based on your memories.
2. After reading the teaching poem, "Kindergarten Creation," write a poem, prose poem, or memoir about your kindergarten or elementary creations or writing experiences.
3. After reading "Weaver's Needle," write your own poem, prose poem, or memoir about a teacher or experience of education or mis-education.

For Your Students: Writing Memories

Instructions for Students

1. What are your writing memories? Reflect upon your experiences with writing throughout your schooling across the disciplines. What were your elementary and high school writing memories? Describe and record your memories.
2. What do writing memories reveal to you about your attitudes, feelings and experiences with writing across the disciplines? Reflect and evaluate.

Chapter 4 Note

1 Twenty-first century research and scholarship in the academy calls for widespread improvement in teaching of creativity and literacy through the development of (a) creative literacy as a field (b) development of a creative writing pedagogy that unites composition and creative writing teaching (c) use of creative writing as an interdisciplinary tool to unite the arts and sciences. (Chik, Costley, and Pennington, 2015; Clark, Hergenrader, and Rein, 2017; Millan and Pennington, 2014; Peary and Hunley, 2015).

Chapter 4 References

Chik, Alice, Costley, Tracey, and Pennington, Martha C. (eds.) (2015) *Creativity and Discovery in the University Writing Class*. Sheffield, UK and Oakville, CT: Equinox.

Clark, Michael Dean, Hergenrader, Trent and Rein, Joseph (eds.) (2017) *Creative Writing Innovations: Breaking Boundaries in the Classroom*. London, UK and New York, NY: Bloomsbury.

Bishop, Wendy (1994) Afterword – Colors of a different horse: On learning to like teaching creative writing. In Bishop, Wendy and Ostrom, Hans (eds.) *Colors of a Different Horse*: *Rethinking Creative Writing Theory and Pedagogy*, 280–295. Urbana, IL: National Council of Teachers of English. https://files.eric.ed.gov/fulltext/ED366967.pdf

Bishop, Wendy and Ostrom, Hans (eds.) (1994) *Colors of a Different Horse*: *Rethinking Creative Writing Theory and Pedagogy*. Urbana, IL: National Council of Teachers of English. https://files.eric.ed.gov/fulltext/ED366967.pdf

Gorrell, Nancy (1989) "Kindergarten Creation." *The Rockford Review* 8: 62. Rockford, IL: Rockford Writers' Guild.

Gorrell, Nancy S. with Erin Colfax (2012) *Writing Poetry through the Eyes of Science: Scientific Literacy and Poetic Response*. Sheffield, UK and Oakville, CT: Equinox.

Mayers, Tim (2015) Creative writing and process pedagogy. In Peary, Alexandria and Hunley, Tom C. (eds.) *Creative Writing Pedagogies for the Twenty-First Century*, 30–51. Carbondale, IL: Southern Illinois University Press.

Millan, Harriet Levin and Pennington, Martha C. (eds.) (2014) *Creativity and Writing Pedagogy: Linking Creative Writers, Researchers, and Teachers*. Sheffield, UK and Bristol, CT: Equinox.

Peary, Alexandria and Hunley, Tom C. (eds.) (2015) *Creative Writing Pedagogies for the Twenty-First Century.* Carbondale, IL: Southern Illinois University Press.

Robinson, Sir Ken (June 2006) "Do schools kill creativity?" https://www.ted.com/talks/sir_ken_robinson_do_schools_kill_creativity

Stewart, Arthur J. (2003) "Weavers Needle." *Rough Ascensions and Other Poems of Science*, 10. Knoxville, TN: Celtic Cat.

Chapter 5

Discarding Baggage: Reframing Myths

> *Come June, many of us suffer from the baggage of "old textbooks." I know I do. Letting go is hard. Change is harder. Not changing is the hardest.*
>
> – Arthur J. Stewart, email correspondence
> (Stewart, November 20, 2017)

PART ONE: A TEACHING STORY

"I Taught That!"

A few years after I began teaching creative writing, a flyer advertising a statewide poetry conference just happened to land upon my desk: Monmouth County College wants you and your students to attend an all-day poetry conference. The only requirement was that all students must submit poetry prior to the conference. I was intrigued. I had never taken a creative writing field trip before or attended any poetry conference. As I boarded a minivan with ten of my student poets, I remember wondering what the day would bring. I imagined my students and myself, together, writing poetry in the ivy halls. Not so. Entering the college auditorium, we were directed by professors to separate workshops – the students to learn about *how to write poetry*; the teachers to talk about *how to teach poetry*.

If the morning was academic, the afternoon proved an eye opener for all of us. After lunch, the auditorium filled with all attendees. The professors were on stage, all smiles. Up to the microphone, they began to read poems and call off the names of winning schools and students. *Winning schools*? I was shocked. I had no idea the poems we submitted were in a competition, a concept I was avoiding philosophically in my classes. There was a 9th grade winner, a 10th grade winner, and so forth, until finally, they got to the best overall poem of the conference. Before the poetry professor read the winning poem, he lauded it for being "deceptively simple." He noted its clarity, conciseness, stark originality, and powerful imagery. Then he read:

Christmas (Portland Oregon, 1969)
by Debbie Busch

My silly Christmas bell
Came off the top of a bakery cake.
It was plastic and covered with cheap glitter.
But it smelled like icing,
And Grandma had given it to me.
And I loved it.
But so did Maria Lisa.

I only let her hold it
Because she promised
Not to throw it in the fireplace.

I could smell it even as it burned.

(Debbie Busch, 1990)

During the reading, the writer of the poem, my student, Debbie Busch, began to slink down in her seat. None of us were prepared for the moment or the ensuing fanfare – the pictures and the attention, least of all Debbie. "Morristown High School, Debbie Busch, winner of the Best Overall Poem!" As my row of students stood and cheered, Debbie, a shy and modest student, trembled in her seat. I nearly had to pick her up and cast her into the aisle so that she could receive her award. Then the professor called me on stage. Afterwards, he marveled, "How did your student create that image? Remarkable the way she ended her poem."

"I taught that" I found myself replying. "She wrote that poem in class as a response to a lesson I teach on recalling recurring images." I don't remember what he said after that, but it didn't matter. It was for me a defining moment. I was embracing the realization that I was responsible for the "birthing" of that poem. I knew it would not have been written if it were not for my teaching and our class. Yes, Debbie was the creative writer that actualized it, but I was the spark that lit the fire. I was a teacher, but I was also a part creator. Would I, could I, become a poet, too? That would come later. It suffices to say that as a result of that conference, I began to walk the path with belief – belief in process, belief in my students, belief in the craft, and belief, ultimately, in myself as a teacher of writing.

What I Learned: Discarding the Baggage of Absolute Authority

The teaching story above became a personal turning point in my teaching of creative writing. Not only because it validated my teaching, but because it helped clarify personal and pedagogical issues that I had been carrying as baggage I needed to discard. The first step in discarding baggage was recognizing the weight of the bags I was carrying. The first bag I noticed occurred at the "eureka" moment itself. Why was the poetry professor asking me how to teach poetry? And why was I, a person who had never really regarded myself as a poet, answering with such conviction? I was still too fresh out of graduate school, too in awe of the academy to realize the wisdom attributed to Ernest Hemingway: *we are all apprentices in a craft where no one ever becomes a master*.[1] I only knew I felt joy – the joy of teaching poetry, the joy of teaching a craft that at that moment seemed egalitarian. There was no one way; there was no one authority, and suddenly I saw the path before me open wide to the excitement, joy, and challenge of teaching creative writing.

The second bag I noticed was that of "anti-competition." Up to that point, I had embraced the philosophy that competition of any kind was anathema to the classroom and the creative process. My reaction to the competition at the conference came as a surprise to me. How would my students feel now that Debbie was a winner? How would Debbie feel? Was the experience constructive or destructive for developing writers? Noticing my students' joy for Debbie, noticing Debbie's newfound recognition that she was a poet, and noticing the inspiration that the community of writers shared with each other, prompted me to reframe my thinking. From that moment forward, I began to break down my classroom walls. I began to encourage my students, when ready, to participate in contests, poetry readings, festivals, and to submit to our high school's literary magazine, the *Tricorn*. Thus began the early validation of our relationship as apprentices and co-learners together.

There were many other kinds of baggage I was carrying at that moment. Perfectionism for one, despite my grandfather's wisdom (see Chapter 3), and it would take years of open eyes, open heart and open teaching to divest myself of that weight. But there were other kinds of baggage I was carrying as well. Baggage from other teachers, from the profession, and the discipline itself. Such baggage is not easily discarded. It takes courage, it takes reframing, and it takes insight to walk the path of becoming a teacher who writes. I like to think of such baggage as myths which we all need to face and reframe as we engage in the art of teaching writing. I offer in this chapter a consideration of the major myths that I believe serve as baggage in need of discard. My hope is that you will consider the myths weighing you down, and that you will redefine and reframe them to enable yourself to teach writing with renewed and reframed creativity.

PART TWO: REFRAMING MYTHS

Myth #1: Writing Teachers Must Be Writers

In *Creative Writing in America: Theory and Pedagogy,* Joseph Moxley outlines "A Writing Program Certain to Succeed" on the high school and college levels. Central to his assumptions is the mantra echoed for decades: "writing teachers must be writers" (Moxley, 1989: 255). As for all myths, this one has inherent truth. But there's a caveat: many high school English teachers do not come to the classroom as writers ready to be teacher-artists. Instead, they find themselves walking the path of being a teacher of something they may not have experienced themselves: the joy of creating through writing, the joy of writing for oneself, the joy of writing what matters, and ultimately, the joy of discovering meaning and self-knowledge through writing.

Myth #1 Reframed: We Are All Apprentices

Reality Check

If it is true, and I believe it is, that very little creative writing is being taught in our high schools, and if it is true, and I believe it is, that the academy continues this trend by separating creative writing teachers and composition teachers, then it stands to reason that the vast majority of our students in high schools have little experience with the art form.

Paradox

The very teachers we need to teach creative writing are themselves products of a system devoid of practice in the art form.

Solution: It's the Process, Not the Product

You don't have to be a writer to begin teaching writing; you just have to be willing to become one – to walk the path of being a work in progress yourself. If you teach writing creatively, that is, as an art form, you will become a writer. Your students will make it so. It's the *process,* not the product; it's your path of becoming. The solution is you believing in the apprenticeship model and actualizing its premises.

Myth #2: You Can't Teach Creative Writing

My uncle is a noted poet and publisher of a poetry press. When I first became a teacher and told him I was teaching creative writing, he chuckled. Then he asked, "How can you teach that?" There is a prevalent attitude shared by scholars in the academy that the great writing as practiced among noted authors and poets "can't be taught." Louis Menand notes that the "skepticism" that "creative writing is something that can be taught" is "widely shared" (Menand, 2009; qtd in Lim, 2015: 252). Stephen Dunn, poet and professor of creative writing, discusses this conundrum in "Poet as teacher: Vices and virtues" where he comments: "As everyone knows, you can't teach someone to be a poet" (Dunn, 1991: 147). He continues, "How a fine poem comes along is mysterious, though when it happens it clearly is transcendence [...]. How many times does lightning strike? How many times does the poet get to traffic with the gods?" (p. 152). Dunn's discussion gets at the heart of the role of the teacher in the process of *creating* writing. If we see the "great" poem as a lofty, mystical experience of transcendence reaching to divine presence, then, to continue the metaphor, we as teachers must become the guiding "angels" in the process. But if we come down to earth for a moment, we can also see the need to get practical, to look at the reality of teaching creative writing in our classrooms with all those poets-in-waiting wishing to take flight.

Myth #2 Reframed: Who is the Creative Writing Teacher that Teaches?

> *Those of us who teach* [. . .] *believe that writing can be taught.*
>
> – Eve Shelnutt, *The Writing Room*
>
> (Shelnutt, 1989: 317)

Reality Check

Despite those who share the myth that creative writing cannot be taught, the fact remains: we are teaching creative writing. Writing workshops, writing centers, writing classes, writing projects, and degree programs abound throughout high school and universities. Eve Shelnutt in *The Writing Room* affirms: "Those of us who teach in writing programs believe that writing can be taught. That is, we believe in *apprenticeship* as a lifelong activity that writers engage in" (Shelnutt, 1989: 317, emphasis added). John Gardner points out, "I can think of only a handful of well-known American writers who have not taken creative writing courses and usually not one course but several" (Gardner, 1934/1981: 17). The question remains: if creative writing cannot be taught, why are teachers teaching it to so many students?

Paradox

One answer lies in the paradoxical nature of writing itself. Writers need both solitude and community to write. They need isolation and quietude to compose and create, but they also need a community of fellow writers to support, nurture, read, and react to their work. Note the axiom: *writers need readers and readers need writers*. That is the role of the class, teacher, and sharing circle or workshop where the readers read like writers.[2]

Solution: Reframe Who is the Creative Writing Teacher

The question remains: Who is the writing teacher that teaches? The answer is not so simple. For creative writers, that "teacher" may be a spark of light in the classroom, literally and figuratively. "Distance and certain light" to quote a line from a poem by May Swenson (Swenson, 2013: 200), can be just the spark to ignite writing, *if* the student sees it. To make sure that happens, we need another spark of light, a teacher, to ignite the student to see the light. The teacher who says to the student, "See the light over there coming through the window onto your desk? Feel it; think about it; now write about it." Or, "Here is a poem by May Swenson. See how she sees the light. Now, how do you see the light?" Or, "look into the light coming from the window; stare at it as long as you can; feel it; then close your eyes; see the light again. Now write about seeing the light." In reframing the myth that creative writing can't be taught, we might reframe the scope of the "teacher" to acknowledge the reality of that need in the process of creation. Such reframing confirms the not only the need of a teacher, but of a place for that teacher. That place is a community, a class, a writer's group or circle, if you will, to foster and collaborate in the role of writing.

Reframing the Role of the Creative Writing Teacher

We know we may not be teaching future Pulitzer prize-winning writers, but we also know we must teach as if we are teaching Pulitzer prize-winning writers. How? By heeding Stephen Dunn's solution: "I treat even the most marginal student's poem as a poem wishing to be a poem" (Dunn, 1991: 147). Each piece of writing must be accorded the honor, respect and importance it deserves in its wish to *become.* And who better to guide that wish than the teacher whether that teacher is in a creative writing class, a composition class, an English class, or in any other classroom, subject, or discipline.

Myth #3: You Can't Teach Creativity

> *Believing that creativity exists in all human beings, and is moreover teachable and can be enhanced, is an important notion for writing pedagogy and for education more generally.*
>
> – Martha C. Pennington, "Toward a Creative Writing Pedagogy"
>
> (Pennington, 2014: 23)

When it comes to creativity, talent, or genius, some believe you either have it, or you don't. Joseph Moxley, in *Creative Writing in America*, decries the destructive nature of this myth:

> Emphasizing the mysterious nature of creativity erects walls around our writing classrooms. With a dismissive wave of a hand, *we should not foster the myth that writers are born, that you cannot teach someone to be a talented writer.*
>
> (Moxley, 1989: 28; emphasis in the original).

Martha Pennington concurs:

> [. . .] [T]he pairing of creativity with innate talent is a main reason why it has not been thought to be teachable. However, work carried out in the second half of the 20th century by cognitive and educational psychologists on motivation and mastery has led to a new view of creativity as something that can be developed in oneself and others.
>
> (Pennington, 2014: 5)

Nevertheless, the destructive nature of this myth persists. Moxley (1989) notes that many students don't enroll in college writing courses because "they've been trained to think they're neither creative nor gifted. Still others avoid writing courses because they perceive English and writing to be an esoteric discipline, an artistic activity dependent solely on divine inspiration" (p. 28). Potentially great writers, internalizing the pessimism of this myth, may lose hope in their ability to tap the resources of their innate creativity. Recall Stefanie DeFronzo's loss of confidence in her writing ability (see Chapter 4). As a consequence of this myth, we may be losing for our discipline the potentially great teachers of writing as well.

We may also be losing potentially great teachers of writing in other subjects and disciplines. If math and science teachers think that teaching creative writing is limited to English teachers, they may avoid teaching creative writing pedagogy, writing-to-learn strategies, and discipline-related writing. For example, they may avoid teaching science poetry to express awe, wonder, perplexity, outrage, and empathy, as explored in *Writing Poetry through the Eyes of Science* (Gorrell with Colfax, 2012, Chapters 9–10) or, as illustrated in this book, math poetry to teach math concepts (see Chapter 8, "O Asymptote," by David Pitt).

Myth #3 Reframed: Teach Students to Discover the Creativity Within

Reality Check

Julia Cameron, a teacher of creativity workshops puts the paradox to rest by explaining it this way: "I teach people to *let* themselves be creative" (Cameron, 1992: xi). Here the concept is that creativity can be taught in the sense that some agent, the "teacher," removes the many "obstacles" and provides the space, environment, atmosphere, and guidance for *letting* students discover the creativity within. Nevertheless, the question remains: is creativity being taught?

Paradox

If we all have innate creativity as many authorities agree, then why teach creativity at all?

Solution: Teach Creative Literacy

Sir Ken Robinson in his TED talk, "Do Schools Kill Creativity?" (Robinson, 2006) argues that "creativity is as important now in education as literacy, and we should treat it with the same status. In another TED talk, he decries the demise of creativity in our educational system and advocates instead for an "educational revolution" (Robinson, 2013). Teachers of creative writing know that to write creatively students need to develop a creative mindset. Martha Pennington in "Creativity and Writing Pedagogy" defines the mindset of the creative writer "as one which has a high tolerance for ambiguity and risk, one that resists premature closure, and is comfortable remaining in an indeterminate and fluid state for long periods of time, and one which seeks out novelty and enjoys playing with language and ideas (Pennington, 2014: 21). This mindset will only flourish if the teacher teaches creativity in a "creative-friendly" environment, one that can be considered a "haven" because it is different from the pedagogy in other academic classrooms (see discussion in Chapter 6).

What I Learned: We Need to Reclaim Creativity

If all writing is a creative act, and all schools teach writing, then why are our schools not havens of creativity? Csikszentmihalyi notes: "It is quite strange how little effect school – even high school – seems to have had on the lives of creative people. Often one senses that, if anything, school threatened to extinguish the interest and curiosity that the child had discovered outside its walls" (Csikszentmihalyi, 1996: 173). Yet if the institution of school is so detrimental to the teaching of creativity, Csikszentmihalyi (1996) affirms that the individual teacher is not. To the contrary, he emphasizes that if schools don't inspire, "individual teachers [can] often awaken, sustain, or direct a child's interest" (p. 174). His findings are instructive for all teachers desiring to teach creativity to students, whether those students are "Large C" creative like Pat Conroy or "small c" creative (see Chapter 1). Case in point: The Citadel military academy was hardly a creative learning environment. Pat Conroy was not only plagued by arbitrary institutional strictures; he lived with daily hazing and oppressive conformity that nearly broke him emotionally. Yet Colonel Doyle "awakened," "sustained," and "directed" the writer within, and Pat Conroy blossomed his senior year into the writer he would become.

What makes teachers like Colonel Doyle so inspiring? Csikszentmihalyi answers by identifying two main factors: first, the teachers "noticed the student, believed in his or her abilities and cared." Second, the teacher showed care by giving the student "extra work to do, greater challenges than the rest of the class received" (p. 174). We as teachers may not be able to change the schools we teach in, but we can teach writing creatively within the walls of our classrooms as long as we are willing to live with the paradoxes and follow a few simple guidelines:

- *Provide respect for the writer.*
- *Provide respect for the process.*
- *Provide a balance between structure and freedom.*
- *Provide a non-competitive atmosphere.*

- *Provide an inspirational, nurturing environment.*
- *Respect and honor difference.*

Clearly, we need to reclaim a place for the teaching of creativity and creative writing in our schools. How do we do it? By discarding the baggage we are carrying, by reframing the myths we believe in and teach by, and by having faith – faith in ourselves, our students, and the process of becoming. If we have faith that all of our students are creative, that creativity is the true nature of human beings, then our essential task as teachers will be clear: to provide the fertile soil for the blossoming of creativity in our classrooms.

PART THREE: INTERDISCIPLINARY APPLICATIONS

Baggage That Cannot Be Discarded: "The Tyranny of the Ts"

> *Standards can support growth and nurture learning. Standardization, on the other hand, can undermine the human relationships that are central to the act of teaching. When standards are coupled with standardization, the result is decay.*
>
> – Julie Gorlewski and David Gorlewski, "From the Editors"
> (Gorlewski and Gorlewski, 2014: 11)

In September 1989, Ted Hipple wrote a prophetic essay in the *English Journal* arguing that some English teachers are almost "tyrannized" by seven Ts – *time*, *tradition*, *textbooks*, *teacher guides*, *tests*, *and "they*." I read that article with personal interest because 1989 was the first year I broke down my classroom walls, *literally* stepping out to attend my first National Council of Teachers of English (NCTE) annual convention. This step proved critical in my path to becoming a writer (see Chapter 11). In his essay Hipple wrote with a sense of urgency: "If afflicted with the tyranny of the Ts, you must try to do something; else you become Prufrock in the classroom. Good luck" (p. 22).

Considering the tyranny of the Ts at the time, I felt more than "lucky." I felt blessed – blessed to be teaching at Morristown High, where I was encouraged to develop a curriculum for a creative writing elective program that I taught for over three decades; where the department decided together not to adopt a textbook approach to literature, but instead, purchased novels for all required English courses; and where I had a supportive supervisor who believed in pedagogical change. Fortunately, I was able to teach creatively and authentically and was not affected by the tyrannies of *textbooks*, *teacher guides*, *other teachers*, and "they."

As for *tradition*, I was greatly affected by it, but I was still able to reframe my teaching, in a way that broke disciplinary boundaries. (See Chapters 10 and 17 for further discussion.)

But what of the Ts impossible to discard? What about *time* and *testing*? To time constraints, this book says you can become a writer while you teach your students to write. Therefore, it takes little or no extra time to do. Testing, institutionally mandated, district, state-wide, and federal, along with core standards is impossible for high school teachers to discard. Yet creative teachers with creative courage and creative literacy will be better able to reframe their teaching to promote creativity even in the age of No Child Left Behind Act of 2001 and the common core standards and assessment movements. To that end, the editors of the *English Journal* devoted the November 2014 issue to articles reframing the teaching of English, literacy, and creativity during the standards movement with the opening editorial statement quoted above.

Although the educational reform and standards movement prevailed in the first decade of the 21st century, this was also the time when Morristown High bridged the "divide" between the arts and the sciences by establishing a Science Academy, a "school within a school" for "average science-minded students." Science Academy students in grades 9–12 took all of their subjects together, co-taught by an English and science teacher. The teachers on each level collaborated to develop a new curriculum in which students learned their subjects "through the eyes of science." I taught English III in the Academy with a biology co-teacher, Erin Colfax, who was the catalyst for discovering *science poetry,* a little known, rarely taught genre. We developed an interdisciplinary curriculum which culminated in a book, *Writing Poetry though the Eyes of Science* (Gorrell with Colfax, 2012). Ironically, all this occurred during the time that Sir Ken Robinson was decrying the lack of creativity in the American educational system with its emphasis on common core standards and testing assessments (Robinson, 2006). Professionally and personally, the Science Academy experience was one of the most transformative times in my life as a teacher and poet.[3]

The Tyranny of the Ts, the Global Pandemic: Baggage That Cannot Be Discarded

One tyranny that Ted Hipple could not have foreseen – the global pandemic – caused cataclysmic consequences for teachers and students in the America. When COVID-19 began to sweep across the country in March of 2020, public schools in every state closed their doors. Teachers became first responders in an emergency which tested their creativity, their ability to teach the spontaneous lesson, their technical know-how, and their resilience – students were frightened, colleagues were leaving, and people were dying. "Remote learning effectively became a policy for the rest of the spring." (Leonhardt, 2022: A18).

Challenges and Failures of Remote Learning: "A Generational Loss"

> *This will probably be the largest increase in educational inequity in a generation.*
>
> – Thomas Kane, author of the Harvard study (qtd in Leonhardt, 2022, A18)

When schools reopened in the fall of 2020, teachers were challenged as never before with an historic teachable moment. The best were able to teach to screens and students unseen with creativity and heart. Yet little did they know that they were engaging in an experiment in the success of remote learning and its long-range effects on education. Two years later, David Leonhardt reports the findings of the scholarship and its meticulous data as a "generational loss.[4]

Returning to In-School Learning 2022

The September 1, 2022 front page of the *New York Times* led with this headline: "Pandemic Set Schools Back Two Decades." Sarah Mervosh reports the "devastating effects on American school children, with the performance of 9-year-olds in math and reading dropping to the levels from two decades ago. The declines spanned almost all races and income levels and were markedly worse for the lowest performing students" (Mervosh, 2022: 1).

It comes as no surprise to this author that the results above affirm the thesis of this book – *to teach is to learn*. And to teach requires first and foremost teachers. And to learn is to be. To be requires a community of learners, face-to-face in a place, in community *becoming*. Since the return of students to school in the fall of 2022, it is this author's hope that the learning will focus primarily on creativity, discovery, and invention, discarding the baggage of the terrible "T" of time-consuming, standardized testing. Only then might our children experience transformational learning – the kind of learning were there are leaps and bounds of knowledge, achievement, and spirit.

For Your Journals: Discarding Your Baggage

1. What baggage are you carrying about teaching? Do you carry the baggage of perfectionism and absolute authority? Have you ever been "wrong?"

2. What myths about writing affect your beliefs and attitudes? Are any of the writing myths discussed in this chapter baggage for you?
3. Write in your journal a list of belief statements about teaching and/or writing that you wish to discard as baggage.
4. Are any of Ted Hipple's Ts – *time*, *tradition*, *textbooks*, *teacher guides*, *tests*, *teachers*, and "*they*" – baggage for you?

For Your Students: Discarding Baggage

1. Ask your students to list their beliefs, attitudes, and feelings about creativity. Can those beliefs be learned or taught? Are any of those beliefs about creativity "baggage" in need of "discard?"
2. Ask your students to list their beliefs, attitudes and feelings about writing. Are any of those beliefs about writing "baggage" in need of discard?
3. Ask your students to list their beliefs, attitudes, and feelings about discipline-related writing across the curriculum. Are any of those beliefs about writing "baggage" in need of discard? Do they pertain to the subject they are presently taking with you?

Poetic Offering on Discarding Baggage – Model Contributor Poem: "Old Textbooks" by Arthur J. Stewart

Old Textbooks
by Arthur J. Stewart

Nothing at all at first.
No feather fluff, no hawk beak, not even a quick
onion, pepper, squash, or leek. I sit. The sun
works over the eastern ridge, steady and slow;
the long shadows of trees
in the yard grow shorter, slowly.
The calico cat
we call Hannah sits on a pile of books

at my upstairs office window, looking out. And
speaking of books, and speaking of
looking out:

> Yesterday I took a full box of old textbooks
> from college classes I had 40 years ago
> to the high school and dropped them off.
> Some are still good. Parasitology, for example,
> has advanced a lot
> in terms of molecular this and that but
> a tapeworm is still a tapeworm, with a life cycle,
> and a life history
> of the fence lizard, *Uta stansburiana*, has not changed
> much
> despite global climate change, urbanization, speeding up
> of the hydrological cycle, or habitat
> fragmentation. Some young student
>
> might yet learn a little, might
> do good things in the world, blow off
> the dust, get
> interested
> perhaps
> by accident.
>
> (Stewart, 2017)

Stewart's Commentary on "Old Textbooks"

> Come June, many of us suffer from the baggage of "old textbooks." I know I do. Letting go is hard. Change is harder. Not changing is the hardest.
>
> (Stewart, November 20, 2017)

Commentary on "Not Changing is the Hardest"

In reference to "discarding baggage," Stewart's "Old Textbooks" presents the image of his cat, Hannah, sitting "on a pile of old books in the office window "looking out." It prompts him poetically:

"speaking of books, and speaking of looking out:" The poem leads us through a physical window that is also a mental window of perspective on change – What to keep? What to discard? What is baggage for you? During the last three years of pandemic and endemic education, each of us as teachers has faced educational challenges we could not have predicted or foreseen. "Not changing may be the hardest." Yet, for our students and colleagues, change prevailed. (See the Conclusion for "How this Book Can Help" and "Teaching Pedagogies in Review" that are effective as pandemic pedagogies.)

Chapter 5 Notes

1 This quotation is attributed to Hemingway posthumously in the *New York Journal-American* (July 3, 1961).

2 The use of the terms *sharing circle* and *workshop* as they align with this author's creative writing pedagogy for high school students is defined first in the Introduction of this book and subsequently illustrated through the chapters' teaching stories and model lessons.

3 The 21st century was paradoxical at Morristown High School, where creativity flourished despite the core standards, assessment, and test-driven faculty workshops and training. Actual teaching in the creative writing class elective was unaffected as were most Honors English courses. Teaching in regular English classes and the remedial classes was mandated test-driven instruction primarily. All teachers were required to align our lessons plan books to common core standards with the exact numerical codes. Creative class teaching gave way to practice test lessons in English, writing and mathematics. Creativity and the arts suffered for a decade as the Federal law of 2001 benchmarked the year 2014 to measure student improvement nationwide. What happened? For the answer to this question, see Gorlewski and Gorlewski, 2014.

4 As David Leonhardt reports:

Researchers compared before and during the pandemic test results based on the K–12 reading and math MAP test. On average, students who attended in-person school for nearly all 2021 lost about 20 percent worth of a typical school year's math learning during the study's two-year window. Some of the losses stemmed from the time they were remote learning in the spring of 2020 […] and some of the losses

> stemmed from the difficulties of in-person schooling as families coped with disruption and illness […]. But students who stayed home for most of 2020–21fared much worse. On average, they lost the equivalent of 50 percent of a typical school year's math learning during the study's two-year window. School closures widen both economic and racial inequality in learning. K–12 education made much progress in the U.S. during the 1990s and early 2000s: math and reading skills improved especially for Black and Latino students. The COVID closures have reversed much of that progress.
>
> (Leonhardt, 2022: A18)

Chapter 5 References

Busch, Debbie (1990) "Christmas (Portland Oregon, 1969)." Qtd in Gorrell (1990: 29).

Cameron, Julia (1992) *The Artist's Way: A Spiritual Path to Higher Creativity*. New York, NY: Tarcher/Putnam.

Cameron, Julia (2002) *Walking in this World: The Practical Art of Creativity*. New York, NY: Tarcher/Putnam.

Csikszentmihalyi, Mihaly (1996) *Creativity: Flow and the Psychology of Discovery and Invention*. New York, NY: Harper Perennial.

Dunn, Stephen (1991) The poet as teacher: Vices and virtues. In Schwartz, Mimi (ed.) *Writer's Craft, Teacher's Art*, 145–152. Portsmouth, NH: Boyton/Cook.

Gardner, John (1981) Forward. In Dorothea Brande, *Becoming a Writer* (new edition). 11–18. New York, NY: Tarcher/Putman.

Gorlewski, Julie and Gorlewski, David (eds.) (2014) From the editors. *English Journal*, 104 (2): 11–12. https://doi.org/10.58680/ej201424637

Gorrell, Nancy (1990) Taking off the mask: Teaching the recurring image in poetry writing. *English Journal*, 79 (7): 27–29. https://doi.org/10.2307/818712

Gorrell, Nancy S. with Erin Colfax (2012) *Writing Poetry through the Eyes of Science: Scientific Literacy and Poetic Response*. Sheffield, UK and Oakville, CT: Equinox.

Hipple, Ted (1989) The tyranny of the Ts. *English Journal*, 78 (5): 19–22. https://doi.org/10.2307/819194

Leonhardt, David (May 6, 2022) Long school closures came with high costs. *New York Times*, A18.

Lim, Shirley Geok-lin (2015) Highways and sinkholes: Incorporating creativity strategies in the writing classroom. In Chik, Alice, Costley, Tracey and Pennington, Martha C. (eds.) *Creativity and Discovery in the University Writing Class*, 252–276. Sheffield, UK and Oakville, CT: Equinox.

Menand, Louis (June 8, 2009) Show and tell – Should creative writing be taught? *The New Yorker*, 106–112. Cited from Lim (2015): 252.

Mervosh, Sarah (September 1, 2022) Pandemic set schools back two decades: Children's reading and math scores suffer. *New York Times*, 1.

Moxley, Joseph. (ed.) (1989) *Creative Writing in America*. Urbana, IL: National Council of Teachers of English.

Pennington, Martha C. (2014) Towards a creative writing pedagogy. In Millan, Harriet Levin and Pennington, Martha C. (eds.) *Creativity and Writing Pedagogy: Linking Creative Writers, Researchers, and Teachers*, 17–24. Sheffield, UK and Bristol, CT: Equinox.

Robinson, Sir Ken (June 2006) "Do schools kill creativity?" https://www.ted.com/talks/sir_ken_robinson_do_schools_kill_creativity

Robinson, Sir Ken (May 10, 2013) How to escape education's death valley. https://www.ted.com/talks/sir_ken_robinson_how_to_escape_education_s_death_valley

Schwartz, Mimi (1991) *Writer's Craft, Teacher's Art*. Portsmouth, NH: Boyton/Cook.

Shelnutt, Eve (1989) *The Writing Room*. Atlanta, GA: Longstreet Press.

Stewart, Arthur J (2017) "Old Textbooks." *Elements of Chance*, 32. Knoxville, TN: Celtic Cat.

Stewart, Arthur J. (November 20, 2017) Email correspondence with Nancy S. Gorrell.

Swenson, May (2013) "Distance and a Certain Light." *Collected Poems*. New York, NY: Literary Classics of the United States.

Chapter 6

Knowing Where You're Going: The American High School

I knew that I once had imagination. That when I was younger, I turned my basement into a dungeon and fought for hours against make believe dragons. But as a teenager, I could not reclaim the same imagination.

– Mark Hess, High School Creative Writing student (2004)

PART ONE: TEACHING CREATIVE WRITING – TRENDS AND FINDINGS

Upon the conclusion of each Creative Writing course I teach, I ask my students to write a reflection of their learning experience. The following is Mark Hess's reflection.

Autobiography of an Emerging Writer
by Marc Hess

Tap, tap, tap. Nothing, nothing, nothing. Despite doing the usual procedures for brainstorming, I couldn't think of anything. I continued to rap my pen against a pad of paper. Tap, tap, tap. I was trapped in an empty room of boxes and my bed. Having just moved to a new house, nothing was in order and my head was no different. How was I to focus on writing an essay when I had just moved to a new house, a new yard, and new neighborhood?

Yet I sat in my bed forcing meaningless words onto a pad of paper. My heart was nowhere near my bed; it was outside swimming in my new pool or chasing my dog around in the yard. I found this to be the case with most of my writing assignments throughout high school. They were forced writing assignments that I wrote halfheartedly. When my parents read what I wrote, they often commented on my writing being too formulaic and brief. I lacked the creativity to go off in another direction or to take a risk in my work.

Reflecting upon my writing memories is a tough task. I knew that I once had imagination. That when I was younger, I turned my basement into a dungeon and fought for hours against make believe dragons. But as a teenager, I could not reclaim the same imagination. It was not until I took a creative writing course that I was able to reclaim what was once mine and evolve to become a better writer.

Commentary on "Tap, tap, tap. Nothing, nothing, nothing."

I have been listening for a long time to students like Mark. Each semester when they enter Creative Writing, I ask them how they feel about writing, what they have written so far in school, and what they have written for themselves. Their writing memories speak volumes about how they learn to write, how they feel about writing, and how they have journeyed within the institution of school to become writers. What happened to Mark's imagination as a teenager? What happened to the boy who fought make-believe dragons in his basement? Why does a student like Mark, clearly a talented, intelligent writer, feel such "writer's block" when faced with assigned writing? Mark sets high standards for himself. He knows the kind of writing his English teachers and the tests want; he is an "A" honors student. Yet he also knows his writing is "formulaic," unimaginative, and forced. Mark, like many students entering my creative writing elective feels a sense of loss somewhere between his younger, "imaginative" days and his "halfhearted" teenage years. He is a man soon to enter college, yet he yearns for the creativity he felt as a child; he yearns to reclaim his inner voice.

Such attitudes reveal a persistent trend well into the 21st century as expressed by Stefanie DeFronzo's high school writing memories. In Chapter 4, she recalls her love of poetry writing in elementary school becoming a mere "background skill" in her high school, where creative writing was not offered as an elective, and she experienced primarily academic writing in her AP English class that focused on "one interpretation for each novel, short story, or poem." Such an approach "seemed painfully one sided" to Stefanie.

The Demise of Creative Writing in High Schools

> *Teachers don't have to profess writing, but they should experience it, and that experience, as any graduate of National Writing Project training will attest, is life changing.*
>
> – Wendy Bishop, "Crossing the Lines: On Creative Composition and Composing Creative Writing" (Bishop, 1994: 194)

Although I cannot speak for the state of creative writing in high schools across the nation, I suspect Morristown High reflects a persistent trend. My students' observations about the demise of their creative writing experiences from a high in elementary school to a low in high school confirm 20th and 21st century scholarship on the subject. Decades ago, James Britton (Britton, 1970) recognized the demise of British students' opportunities for creative expression as they got older. In 1981, Arthur Applebee's nationwide study of writing in American secondary schools (Applebee, 1981) confirmed a similar trend. American teachers were assigning very little creative writing: 8.2 percent of 9th graders' writing and only 7.2 percent of 11th graders' writing involved stories or poetry (Moxley, 1989: 28–29).

The persistent trend of demise of creative writing experiences is not surprising when one considers its historic and systemic roots. These roots reflect a pedagogical "imbalance" between the modes of discourse students experience. In 1970 James Britton identified three modes of discourse students should be taught – *expressive, poetic and transactional* – each with separate purposes (Britton, 1970).[1] "In 1975 Britton and his co-researchers found that the bulk of secondary school writing in England was 'transactional' (63.4 percent) with writing as 'creative art or poetic' at 17.6 percent and just 5.5 percent allotted to 'expressive'" (Britton et al., 1975; qtd in Peary, 2015: 202). According to Peary, this "imbalance" in which students spend the large majority of their writing time in transactional experiences such as "exam questions, note-taking and other rote tasks which generally involve the recall of instructor-provided information rather than students generating new thoughts" is viewed by "some writing-across-the curriculum (WAC) theorists less than positively" (p. 201).

Unfortunately, teaching creative writing in high school is often more dilemma than solution. Despite a half century of research and practice on the value of teaching creative writing – observation, description, narration, and poetry – the foundation and bridge for developing higher level thinking, language, and writing skills (Peary, 2015: 195) – our high schools continue to relegate creative writing to elective programs serving a relatively small group of the student population. This is not surprising since the "divide" still persists in the academy. Shirley Lim confirms:

> There has been little interchange between creative writing and composition programs nor between creative writing teachers and faculty teaching composition, that is, academic writing. The common understanding is that there is no common ground between the two teaching enterprises [...].
>
> (Lim, 2015: 253)

Nevertheless, in the late 20th century, pioneers in the workshop model of teaching creative writing inspired generations of teachers to teach more creative writing to students, grades K–12. James Moffett's *Student-Centered Curriculum* and *Active Voice* series (Moffett, 1992) provided sequential writing programs for students K–12, and Nancie Atwell's *In the Middle* (Atwell, 1987/1998) modeled innovative creative writing practices from her writing center in Maine. Since the founding of the National Writing Project (NWP) in 1974, projects in California, Oregon, and New Jersey have spearheaded teacher training initiatives in process writing pedagogy substantiated by extensive research and practice in the field. Yet despite these initiatives that continue as models of best practice in the discipline, somewhere between middle school and college, we are still losing something vital, something irreplaceable: we are losing the *creative* spirit and skills of many of our high school students.

The Dilemma: Very Few Teachers Do It

In *What is English?* Peter Elbow, in response to the 1987 English Coalition Conference, questions why the profession has historically privileged the teaching of literature and the critical essay over the teaching of creative writing. He asks:

> Why doesn't every high school or university literature class ask students as a matter of course to do an equal amount of rendering or imaginative writing as critical writing? Why don't we normally ask students to write stories when we read Hawthorne, poems when we read Emily Dickinson, a play or some scenes when we read Shakespeare? After all, to respond to a work doesn't necessary mean to write critically. It means, perhaps even more helpfully, to answer – to write back in the same mode or theme […]. *Very few teachers do it.*
>
> (Elbow, 1990: 189–190)

Why don't more English teachers "do it?" I too have been wondering why so many of my skilled colleagues do not teach more creative writing in their English classes. Elbow (1990) offers some explanations for English teachers:

- *We value imaginative writing so highly – the "great literature" – that we don't think we or our students can "do it." The "masters on the pedestal" syndrome.*

- *Stories and rendering of one's experience are "too easy, too thoughtless, too based on feeling." It doesn't require enough critical thinking or analysis.*
- *"I mustn't ask students to do something I can't do, and I can't write stories or poems or personal experiences."*
- *"I can grade essays, but I can't grade stories and poems." There's no agreement how.*

(pp. 190–191)

Facing the Dilemma: High School and the Academy

It's possible, I guess, to teach writing without ever having felt like a writer, but shouldn't we insist it be otherwise?

– Wendy Bishop "Crossing the Lines: On Creative Composition and Composing Creating Writing" (Bishop, 1994: 194)

The dearth of required high school creative writing experiences, save, perhaps, a creative writing elective offered for all four years of high school, speaks volumes about what we as teachers value, not only in writing skills, but in creativity and creative literacy. The dilemma of the demise becomes even more egregious when one considers that a high school creative writing elective may be the last opportunity a student may have to write personally, imaginatively, expansively, and authentically depending upon that student's major, career aspirations, and possible exemptions from English composition. I teach an abundance of poetry writing in both my English and creative writing classes with that thought in mind.

"Academically Adrift: Limited Learning on College Campuses," a 2011 study (Arum and Roska, 2011), found that 50% of United States undergraduates are not enrolled in a class expecting more than twenty written pages during a semester. Peary (2015) cites this study, suggesting the 50% statistic as "one explanation for why 36% of students do not show any improvement in critical or analytical learning over four years of college (p. 195). She also cites the 2010 National Survey of Student Engagement, where first-year students reported writing a "paltry one or two papers or reports, five to 19 pages long over the course of one year" (p. 195).

The statistics above are alarming but once again not surprising, given the dearth of creative writing in our high schools, which feed colleges and universities that continue to wrestle with the dilemma. Most importantly, how are prospective teachers in the field of English and other subjects going to be able to teach creatively with discipline-related writing strategies if they have never written creatively, authentically, and personally themselves? Consider again Bishop's compelling question: "It's possible, I guess, to teach writing without ever having felt like a writer, but shouldn't we insist it be otherwise?" (Bishop, 1994: 194).

Solving the Dilemma: Becoming a Teacher Who Writes

Given the plethora of books, workshops, professional organizations, and state and national writing projects which have endeavored to promote best practices in the teaching of writing, why hasn't there been more widespread change in attitude and practice within the profession? The answer I think lies within the heart and spirit of the teacher. What motivates us to do what we do? Is it intellect? Is it theory? Is it belief? Or, is it heart? Yes, intellect, theory, and belief are all important, but as human beings we do what gives us *joy*. And what gives us joy is the process of becoming, the process of creating, and the process of being.

Once you taste this joy, I don't think you will need convincing to do it. But you will need, as we have seen in earlier chapters, *courage* – the courage to create and the *courage to teach*. Such courage is necessary to "walk the path" of becoming a teacher who writes. To quote Rainer Maria Rilke, each one of us must "go within" and search our hearts to find our creative spirit (Rilke, 2000: 11). "Go within" yourself – discover, become, teach. In the process, you will learn how to balance and navigate the landscapes of your inner and outer teaching worlds.

PART TWO: THE CREATIVE WRITING CLASSROOM

Creating a Haven

How is it possible for the creative writing classroom to find its place in the dilemma of academic debates that frame the outer world of the American high school? The answer? The creative writing classroom must be different; it must offer an alternative environment operating under an entirely different set of norms. These norms establish an atmosphere or sense of community that supports, encourages, and honors, difference, originality, imagination, risk taking, nonconformity, creativity, the individual voice, and the art of writing. Whereas most classrooms function on overt and covert competition, the ethos in the creative writing classroom is non-competitive. If we are all apprentices in a craft where there are no masters, then "stars" are anathema to the creative process. "Favorites" or "favoring" is also anathema. The norms provide that we are all works in progress, all co-learners on the path of becoming, all together, in a community where "to teach is to learn, to learn is to be" and *writing* – not the student or the teacher – sits at the center of the classroom.

In sum, if you find yourself in a creative writing classroom – the creative writing elective – or if you choose to create one inside the required English classroom, you must strive to make that classroom a haven, not only for your students' blossoming creativity and writing, but for your own. In such a reframed classroom environment, you the teacher can blossom and grow, too. You can take risks, experiment with new lessons, close the plan book, and teach a spontaneous lesson just like I did when the grasshopper flew into my classroom window, as I describe in the Prologue.

But creating such a haven requires a paradigm shift from classroom, to community, to workshop.[2] In that haven, the community fosters common norms, purpose, and connectedness; the workshop models the communal skills of craft. Teachers and students become co-learners in an art form in which process becomes paramount; voice becomes authentic; feedback replaces critique or criticism; and assessment becomes multifaceted using portfolios, conferencing, self-evaluation, and the ultimate assessment beyond classroom walls of self-publication, in-school publication, public readings, writing contests, teen arts festivals, and poetry readings, and slams.

In such a haven dream teaching occurs at unexpected times. Students become transformed; they take on with seriousness the identity of "writer," and they begin to write what matters. The change will be profound and palpable. Often it will be contagious and spread quickly, so if there is any naysayer in the class, they too will join in to write.

Establishing the Community of Writers

How can you create this haven of creativity? Here's the caveat: you must do it on Day One, and then nurture, practice, and model it throughout the course. From the moment the students walk into your classroom, they must sense that "something is different." I play classical music as students enter; there is usually chatter, socializing, and noise. I direct them to their assigned seats. Each seat has a student's name and a blank piece of paper. On the board are instructions: Listen to the music; write freely whatever you are thinking; there is no talking while the music is playing. Soon the class settles down. I take attendance while students are writing. I model quiet. I never say anything during this period of writing reflection. If students look puzzled, I just put my finger to my mouth to indicate "quiet" and whisper to them, "Just write anything. It's ok." After about 15 minutes of freewriting, I turn off the music and give a brief "pep talk." The pep talk covers the basic norms of the course. I reserve discussion of course goals, philosophy, procedures, and grades for the following class. On Day One, I want them to engage immediately in the writing process. I deliver the pep talk with excitement and seriousness of purpose. It goes something like this. . .

Day One Pep Talk: Establishing the Atmosphere and Norms

Welcome to creative writing. This class is going to be very special. It's going to be unlike anything you have ever experienced in high school before. How do I know? Because I love (or I'm passionate about) writing. I want you to love writing, too. This class is for everyone, whether you've written volumes of poems and stories or whether you have never written before. As long as you have an open mind and a willingness to create and write, you are in the right place. We're going to begin with simple, short, and fundamental writing exercises to develop your creativity and writing. Whether you are an experienced writer or a beginner, these writing exercises will be useful and challenging. I am a writer now, but I wasn't always a writer. It took me a long time to learn to write because learning to write is a lifelong process. Teaching writing has helped me in this process. I have much to teach you about writing, but I also know you have much to teach me in equally important ways. In this course, we will all be learning and writing together.

And together means we need to help, nurture and support each other in the process. In other words, we need to become a *community of writers*. All communities have common values. I'm going to call these rules our *norms*. It means how we are going to relate to each other as writers. Our norms are simple: honor the writer, honor the writing, and honor the creative process. Now it's time for me to stop talking and for you to start writing. From this moment on, we are writers, thinking like writers, looking at the world like writers, and doing what writers do. So, let's begin now, doing what writers do.

Adjusting the Pep Talk for Yourself and Your Classroom

Whenever students write creatively, expressively, and imaginatively, the creative writing classroom emerges. Whether this classroom is an elective course, or part of an English literature class, you as the teacher have the opportunity to teach writing as an art form in a workshop environment. You just need to establish the norms, attitudes, and mindset which will unite your community of writers. Accordingly, the fundamentals of your Day One pep talk need to be adjusted for your particular point in the journey of becoming a writer. Your goal is to establish a writing-respectful atmosphere, with norms and behaviors that will establish a sense of community, a sense of reciprocal roles of students and teacher, and a noncompetitive, engaging and excited atmosphere for creating.

Day One Writing Exercise: Non-Stop Writing

I now engage the students in an opening writing activity to warm them up and to whet their appetites for writing. In my creative writing elective class, I like to begin with students working with the tools of their trade – words – and the *warm-up* exercises of *non-stop writing*. I want to get them to feel playful, to ease into experimentation, to use their imaginations and to feel as if they are functioning as writers in a craft. The opening activity has to be "no-fail," in other words, confidence building. Non-stop writing[3] works beautifully for this.

I write on the board "Non-Stop Writing." Then I explain that writing is a physical act which requires, like athletics, a "warming up" of our muscles, our writing implements, and our brains. I tell them that non-stop writing requires just that, writing non-stop about anything that pops into their heads. I tell them it doesn't have to make sense; they just must keep their pens or pencils moving on the paper. I encourage them to repeat words if they can't think of anything to say like, "I don't know what to write; I don't know what to write," or "tired, tired, tired." I assure them there is no wrong way to do this exercise as long as they keep writing. I check the time on the clock, and tell them to write for five minutes. This might seem like a short time, but writing non-stop for five minutes produces considerable material. Then I say, "Begin!"

The classroom is quiet and energized as everyone is writing. After five minutes, I say, "Stop. Read over your writing." Next, I ask, "Does it make sense?" We discuss the meaning of "making sense" as part of the writing process. What is sense? Who decides what makes sense? The difference between making sense for oneself and making sense for someone else – the concept of audience-directed writing. Finally, I ask them to count the number of words they have written. This is fun and gives me an opportunity to praise and be playful. I ask: "How many wrote 150 words or more?" Many raise their hands. I raise the number until we get to the maximum words written in the five minutes. After praising, I pose the following question: "If I assign you to write a 150-word essay for homework, should I expect it to take you only five minutes?" Students always laugh at the thought and readily challenge the logic. Here is the moment to distinguish between personal writing for oneself and writing on demand, for a teacher, test, or assignment.

Then I point out the tools of the trade – words, phrases, sentences. I tell them that lots of time in writing we have "diamonds," or sparkling gems, hidden in the "rough" of our words. I ask them to circle their favorite word in their non-stop writing. Next, I ask them to underline their favorite phrase or line. At this point, I ask them to choose *one* word or phrase to give voice. On Day One, I not only want them to experience the act of writing, but I want them to hear their own emerging voices. I tell them we are going to do a choral reading of their favorites, and that they must voice their words or phrases with passion and energy. I demonstrate with histrionic flavor the voicing of a word into the air space. Often there is laughter once again. In addition, by asking each student to voice the minimum – one word or line – even the most reluctant or shy students participate in the choral reading without hesitation.

On Day One, this sharing begins our sense of community. Time permitting, we discuss or note any sense in the randomness of the choral reading. I point out that often creativity works this way, with playful, random connections. I stress the role of audience and reader in meaning-making or making sense by calling on students to point out any logic or coincidence by chance in any of the random juxtapositions.

Lastly, I pass around a piece of paper and ask each student to write down from their non-stop writing their favorite word, phrase or line. I tell them, "I want to get to know the creative writing side of you. Think of this exercise as an introduction of your creative writing self. We will use these introductions as your first writing sample."

Student Non-Stop Writing Prompt

- Circle your favorite word, or underline your favorite phrase or line, and *begin* a new piece of writing with it. It could be a poem, a short prose piece, a description, or a story. You can write any form you want, but use your "favorite" as a prompt to begin.
- Or, use your favorite word, phrase, or line to *end* a new piece of writing.
- Use all of the class's "favorite" words or lines voiced in our choral reading to create an original poem, prose piece, or story. Underline and number the favorite words or line as you use them. (class "favorites" provided by teacher)

This Day One writing activity serves multiple purposes. It builds enthusiasm, confidence, interest in the craft, and a sense of emerging community. It says to the students, we are on a journey together. We are going to write together, voice together, collaborate, and share together. When students exit my creative writing or English classes the first day, I want them to feel a sense of wonder. I want them to think: *Yes, I can do this!*

Note on Grading in the Creative Writing Elective

On Day One, I do not discuss the grading system with the students. If students ask, "How will the non-stop writing exercise be graded?" I reply, "It's just a writing sample, and I will discuss the grading system in our next class." In the creative writing elective, I use a contract grading system and portfolio assessment for evaluation.

Letter grades are not placed on students' works in progress, final drafts, or portfolios. Students "contract" for the grade they will work for from a list of required writings distributed in the syllabus. Students receive a final grade for the course based on their achievement of the contract. In other words, they can "contract" for whatever grade they would like to receive.[4]

Model Student Non-Stop Writing and Poem by Lauren Glanville (Palmer)

Description of Process

Step One, the nonstop notes, were written in class in Lauren's journal, on February 4, 2004. The following day, for Step Two, Lauren chose to focus her writing on one word, *protection*, as the "diamond in the rough" of her words. Lauren's deceptively simple poem from the class exercise speaks for its time and all time. Historical context is important here. Her poem was written post-9/11 and less than a year after the onset of the Iraq War.

Step One: 173 non-stop words by Lauren Glanville (Palmer)

> *The rabbit is under the bush hiding but poking his little head out once in a while the trees are so pretty covered in snow, the sight is a beautiful thing to see this blanket of snow covers the world nothing can escape its path cold wind blows and the rabbit is tickled by the cold air his nose is pink and his fur is white as he sits under the bush the protection from the snowy world around him but he can't escape the snow he just sits and waits for it to stop so he can continue on. . . he could continue now but it's so hard to see with the snow constantly blowing the woods are silent except for the wind not a creature makes a noise the bear is in his cave and he sleeps warm and cozy until spring time the animals huddle close to each other looking for warmth and love the wind is so snappy it stings the animals but the rabbit stays still he waits. . .*

Step Two: Poem, "Protection" by Lauren Glanville (Palmer)

Protection
by Lauren Glanville (Palmer)

Protection,
Safe in your world,
Loved ones all around you.
Protection.
Secure in your mind,
Happy with the person you are.
Protection,
Not sad or alone,
Content with your life.
Protection,
Heroes come home,
Life is simple routine.
Protection,
Cuddled up, warm,
Soft and at peace.
Protection,
Feeling perfect,
And being with you.
Protection,
Too much to ask for
In this world full of hate.

What I Learned: Finding a Place for Creative Writing

Too often high school English teachers of reading and literature defer the creative writing experiences of their students to elective or specialty writing courses. However important such electives are as havens in the lives of student writers, they alone cannot provide the wealth of creative writing which students need to experience. In the context of paucity, the roles of the creative writing elective, and the creative writing workshop, within the required English classroom, become even more critical. They serve not only as places to immerse and nurture students in the art form, but they also must serve as correctives for many students like Mark and Stefanie, who grieve the loss of their imaginations and creative spirits.

Questions to Consider about Creative Writing

- *Should creative writing be taught as an integral part of all English classes?*
- *Should creative writing have parity with critical and academic writing in the English class?*
- *Should all English teachers be prepared to teach creative writing?*

This book's pedagogy suggests an affirmative answer to all of the questions above. We need to teach more creative writing not only in creative writing electives, but for all students in required English classes as well. The teaching of creative writing serves different purposes in each of these classrooms. Specialty courses serve the need for immersion in the discipline. Here students can develop their creative writing skills as an art form as they explore all aspects of the craft. Creative writing in literature classes serves a different purpose. There creative writing enables students to enter literature as writers; that is, to read literature as writers would read it, and to respond to literature as writers would respond, modeling the same form, style or genre. Most importantly, educators need to expand this creativity and writing literacy across the curriculum to further expose students to the wide range of writing genres and discipline-related writing skills.

PART THREE: INTERDISCIPLINARY APPLICATIONS

Creative writing is an invaluable transferable skill: students who have taken a creative writing course see improvement specifically

> *in areas of critical thinking, the maintenance of a healthy writing process, and close reading.*
>
> – Alexandria Peary, "The Pedagogy of Creative Writing Across the Curriculum"
> (Peary, 2015: 196)

Questions to Consider about Writing Across the Curriculum

- *Should creative writing be taught across the curriculum?*
- *Should teachers in all subject areas experience* writing to learn *(WTL) strategies?*
- *Should all students experience discipline-related and subject-related writing, that is,* writing in the disciplines *(WID)?*

What a Student Has to Say: The Value of Science Poetry

I can think of no better answer to these questions than my student Alex Davis's comment on first learning about science poetry:

> *My interest in writing and my interest in science seemed so far apart that I wondered if I could ever be successful in either if I continued to devote thought to both. Science poetry changed my viewpoint. I learned that my interest in science could inform my poetry. Thought devoted to science is not wasted when my mind turns to poetry* [. . .]. *I loved the science poetry unit. It commanded my attention in a way that school rarely can.*
>
> (Alex Davis, 2012b; emphasis in the original)

Science poetry, a little known literary genre serves as a valuable interdisciplinary literacy tool for teachers of both the arts and the sciences (Gorrell with Colfax, 2012). Consider Alex's first science poem as he transfers his knowledge from his AP science class to write a poem for his AP English class.

Model Student Science Poem: "The Second Law of Thermodynamics" by Alex Davis

The Second Law of Thermodynamics
by Alex Davis

Everything is falling apart.
First the stars die, and light leaves the universe.

Then the galaxies disintegrate, and every unseen corpse of a star is alone, until the atoms that compose it finally evaporate.

Black holes rule the blackness until they disappear, and the universe reaches the state of perfection it has been chasing for eternity.

Sometime between the beginning of everything and the death of the stars, something begins, and ends, and calls itself – Alex.

(Alex Davis, 2012c)

Commentary on "The Second Law of Thermodynamics"

When Alex shared his science poem in progress, there was a palpable sense of awe in the room. In a mere ten minutes of writing time, Alex had somehow come face to face with the universal struggle to find one's place in the universe. What better task for science poetry? Drawing on his scientific knowledge, Alex takes an intergalactic leap, from the universe of science to the universe of self – from "disintegration," "an unseen corpse of a star," "black holes rule the blackness," to "sometime." Here the transition word *sometime* reverberates for the universe of science as well as for Alex and the students listening to his poem. How much time? For a brief time, we are able to connect ourselves with time, space, and our own place in the vastness of the universe. The contrast of this vastness and the singularity of Alex is astonishing and strikingly authentic.

Alex's Reflection on "The Second Law of Thermodynamics": The Last Word is Alex

> *Some people in class laughed when they heard the last line as if it was a relief of tension. One girl commented, 'I love how it starts so dark and ends on a light note.' That's not how I see it at all. I see two sides to it. One is my insignificance in the face of eternity. I communicated this in part with 'something begins, and ends,' with nothing in between the beginning and the ending. The last line is like an engraving on a gravestone. Something lived and died and this is what it was called. There is nothing between the first date and the last date but a hyphen. The other side is a rejection of this anonymity. In the grand story of all time and mass that exists, Alex must be mentioned. The last word is Alex; he is more important to this story than the death of light. I wouldn't call this a 'lighter' note.*
>
> (Alex Davis, 2012b)

(See Chapter 18 for science poetry defined, science poetry pedagogy, and additional model student science poems.)

For Your Teacher Journal: Non-Stop Writing Exercise

1. Practice the warm-up technique of non-stop writing for two weeks. Time yourself. Allow five minutes of non-stop writing every day.
2. After two weeks, reread all of the non-stop writing entries. Find the "diamond in the rough" of your entries.
3. Reflect on your "diamond" or favorite entry. Write a new draft of that entry, or expand the entry.
4. What have you discovered about yourself as a writer in the process?
5. When so inspired, write another draft in any form you want – poem, short prose piece, a description, or a memory from any starting point.
6. What have you discovered about the writing process?
7. What have you discovered about your discipline and/or discipline-related writing?

For Your Students: Model Student Non-Stop Writing by Stefanie DeFronzo, Biochemistry and Molecular Biology Major, Drew University

Light/Refraction
by Stefanie DeFronzo

Light

Sizzle
Stress
Not manageable
Without the lid
The vegetables simmer on the stove top
In oil
Sitting
Spitting
Squishing
Next to one another
Pieces in the pan
Children in the sandbox
Tan, grey, green, orange, red, black, brown
In one sauté
On one cast iron
Fire in the hole
Like a belly

Refraction

Tan, grey, green, orange, red, black, brown
Pieces in the pan
Children in the sandbox
Crayons in the box
Each unique
Respected
And equal
Colors
Vegetables

Human beings
For love
Is not blind
But bountiful
And colors are not dividers
But reasons to celebrate
The complexion of life

Stefanie's Reflection on "Light/Refraction"

The "light" of this work stems from emotions I found within myself on a given day during the COVID-19 crisis. I was sitting in the kitchen while my parents were cooking dinner when I decided to start the non-stop writing prompt. Crowded by so many diverging thoughts and feelings, my senses seemed to help my brain focus on the concrete things around me while still allowing it to wander to raw sentiments.

(See the Epilogue, "The Students in the Window," for Stefanie's complete discussion of her poem.)

Chapter 6 Notes

1 James Britton defined three modes of (written) discourse in *Language and Learning* (Britton, 1970) and again in *The Development of Writing Abilities* (Britton et al., 1975). *Expressive discourse* is informal writing resembling ordinary talk and often informing the foundation of *poetic writing* and *transactional writing* (Britton et al., 1975: 82–83). Transactional writing is for the purpose of conveying information "to meet the demands of some kind of participation in world affairs" (Britton, 1970: 174–175). *Poetic writing* or creative writing is an aesthetic artifact – it's "MAKING something with language rather than doing something with it" and in the positive case evokes an appreciative response in its reader (Britton, 1982: 158–159). Detailed discussion of Britton and these modes can be found in Peary (2015: 201–202).

2 The use of the terms *workshop* and *sharing circle* as they align with this author's creative writing pedagogy for high school students is defined first in the Introduction and subsequently illustrated through chapter teaching stories and model lessons.

3 I credit the concept of non-stop writing to Peter Elbow's pioneering pedagogy of regular freewriting exercises to improve writing (Elbow, 1973/1998). He describes "writing without stopping" or "whatever comes to mind," but to my knowledge, does not use the term, *non-stop writing.* The pedagogy I adapted from Elbow's (1973) *Writing without Teachers* takes non-stop writing to its logical conclusion by forcing students to write literally without pause to force an unedited stream of consciousness in order to paradoxically release the thought process or writers' block.

4 Almost all students under this system receive final grades of "A" or "B." Students who have not completed the required writings receive lower grades. No student has ever failed Creative Writing. But a few have received grades of "C" or lower for not submitting the required number of writing assignments. One other caveat: lateness. Respecting writer's creativity, some occasional lateness is recorded but acceptable. A pattern of lateness is not. I tell students that our exercises are sequential, to build their skills, and that they cannot do well in the course and do all of the exercises at once and expect a good grade. A pattern of lateness, will result in a "late penalty," as an achieved grade of "A" will be recorded as "B." The value of a contract grading system is that it takes the focus off of grades and places it where it should be – on the writing. I say to my students, you can have whatever grade you want. I'll help you do it. I'm absolved of any grade averaging, and students are absolved of grade consciousness.

Chapter 6 References

Arum, Richard and Roska, Josipa (2011) Academically adrift: Limited learning on college campuses. Cited from Peary (2015: 195).

Atwell, Nancie (1987/1998) *In the Middle: Writing, Reading and Learning with Adolescents* (2nd edition). Portsmouth, NH: Boyton/Cook Heinemann.

Bishop, Wendy (1994) Crossing the lines: On creative composition and composing creative writing. In Bishop, Wendy and Ostrom, Hans (eds.) *Colors of a Different Horse*: *Rethinking Creative Writing Theory and Pedagogy*, 181–197. Urbana, IL: National Council of Teachers of English. https://files.eric.ed.gov/fulltext/ED366967.pdf

Britton, James (1970) *Language and Learning*. Coral Gables, FL: University of Miami Press. Cited from Peary (2015: 201).

Britton, James (1982) Spectator role and the beginnings of writing. In Pradl, Gordon M. (ed.) *Prospect and Retrospect: Selected Essays of*

James Britton, 46–67. Upper Montclair: Boynton. Cited from Peary (2015: 202).

Britton, James, Burgess, Tony, Martin, Nancy, McLeod, Alex and Rosen, Harold (1975) *The Development of Writing Abilities*. Basingstoke, Hampshire and London: Macmillan. Cited from Peary (2015: 201).

Davis, Alex (2012a) Alex's commentary on "The Second Law of Thermodynamics." Qtd in Gorrell with Colfax (2012: 146).

Davis, Alex (2012b) Comment on first learning about science poetry. Qtd in Gorrell with Colfax (2012: 36).

Davis, Alex (2012c) "The Second Law of Thermodynamics." Qtd in Gorrell, with Colfax (2012: 145).

Elbow, Peter (1973/1998) *Writing Without Teachers* (2nd edition). New York, NY: Oxford University Press.

Elbow, Peter (1990) *What is English?* New York, NY: Modern Language Association of America and Urbana, IL: National Council of Teachers of English.

Emig, Janet (1977) Writing as a mode of learning. *College Composition and Communication*, 28 (2): 122–128. https://doi.org/10.2307/356095

Gorrell, Nancy S. with Erin Colfax (2012) *Writing Poetry through the Eyes of Science: Scientific Literacy and Poetic Response*. Sheffield, UK and Oakville, CT: Equinox.

Lim, Shirley Geok-lin (2015) Highways and sinkholes: Incorporating creativity strategies in the writing classroom. In Chik, Alice, Costley, Tracey and Pennington, Martha C. (eds.) *Creativity and Discovery in the University Writing Class*, 251–276. Sheffield, UK and Oakville, CT: Equinox.

Moffett, James (1992) *Active Voice* (2nd edition). Portsmouth, NH: Boyton/Cook Heinemann.

Moxley, Joseph (1989) Tearing down the walls: Engaging the imagination. In Moxley, Joseph (ed.) *Creative Writing in America*, 25–45. Urbana, IL: National Council of Teachers of English.

Peary, Alexandria (2015) The pedagogy of creative writing across the curriculum. In Peary, Alexandria and Hunley, Tom C. (eds.) *Creative Writing Pedagogies for Twenty-First Century*, 194–220. Carbondale, IL: Southern Illinois University Press.

Peary, Alexandria and Hunley, Tom C. (eds.) (2015) *Creative Writing Pedagogies for the Twenty-First Century*. Carbondale, IL: Southern Illinois University Press.

Rilke, Rainer Maria (2000) *Letters to a Young Poet*. Novato, CA: New World Library.

Chapter 7

Knowing Your Students: Times of Transition and Transformation

At the start of my junior year, I was forced into a creative writing course by schedule default [...]. I remember sitting in class thinking to myself how terrible the semester was going to be[...] I went to lunch and complained to my friends. "Man, this is not fair, I hate that class, it is going to be the longest three months ever." Wow, I was so wrong.

– Judd Hauser, creative writing student

PART ONE: TIMES OF TRANSITION AND TRANSFORMATION

A Time of Transition: "Here's to 18" by Sarah Beth Kaufman, Creative Writing Senior

Here's to 18
by Sarah Beth Kaufman

11 nights before graduation,
we sit on my bed.
She flips through a magazine,
and I try to write my last-ever official paper for high school English.
"My god," I say. "I don't know if I'm ready to be old.
I'm not sure I feel old."

She looks up. "So write about rainbows," she says.
"Write about rainbows and unicorns like we used to in third grade."
She looks down.
But I am already gone.
I am running on the playground, pigtails in the wind,
where boys have cooties
and we race to get the best swing,
and all I want is to be the line-leader
so I can get a gold star from Mrs… Mrs. someone
whose name I already can't remember and I
don't even know the names of my professors next year,
and I can't write about third-grade rainbows
because they're fading
and now,
suddenly,
it is time to make my own.

I look around my room.
She's still reading.
My calendar on the walls says it's April
But it's June 7. I never used to forget to change the months.
Maybe I'm scared to let them go.

"I can't write about rainbows," I tell her.
"My paper is on the writing technique of Charlotte Bronte."
She smiles. "Just don't forget how," she says.

I put down my paper and take her hand.
We drive to the playground and play on the swings
In the dark silent night, the streaks of our hair
make rainbows in the wind.
In the morning I will change my calendar.

Commentary on Times of Transition

Sarah's poem illustrates defining characteristics of many of the students who find their way into my creative writing elective course.

They are at once adults, anticipating the world of independence, responsibility, and self-actualization, and at the same time, they are children at heart, longing for the innocence and playfulness of childhood. I imagine them straddling two canoes on a lake; one foot in the "canoe" of childhood, the other foot in the "canoe" of adulthood. They balance precariously on this lake of life, never able to separate the two, for both canoes are part of their emerging identities. From one, they look back, from the other, they look forward; the balancing act enables them to stay afloat, as challenging as the task may be.

For over three decades, I have taught creative writing to juniors and seniors at Morristown High School, Morristown, New Jersey. I see them enter my classroom filled with the pressures of daily school life and high-stakes decision-making – jobs, summer schooling and employment, college, tests, grades. They also bring to the classroom a wealth of life experience – of separation, loss, death, betrayal, prejudice, racism, violence, love, sex and friendship to name a few. Some enter class having already shouldered adult responsibilities – living in foster homes, taking care of younger siblings, and managing demanding work schedules outside of school. They are men and women; but when I ask them to remember playing with a favorite childhood toy, they smile knowingly and write with joy. When I ask them to imagine eating ice cream on a hot day, they savor it with a special taste of recognition. When I ask them to write about a place they'd rather be, they write with abandon. When I ask them to go outside with me on a rainy day, "feel the rain on their faces, taste it, and hear it, and then write about it," they look at me as if I am odd, and then, once outside, I see them jumping in puddles and splashing each other in laughter. There is so much they need and want to write about.

The creative writing needs of this age group are often neglected in the maze of launching them into the world of college, workplace, and for some, military service, and war. Yet in the world of writing, *this is the time*. This is the time when they are most able to reflect with maturity on their childhood and their past. It is also the time when this self-reflection is most critical to their identity formation and decision-making. *Who am I? Where have I come from? Where am I going? What do I want to be? What do I want to do?* They are ripe for mature writing, and they savor it. For many, the creative writing classroom provides the first opportunity for self-reflection and self-discovery. How do I know? I have been reading their writing, and I bear witness on a daily basis to their revelations, realizations, and transformations. I also bear witness to their emergence as writers. For many, the closure of the K–12 educational milestone is a time of intense, personal transformation.

A Time of Transformation: "Transformation of a Resistant Writer" by Judd Hauser, Senior

Judd wrote the following reflection for his creative writing course evaluation. As his teacher, I suggested he submit the following reflection as his college essay. He did.

Transformation of a Resistant Writer
by Judd Hauser

At the start of my junior year, I was forced into a creative writing course by schedule default. This first day I was supposed to be in that class was September 11th. Due to the tragedy, I didn't end up going to class until the next day. I remember sitting in class thinking to myself how terrible the semester was going to be. I thought that elective courses were supposed to be easier than other classes. It seemed to me that I was going to have to write so much every day and I hated to write. I was very upset, and now I was being told to write about the previous day's events. I looked to my right, wanting to complain to my neighbor, but he had already started to write. I looked to the left to do the same, and all of the students were writing. Everyone was writing but me, so I started to write down a few things, but I wasn't trying to do my best. Finally, the lunch bell rang and I ran to see my guidance counselor. I told her that creative writing was not for me, and that I wanted to switch out immediately. She told me that

I couldn't leave because there were no other classes available. I went to lunch and complained to my friends. "Man, this is not fair, I hate that class, it is going to be the longest three months ever." I told everyone. Wow, I was so wrong.

First there were two surprises that made it impossible to hate that class. One, my teacher, Mrs. Gorrell was enthusiastic and talented. And second, I found out that I could write quite well. But there was a rough start. The first week or two, I didn't allow myself to really take part in the lessons or activities. I remember my second day of class, Mrs. Gorrell took out a picture of a tree that supposedly had all these other images inside of it. Everyone else in the class had their own creative response to the picture. But all I saw was the tree itself. I thought it was so dumb. I suppose I thought I was too cool for art. I never gave any input, and I never even wrote the response to the picture that everyone else did. I told myself, just a couple of months, and I'll be out of here.

Next, one day Ms. Gorrell called me up to her desk to tell me I wasn't doing well in the class. Not a surprise, but I was upset. So, I decided, while I didn't like the work, I had to complete it. That day we went to the computer lab to write a description that could make the reader feel a certain mood that we desired. I tried my best, and when I handed it in, I thought it was pretty bad. A few days later I got my paper back with comments. Mrs. Gorrell thought it was great! I was upset, and I didn't know why. I just got a great comment, I should have been thrilled. But I was upset because I thought it was bad to be able to write well. My friends always thought that the kids who were artistic were "dorks." I didn't want to be a dork, so I didn't want to be able to write well. Then it all changed.

Soon after, I started to write about what was bothering me in my journal. I would actually come home from school and go up to my room and write. I wrote songs or poems about things I felt during that day. Slowly, I started to lose that ridiculously immature feeling I had that told me writing was for dorks. I started to love writing. Every day I wrote several poems on different subjects. I started handing in extra writings to Mrs. Gorrell. When she returned them, she would always give me a good response.

I loved getting my poems back. It was the best feeling in the world when she would say she thought they were good. She started asking me to read some of them out loud in the sharing circle. Of course, I said "no." I was far from ready to admit that I could possibly like writing. Even though I did really enjoy it, I didn't like the fact that I did. So, for weeks I went on writing all the time, but keeping it to myself.

Luckily, I had some great kids in my class who were far more mature than I was. They started to encourage me to read some of my poems out loud. But I still didn't want to, so I didn't. But I continued to write more and more, and I started to get better and better. Sometimes I would be so excited during block five that I was going to be able to go home and write, I just couldn't wait for the bell to ring. I was writing all the time. It was therapeutic, fun and rewarding. At the same time, my social life was becoming better and better. I suppose writing was completing me as a person, and helping me interact with other people.

When it came towards the end of the semester, I had grown so much. When I was writing, I was constantly discovering new things about myself. I started to see reading out loud to the class as my last mountain to climb. By the last two weeks, I was reading poems out loud. I began reading my least personal ones, but by the end of the course, I was reading my favorites. And to my surprise, people really like it. A few girls came up to me after I read and told me how much they enjoyed it. Then my best friend in the class, the kid who I once sought out to complain to, told me how good a writer he thought I was.

When I was reading out loud, I would always look at Mrs. Gorrell's face and the warm smile on her face was something I still can't describe with words. It was the best time of my life, and it changed me forever. Still today, I write all the time, and I'm proud to say that.

On the last day of that class, I went to Mrs. Gorrell and asked to see that picture of the tree.[1] I looked at it, and I saw tons of little things. One thing I didn't see was the tree.

What I Learned: The Power of the Community of Writers

Judd exemplifies the student who enters creative writing class having internalized negative attitudes and stereotypes about writing. Judd honestly admits he "hated" writing and didn't write well because he didn't want to be a "dork." He had a poor self-image, lacked confidence in his own voice and abilities, and refused initially to do the exercises or participate. What enabled Judd to be transformed in relatively short time into an independent, self-proclaimed writer?

Judd's story attests to the power of the community of writers to bring into the fold even the most reluctant student. Fortunately, most of the students in creative writing class are present because they have positive attitudes and want to learn the art of writing. Such students model writing in class by responding freely to given prompts. They write with sustained flow, focus, and enthusiasm, producing on-the-spot works in progress that they feel confident enough to share with the class. Students like Judd observe these writers and usually follow suit. No one wants to sit in front of a blank piece of paper when everyone else is writing. Judd of course became an unusual case. Not only was he resistant initially to composing, but he held out to the end the sharing of his writing with the class.

Judd's story also attests to the power of praise to engage a student in the process of writing. I begin creative writing with considerable freewriting, short exercises, extensive journaling, and fundamental lessons that easily engage. My comments always seek the strengths of the writing, and I comment with heaps of textually supported praise. No student will write for a teacher who does not believe in them or their work. Initial and sustained praise are the most important motivators for beginning writers. Without fear of criticism or judgment, they are able to write freely, and therefore, produce more. And that is so important in an introductory course – getting students to write more expansively and productively.

Judd's story also attests to the critical importance of developmental time. Such time is needed for some students to mature and develop confidence in their writing. Judd clearly was one of them. He did not share until the end of the course despite seeing most of the other students eagerly sharing. During the sharing circle, some students began to aggressively urge Judd to share his work. Such peer pressure must be discouraged. The class norm is that the "pass" is accepted by the circle without comment. I never compel students to read or share their work. Any student may "pass" when they do not feel so moved to share. It's important to note that although Judd was not so moved, he was writing. And he was producing good work. The first piece he actually shared was at my suggestion. I praised one of his poems and suggested he read it during the circle. Of course, I had been doing this gentle "suggesting" for quite some time, but Judd finally took the encouragement. Time and patience on the part of the teacher succeeded with Judd.

Lastly, Judd's story attests to the ultimate powers of the writing process to transform. Gradually, Judd began to write for himself. He began to discover issues of self, issues of personal identity, and he began to discover his voice. In relatively short time, he transformed himself into an independent, self-proclaimed writer. He notes the convergence of his emerging maturity and the improvement in his social life. Judd attributes this transformation to his newfound identity as writer.

PART TWO: WHO TAKES CREATIVE WRITING?

A Mélange of Students

Although one might think that only avid writers "elect" creative writing, the truth is that creative writing is a mélange of students, with a host of reasons why they are there: they want to try something different; they think it will be easier than other courses; they think they will get a better grade; their counselor made them do it; nothing else fits into their schedules; they think they are weak writers and it will help them improve; and yes, they just might love to create and to write. At Morristown High School, Creative Writing I, the introductory course, is open to all students who have completed sophomore English. That makes creative writing one of the most diverse and heterogeneous courses in the school, save physical education. Many, like Mark in Chapter 6 ("Knowing Where You're Going: The American High School"), are searching to reclaim their creativity and imagination. Others, like Sarah above, want to write to discover their evolving selves. Always, there are some writers biting at the bit to learn the craft. These writers form a comfortable community within the classroom with the inter-arts students – art, music, film and drama students – who eagerly find their way into creative writing as well.

Such arts students initially form the core of the writing community, inviting into the circle, students like Judd above, who enter with negative experiences and attitudes. Yet a significant portion of any class consists of the cautionary, reluctant students, there for a host of reasons besides the love of writing. High school guidance counselors play a major role in placing these students into creative writing: fifth year seniors who have to double up on English courses to graduate; "classified" students who can't read well and would rather just write; exceptional juniors who need to double up on course credits to graduate early; and the host of "lost souls" that don't seem to fit into anywhere. In his study, Csikszentmihalyi (1996: 176–177) calls these years the "awkward years," noting that "talented teenagers" reported "marginality, the feeling of being on the outside, of being different" from their peers as a common theme.

And yet, none of this is of any significant consequence, for once the students enter your classroom, you will regard them all as works in progress. Once the process takes hold, once the community of writers forms, you and your students become co-equals in the ongoing process of transformation. Stereotypes dissolve, ability "levels" disappear, and the individual voice prevails.

A Diversity of Voices

One of the greatest pleasures in teaching creative writing is witnessing the power of the diversity of voices to teach, to motivate, and to inspire not only writing, but the transformation essential to writing. Students of all abilities, all walks of life, all attitudes and experiences form a web of humanity in creative writing class, replicating life itself. Nothing could better prepare senior high school students for the diverse world than this mélange. For many who have been tracked for years in Honors, AP, basic skills, or special education courses, this diversity opens eyes, breaks down barriers and stereotypes, and brings unlikely students meeting together for the first time.

Polar Opposites: Models for Each Other[2]

In the early days of my teaching, I discovered the power of this diversity when two boys, polar opposites, entered my advanced Creative Writing II elective. One boy, Rob, was the soon-to-be salutatorian of the graduating class. A straight-A student, he had an outstanding record of school achievement and service. He was undeniably intelligent, mature, and successful by all measures. Sporting a short haircut (considered clean-cut in those days), he had already been accepted to Washington University in St. Louis and was waiting to hear from Harvard. He clearly was his parents' success story. Sitting next to him was Thomas.

Thomas was a fifth-year senior, repeating required English and American History in order to graduate. He had long, unruly hair (a signature mark of freedom at the time) and an attitude that said, "I do my own thing." He made no bones about the fact that he lived alone and was just waiting to get out of school so he could travel to the West coast. Grades, class rank, or any other aspect of societal conformity didn't interest him. Walking to the beat of his own drummer, he seemed confident, independent, and self-assured.

I'll never forget the first day of class when I saw Rob glance over at Thomas with a look of disdain. Throughout the course, that look would change several times, from shock, to surprise, to respect and then to awe. How did Thomas look at Rob? Not even a glance. In the beginning, Thomas barely acknowledged Rob's existence. In a world of his own, he kept up his guard. But gradually, Thomas changed, too. By the end of the semester, the two boys shared not only mutual admiration, but each became the other's muse.

How did this transformation happen? It was the matching of opposites, each one possessed with an inner strength the other needed. Rob was the model student and the model writer. His prose was technically perfect, concise, neatly typed, and correct to a fault. Whatever the exercise, Rob modeled it perfectly, and his work was always turned in on time. Yet his writing did not seem authentic. Nothing had a distinct voice that was his own. Rob wrote what he thought great writing should sound like; what great writing should be about. But it wasn't Rob, and he knew it and struggled.

The first time Rob shared in the circle, he read his story about a soldier. It was skillful but forced, falling into cliché. I remember Thomas looking somewhat amused. Yet something in what Rob read spoke to Thomas, and he volunteered his own evolving story, chicken-scratched on a tattered piece of paper (Thomas never typed up his writing). It was about a boy leaving home. When he was finished reading, the class was quiet; Rob looked surprised. Thomas had a voice of his own, and it was manly and mature. From that day forward, I could see that Rob was eager to hear Thomas's writing.

I could also see that Thomas was eager to write for Rob. For the more Rob look surprised and then amazed, the more Thomas wanted to write. After that, Thomas's work came rushing in torrents of inspiration. One day during peer editing, the two boys paired up. Thomas's story was only half-way typed, and Robert commented that he couldn't read all of it. After that, Thomas almost always had his work typed. But more importantly, he also started to value Rob's feedback. Rob knew literature, and when he told Thomas that his poetry was as good as Allen Ginsberg's, I knew Thomas valued the comment.

Thomas modeled for Rob the joy of uninhibited, freewriting. His poetry was his voice singing, and his stories were about himself. Each time Thomas read, I could see the admiration and wonder growing on Rob's face. Rob longed to be a serious writer. Rob needed to take risks, and I could see him slowly realizing this in his writing. Gradually, Rob began to write about subjects closer to his experience, and closer to matters important to him. At the end of the course, Rob wrote a story about a boy in conflict with his parents. Thomas helped Rob find his voice.

The story of Rob and Thomas is just one example of transformations I have witnessed over the years in which the power of the diversity of voices transforms student writers, accelerating their maturation. Such acceleration works hand in hand with fostering, inspiring, and producing the mature writing I hope to teach for and create with my students, and I hope you can teach for and create with your students as well.

For Your Journal: Times of Transition and Transformation

Reflecting

1. Recall your last two years of high school. Was it a critical time of transition for you? Did you change or transform in those years?
2. Recall a time when you felt the conflict between your inner child or longing for childhood and your emerging adulthood.
3. Recall an age that was transformational for you. It may be a time of transition or change. How does this knowledge inform your teaching?
4. How does reflecting about times of transition and transformation inform your teaching?

Responding: Writing Prompts

1. Write freely in your journal what you can recall about a time in your life of transition.

2. Write freely in your journal what you can recall about a time in your life of transformation.
3 Write your own age poem or memory piece or memoir about a significant age from your past. For example: "Here's to 18" or "Age 18" or "Age 10" or "Age 6."

For Your Students: Writing Prompts

Instructions

1. Recall your junior or senior year of high school. Were those years a critical time of transition for you? Did you change, mature, or transform? Reflect about this time in your life. Then write a poem, prose poem, memoir, or story titled "Age 17" or "Age 18."
2. Recall a time growing up when you longed for your childhood. Reflect and then describe that time in a poem, prose poem, memoir, or story.
3. Choose any age that was a time of change or transition for you. Write a poem or prose poem about that age and that time. You can entitle it for example, "Age 10" or "Age 13."

Model Student Poem – A Time of Change or Transition: "Humanitarian at Age Six" by Sarah Beth Kaufman

Humanitarian at Age Six
by Sarah Beth Kaufman

She remembers distinctly
the sound of cold rain falling
on her shiny red raincoat with the little ducks on it
as Mommy and Daddy and She
step out from the opera onto the city streets.
The rain was cold
but She was warm
shelter between two big protectors.

She also remembers
the wet ragged man
who grabbed at Mommy's shoulder,
and pleaded for a dime and some mercy.
But Mommy, used to the big city,
whisked by
and the family hustled into the car.

Mommy turned on the heat and
Daddy rubbed big hands together,
But She looked out the foggy window
at the faded man
and cried.

Humanitarian at age six.

PART THREE: INTERDISCIPLINARY APPLICATIONS

The Awkward Years

> *Marginality – the feeling of being on the outside, of being different* […] – *was a common theme* [of talented teenagers who were interviewed].
>
> – Mihaly Csikszentmihalyi, *Creativity: Flow and the Psychology of Discovery and Invention*
> (Csikszentmihalyi, 1996: 176–177)

Csikszentmihalyi's study of the "The Awkward Years" describes talented teenagers across the disciplines. Whether they are the budding artists scientists, musicians, or mathematicians, none remembered being popular in adolescence (p. 177). (For further discussion, see Chapter 8: Knowing the Creatively "Gifted" Student.) Regardless of discipline, students in the last years of high school experience *times of transition and transformation* which universally relate to childhood, growing up, change, and maturation. That maturation may or may not be associated with a particular discipline, a particular age, a particular teacher, or a particular teaching experience. Teachers across the disciplines are encouraged to adapt the writing prompts in this chapter for their particular students and discipline-related writing as well as creative writing within their subject and courses.

Model Contributor Prose Poem, "A Handful of Knowing, Part 1" by Amy Uyematsu, Mathematics Teacher

A Handful of Knowing, Part 1
by Amy Uyematsu

> Even as a child she prefers their company. Each day the girl goes to Stone Mountain and chooses one of the ten thousand stones which lie at its base. Sometimes she picks a jagged rock, studies it from different angles to see it brighten and darken in the shifting light. Or she might spread a handful of pebbles on her outstretched palms marvel that no two are exactly the same size or shape. If she finds a boulder big enough for her to recline on her back, she can take in the sky. Before long the girl is able to touch each granite gem with the deft fingers of a sculptor, delighted when a once grainy surface turns glassy and smooth. Sitting among the rocks and pebbles, she listens with them to a world that stirs, grateful when something new flurries in and glad when mountain quiet returns. As time passes, the girl grows so intimate with the stones that no one notices she's become old and weathered and silent like them. Song birds and lizards rest on her. Small fingers trace the lines on her face.
>
> (Uyematsu, 2016: 65)

On Transition and Transformation: "A Handful of Knowing"

The model contributor prose poem by Amy Uyematsu offers a poetic response to *times of transition*, *times of transformation* when a child grasps "a handful of knowing," literally stones, and "as time passes, the girl grows so intimate with the stones" that she transforms, becoming "old," "weathered," and "silent like them." Poetically, she has become "stone," or transitioned to adulthood, maturity, or old age. Birds "rest" on her like a grave. Is she dead, "stone" dead? "Small fingers trace the lines on her face." Who would do this other than a child ("small" fingers) or progeny? Or, someone, poetically, who wants to know a "handful of knowing." Such tracing by "small" fingers will bring stone to life, dead to living, poetically transitioning "the handful of knowing."

Chapter 7 Notes

1 "The picture of the tree" that Judd was looking at was in actuality a print of *Hide and Seek*, a painting by Pavel Tchelitchew.

2 "Polar Opposites" uses pseudonyms for student names.

Chapter 7 References

Cameron, Julia (2002) *Walking in this World: The Practical Art of Creativity*. New York, NY: Tarcher/Putnam.

Csikszentmihalyi, Mihaly (1996) *Creativity: Flow and the Psychology of Discovery and Invention*. New York, NY: Harper Perennial.

Uyematsu, Amy (2016) "A Handful of Knowing." *Basic Vocabulary*, 65–66. Pasadena, CA: Red Hen Press.

Chapter 8

Knowing the Creatively "Gifted" Student

The "geniuses" – are those who were able to free more of that faculty for use in their lives and in their works of art than the rest of mankind.

– Dorothea Brande, *Becoming a Writer*
(Brande, 1934/1981: 157)

If we were purists, we would not speak of a 'creative person,' but only of a creative act.

– Rollo May, *The Courage to Create*
(May, 1975: 43; emphasis in the original)

PART ONE: A GIFTED TEACHING STORY

We all possess creative potential, talent or "gifts" if you will, but clearly, some of us possess more talent or gifts than others. Or, is it that some just know how to actualize their gifts better than others? As noted by Rollo May in Chapter 2, "If we were purists, we would not speak of a 'creative person' but only of *a creative act*" (May, 1975: 43; emphasis in the original). If a student does not actualize that potential, how are we as teachers able to recognize it? For teachers of writing and teachers across the disciplines, there exists a group of students, the creatively "gifted," who readily display their gifts.[1] The creatively gifted students form a vital portion of every creative writing class. When they enter class, they are eager and ready. Some have produced creative acts in the form of portfolios of poetry or stories. Others, unaccomplished, at the moment, are also ready, but in a different way. Like Pat Conroy, many have experienced a wealth of life's hardships and struggles, and they are yearning to find and express their creative spirit. The common axiom goes: *If the pupil is ready, the teacher must* appear. And that is our challenge: how to appear? How to be there – ready and able to identify, mentor, and teach the creatively gifted student.

We face this significant challenge through our creative teaching. Considered the following story of one "gifted" student writer ready, and one "gifted" English teacher willing and able to appear.

Pat Conroy, "Gonzaga High School"

Pat Conroy, in his memoir, *My Losing Season*, credits his scholarly and charismatic English teacher at Gonzaga High School, Joseph Monte, for a transformative moment which forever unlocked for him the mystery of literature and inspired his passion for writing. In trying to help Pat understand his reading of *The Sound and the Fury*, Mr. Monte suggests to him to consider Act 5, Scene 4, of *Macbeth.* Later Mr. Monte encounters Pat and asks him if he has something to discuss with him. "Out, out" he says to "Mr. Conroy" his eyes twinkling at the play on words. Pat replies that Macbeth says, "Out, out, brief candle" when he hears of the queen's death. Mr. Monte probes Pat further – what does that mean? Pat answers "life is short." Again, Mr. Monte probes by asking what the phrase says about Faulkner's book. Pat says it occurs later in the speech when Macbeth says, "It is a tale told by an idiot, full of sound and fury, signifying nothing." Then he tells Mr. Monte why he was confused reading the passage. Pat says it's because the tale is told through the eyes of Benji, an idiot.

To Pat's shock, Mr. Monte opens his grade book and enters an "A+," double credit. He tells him it is a "good moment in both their lives; one they both should cherish (Conroy, 2003: 62).

Teaching the "Gifted" Writer: "We Should Both Cherish It"

> *If the school itself rarely gets mentioned as a source of inspiration, individual teachers often awaken, sustain, or direct a child's interest.*
>
> – Mihaly Csikszentmihalyi, *Creativity: Flow and the Psychology of Discovery and Invention* (Csikszentmihalyi, 1996: 173–174)

Mr. Monte had great wisdom. He knew that both student and teacher shared in the process of becoming and that both should "cherish" it. Just think, someday you might be teaching a future Hemingway, Angelou, or Conroy. Will you be ready? Although the creatively gifted defy easy generalization, we can learn much from Mr. Monte. Clearly, Mr. Monte had faith in Pat Conroy's innate creativity. He believed in his student; he cared and showed his caring by giving Pat extra attention and challenges. In addition, he recognized the art of all great teaching: balancing challenge with encouragement. As he commanded, "Out, out with it, Mr. Conroy," there was a "twinkle in his eye." The creatively gifted need challenge, but they also need challenge coupled with faith, validation, and encouragement. It seems so simple, but when it works, miracles happen. For in the process, both student and teacher are transformed. In his memoir, Pat confirms Mr. Monte's transformative influence: "All I knew was, I was not the same boy who walked into Gonzaga that previous fall" (Conroy, 2003: 63).

In the spirit of teaching and cherishing, the question remains: how can you identify the creatively gifted writer in your class? Whether you are an English teacher or a teacher of another subject, the following case study illustrates one creatively gifted, multitalented writing student.

PART TWO: A CASE STUDY

Mike,[2] a Sixth Grade Student: "The Story of My Life as a Writer in the Making"

The Story of My Life as a Writer in the Making
by Mike

Sixth Grade English

Back in the sixth grade my English teacher, Mrs. Baiel, had one of the coolest projects every created. We were asked to write and illustrate our very own children's story. They were going to be sent away to a company, and then printed in a hardbound cover. My story was titled "Lenny, the African Flying Spider Frog" and it was definitely a good read. Well, for sixth graders anyway. After the project was finished, our class was asked to read our stories to a first grade class at the Mountain Way School. A lot of the younger kids liked that we simply came, let alone the fact that we came with stories. Despite that, the little kids seemed to really love "Lenny, the African Flying Spider Frog" a lot. Later, Mrs. Baiel confronted me in class and asked if she could keep the hardcover copy of my story. I asked her if she needed it to demonstrate to future classes what the finished product looked like. She said, "No." It was because she loved my story, and she wanted to keep it for herself if I didn't mind. I didn't, mind that is.

AP History

History I AP, sophomore year of high school. Mr. Lockman was handing back the essays we had taken the week before. He slid his loafers in a scratchy swagger and told us that we were getting better with our essay writing, but we still had a long way to go. Even though he continued to speak about ways we can improve and how we all failed to miss the bar, I thought of one thing. How many weeks I would spend grounded for another bad history grade. One by one, my fellow classmates fell like dominos. Folded paper, read the grade, put your head down in shame. Folded paper, read the grade, put your head down in shame. It was like watching the same student over and over again. Time for my row to get their essays back. The first girl got a 5.5, I could see it from my seat. The girl in front of me got a 4. Ouch. The next paper had a nice big 3 on it and I sighed in despair. But for some odd reason, at that moment, Mr. Lockman's order of passing out papers skipped a heartbeat and he moved right passed me and handed the 3 to the kid behind me. His hand popped over my shoulder and flopped my essay on my desk. It hadn't been folded, because he knew that I didn't have to worry about covering my grade up. My paper read simply: 10 "Wow, Mike!"

Band Lyrics

"Hey Mike, I'm really diggin' these lyrics, bud." My friend rifled through some papers the drummer had printed off of our band's website. Up until then, no one in our band knew what I sang or that it meant anything.

"Thanks man, I worked really hard on those." My friend then asked me to tell him what it meant. Despite him liking it, the lyrics were confusing and very odd. I told him that I wouldn't know what they meant for a few more days. With his puzzled look, I explained to him that when I write lyrics, it doesn't make sense for a few days. Then I get an emotion, more like an inclination of what feeling I'm trying to express. Then it all comes to me. He stood completely plain-faced. Then he let a big smile open up his face and he began to bear hug me.

Drama, Creative Writing

It was late one night about a week ago. My friends and I were still at play practice. It had been a slow day; everyone was irritated at each other. Nothing was coming along smoothly. The main cast was asked to meet in the hallway in front of the Senior Stairs for a line rehearsal because, well, we needed it. My friend Martin and I have small male parts, poking in every now and again once or twice in every act, so as you can imagine, there was a lot of downtime for him and me to relax. The supervisor, a very angry assistant stage manager, led the run-through. She had made it quite clear that she didn't want anyone talking. I decided to look over some of my creative writing assignments for submission to *Tricorn*, our literary magazine, and for the final course project. Without me noticing, Martin picked up my folder, opened it up. I was busy thumbing through a George Carlin book, completely unaware that he was reading anything. After fussing through my work, Martin arranged the folder neatly and placed it back on the second highest stair where I had left it. A few minutes later, I picked up my folder and opened it. On one of my pieces, Martin had strewn across it in big letters his praise and admiration of me as a writer.

Mom/Writing Portfolio

I was coming home from play practice. My mom was driving and she seemed very nervous or on edge. I didn't know what she was flipping out about, but I wanted to know, so I asked. She said that nothing was wrong, but I knew her all too well. Finally, she told me that the night before she had looked through the poems I had written in Creative Writing. I thought, *oh, boy here it comes. The editor part of her is going to edit me, and the parent part of her going to tell me what I can and cannot write about*. Instead, she said, "I was amazed. They were really good. Like, I don't know, they were just amazing." All I can say is that was a very comfortable ride home.

Identifying the Creatively "Gifted" Student Writer

From the moment Mike walked into the class, I knew he was going to be a "creative" student. He had the look of wonder and awe on his face; he was always focused, alert, on task and just filled with the joy to write. From day one, his enthusiastic smile electrified the class. Most definitely an extrovert, Mike was open, outgoing, and friendly. He exemplified many of the creatively gifted who I like to think of as inter-arts students who move easily from one creative field to another. In Mike's case, he writes, acts, sings, and composes song lyrics.

His story, told in a series of anecdotes, illustrates how teachers from levels and disciplines are able to readily identify giftedness in writing. But Mike made it easy. His creativity was observable through overt acts: his writing, book publishing in 6th grade, song writing and singing. From his middle school teacher, high school history teacher, friends, and parents, Mike's creativity was actualized, acknowledged, and affirmed to his great pleasure and encouragement.

Despite all this affirmation, there is another side of Mike: the face of the writer still unaware or unsure of his own creativity and gifts. Note that Mike was completely surprised by Mrs. Baiel wanting to keep his book. It wasn't because she loved the form or cover; it was because she loved his writing. He was clueless as to his writing skill in history class, believing he was going to be "shamed" like all the others with a score of 3 when he actually got a 10. Later, he was still surprised when his friends and his mother admired his writing. Mike, like other creatively gifted students, needed encouragement and validation to pursue the art form. His creativity may be a given, but the expression of that creativity is not. It is dependent upon a host of factors, among them, the vital role of the teacher and the writing community or class.

Guidelines for Teaching the Creatively Gifted

Although the following guidelines are essential for fostering the innate creativity possessed by all our students, they remain particularly essential for our creatively gifted students. In this regard, how can we best teach students like Mike?

The first guideline is: *Provide freedom*. Students like Mike, humble and in awe of the creativity of others, often place high standards and expectations on themselves. For such students, considerable freedom must be given so that they can immerse themselves in the totality of the creative process *without fear of judgment or failure*. Unlike many other writers, Mike would not plunge head first into a writing prompt in class. I often saw him waiting, thinking, and puzzling before and during the composing process. It was always clear to me that his writing was "1% inspiration and 99% perspiration," as the well-known Edison axiom defines it. Creative gifts do not actualize easily, and Mike worked hard on his poetry, drafting and revising.

The second guideline is: *Provide structure*. Creatively gifted students want to learn skills; they love to challenge themselves with exercises, and they are accustomed to the discipline of sequential exercises from other art forms. In creative writing class, I provide those sequential exercises which build fundamental writing skills. Mike loved the exercises. They were creative, the goals were clear, and he felt success. Such writing builds confidence and leads to the more personally meaningful work.

The third guideline is: *Be a good reader*. Engage in meaning-making with student writers by responding to their writing. What the creatively gifted need more than anything else is a clear understanding of their writing. Notice how aware Mike was that he needed to wait a few days before the "meaning" of his own lyrics became apparent. Mike would continually give me his poems. I would simply read them and tell him *how I understood them*. With that check of validation, Mike would then revise or not revise his poetry. Often, I would see him reading his poem aloud to his neighbor in class, or mouthing the rhythm or words to himself as he composed on the computer. Although I never tampered with his voice by adding words or rephrasing lines, I would frequently point out unclear lines, places to cut, or suggestions for titles. (Many students, even the most gifted, are at a loss for titles.)

The fourth guideline is: *Provide challenges that enable student writers to function as professionals*. For as long as I have been teaching creative writing, I have been encouraging my students to submit their work to contests and publications when they feel they are ready. Such challenges must be voluntary; not every student is ready to go public with his or her work. Often the best work may be too private to reveal, or a student may not feel it is good enough, no matter how good the teacher believes the work to be. Other students may just not be emotionally ready for rejection. I encourage my students, but I also prepare them for rejection, telling them that this is what all writers go through. It's part of the process.

After a semester of creative writing, Mike was ready to take up the challenge. I encouraged him to submit his poetry and stories to one of the most prestigious state competitions for student writers, the New Jersey High School Writing Contest, sponsored by the New Jersey Council of Teachers of English. In this contest, students are allowed to submit only one poem in the poetry category. Mike struggled to select his best poem. Finally, he decided to submit a poem written for one of our class exercises which was "searching for your writing muse." For this exercise students read many other poets' works until they found one that inspired their writing. Mike submitted his muse poem, inspired by Allen Ginsberg's "Howl" (https://www.poetryfoundation.org/poems/49303/howl), titled "Howling Back." His poem won first place, affording him the recognition of the "Best High School Poem in the State of New Jersey." Such an honor confers to students an additional award given by the Governor each year, the Governor's Arts Award Medallion. In all my years of teaching award-winning gifted student writers, no one has ever won this award in the junior year of high school. Mike acted a bit overwhelmed by all the attention. He was proud to be recognized, but he was also quite humbled about it.

A final guideline is: *Do no harm*. In consideration of the nature of our educational system, which negates creativity in so many spheres, and also in consideration of the gifts of the gifted, which are so often neglected, unrecognized, or stifled, we must teach above all else in such a way as to *do no harm*. Creatively gifted students are often *risk takers*, assuming challenges that others might ignore. As teachers, we need to support such risk-taking, for it is often a major catalyst for creative growth. Given the proper encouragement, environment, and community of support, creativity will surface naturally, itself, as water rises to its level of equilibrium.

Mike in Science Class: "Under the Teacher Radar"

When I think of Mike, I think not only of adaptability but its close partner, *risk-taking*. For how else do you adapt without also taking a risk, making a change, imagining creatively? I knew Mike was a gifted arts student, but I didn't know about science until one day after class when he told me about his science project:

> In science I was told to write about an important and untapped source of energy in the world. Some kids said solar power; others said static electricity. I chose to write about the power of a hamster wheel. It was original and my teacher got a kick out of reading about it. Sometimes teachers will seem to want their kids to conform to the lesson plan and not stray from the beaten path. In that case, you just have to be more creative and think of a way to be original and still "pass under the teacher radar.

I was ready to give Mike an "A+" right then and there for transferring his creativity to other subject areas like science and for taking the risk to be original, both key elements of the gifted personality. And I'm certain his science teacher "cherished" it too.

The Ten Dimensions of Complexity: The Creative Personality

What is the creative personality? Csikszentmihalyi (1996) answers that question with one key word, *complex*. He describes complex as "being able to express a full range of traits that are potentially present in the human repertoire" (p. 57). He then identifies ten pairs of antithetical traits that are both present and integrated in creative individuals in a dialectical tension. These are listed below, followed by my own reflection on them and how they apply to my student, Mike.

The Paradox of the Creative Personality

- *Creative individuals have a great deal of physical energy but they are also often quiet and at rest* (p. 58). They can work long hours with great concentration while projecting an aura of freshness. This is Mike to a "tee," full of energy, able to write for long periods of time without tiring.
- *Creative individuals tend to be smart, yet also naïve at the same time* (p. 59). This is Mike as well, definitely intelligent, but with a charming innocence that makes him seem always to be filled with a sense of wonder.

- *Creative individuals tend to be playful and disciplined, responsible and irresponsible at the same time* (p. 61). A playful attitude is typical of creative individuals. But this playfulness doesn't go very far without its antithesis, a quality of perseverance. The ability to be "playful" and then to know when to stop and be "disciplined" is critical to all creative writing classes. Mike can be playful and then immediately disciplined and on task in class.
- *Creative individuals alternate between imagination and fantasy at one end, and a rooted sense of reality at the other* (p. 63). Both are needed to break away from the present without losing touch with the past. The recommended sequencing of writings for my creative writing elective move from the realms of the present, to the past, and finally to the world of the future. The creatively gifted, like Mike, move easily on this continuum.
- *Creative people tend to harbor opposite tendencies on the continuum between extroversion and introversion* (p. 65). The stereotype of the "solitary genius" is strong and gets ample support from the study's interviews. "After all, one must generally be alone in order to write." Yet the importance of seeing people, hearing people, exchanging ideas, getting to know another's work and mind are stressed by creative individuals. Mike, the proverbial extrovert, can isolate himself for long periods of time to write, but then he is eager to share and collaborate with others in creative writing class, drama, and his band.
- *Creative individuals are remarkably humble and proud at the same time* (p. 68). Mike was so proud when his writing was recognized by the larger community, and yet he was exceedingly humble and somewhat uncomfortable about all the attention.
- *Creative individuals to a certain extent escape rigid gender role stereotyping of our culture* (p. 70). They are more likely to be able to express a full range of masculine and feminine

traits. I would add to this my own observation that, accordingly, creatively gifted students tend to be highly tolerant and accepting of difference.

- *Creative people are thought to be rebellious and independent* (p. 71). I have seen this paradox reflected in Mike's poetry. Although Mike loves performance poetry, hip hop, and slam, and although his muse is Allen Ginsberg, Mike continues to choose to write in fixed verse and closed forms (that is, types of poetry that have a set structure, such as a sonnet or villanelle).
- *Most creative people are very passionate about their work, yet they can be extremely objective about it as well* (p. 72). This paradoxical trait is highly important. Mike is passionate about every piece he writes, but at the same time, he can be objective, stand away from it, and see it for what it is.
- *The openness and sensitivity of creative individuals often exposes them to suffering and pain yet also a great deal of enjoyment.* I have seen Mike display empathy towards his peers in class and those less fortunate. He takes great joy in the success of struggling writers in class and is a champion of the "underdog."

What I Learned: Teaching the Creatively Gifted

Let's consider for a moment the practical application of the gifted personality. Experience in the classroom confirms the creatively gifted are most certainly paradoxes of strength and resiliency. They bounce back and forth easily from freedom to structure, playfulness to discipline, fantasy to reality. They love to move from their "inner child" to their emerging manhood and womanhood, all in one moment. They can run outside of your classroom to taste snowflakes on their tongues and in the next moment return to write a serious poem about the experience. This "dancing" describes the rhythm and tempo of many creative writing classes: lots of initial energy, hands on playful experience followed by disciplined, solitary writing, quiet time if you will, followed by communal voicing or sharing. This wave-like flow defines the creative spirit that permeates the creative writing classroom. In such an environment, the creative personality delineated above finds its haven and home.

Caveat: Teach All as Creatively Gifted

This chapter has been devoted to an understanding of the creatively gifted student who expresses and actualizes the gift. But what about the creatively gifted who are as yet unaware of their gifts, who are not in touch with their creative spirits, who have yet to act or produce in any way? How do we teach those students who dare not give us a clue through either spoken or written word or example? ("The Quiet One," in Chapter 17, offers continued discussion on this question.)

The answer? Easy in its simplicity but, difficult in application: *we must teach all students as if they are creatively gifted.* Think about it for a moment. The creative teaching strategies in this book are inclusive (see Chapter 1, "Works in Progress"). I have a little bird that sits on my shoulder when I teach. It says to me: *What's good for creativity is good for all*. And so I teach all with a balance of freedom and structure, playfulness and challenge, and I try not to do harm. Thinking that some in my class may not be as creative as others is doing harm. If higher teacher expectations mean higher student achievement, then we can do no harm by teaching through practice and example the complexity of creative personality traits. Knowing the personality traits will help us identify earlier than not, the hidden and emerging creatively gifted student. But it takes patience, awareness, and creative teaching.

For Your Teacher's Journal

Reflecting

1. Do you consider yourself a creative person? If so, how? If not, why not?

2. Recall the most creatively gifted student you ever taught. Did you see this student as a complex personality?
3. Given your awareness of the ten dimensions of the creative personality and its contrasting traits as identified by Csikszentmihalyi (1996), has your understanding of gifted students in general or your own gifted students in particular changed?

Responding: Writing Prompts

1. What personality traits do you possess that you believe are creative or gifted? List in your journal.
2. If you have taught a creatively gifted student, what were the challenges for you? List them in your journal.
3. How might you change your teaching methods or lessons to better teach creatively gifted students?
4. Write a poem, prose poem, or memoir of a creatively gifted student you have observed, taught, or known.

PART THREE: INTERDISCIPLINARY APPLICATIONS

Teaching the Creatively Gifted: The Highest Achievers

Consider this: if you are teaching a required subject like English III, and you are the only teacher teaching the Honors sections, then it stands to reason you are teaching the highest achievers in the class. Among those highest achievers will be some of the schools' most talented and gifted students.[1] I taught those students for over three decades, never considering that those students were also gifted in science and math. It wasn't until I was teaching in the Science Academy at the end of my career and discovered with my co-teacher the little-known genre of science poetry that all that change. I broke boundaries, built bridges, and began to teach my Honors English students to "see poetry through the eyes of science" (see Gorrell with Colfax, *Teaching Poetry through the Eyes of Science,* 2012). Testimony from my students confirm how transformational the experience was for them (see model student science poems in Chapter 18).

Conversely, consider this: if you are teaching a required subject like science, and you are the only teacher teaching an Honors section, then it stands to reason you may be teaching "highest achievers" in that class as well. Among those highest achievers will be some of the school's most talented and gifted student writers. How will you best teach and reach those students? One suggestion is to give them the opportunity to express their scientific literacy, knowledge, and passions in another form, that of *science poetry.* My colleague, Erin Colfax, did just that. She also uses science poetry as a means of alternate assessment in her biology classes. If you are a science teacher, you might find it eye-opening to read about how Erin and I worked together to bring out the creativity in science students through poetry. (Recall Alex Davis's science poem, "The Second Law of Thermodynamics," in Chapter 6.)

Confirming Creativity Scholarship: Highest Achiever Math Poetry

The gifted math-minded students in my Honors English classes produced highly creative math poems as well. They were able to transfer their knowledge to poetic and imaginative expression producing math poems with authenticity in an individual voice. In the following poem, David Pitt expresses his awe and wonder of "asymptote," defined mathematically as a line that continually approaches a given curve, but does not meet it at any finite distance. What better form to express his passion for the elusive "asymptote" than the ode?

Model Student Math Poem: "O Asymptote" by David Pitt, Honors English Student

O Asymptote
by David Pitt

O asymptote
the noting I can never reach
    for ever
However infinite I am
I stretch, I pull myself
    so thin.
        Approaching zero.

It's silly
To be so close.
(less than 1 away!)
And nearing
    rapidly.
    And I can strive forever.
        Obsessively augmenting x or y.

But past a certain point
The more I try
    the less a point
        at all.

        O asymptote.

(David Pitt, 2012)

Model Contributor Poem: "The Weight of Nothing, Part II" by Amy Uyematsu, High School Mathematics Teacher

The Weight of Nothing, Part II
by Amy Uyematsu

II
the student's assignment—
concentrate on nothing
for fifteen minutes a day.

she tries to empty her head
but can't figure out how.
after all, she doesn't know what
nothing sounds or looks like,
and the teacher won't give
the slightest clue. yet
she's got a good hunch
the exercise might quiet
all that shriek and clatter
trapped between her ears.
so like a good pupil,
she devotes an entire year
searching for nothing.
some days she's as still
as a stone, but can't
escape the distractions
of river and wind,
footsteps approaching,
birds calling in the trees
overhead. or closing
her eyes, she'll focus
on a cloudless blue sky.
pillows and planes and purple
sunsets keep interrupting.
she silently repeats words
like *ocean* or *why*,
chants sounds that dwell
low in her throat
like *maah* and *uhmm*.
at year's end her teacher
asks if she's found nothing.
she tells him she's found
everything but nothing.
he smiles, *you're closer*
than you think. now
try for twenty minutes.

(Uyematsu, 2005: 72–73)

(See Appendix B for the complete poem.)

A Gifted Teaching Assignment: "The Weight of Nothing"

The student assignment in Part II of Uyematsu's poem, "The Weight of Nothing," may be considered a "gifted" teaching assignment. In that context, Csikszentmihalyi's research findings are worth revisiting: "If the institution of school is so detrimental to the teaching of creativity, the individual teacher is *not* (p. 174). From an instructional point of view, the teacher's assignment in Uyematsu's poem "awakens" interest, "sustains" that interest until "the year's end," and "directs" that interest with affirmation – "he smiles," and offers care, and encouragement: "you're closer than you think." But most importantly, he provides further challenges, "Now try for twenty minutes." Poetically speaking, this poem speaks of the "weight of knowing," when the gifted student has found "everything" that means something to her but "nothing" to do with the assigned task – "concentrate on nothing for 15 minutes a day." In this she is confirming poetically how she found "everything but nothing" – while also confirming the paradoxical, complex personality of the talented and gifted student who walks to the beat of a different drummer.

Amy Uyematsu's Commentary on "The Weight of Nothing Part II" (email correspondence, August 6, 2019)

Q: What was the inspiration for this amazing poem that starts in part II with "the student's assignment" and the "teacher won't give the slightest clue?" It seems to be about teaching – or "nothing" – but so much more. It's paradoxical, poetic, and so thought provoking. Please comment on "nothing."

A: In the 90s I saw a calligraphy scroll by a Japanese artist named Munakata; the character he displayed in ink was "mu," a key word in Buddhism and Zen that is related to the idea of without, nothingness, and emptiness. At the time I was also attending writing classes with Zen poet Peter Levitt, and that idea was discussed. Several of Peter's students did sitting meditation with him. I tried but wasn't too effective – the student in the poem is me. I do like the title of the poem. The other meaning of "weight" as "wait" – since there is a lot of waiting and patience involved in meditation and spiritual awakening.

Q: Who is the student in the poem?
A: The student in the poem is me.

Chapter 8 Notes

1 The terms best and brightest and talented and gifted are complex, politically and educationally charged terms, resulting in classification and tracking systems within schools and teaching. They do not reflect the ethos and philosophy of this book or my pedagogy. Nor are the terms mutually exclusive. Not all creatively "gifted" end up in Honors classes. Those nonconformists who walk to the beat of different drummers (often less motivated by grades) find a home in creative writing. The term "talented and gifted," also known as "TAG" in my school system, served in the 1970s and 1980s as an independent enrichment program for gifted students grades 9–12 that I taught.

2 Mike asked for only his first name to be used.

Chapter 8 References

Brande, Dorothea (1934/1981) *Becoming a Writer*. New York, NY: Tarcher/ Putnam. Originally published by Harcourt, Brace.

Conroy, Pat (2003) *My Losing Season*. New York: Bantam Dell Random House.

Csikszentmihalyi, Mihaly (1996) *Creativity: Flow and the Psychology of Discovery and Invention*. New York: Harper Perennial.

Gorrell, Nancy S. with Erin Colfax (2012) *Writing Poetry through the Eyes of Science: Scientific Literacy and Poetic Response*. Sheffield, UK and Oakville, CT: Equinox.

May, Rollo (1975) *The Courage to Create*. New York, NY: W.W. Norton.

Pitt, David (2012) "O Asymptote." Qtd in Gorrell with Colfax, *Writing Poetry through the Eyes of Science: Scientific Literacy and Poetic Response*, 297. Sheffield, UK and Oakville, CT: Equinox.

Uyematsu, Amy (2005) "The Weight of Nothing, Part II." *Stone, Bow, Prayer*, 72–73. Port Townsend, WA: Copper Canyon Press.

Uyematsu, Amy (August 6, 2019) Email correspondence with Nancy S. Gorrell.

Chapter 9

Balancing Freedom and Structure: The Paradox of Boundaries

That's the beauty of creative writing. There are no boundaries. Your writing can go as far as your heart and imagination will allow it to go.

– Lauren Glanville (Palmer) Creative Writing student (2004)

PART ONE: THE BALANCING ACT

Upon the conclusion of each creative writing course, I ask my students to write a reflection of their learning experience. I have selected a reflection written by Lauren Glanville (now Lauren Glanville Palmer) at the end of the course in 2004 as a starting point for this chapter.

"There Are No Boundaries"
by Lauren Glanville (Palmer)

Learning can change a person's perspective on life entirely. Everyone knows this. One day you learn how to walk. It's just that simple, and now you can go places. You enter school and you suddenly have someone with so much more knowledge than you trying to teach you the colors. It takes a while to get them all straight, but you eventually figure it out. And from that point on, learning is unlike any experience you have ever had.

You have no input on what you learn; the superior beings (also known as your teachers) choose for you. This is not necessarily a bad thing; it's just is a fact. As the years fly by, you get used to learning like this; just trying to comprehend the knowledge that your teachers are spoon feeding to you.

But then you enter a creative writing class. And on the first day of class, you realize this is unlike any other course you have ever taken. This class reverts back to the days of old, where you learned to walk on your own (with a little help from mommy). Creative Writing is like taking your first step; you might fall a couple times, but you will get back up again. And all along you have a teacher there to guide you, but not to put ideas into your head. She's there to help you think for yourself, to break all the rules that you have followed so far in your school career. You have taught yourself to conform to the classroom and the teacher and the subject, but now you are given the freedom to think for yourself and to express all the emotions that have built up inside you. It's such a release.

Writing makes your heart soar, and once you get up, you can't come back down. One teacher guides you a little, and then you can start finding your own style, learning how you want to learn, and writing how you want to write. That's the beauty of creative writing. There are no boundaries. Your writing can go as far as your heart and imagination allow it to go.

Commentary on "There Are No Boundaries"

When I read Lauren's reflection of her creative writing class experience, I was amazed, because her words expressed exactly how I want all my students to feel – that *there are no boundaries*, and that they can "soar" and never "come back down." Yes, that's exactly how I want them to feel, although I know it's not entirely true. There are boundaries in creative writing class. Lauren, I believe, knows that too, but she doesn't sense them as confining, conforming, or limiting. She lives and learns easily in the land of paradox that defines the teaching and learning space of the creative writing class

– a place, first and foremost, of freedom and spontaneity in which students are able for to explore, express, and discover freedom.

This feeling of freedom defines the space that surrounds creative writing class. It must be there if students are to get in touch with their creativity. It must be there if the "haven" described in Chapter 6 is to exist. And it must be there if students are to produce authentic writing that matters to them. I sometimes like to think of this feeling of freedom as play, the kind we all did as children. There has to be imaginative play, or fun if you will, within a relaxed but energized space within the classroom to create.

Yet students will accomplish little if there are no boundaries; that energy needs to be harnessed, focused and given direction. The haven described in Chapter 6 cannot exist without order and norms. In essence, creativity cannot function without the challenge of limits. Thus, we as teachers teach in the land of paradox – the act of balancing freedom and spontaneity, on the one hand, and boundaries and limits, on the other.

Given the complexities of the creative personality, creative writing students seem to flourish in an environment that recognizes and supports the paradoxical balancing act. This idea I made clear to my students from Day One – the center of our attention and classroom is not what I want, or what they want, but what is required and demanded by the discipline of writing, itself. Our boundaries are clear: *if writers do it, we can do it.* When I established the boundaries of "going outside" in Chapter 2 "poetry watching," the students felt free but the boundaries were clear. There were no voices demanding the opening of the boundaries such as "Can we go here instead of there?" or "Can we write this instead of that?" I am always surprised at how grateful my students are for what seems to be such little freedom, and that gratefulness makes me, as a teacher, ever more comfortable teaching and living within the daily balancing act.

The Paradox of Boundaries: The Expansive Nature of Limits

> *Confronting limits for the human personality actually turns out to be expansive. Limiting and expanding thus go together.*
>
> – Rollo May, *The Courage to Create*
>
> (May, 1975: 115)

Rollo May, in his chapter "On the Limits of Creativity," notes the positive value of limitations to birthing creativity: "Creativity arises out of the tension between spontaneity and limitations, the latter (like the river banks) forcing the spontaneity into the various forms which are essential to the work of art or poem" (May, 1975: 115). If I had allowed my students to spontaneously go outside to write, as they initially requested when they saw the hawk watch, they certainly would have written, but the writing have been unstructured, freewriting. But for instructional purposes to facilitate skills, I like to build in boundaries. May points out the paradox: "The struggle with limits is actually the source of creative productions" (p. 115).

In creative writing class, I prefer to think of the "struggle" that May describes as challenges which foster imagination and creativity. These challenges come from specific prompts or requirements of structure or form. In this sense, limits become "expansive," allowing the imagination to expand into new directions and terrain. In this spirit, I call the writings we do "exercises" rather than assignments or homework. The term "exercise" carries with it the mastery of skills common to the arts and sports. It connotes to students the essence of practice and process. The writing does not have to be "great," which helps to dissolve writer's block, but only to demonstrate mastery of the specific required skill. Rather than causing frustration, these challenges provide specific writing goals which enable students to feel secure in their accomplishments. I, as well, can feel secure in my ability to evaluate the outcomes of each student's piece of writing without fostering grade competition or grade consciousness. The remainder of this chapter illustrates how boundaries or limitations fosters creativity, imagination, and a sense of freedom and joy.

PART TWO: ON FREEDOM IN WRITING

On Freedom in Writing: Freewriting Exercises

> *To begin with, you must teach the unconscious to flow into the channel of writing.*
>
> – Dorothea Brande, *Becoming a Writer*
> (Brande, 1934/1981: 69)

The "freest" type of writing, the type of writing without any limits or boundaries, is called *freewriting.* Writing teachers have long advocated this type of writing to help writers warm up, and get the flow of their thoughts on paper. That flow emerges from the depths of consciousness at various moments of the day when first arising in the morning, when going to sleep at night, or day dreaming at any time. The first long-range assignment to all my students is to get their own personal journal, carry it with them wherever they go, and freewrite in it every day for a two-week period of time. I tell them: "If you are a morning person, write in it for fifteen minutes before you get out of bed." They laugh because most teenagers are not morning people. Then I tell them, "Write before you go to bed each evening." This first exercise I credit to Dorothea Brande's *Becoming a Writer*, where she recommends "rising a half an hour or a full hour earlier [. . .] in the twilight zone between sleep and the full waking state, simply to write" (Brande, 1934/1981: 73) Her instruction: "Write anything that comes into your head [. . .] rapidly, uncritically, without rereading what you have done" (pp. 72–73). Brande pioneered the idea that students of writing "must teach the unconscious to *flow* into the channel of writing" (p. 69). She called it "effortless writing" or "harnessing the unconscious," thereby framing a century of creative writing pedagogy (p. 71).

Over the years, I have encountered writing teachers naming this type of writing in various ways: Peter Elbow (Elbow, 1973/1998) and Ken Macrorie (Macrorie, 1968/1976) call it *freewriting*; Julia Cameron calls it *morning pages* (Cameron, 2002). I use ten minutes of freewriting in journals to begin every creative writing class for the first two weeks of the elective course. Here are the objectives:

- *To "warm up." Writing is a physical act that needs warming as does any physical act.*
- *To quiet the brain from the "buzz" of the day thereby getting rid of distractions.*
- *To quiet the brain so that students can listen to their inner voices.*
- *To get into the flow of inner consciousness.*

More often than not, I play instrumental, classical music as background for this freewriting. I choose pieces that express different moods – elation, mystery, tranquility, energy. Sometimes we write to silence; sometimes we write in darkness. Students love when I turn off the lights. The sense of communal writing is literally a breath of fresh air as we all seem to breathe together. I too enjoy this writing time, and often write with my students. After the ten minutes, they are relaxed, focused, and ready for the writing exercise at hand.

Freewriting Exercise: Long-Range Journal Assignment

Write freely for ten minutes every day in your journal for two weeks. This writing should be a continuous *flow* of consciousness on paper. Just write whatever is in your head at the moment. If you are a morning person, write for fifteen minutes before you get out of bed. If you are a night person, write for fifteen minutes before you go to bed. Or, write during the "daydreaming" moments of the day. The more freewriting you generate, the more material you will have for future writing. Be sure to date every entry.

Boundaries in Freewriting Exercises: Non-Stop Writing and Interrupted Journal Writing

Non-stop writing and interrupted journal writing are variations of freewriting that build in challenges. The Non-Stop Writing Exercise in Chapter 6 shares with freewriting many of the same objectives, but there is a critical difference: students must not stop writing. The hand must keep writing the "stream" that the mind is sensing. That demand alone makes it not as free as freewriting, which allows pausing or stopping. As a consequence, non-stop writing may produce more forced or nonsensical writing and greater quantity of writing. At least that is the case in theory, although I have discovered that the outcomes are usually quite similar. Rarely, do students produce nonsense writing. Both types of writing seem to result in a stream of consciousness which is generally fluid, expansive, and often makes sense.

Another variation of freewriting which I use to build in challenges is *interrupted journal writing*. I use this variation after a week or two of general freewriting. Students love it because I give them writer's choice to take the challenge or not. The challenge is simply to interject a prompt at various intervals during the journal writing session. For example, after a few minutes I might say, "red." At that moment, students may respond to "red" or they may continue their writing. These interruptions voice concrete images to prompt further writing. They are especially useful for students who need to develop greater fluency in their writing.

The Expansive Nature of Freewriting: Fiction Writing

In Creative Writing class, I begin fiction writing with a warm-up exercise in expansion. I explain to students that there are two universal and opposing skills demanded of all writers – the skill of *expanding* their writing, and the skill of *tightening* or cutting their writing. "Sometimes you have written one page and your editor will say it has to be three pages long; then you, the writer, will have to expand your writing while still saying something that matters.

Other times, you may have written more, and your editor will say, it can only be one page. Then you have to cut it down while keeping the essence. Expanding and tightening are professional skills we will practice throughout the course."

How does it work? By the introduction of challenges: one starting prompt and several specific elements to integrate into the narrative. As May (1975) would note, these boundaries are not "limitations." Rather, they become expansive, providing for students a structure upon which to expand their imaginations and consequently, their narratives.

Student Expansion Warm-Up Exercise

Instructions for Students

This is an exercise in expansion using your imagination to add material to a given text. Write continuously for 30 minutes. You must begin your story with the following prompt: *My uncle had a mustache made of spinach.*

In addition, you must use in your story the following elements:

- *the name of a Greek god or goddess*
- *some type of weather*
- *the title of a famous book or film*
- *a type of ice cream*
- *an SUV, RV or type of vehicle*
- *an animal or creature*
- *an additional element chosen by the class*

Be sure to underline, number, or boldface each element used in your story.

Instructions for Teachers

Before students write, I stress to them not to be overly clever and circumvent the intent of the exercise by combining all of the elements in a couple of sentences – an example of compression, not expansion.

PART THREE: ON BOUNDARIES IN WRITING

Form provides the essential boundaries and structure for the creative act.

– Rollo May, *The Courage to Create* (May, 1975: 117)

Boundaries in Poetry Writing: The Imitation Poem

The *imitation poem* is useful for teaching poetry to novice and advanced poets alike. Stephen Dunning and William Stafford suggest the use of imitation as a first-step exercise for novice poets by "copying poems of others" in *Getting the Knack: 20 Poetry Writing Exercises* (Dunning and Stafford, 1992: 84). On more challenging levels, this method – the ancient practice of *imitatio* from the Latin, or *mimesis,* from the Greek – can be used in English and language classes with students turning foreign language poems into English.[1]

Tom C. Hunley and Sandra Giles advocate that students first "copy a passage of poetry or prose they admire" and then "identify the features that draw them to it" (Hunley and Giles, 2015: 24). Ron Padgett's *The Teachers & Writers Handbook of Poetic Forms* (Padgett, 1987/2000) includes a section on the *imitation poem*, referencing Robert Lowell's use of the word in his (Lowell's) collection titled *Imitations*, in which Lowell translated the poems of other poets, discovering that his translations took on a life of their own, "a life that was different from that of the original text" (Padgett, 1987/2000: 89).

Bounded Imitation: Searching for Your Poetic Muse

I use a bounded imitation exercise at the conclusion of the advanced creative writing elective that inspires my students. I call this culminating exercise "Searching for your Poetic Muse." Although students have the freedom to search and find their muses, they are bound by the form and of the response. Students do not struggle with this challenge. They often seem to know their poetic inspirations or muses, and the poems they "imitate" or create become truly their own.

Consider Lauren Glanville Palmer's choice of muse. She chose William Carlos Williams as her muse and his poem, "Between Walls," as her inspiration. Williams, a modernist poet and practicing pediatrician from Paterson, New Jersey was noted for his imagist poetry. (William's poem "Between Walls" is available at www.poetryfoundation.org.)

Model Student Muse Poem: "A New Hope" by Lauren Glanville (Palmer)

A New Hope
by Lauren Glanville (Palmer)

in the fence
of the

prison yard
grows the vines

of the morning
glory

and the blue
flowers

keep the hope
alive

Boundaries in Poetry: Closed Forms and the Freedom of Writer's Choice

Limits are most evident in fixed or closed form poetry. I reserve teaching such bounded forms for the advanced elective, Creative Writing II. In a sonnet, for example, students are confronted with the boundaries of meter, number of lines, and a particular rhyme scheme. Strict limits prevail. Sometimes my students exhibit frustration, preferring to write in the open and free verse forms of the introductory elective. Yet even with the most bounded forms, there exists the freedom of writer's choice. This freedom prevails even within the boundaries of closed forms. For example, some modern sonnets that are 14 lines dispense with meter, and contemporary English language haiku dispenses with the 5/7/5 syllable form and "count" sounds not syllables or lines.[2]

Consider the model student villanelle by Mark Hess as an example of a bounded form. You may recall Mark Hess, the high school senior in Chapter 6 ("Tap, tap, tap") who was struggling to regain his imagination, struggling to find his creativity, and struggling to find his voice. And yet Mark found success composing his villanelle, "Wondering Around My Home Asleep."

Reflection on Boundaries by Mark Hess, Creative Writing II Student

> *The poetry lesson I enjoyed the most was writing in fixed forms. Most of the poems I wrote were in class, but the one I liked the best I wrote at home on my own. It was a late-night poem that I started writing in the moment. It was inspired by a feeling I was having about sleepwalking. My poem was written in the villanelle form. The completion did not take that long which was surprising because any other attempt at the villanelle form took me a long time. I made several revisions in the morning after because grammatically I had made some mistakes. The final result was* "wondering around my home asleep." *I liked the challenge of the villanelle form. But also, I felt I was able to expand on the villanelle and include poetry that was more meaningful for me. I did not think that I would be able to write a villanelle but I was able to communicate a feeling that I had previously not been able to put on paper before. I hope that I would be able to connect with someone who has the same feelings.*

Model Student Villanelle by Mark Hess: "Wondering Around My Home Asleep"

Wondering Around My Home Asleep
by Mark Hess

Wondering around my home asleep
I should have awoken before
Wake up, wake up, I continue to creep

Rising in the morning is much too steep
My body tired and sore
Wondering around my home asleep

Voices and noises always peep
All I do is lay on the floor
Wake up, wake up, I continue to creep

Papers to read fall in a heap
And shoved into a dark drawer
Wondering around my home asleep

My life becomes about jumping sheep
Most exciting events are just a bore
Wake up, wake up, I continue to creep

Minutes to hours, hours seep
To wake and snore
Wondering around my home asleep
Wake up, wake up, I continue to creep

Commentary on "Wondering Around My Home Asleep"

Mark clearly enjoyed his success at composing a villanelle, but he didn't realize at the time the full extent of his remarkable word choice – "wondering" (the mindset of sleepwalking) instead of "wandering" (literally, a term that suggests a walk). His villanelle is actually a dual genre poem, a villanelle and a *walk poem*, "A poem that reflects the way the mind works during the walk"

(Padgett, 1987/2000: 201; see Chapter 18 for further discussion of walk poetry).

What I Learned: The Value of Balancing Freedom and Structure

This balancing act has served as the guiding principle for my course organization, my classroom norms, and my writing lessons, and exercises. It enables students to function as writers in developing the skills of their craft and the attitudes that go along with those skills.

For Your Teacher Journal: Long Range Exercises

Responding and Reflecting: Free Writing Exercise #1

1. Begin freely writing daily in your journal. Write in either the morning or evening for at least 15 minutes. Make this your creative practice. Try to increase your writing output gradually. Write rapidly, do not reread, and write whatever comes into your head at the moment.
2. After two weeks of freewriting, read over your work. Reflect. What does your freewriting reveal to you? Have you developed greater ease and fluency? What have you learned about a yourself becoming a writer? Respond in your journal.

Boundaries in Writing: Exercise #2

1. Challenge yourself with an exercise involving boundaries and limits.
2. Follow the instructions for one of the expansion exercises or make up one of your own. Give yourself 5–10 elements to integrate into a text. Be as expansive as possible in your narrative response.
3. Try your own fixed form poem. You may wish to consult Padgett's (1987/2000) *The Teachers & Writers Handbook of Poetic Forms* to select a poetic form that inspires you.

4. Reflect in your journal. How did writing with boundaries and limits make you feel? Did limits enable you to expand and develop greater fluency? What challenges did you experience?

PART FOUR: INTERDISCIPLINARY APPLICATIONS

Questions to Consider about Freedom and Boundaries

- *What is the balance between freedom and boundaries or structure in your subject, classroom, and discipline?*
- *How do you plan to use writing and/or creative writing in your subject, course or discipline? Writing to learn? Writing to express feeling? Writing to clarify thinking? Writing to create?*
- *What subject, genre, or discipline-related writing do you teach?*

Suggestions for Using This Chapter's Exercises

The following interdisciplinary poems from our model contributors address these questions, one by Arthur Stewart, speaking of boundaries, the other by Amy Uyematsu, the paradox of limitless freedom. Teachers across the disciplines may find the brief, "non-stop" writing exercise a useful way to introduce and discuss the elements of writing you will do in your course subjects. Use this exercise as a confidence builder to show students they can write, logically as well as freely, and then explain your expectations and the kinds of writing (for various purposes) they will do in your discipline. You may also want to share the science and math poems below for discussion with your students as they relate to your pedagogy and discipline. Use these poems as teaching poems for your subject and course.

Model Contributor Poem: "Getting it Right" by Arthur J. Stewart

Getting it Right
by Arthur J. Stewart

In lab I ask them not to slop
the acid for titration; and please use
just a pinch of indicator; keep your thumbs

out of the glassware, do you have any idea
how much phosphorus you can add
to the surface of glass

just by touching? And dry weights
of glass-fiber filters – watch them
rise like mercury rises, numbers

increasing on the Mettler balance, for samples
taken directly from the oven and left
unmeasured in lab air too long: it's

just one thing after another
constantly
trying for perfection.

(Stewart, 2010)

After Reading "Getting it Right"

Teacher Instructions

1. Have your students read Stewart's poem "Getting it Right." Then discuss with your students "getting it right" in science and math class. How do scientists "get it right?" Through proof? Disproof? Discuss "getting it right in your discipline or subject course. Do your students have to "get it right?" In what sense and context? Do they have to strive for "perfection?"
2. Contrast "Getting it Right" with Stewart's other science poem, "Learning" (Chapter 16). Compare the two different ways of

teaching science. How do these ways inform your classroom pedagogy?

3. How do these two ways inform the teaching and learning of creativity, literacy, and writing across the disciplines?

Model Contributor Poem: "This Thing Called Infinity" by Amy Uyematsu

This Thing Called Infinity
by Amy Uyematsu

Then again, a very different sort of infinity may well be free-wheeling you.

– Natalie Angier, "The Life of Pi, and Other Infinities"

Impossible to grasp yet I'm sure it exists,
sure as the fact that I won't be around by 2047—
which would make me a century old—
and my little grandsons close to middle age.
I know about infinity whenever I admire a passion flower,
feel myself pulled into its oddly perfect symmetry.
Or ponder snowflakes, shooting stars and soap bubbles.
Scientists tell us there are different kinds of infinities—
some are flat, others hunchback, inflating, explosive.
Mathematicians are the real jokesters when it comes
to playing with the mind—how counting from 1 to forever
is somehow smaller than the set of all values
between 1 and 2, or as I used to ask my students,
take half of a half of a half and never stop.
Some notions of the infinite can rattle the nerves—
like the possibility there are many earths
and someone exactly like you or me
with a totally opposite or identical life,
or there are galaxies of multiplying gods,
planets that will never be at war.
And what about time? These last hours I count
in my brief life—the way grief can make time endless
and delight mere seconds which tickle and tease us

in unending supply. Old Man Pythagoras
was insecure about the whole matter—
deeming the finite masculine and good,
while infinity was feminine—both had to be
subjugated—as if either could.
I rather like being a woman who tries
to embrace the ever-emerging infinite, especially
when it comes to love and my own unfolding
of wonder after wonder.

(Uyematsu, 2016)

Commentary on Poetic Freedom and Boundaries

"This Thing Called Infinity" is a model of the paradox of limitless yet bounded freedom. The poem itself, in free verse, flows like a stream of consciousness from one thought to the next, artfully weaving the poet's conscious preoccupation with the "impossible to grasp" infinity. And yet, from the first line, she grasps the paradox, fully aware of "what she knows" of infinity "when she admires a passion flower," or tries to explain infinity to her students regardless what mathematicians ("the real jokesters") or scientists say. (Is it possible to make infinity concrete enough to explain its limitless boundaries?) Uyematsu ends her poem with the freedom of self-affirmation: trying to "embrace the ever-emerging infinite, especially/when it comes to love and my own unfolding/of wonder after wonder. Like infinity, there is no end, there is no boundary or limit to the "wonder after wonder" – Of love? Creative bliss? Awe? Or curiosity, the motivator of all discovery? The end image is as open to interpretation and as vast as infinity itself, yet bound by the moment, and the primacy of the poet's never-ending vision of "wonder."

Chapter 9 Notes

1 See Hunley and Giles, "Rhetorical Pedagogy," for an in-depth discussion of *imitation* as it relates to practical student writing, critical, and analytical thinking activities, and creative writing studies.

2 For a useful resource for the modern sonnet, English language haiku, and villanelle forms, you can refer to *The Teachers & Writers Handbook of Poetic Forms* (Padgett, 1987/2000) and *The Haiku Handbook: How to Write, Share and Teach Haiku* (Higginson, 1985).

Chapter 9 References

Brande, Dorothea (1934/1981) *Becoming a Writer*. New York, NY: Tarcher/Putnam. Originally published by Harcourt, Brace.

Cameron, Julia (2002) *Walking in this World: The Practical Art of Creativity*. New York, NY: Tarcher/Putnam.

Csikszentmihalyi, Mihaly (1996) *Creativity: Flow and the Psychology of Discovery and Invention*. New York, NY: Harper Perennial.

Dunning, Stephen and Stafford, William (eds.) (1992) *Getting the Knack: 20 Poetry Writing Exercises*. Urbana, IL: National Council of Teachers of English.

Elbow, Peter (1973/1998) *Writing without Teachers* (2nd edition). Oxford, UK: Oxford University Press.

Higginson, William J. with Harper, Penny (1985) *The Haiku Handbook: How to Write, Share and Teach Haiku*. New York, NY: McGraw-Hill.

Hunley, Tom C. and Giles, Sandra (2015) Rhetorical pedagogy. In Peary, Alexandria and Tom C. Hunley (eds.) *Creative Writing Pedagogies for the 21st Century*. Carbondale, IL: Southern Illinois University Press.

Macrorie, Ken (1968/1976) *Writing to Be Read* (2nd edition). Rochelle Park, NJ: Hayden.

May, Rollo (1975) *The Courage to Create*. New York, NY: W.W. Norton.

Padgett, Ron (ed.) (1987/2000) *The Teachers & Writers Handbook of Poetic Forms* (2nd edition). New York, NY: Teachers and Writer's Collaborative.

Palmer, Parker (1998) *The Courage to Teach*. San Francisco, CA: Jossey-Bass.

Stewart, Arthur J. (2010) "Getting it Right." *Circle, Turtle, Ashes*, 91. Knoxville, TN: Celtic Cat.

Uyematsu, Amy (2016) "This Thing Called Infinity." *Basic Vocabulary*, 102. Pasadena, CA: Red Hen Press.

Williams, William Carlos (1938) "Between Walls." https://www.poetryfoundation.org/poems/49849/between-walls

Chapter 10

Breaking Boundaries Within Your Discipline

I walk at the edge/ of poetry and science; I live day by day/ on an edge.

– Arthur J. Stewart, "Edges"
(Stewart, 2017)

PART ONE: BREAKING PHYSICAL BOUNDARIES

Physical Boundaries

The belief that the physical environment affects our thoughts and feelings, and therefore must surely affect our creativity, seems common sense. To the contrary, Csikszentmihalyi (1996) concludes after 30 years of research: "There is no evidence, and probably there never will be, to prove that a delightful setting induces creativity" (p. 135).

I have a dream. I am sitting with my students on a beautiful beach. Everyone is writing quietly to the sounds of the waves and gulls. Common sense tells me that my students will write with more passion and inspiration in such an environment than in the stuffy, stale air of the four walls of our classroom. And so, in my teaching, we often "break down the classroom walls" and expand our physical space by going outside or on field trips to write. The students seem to appreciate it, and they do produce inspired writing, but is that writing any more inspired than what might have been produced within the bounds of our classroom walls? I wonder.

Csikszentmihalyi admits that "[w]hile novel and beautiful surroundings might catalyze the moment of insight, the other phases of the creative process – such as preparation and evaluation – seem to benefit more from familiar, comfortable settings" (p. 139). Perhaps we as teachers are lucky in this respect. For the most part, our classrooms are far from beautiful. Despite our efforts to enhance our rooms with posters, artwork and plants, walls remain walls. Our students know where they are, and little can be done with desks even if we put them in circles or replace them with tables and chairs. White boards, smart boards – a board is a board. I have taught for over four decades in dozens of classrooms in my high school, not all my own. Often by necessity, my classroom looks generic; at times the desks have been kept in rows for the other teachers who use the same room. Thank goodness for windows. And yet, creativity still flourishes whether that classroom looks like a "beach" or a "garret."

Bounded by More than Walls

Many a text begun in school has finished in the world.
– Robert Scholes, *Textual Power: Literary Theory and the Teaching of English*
(Scholes, 1985: 10)

As Robert Scholes so aptly points out, "Many a text begun in school has finished in the world. The 'real' and the 'academic' deeply interpenetrate one another" (Scholes, 1985: 10). For example, Mike's poem "Howling Back" in Chapter 8 originated in creative writing class but finished in the world with performance poetry, a slam competition, writing contests, and a prestigious writing award. The physical space you teach in is more often than not a given – an assigned space, most likely, shared. If you think about it, you are bounded by more than walls. You are bounded by arbitrary time periods, deadlines, bell signals, and most importantly, scheduling systems. These givens vary within each high school, but they are givens, and they are arbitrary.[1]

They are so accepted that Lauren didn't even consider them "boundaries" when she thought of herself as so "boundless" (Chapter 9). Yet I don't know how many times my students have complained, "The class is over already? Or, I really don't want the semester to end, Ms. Gorrell. I'm just beginning to flow in my writing." Closure is a boundary; it's a deadline, a time for grades and evaluation, yet another boundary. In this respect, creative writing is no different than other classes. With one critical exception, and that is, you, the *creative* writing teacher, aware of the paradox of boundaries and the paradox of structure and freedom as discussed in Chapter 9.

Breaking Physical Boundaries: Beyond the Classroom Walls

> *Writing doesn't really care about where you do it. It cares that you do it.*
>
> – Julia Cameron, *Walking in this World: The Practical Art of Creativity*
>
> (Cameron, 2002: 16)

The Poem Pals Project

Before there was email, there was "Poem Pals," later referred to as the "Poem Pals Project." It was an idea born while teaching poetry to Honors English III students. In the *Poem as Process*, David Swanger discusses how "difficult it is for students talk about poems" in the classroom (Swanger, 1974: 62). I had been having a similar experience, struggling to find poems to inspire and excite my students, not realizing this was a thankless task. The poems I found were instructive, but they were my poems. Students needed to choose their own poems to discuss; they needed an authentic reason to discuss those poems; and they needed to read more poetry. Eureka! The idea for "Poem Pals" was born. But what they would they talk about and how they would share and exchange poems had to be structured and instructive. The solution was a pedagogy based on a reader-response approach in which each student was required to "find" the most exemplary poem in each of five categories in our classroom contemporary poetry anthologies: the most beautiful, shocking, emotive, thought-provoking – and, finally, a free-choice category poem (Gorrell, 1990: 38–39). "Poem Pals" began in my Honors III classes as a unit of study where student "pals" paired and shared their poem selections in class.[2]

Then, in 1989, I attended my first annual NCTE convention. There I met poetry-minded teachers from the west coast who were interested in collaborating to form a cross-country Poem Pals Project. Students from New Jersey, California, and Arizona would exchange their favorite poems with their Poem Pals from other states based on the reader-response pedagogy of the "five category poems" strategy. We waited weeks before we received our large packet of poems and letters from our "pals." But the anticipation and the waiting were worth it. Students were so excited to receive their letters. Our method of exchange that required teachers to mail letters together to ensure all students received responses from their "pals" at the same time worked. Students developed Poem Pal friendships from coast to coast in the process.

In retrospect I wonder if the Poem Pals Project would have been so successful with email and the internet. With virtual communication, would students take the time to reflect on the poems? And what about all that wonderful anticipation? *Did the letters come yet?* It was not long after that when a student in creative writing class came running in to tell me in passing, "Something's coming, Ms. Gorrell. It's a super highway. It's going change everything." I didn't know what she was talking about but, it wasn't long before a cube-like tower was sitting on my desk – my first Apple computer.

PART TWO: BREAKING DISCIPLINARY BOUNDARIES

Breaking Tradition

The most persistent and thorniest "Tyranny of the Ts" that Ted Hipple identifies remains *tradition* (Hipple 1989: 19–22). Although I did not indicate that tradition affected me while discussing different kinds of baggage in need of discard in Chapter 5, it most certainly affected my teaching. Tradition cannot be discarded or put aside in the same way as other Ts because it is embedded in our disciplines, in other teachers, and in the discourse of "*they,*" and it dominates debates and divisions within our high schools as well as the academy. From the moment I sat in my first English department meeting, I heard the lament from the naysayers and grammarians: "They can't write. They need grammar." The year was 1972. Their solution was simple and "hardcovered," and it sat on dusty shelves: *Warriner's English Grammar and Composition* (Warriner, 1982). The book was "unteachable," the grammarians were unmovable, and the debate continues well into the 21st century (see Warner, 2018), as does the discredited formulaic five- paragraph essay that was taught and favored by many in my department.[3] Yet these teachers were my colleagues and friends. On a personal level, such academic debates did not affect our relationships. We coexisted. But what about our students? Most were tracked in required English courses, not experiencing much creative writing.

At the time I did not think of myself as "breaking boundaries." I just knew "I could not teach that way," to echo Bishop. And so I just taught. In my classes, I acknowledged to my students my grammarian colleagues, praising their efforts, but also opening my students' eyes to alternate ways of writing academically. Since the main grammarian taught AP English to seniors using the five-paragraph essay approach exclusively, I considered Honors English III as my students' last chance to write and view literature in other ways. Wrestling with what's best for my students, compelled me to become the teacher I wanted to be.

Breaking Disciplinary Boundaries

> *We need to be crossing the lines between composition and creative writing far more often that we do. In fact, we may want to eliminate the line completely.*
>
> – Wendy Bishop, "Crossing the Lines: On Creative Composition and Composing Creative Writing" (Bishop, 1994: 181)

Wendy Bishop's seminal essay, "Crossing the Lines: On Creative Composition and Composing Creative Writing" (Bishop, 1994) is a call to action to her fellow academics from a deeply passionate composition specialist on how best to teach writing. Her position, one I practiced from the earliest days of my teaching of writing in middle school – that creative writing should be taught *first*, before academic writing – endures as fundamental to the discipline. Bishop advocates for college freshman: "I believe we should teach 'creative' writing in the first-year program. "Students are well prepared for future academic writing when they explore creativity, authorship, textuality […] together, at once" (p. 129).

Teaching in the 1970s and 1980s in high school, I was unaware of Bishop's work, but I was not shielded from the academic debates that trickled down from the academy to my department. Nevertheless, based on my early reading of pioneers like James Moffett (Moffett, 1973) I began teaching student-centered, process writing in my English classes with his rhetorical approach of observation, sensation, description, and narration. In reality, I was teaching "creative composition" in English class, while teaching "composing" in Creative Writing and Composition electives. In addition, I was heavily influenced at the time by *Experiential English* (Fluck, 1973) which inspired the development of my creative writing teaching and thus enabled me to walk the path to become the teacher I wanted to be.

Breaking Boundaries: Honors English III and the Academic Essay

Step One: Re-Framing the Five-Paragraph Essay

Well before Wendy Bishop had written her essay (Bishop, 1994), I was telling my Honors English III students, "We are going beyond the five-paragraph academic essay. In fact, we're not going to be limited by it, and more importantly, in most cases, we're going to eliminate it." Why? Because it limits thinking, reflection, and creativity. It's formulaic, unoriginal, and arbitrary: there is no set number of paragraphs for writing an essay or making an argument. Furthermore, it's discredited by colleges and universities." When I say this, there is not a student that seems to disagree.

Neither do the critics. John Warner sums up the argument in *Why they Can't Write: Killing the Five-Paragraph Essay and Other Necessities* asserting: "They don't write well because they haven't been taught well" (Warner, 2018: 29 –31). He points to the test-driven "writing related simulations" and the five-paragraph essay" as major factors. As a university professor who taught writing for two decades, Warner argues that decades of educational reform rooted in standardization, assessments, and accountability have made students passive and disengaged, writing more for "proficiency performance" than to think and learn.

Step Two: Teaching Alternate Ways to Write the Academic Essay

I teach students that the five-paragraph essay introduction, based on deductive logic, moves from a broad generalization to a specific point. Drawing an inverted triangle on the board, I offer a "creative approach" to the academic essay based on inductive logic, moving from a specific point to a broad generalization. The specific point, an example, quotation, literary allusion, or narrative illustrates the thesis, engaging the reader. This approach, typically followed by a deductive paragraph, enables students to introduce personal experience. Drawing on the board a diamond shape to model this inductive-deductive structure, I use models from journalism in persuasive and personal forms. I advocate the "diamond" introduction approach to my students for their Honors Thesis and especially for reader response essays. I also suggest to them the utility of this writing approach for subjects like history and science, in which creative and illustrative introductions are appropriate (see Handel's Model Contributor Essay in the "Interdisciplinary Application" section of this chapter). I also dispel a few misconceptions by telling students that in my Honors class you will be able to write what you think, using first person *I* when appropriate in academic essays; you will be able to write academic essays in any number of paragraphs; you will be able to write expansively, without limits; you will analyze literature with multiple interpretations; and you will be able to choose some of the novels you will read.

Step Three: Creating an Honors Thesis as an Exit Project

From its formulation, my supervisor wanted the Honors III curriculum to be different from other Honors tracks, one "differentiated" as he described it, not only by reading level or number of readings alone. As a result, I recommended a written thesis component. The Honors Thesis became a year-long, independent study project based initially on Ken Macrorie's "I-Search" paper. The thesis involved initial conferencing with each student to develop the readings and secondary research based upon an interest, experience, or subject that the student was personally connected to or passionate about. After conferencing with each student, I would suggest appropriate topics and readings, each uniquely tailored to the individual student. In the end the Honors Thesis became not only a legendary hurdle for honors students, but a transformative and memorable one as well.

Step Four: Teaching Alternate Ways to Analyze Literature

The English department at Morristown was dominated by the grammarians with their complete devotion to one method of literary analysis, New Criticism. Therefore, in addition to the five-paragraph essay, there was one way to approach literature in a mostly literature-based department that taught little creative or poetry writing. From Day One, I taught my Honors classes a full range of ways to view, read, and analyze literature: reader-response; feminist analysis; archetypical analysis; and psychological, political, sociological, religious, and historical analysis, to name a few. With their eyes open to multiple ways of analyzing literature, students were better able to select, approach, define and research their thesis topics.

Breaking Boundaries: Teaching Composition with a Rhetorical Approach, Creatively

In teaching a Composition elective to juniors and seniors, I credit *Twenty Questions for the Writer: A Rhetoric with Readings* by Jacqueline Berke (Berke, 1972/1981). Her scaffold includes twenty questions that define the purpose of the essay aligned with twenty answers that form the type of essay. The first question she asks is: "How can X be described?" aligning the question with the type of essay, description, followed next by "How did X happen?" aligning the type of essay, narration. Berke's rhetorical method, first published in 1972, predates Wendy Bishop's essay by almost two decades, but Berke would certainly agree on teaching "Creative Composition" first. Description and narration form the foundational skills of creative writing – not only Bishop's recommendation for university students, but James Moffett's (Moffett, 1973) recommendation for all students K–13 as well. Most importantly, Berke's rhetorical approach teaches interdisciplinary and discipline-related writing models. For example, Berke teaches both *describing to inform* (exposition) as well as *describing to create mood and meaning* – the former for explanation and technical writing, the later for creative or imaginative writing. Her models for the former, a description of "Evaporation" from a chemistry textbook and a technical description of a grasshopper from *The Book of Popular Science*, anatomical diagram included (Berke, 1972/1981: 35–37), demonstrate creative writing as a foundational pedagogy for writing across the curriculum in both arts and sciences.

Berke's rhetorical approach proved exceptionally successful for the Composition I elective, designed for a heterogenous group of students, grades 9–12, working in a writing lab classroom. I taught the composition elective with the same procedures, methods, and norms as I did in my Creative Writing I elective, and students produced portfolios of quality and quantity. For some, that quality and quantity garnered national award recognition. Michelle Kim won Scholastic Writing Award's highest honor, the Regional Gold Key in its Non-Fiction Portfolio Division for her composition portfolio. She also won the James B. Reston Portfolio Silver Award and a New Jersey Governor's Arts Award in Writing.

Model Student Essay of Definition: "Idiocy? What's Love Got to Do with It" by Michelle Kim, Composition I Elective

Idiocy? What's Love Got to Do with It
by Michelle Kim

> When I think of idiocy, I immediately think of my friends, whom I shall refer to as Mindy and Adam. These two people were the perfect example of true deep, lasting, love and friendship, as well as that of idiocy. I am by no means saying that love and idiocy are synonymous, though Mindy and Adam's story might suggest that. The two started out as friends who caught each other at weird times. Both were extremely depressed, and found comfort in each other. Love was growing with their bond and a little less than a year later, they found themselves happy and very much in love. The two could not have been more compatible or compensating for each other; I honestly believed that this was a perfect match. Apparently, so did both Adam and Mindy. But Adam grew scared of this overwhelming feeling, and one day, completely broke off all contact with Mindy, after some ridiculous explanation and excuses. I have spoken with both of them since, and I repeat that when I think of idiocy, I think of their story

Mindy too was an idiot. She was idiotically in love, and idiotically dared to believe Adam loved her the same. She thought that love could last, withstand all distances, and survive any test. What an idiot. Love rarely can make it through those poetic fancies, especially when its participants are young and foolish. She gave herself up too easily and left herself wide open for injury, which was a very idiotic mistake. What is more, now that the relationship is over, she cannot find it in herself to move on, regardless from the coaching she gets from me and other friends. She is being an idiot, and she knows it.

So what exactly is idiocy? Though my mind's definition is "Adam and Mindy," and that suffices for me, I was curious as to what those that are ignorant of the idiotic archetype used as a definition. *The American Heritage Dictionary of the English Language* claims that "idiocy" is an "extreme folly or stupidity," "a foolish or stupid utterance or deed," and using the lexicographer's typical evasion strategy, "the state or condition of being an idiot." Leaving the last definition aside (its style reminds me too much of Adam – wishy, washy and pathetic), I concede that the *American Heritage* is not far off the mark. Mindy's actions were folly; Adam's stupidity. Adam said perhaps one of the most foolish utterances in the history of utterances when he made his poor excuses. Mindy committed a stupid deed, and continues to commit them, by believing that somehow this mess with her one, her only, her true love will resolve itself to her liking. At this point, I am wondering if the *American Heritage* also had Adam and Mindy in mind.

Practically speaking, my definition of idiocy is too specific, as love does not have to be directly linked to idiocy, as it was here, and the dictionary's is . . . well, it was written by those delightful people who write dictionaries. If I was so ever inclined, I would suggest that the authors of *American Heritage* and their colleagues change their entries of "idiocy" to: Idiocy. 1. departure from one's own judgement and common sense, resulting in a potentially detrimental situation to one's own well-being. 2. an attachment to the belief that "everything will be all right." 3. Adam and Mindy.

PART THREE: INTERDISCIPLINARY APPLICATIONS – BREAKING BOUNDARIES

Model Contributor Editorial: "Birnam Woods, Moving Closer, Shadows Our Work" by Steven Handel, Plant Ecologist

Steven Handel's artful editorial for *Ecological Restoration* demonstrates the value of creative writing strategies in scientific writing and scientific journals. He opens his editorial using a literary allusion to Birnam Woods to relate to "our reality of escalating climate change and its biotic consequences" (Handel, 2019: 1). This can be considered Handel's use of a "diamond" structure as a creative approach to the academic essay. (Recall discussion of the "diamond" introduction earlier in this chapter.)

Birnam Woods, Moving Closer, Shadows Our Work
Steven Handel

> The impossibility of a forest that could move served to quiet fears of the future for a troubled king:
> Apparition:
> *Macbeth shall never vanquish'd be until*
> *Great Birnam wood to high Dunsinane hill*
> *Shall come against him.*
> Macbeth responds:
> *That will never be*
> *Who can impress the forest, bid the tree*
> *Unfix his earth-bound root?*
> (Macbeth, Act 4, scene 1)
>
> (Handel, 2019: 1)

The apparition warns: Macbeth shall never be vanquished until Birnam wood comes to high Dunsinane hill. Macbeth responds: "That will never be" because "Who can impress the forest" or "bid the tree" to "Unfix his earth-bound root?" With this specific question in mind, Handel (2019) answers with dramatic flair: "Then in one of the play's most vivid scenes, it happened. Soldiers masked by tree boughs marched through Scotland towards the king, and his terrifying fate, once impossible to imagine, unfolds" (p. 1). Handel moves from "ancient literature" to the "feckless present," and begins his editorial argument:

> With global warming, the distributions of land and sea species may move to a place where the migrating favorable climate can be found. [. . .] Many surveys have shown that trees, insects, and other taxa have already moved beyond their historic zones because of climate change.
>
> (p. 1)

Using the aforementioned "diamond structure," a poetic title, and an opening allusion from Shakespeare, Handel engages his readers (scientists) to his advocacy, broadening and then narrowing to his main thesis: "The change in vegetation zones that is occurring corresponds in our time to the moving woods that Shakespeare fancifully created in his *Macbeth*" (p. 1). Handel concludes his editorial, "Art has become reality" (p. 1).

Ecological Restoration Restores 21st Century Communication

Handel's use of creative strategies for scientific writing reflects two decades of serious debate and controversy in scientific disciplines, beginning in 1997 with James Glanz's article in *Science*, "Cut the Communications Fog, Say Physicists and Editors" (Glanz, 1997). The problem? According to Glanz, "In the past, physicists have fretted over their inability to communicate with the lay public. Now the flood of unexplained acronyms, cryptic symbols, nightmarish graphs has risen so high [. . .] that physicists can no longer understand each other (Glanz, 1997: 895). Most importantly, Glanz emphasizes: "No one is claiming the problem is unique to physics [. . .]. [I]t is about the same in astronomy, chemistry, and biology (p. 895). Creative strategies, the kind employed by the journal *Ecological Restoration* and in Steven Handel's editorials, underscore the urgent need to communicate scientific information to the lay public.

Model Contributor Term Paper: "The Emergence of Yellow Power in America" by Amy Uyematsu, Mathematics Teacher

In 1969, Amy Uyematsu, a senior at the UCLA, broke boundaries when she wrote a historic term paper, "The Emergence of Yellow Power in America," for the first Asian American Studies class offered at UCLA. When asked why she wrote the term paper, she replied, "Initially, to protest and wanting to be an advocate for a positive, non-stereotyped Asian American identity" (Uyematsu, 2020). If that was not ground- breaking enough, there was more – something perhaps less noteworthy at the time, but equally significant. Uyematsu wrote three poems that accompanied her term paper. In her email correspondence, she explains: "I consider those college poems written with my senior term paper my first poems" (Uyematsu, 2020). As a mathematics major at UCLA, what inspired her to write poetry and attach those "first poems" to a ground breaking academic paper calling for yellow power? In her words, "I was experiencing tremendous emotional upheaval and political insights that could not be expressed in a college essay – poetry seemed a vehicle in which I could better express all that I was going through" (Uyematsu, 2020). Not only did Uyematsu break disciplinary boundaries by inclusion of unassigned protest poetry in an academic paper; the paper itself broke boundaries, contributing to a new field of study, Asian-American studies.

Uyematsu explains how it happened:

> The three poems I attached to my term paper were Asian American identity/protest poems. They weren't assigned. I wrote them while I was writing the term paper. The poems were able to express some of the intense emotional changes I was experiencing as a result of my taking the first Asian American Studies class at UCLA. It was titled 'Orientals in America' because the term Asian Americans didn't exist yet. One of the students

who helped get the course at UCLA was also a co-founder and co-editor of the movement newspaper GIDRA (1969–1974). He published my poems first, in an early issue of Gidra; a few months later, he published the term paper. That was fortuitous since it led to my being hired by the new UCLA Asian American Studies Center in October, 1969.

(Uyematsu, 2020)

Model Contributor Article: "On the Need for Poetry by Scientists" by Arthur J. Stewart, Aquatic Ecologist and Ecotoxicologist

In April 1999 Arthur Stewart, broke boundaries "while contemplating the need for bridge-building." He wrote for the *Bulletin of the Ecological Society of America* "On the Need for Poetry by Scientists," which Stewart describes as his "first formal attempt to bridge poetry and science from the science shore" (Stewart, 1999b: 133). In the context of C. P. Snow's "Cultural Divide," it was a courageous article at a critical time.

The "Cultural Divide" found its most controversial expression in 1959 when C. P. Snow, English physicist turned novelist, delivered a landmark lecture identifying an unbridgeable gap between "Two Cultures," one the science culture, the other the arts or literary culture (Snow, 1959/2007). Critics described the "two cultures" as forming two "distinct and separate realms: the first material, tangible, measurable, and real: the second, immaterial, intangible, unquantifiable and imaginary" (Morris, 2006: 147). According to Stewart, 1997 was a critical time, prompting him to write his article, "On the Need for Poetry by Scientists."

As an aquatic ecologist and ecotoxicologist from Oak Ridge National Laboratory, Stewart presented his case "On the Need for Poetry by Scientists" modestly: "I function as a credible scientist. However, I also write and publish poetry in literary magazines. I think it's a good thing to do, by offering something tangible and closer to the heart" (Stewart, 1999b: 133). To that end, he shared with his colleagues two of his science poems, "What they Found" followed by "Learning" (see below) explicating their meanings, value, and utility for science.

What They Found
by Arthur J. Stewart

They found
telemerase in a cell
adding bits
of DNA to the ends

of chromosomes
thus compensating
for losses that occur
with routine

cell division and this means
could we live forever
ageless?

(Stewart, 1999c)

In his commentary on his poem "What They Found," Stewart (Stewart, 1999b) explains to his colleagues that it is "not about telomerase at all" but a metaphor for

> a deeper issue of science itself. What one finds in asking any good scientific question is a path leading to another question only. That's what "they" in the poem really found: a new question, imbued with its own plethora of ethical and moral issues – a question relating to the possibility of learning to significantly extend the length of human life. Fascinating!
>
> (p. 133)

In his poem "Learning," Stewart tackles the development of his personal understanding of science while teaching science.

Stewart's Commentary on His Poem "Learning"

> There is much we don't know scientifically about how iron-weed "by slamming purple softens / wild hills in autumn," because the aesthetics of nature extend well beyond our primitive ability to write equations, and human perception is deeper than any tools science presently has to offer […]. One must teach the tools of science, I think, and help students *see* the science to which the tools can be applied. And "[…] when I look up at last / I must stop and lean forward, learning […]" the message is complete, encapsulated and installed; I realize that one or more of the students realizes that the facts are naught but tools: the bond is created. I see then, in that instant that *I* have learned from the students I am trying to teach.
>
> (Stewart, 1999b: 133)

******

Envoi

I can think of no better poem to conclude Section One, *The Teacher Self*, than "Learning." It expresses the core belief of this book that we are co-learners, reminding us – *to teach is to learn. . . to learn is to be.*

Learning
by Arthur J. Stewart

My nine and duckling students dear –
I cannot teach you how iron-weed
by slamming purple softens
wild hills in autumn.

So on this bold day I say just
iron-weed blooms, and dig in stitching
raw data with statistics,
explaining the need to round
to whole near numbers, values
that have clear meaning.

But when I look up at last
I must stop and lean forward, learning
in your young eyes
how beautifully these tumbling
fragments of knowledge adorn you.

(Stewart, 1999a)

Chapter 10 Notes

1 In 1974, when I wrote the Creative Writing I and II elective curriculum, I did not imagine teaching it under every possible scheduling system. But that is what happened given my four decades of teaching at Morristown High. What it proved was the adaptability of the pedagogy and the student writers to write under two types of methods: immersion writing when there is little time and reflective writing courses under block or A/B scheduling. I wrote the curriculum and taught CWI for many years when students met every day and for 50 minutes for a semester. They advanced if they elected to do so the following semester to CWII. In this system, students could elect to take a full year of creative writing. Then Morristown changed to block scheduling, when students did not meet every day but rotated through a daily sequence of classes. It was a drawback to meet irregularly for writers, but the 90-minute block classes were productive for student writers motivated to write in class and writing labs with computers. I taught the curriculum as a quarter course, a semester course, and under block scheduling for over a decade.

2 For a complete discussion of the pedagogy supporting "Poem Pals," see "Poetry to Engage the Person" (Gorrell, 1990). There you will find a five day "no fail" unit lesson plan for teaching poetry to engage students of all levels and abilities using a reader-response approach.

3 Refer to John Warner's *Why They Can't Write: Killing the Five-Paragraph Essay and Other Necessities* (Warner, 2018). As a university professor who taught writing for two decades, his thesis is that decades of educational reform rooted in standardization, assessments, and accountability have made students passive and disengaged. They don't write well because they haven't been taught writing well, pointing to test-driven "writing related-simulations" and the limited academic essay response to literature of the five-paragraph formulaic essay.

Chapter 10 References

Berke, Jacqueline (1972/1981) *Twenty Questions for the Writer: A Rhetoric with Readings* (3rd edition). New York, NY: Harcourt Brace Jovanovich.

Bishop, Wendy (1994) Crossing the lines: On creative composition and composing creative writing. In Bishop, Wendy and Hans Ostrom (eds.) *Colors of a Different Horse*: *Rethinking Creative Writing Theory and Pedagogy*, 181–197. Urbana, IL: National Council of Teachers of English. https://files.eric.ed.gov/fulltext/ED366967.pdf

Cameron, Julia (2002) *Walking in this World: The Practical Art of Creativity*. New York, NY: Tarcher/Putnam.

Csikszentmihalyi, Mihaly (1996) *Creativity: Flow and the Psychology of Discovery and Invention*. New York, NY: Harper Perennial.

Emmert, Mark A. (1997) Poets, painters, and the future of science. *Science*, 278: 1381.

Fluck, Sandra (1973) *Experiential English*. New York, NY: Glencoe Press.

Glanz, James (1997) Cut the communications fog, say physicists and editors. *Science*, 277: 895–896. https://doi.org/10.1126/science.277.5328.895

Gorrell, Nancy (1990) Poetry to engage the person. In Patricia Phelan (ed.) *Literature and Life: Making Connections in the Classroom*, 35–43. National Council of Teachers of English: Urbana, IL.

Handel, Steven N. (2019) Birnam Woods, moving closer, shadows our work. *Ecological Restoration*, 37: 1–2. https://doi.org/10.3368/er.37.1.1

Hipple, Ted (1989) The Tyranny of the Ts. *English Journal*, 78 (5): 19–22. https://doi.org/10.2307/819194

Kim, Michelle (2004) Idiocy? What's love got to do with it. *Tricorn Literary Magazine*, 39: 26. Morristown, NJ: Morristown Public High School.

Macrorie, Ken (1988) *The I-Search Paper* (revised edition of *Search Writing*). Portsmouth, NH: Heinemann.

Moffett, James (1973) *A Student-Centered Language Arts Curriculum Grades K–13: A Handbook for Teachers*. Boston, MA: Houghton Mifflin.

Scholes, Robert (1985) *Textual Power: Literary Theory and the Teaching of English*. New Haven, CT: Yale University Press.

Snow (1959/2007) *The Two Cultures* (10th edition). Cambridge, UK: Cambridge University Press.

Stewart, Arthur J. (1999a) "Learning." On the need for poetry by scientists. *Bulletin of the Ecological Society of America*, 80 (2): 133.

Stewart, Arthur J. (1999b) On the need for poetry by scientists. *Bulletin of the Ecological Society of America*, 80 (2): 133–134.

Stewart, Arthur J. (1999c) "What They Found." On the need for poetry by scientists. *Bulletin of the Ecological Society of America*, 80 (2): 133.

Stewart, Arthur J. (2017) "Edges." *Elements of Chance*, 51. Knoxville, TN: Celtic Cat.

Swanger, David (1974) *The Poem as Process*. New York, NY: Harcourt, Brace, Jovanovich.

Uyematsu, Amy (2018) Five decades later: Reflections of a yellow power advocate turned poet. In Schlund-Vials, Cathy J. (ed.) *Flashpoints for Asian American Studies*, 21–35. New York, NY: Fordham University Press.

Uyematsu, Amy (August 6, 2019) Email correspondence with Nancy S. Gorrell.

Uyematsu, Amy (May 6, 2020) Email correspondence with Nancy S. Gorrell.

Warner, John (2018) *Why They Can't Write: Killing the Five-Paragraph Essay and Other Necessities*. Baltimore, MD: John Hopkins University Press.

Warriner, John E. (1977) *English Grammar and Composition: Complete Course* (Series). New York, NY: Harcourt Brace Jovanovich.

SECTION TWO: THE WRITER SELF

Chapter 11

Discovering the Creative Writer Within

> *Go within and scale the depths of your being from which your very life springs forth.*
>
> – Rainer Maria Rilke, *Letters to a Young Poet*
>
> (Rilke, 1875/2000: 9)

PART ONE: THIS IS HOW IT HAPPENED

For a long time, I am teaching. I am teaching English and creative writing. While I am teaching, I am a working mother and I am very busy. But I find that my life is not complete without teaching. Why is teaching so important? I don't know; I just feel I love to go to work every day. But it's not "work." It's something essential, something else that I can't put my finger on. Gradually, I come to recognize that what I love is *learning*. And that learning, is learning to teach *creative* writing. I name myself: *creative* writing teacher. There are no teachers in my school to mentor me. I read books by writing teachers. I teach as I learn. I learn as I teach.

Then, without my realizing it, something else happens. I am becoming a *writer.* How could I not? I am teaching my students how to write; I am writing along with them in the classroom and on our walks. I am becoming a writer too. But I don't know it yet. I still think of myself as a teacher first, a creative writing teacher, but a teacher. Then the moment of occasion calls, and I find myself writing. It's "real" writing, not just writing for an exercise with my students, and it comes from "within." I sense the difference. I am an English teacher, but I am also becoming a *writer.*

PART TWO: THE MOMENT OF OCCASION

The Old Nut Bowl: "Going Within"

The moment of occasion was my grandfather's 80th birthday and I did not have a present. I knew from experience as a young child that you could not buy a present for grandpa. He always said, "I need nothing." If you bought him anything, it was quickly returned. As a child, I made him pictures, ash trays, and fishing lures for his tackle box. In college, I knit him scarves. But for his 80th birthday, I was out of ideas and time. Then it occurred to me, what do I spend the most time doing? *Teaching*. Remarkably, I took the first step and started to "go within." I thought about a writing exercise I was teaching to my students. It was a warm-up exercise I used for beginning memory writing, *memory association technique*.

Memory Association Technique: Chaining

In this exercise, I tell my students to think of some object to prompt their memories: a childhood toy, a special photograph, or some kind of music. Then I tell them to use the object to begin a "chain" of memories. The idea is to let memory flow naturally, in a stream of consciousness, bouncing back and forth within the time of one's life, one association prompting and "chaining" to another. Suddenly, I was thinking of the dark, wooden nut bowl my grandfather had recently given me. As a child, I played with the nut bowl on the parlor table. There were no other "toys" in his house. In the nut bowl, my grandmother placed whole walnuts along with the nutcracker, a fearsome thing with a pirate face. My sister and I played with the nut bowl for hours, she often chasing me while opening the nutcracker's face. But the best part was the music.

When I cranked it just so and lifted it off the end table, it played the most delicate tune. I listened again and went "within," writing.

> *I turn the stiff key of the dark old wooden music box, a nut bowl in its prime . . . chimes. . . bells. . . light. . . airy. . . warm, loving feelings. . . I'm six years old. . . long stone steps up to the towering apartment. . . "be careful" my mother says. Grandpa answers the door. . . arms wide, face like lightning. . . Beethoven plays in the background, somber and powerful. Grandpa swings me up into his arms. I circle round and round. Up to the window: I'm going to throw you in the river! One! Swing. Two! Swing. Three! Swing. . . Down, down, down I go. . . onto the floor. Games are over. Now grandpa asks: what did you learn in school? His principal face is on. . . pointy eyebrows. I recite what I know. His face gleams. He tries to stump me. . . I'm fooled and feel ashamed. He prods me on. . . He wants me to know. I want to know for him. I get the right answer. Joy! Lesson over for now. . . He hugs me. I'm ambrosia to him. That's how good, that's how sweet. He asks, "What is ambrosia?" I reply, "The nectar of the gods." I'm that special. My sister is nectarine, his favorite fruit. Grandma comes out of the kitchen: sparkling blue eyes, flushed cheeks, soft, beautiful white hair. . . she cooks. . . the aroma of two worlds. . . Grandpa: smells "fooey" "Never use grandpa's towel!" grandma warns. His world: music, dark, sober, Beethoven, learning. One portrait says it all: the old fisherman with overnight stubble, weathered sagging skin, battered hat looking out over the perpetual lake. Grandma: another world. . . pure, alabaster skin, all sparkles, walks in circles of good food and clean living. Grandpa says, "Your dizzy grandma!" always busy. . . fussy. . . plastic covers on the lamp shades. . . I called her busy when I was three. . . everyone laughed. "I'll tuck you in as snug as a bug in a rug!" Grandma kisses. Grandpa never kisses. . . Dinner ready. Grandpa sits majestically at the center stage. Grandma never sits. in/out. . . in/out. . . in/out of the kitchen. "Grandma, sit down!" we all know she never will. Grandpa directs the meal, but always first giving thanks: we are all here. . . we are all healthy. . . we are all together. He glares at*

me in fun. . . pointy eyebrows again, pinches my cheek. "I have the stinkiest grandchildren in the world!" I know he's joking but I'm still scared. It always hurts. Grandma comes, "Sam, don't frighten the children!" Grandma serves hearty soup, hot steaming, all glistens, all is perfect: sweet potatoes with marshmallows, deepest red cranberries. . . grandpa gives thanks again. "Do you know there are children starving in this world?" I don't know but I feel guilty for the moment as I eat my bread. Dinner over. . . I settle warm and heavy by grandpa's side. He tells stories from his head. . . no book, no pictures. . . I can close my eyes. . . we listen. . . for hours. . . my favorite: the bell of Atri. . . an old faithful horse, mistreated by his ungrateful master, rings the bell of Atri – the bell of justice – the town listens and punishes the evil master. . . I have a lump in my throat for the horse. . .[1]

At this point in my memory chain, a poem suddenly surfaces. I stop composing at my electric typewriter and take up a pen. I still have the original notes, in my own hand. I save them to share my process with my students. After a few minutes of drafting, I complete my first "real" poem which I present to Grandpa on his 80th birthday:

To Grandpa
by Nancy Gorrell

You who have pulled this child-rider
through soft-leathered journeys,
You who have carried her always
with golden reins through fertile fields,
You who have called her Ambrosia
and placed her in blue among the gods,
You who have labored and sowed your oats
and now, stand weary and stabled.

Listen to this child-rider
She has learned her lesson well.
Your home is not Atri

You shall never need the bell,
This child-rider remembers
And reveres her faithful horse.

What I Learned: Writing as Self-Discovery

I truly do not know why this "going within" did not occur earlier in my teaching. Perhaps I needed a prompt, a moment of occasion, to compel me to stop, reflect and go within. Whatever the reason, the moment of occasion was for me a turning point in my process of becoming, for I had taken the first steps in making my teaching life and my writing life one creative act. I had become my own student, and I loved it. I experienced what I had been teaching all along – that writing is a *path to self-discovery*. From this brief memory writing exercise, I came face to face with feelings I had been burying – fear of my aging grandfather's dying and guilt and worry how we could honor him and take care of him in his final years.

The childhood story of the bell of Atri gave me the language, the metaphor to say what was so difficult to say to my grandfather: that I loved him, I was worried about him, and that I always wanted to be true to him. My grandfather received the poem with delight. For the first time that I could remember, he was wordless and didn't correct my writing. Later, my uncle, the poet, read it with a critical eye. "It's a poem," he said matter-of-factly, and continued eating his dinner. From that moment on, I began to think of myself as a writer, someone who could write what matters for myself and others.

And that is of course, what I had been teaching my students to do all along – write from experience; write what matters; write from within. Now I was able to teach with a greater sense of personal authenticity. I could teach from my own life. I could teach from my own struggles with writing. I was a teacher. I was a writer. Although I had yet to integrate the two in my mind and heart, I had taken the first step in becoming a writer. I reveled in the joy of that *becoming*.

Whenever I begin teaching memory writing, I take out the old wooden music box. I turn the key and let my students listen. Then I read from my notes. Afterwards I say, "You don't know my family, and you don't know my grandfather. But can you understand what I have written?" They always nod, "Yes." I point out the paradox: the universality in the particular. I encourage them: "Write for yourself. Do not explain your memories. We will be able to understand them." They begin their "chains." After they have written for twenty minutes, I show them the process of writing "To Grandpa." I tell them, "When you are writing your own memory chain, if you feel a poem coming, stop the chain (which theoretically has no end), and write your poem. That's what I did with my poem." I tell them that was how it happened for me. Then I explain the background of the moment of occasion. I suggest to my students that their memory writing may produce poems, prose poems, or memory pieces worthy of gifts. I urge them to write for occasions whenever the moment arises. I say, "The power of such gifting is the ultimate power of writing."

I also mention how potential poems may be "buried" within their memory association notes. I point out that my memory of the window game, "One! swing Two! swing. . ." later became a poem I titled "The River" – another early childhood memory of "grandpa" buried deep in my subconscious until the association exercise unearthed it.

The River
by Nancy Gorrell

I never actually saw
the river, the flowing
of the currents, the deep
blue driving sweep
of the tugs and barges,
pulling us to and fro,
out and away,
I only saw the window

of grandfather's apartment
and my sister standing
waiting her turn
to be thrown into the river.

Each and every time
he would come to the door,
the river on his breath,
his bold arms sweeping us
up and away to the window
where we'd play one,
swing, two, swing, three
swing and into the river

And we wondered,
as we tempted space
and his embrace and
the floor became sky
and our feet air
and our stomachs
uncertain waters,

what lesson did we learn
from the river
game whose currents
took us nowhere?

(Gorrell, 1993)

For Your Teacher Journal: Memory Association

Reflecting

Find a prompt to begin your "memory chain." It could be an object (a key, a glove, a ball), a song, or a recollection of a place.

1. Let your memories flow for as long as you wish in a "stream of consciousness," or a chain of associations. Let each association suggest the next.

2. If a moment of self-discovery surfaces in your chain, you can focus on that moment or memory.
3. When the moment occurs for you, write a more focused poem or memory association from your chain.

Responding: Memory Association Prompts

1. Seize the moment of any occasion and write a poem, prose poem, memory association, or memoir.
2. Return (in memory or life) to a particular place that's important to you. Start your memory chain from that "place of return." Go as far as you can in your chain.
4. Write a poem, prose poem, or memoir about a place of return or a place dear to you.

For Your Students

Teacher Instructions

1. Use the "Memory Association Writing Prompts" above to inspire student to enter the stream of their own memory chains.
2. After completing your own memory chain and your writing results, share your work, if appropriate, with your students.

PART THREE: INTERDISCIPLINARY APPLICATIONS

The memory association exercise in this chapter is applicable for students in the arts, humanities, languages, science, and mathematics, as well as English and creative writing. The association exercise will engage students across the curriculum to use their creativity and imagination in original and discipline-related ways. Teachers becoming writers should share their writings in progress with their students to further creativity, literacy, and discipline-related writing.

Interdisciplinary Memory Association Models

The three writings below – the first by a science major, the second by a practicing plant ecologist, and the third by a high school student – model writing responses with "eyes" to science. Stefanie writes her "stream of thoughts" with her eye literally staring at the moon. Her association stream is "moon-struck," full of awe and wonder, "One small step. . . One giant leap." And the allusion looms farther than the room.

Model Student Response: "Stream of Consciousness" by Stefanie DeFronzo, Biochemistry and Microbiology major, Drew University

Stream of Consciousness
by Stefanie DeFronzo

1:34 am

Flashlight
Moonstruck
Curled up in the corner of my bed
With the moonlight
With my head
And my stuffed owl
Who sees all
I look at him trying to figure out
what he thinks of me
Maybe I'm just trying to figure out
what I think about myself.

Like sitting on a marshmallow
Or peering into a coconut
A bleeding cross
Between the folds of my sheets
Seems to just get bigger and bigger
the longer I stare
The longer I walk on it

One small step on the corner
of my bed
One giant leap to sleep

I wonder if she knows
we're talking about her.

Stefanie's Reflection on "Stream of Consciousness"

I stared at the moon for about 10 minutes before I wrote my stream of thoughts.

Model Contributor Memory: "Beginning at the End" by Steven N. Handel, Plant Ecologist

Steven N. Handel was raised in Far Rockaway, at the ocean end of Queens, near Kennedy Airport. Decades later, as a university researcher, he came back to this landscape to study Jamaica Bay and the effect of sea-level rise and storms on natural and human communities. Here are his memories and a perspective of a life that started at "The End." Notice how he artfully weaves detailed observations, childhood memories, and sensory experience with his passion for ecology. You can smell the beach!

Teachers across the disciplines will find Handel's memory piece a useful model for high school students searching for their future path while reflecting on their roots.

Beginning at the End (Excerpted)
by Steven N. Handel

The Beginning, Part One (Excerpted)

Brooklyn was too crowded, too dominated by our extended immigrant family, so my parents took their three young sons and moved out to the Rockaways, to the end of the New York landscape, where they could raise us with more freedom. My grandmother, I've been told, came out to the street terrified the day the moving van came. "You're leaving me here; you're leaving me here to die," she wailed. The idea that her oldest son would move a few miles away was impossible for her to understand. This would never happen in the Old Country, in Galicia. What was America doing to her family?

I was four years old, a time when my life memories began. Far Rockaway was quiet, its streets lined with big green trees. As a child I liked watching the maple seeds fall in the spring, watching the leaves turn color and pile up during the fall. The plants were so pretty. Later, when I applied to college, I wrote "I collect deciduous tree leaves" under "interests." I didn't know it then, but curiosity about plants would become my life's work. Eventually I became a botanist, a plant ecology professor. This all started when I was a child surrounded by those maple seeds.

We lived just a few blocks from the beautiful white beach. My parents never traveled anywhere for a vacation, too expensive. Why would they when the ocean's waves and the soft sand were right there? My landscape of experience was simple: just the beach, the empty lots, and my school friends from the small community. In the summer months my buddies and I had a simple routine. In the morning we would go to Jamaica Bay with a glass milk bottle. We put a crushed mussel in the bottle, tied a string around its neck, and threw it in the water. After just a few minutes small fish, killifish we called them, swum in to nibble the shellfish and we pulled the bottle out of the water. The fish became bait for our daily fishing on the rocks by the ocean. We would sit on the white barnacles and blue mussels of the jetties, cast our lines, and waited to catch a flounder or a bass, every day. I would look down at the green, the red, the brown seaweeds in the water. So pretty, did they have names, I wondered? Why are they different colors? An understanding of evolutionary adaptation in photosynthetic pigments was part of my adult life, far from my childhood years. One day I saw a lobster! I still remember it.

The street and community names were Seagirt, Edgemere, Bayswater, Broad Channel, Belle Harbor, Beach Channel Drive, Breezy Point, and Ocean Crest. The high school teams were called the Far Rockaway Seahorses. I never even noticed how our boundaries screamed of the sea. We would wander on the wooden boardwalk skirting the beach, visiting the shops: penny arcade games, cotton candy, knishes, hot dogs, Far Rockaway Bagel Factory, painted pails and small shovels for making sandcastles, rental chairs and umbrellas. The commerce of a beach community at the End was far from Wall Street's concerns.

In the fall and winter, the beaches were empty of people seeking their suntans, teenagers flirting with the lifeguards, seniors playing cards on their folding tables. Kids collected seashells that covered the wet sand: surf clams and razor clams and moon shells and oyster shells and purple-spotted cherrystones. In the Rockaways, most gardens were lined with rows of surf-clam shells, a signature of life in our town.

We used the empty lots full of weedy plants, the mundane and rough patches celebrated in this book, as our playgrounds. We'd stomp down thin paths through the giant reeds, *Phragmites*, until we got to the middle of a patch and pushed down more stems to make a secret hideout, our clubhouse. We'd sit on old milk crates and cinderblocks and made believe we were hiding from the bad kids, the pirates. On the bay, horseshoe-crab shells, prehistoric but still so common, littered the high tide line. We'd twist off the long tails; they became seashore daggers to use in our pirate games.

Sometimes we'd break off the two-meter-long straight shoots of tree-of-heaven, *Ailanthus*, and use them as spears when we played Tarzan fighting in the jungle. Much later I learned these plants were a non-native environmental problem, but for Rockaway kids they were our playthings, part of our natural escape from the daily routines of childhood.

The public school teachers were wonderful. I was bad at sports but good at school. We were poor and one day I got a letter: a full scholarship to Columbia University. My world became bigger. I could take the subway from Far Rockaway, the last stop, to Columbia's campus in upper Manhattan an hour and a half away. I moved from the End to the center of New York City and a new life unfolded.

I was sixteen years old; the Rockaways, The End by the ocean, had been my whole life.

(Handel, 2019: 522)

Model Student Memory Association: "A Window in Time" by Ella Pfahler

Ella Pfahler grew up in the "windy city." She returns through a particular "window in time" in a chain of sensory and memory associations that evoke her childhood as well as the moment of return. In addition, note that Ella's poem was written as well in response to the pandemic (see Epilogue).

"A Window in Time"
by Ella Pfahler

With green rims that stretch endlessly up brick walls, the transparent glass presents the landscape of the Windy City. Seldom am I at this window, yet the sight of the old factory building and the colossal skyscraper with its two spires shooting towards the cloudy sky is instinctive. Below, I see the cars that line the idle streets of Fulton Market. My hands leisurely grip the handles of the window and fight against the rust as I pull up. Instantaneously, I can hear the howling of the wind and the chorus of train bells. I stick my hand out of the window, feeling the sharp cold air and the billowing wind, whose strength prods my hand and teases me with its flowing path. Its sharp and unforgiving force evokes feelings of loneliness and a sense of being out of place.

I lived with this window for one year before my parents separated, propelling me to another state with just my mother. Its setting elicits memories of the strained relationship with my father, who I visit now and then. In moments, I am pulled out of the wind's trance as the scent of hot chocolate ensnares my senses. The sickly smell reminds me of my childhood, when the mornings in Chicago were filled with cups of steaming hot chocolate paired with a croissant for dipping. Memories surface of hours spent gripping crayons and revealing artistic masterpieces, which my father would enthusiastically praise. Although sweet, these memories are ripe with age.

Now, instead of feelings of comfort that innocence entails, unspoken truths of sorrow and anguish litter the atmosphere. Quite like life itself, this window stirs meaningful and painful memories. It has witnessed moments of love and warmth in addition to moments of anger and despair. Fundamentally, this window represents the agonizing unpredictability and calamity of life as well as the unveiling of ignorance that growing up brings.

For Your Students: Memory Association Exercise

Teacher Instructions

For teachers across the disciplines, suggest to your students to begin their memory chains with an object, photograph, microscope, lens, piece of art, or element of nature that relates to the course or subject at hand. List and brainstorm associations with students or let them choose one that comes to mind:

- ***Art***: *a brush, an empty easel, a piece of charcoal, a piece of art*
- ***Science:*** *a specimen or a specimen jar, a measuring tool, a scope*
- ***Math***: *a number, a sign, a symbol, a chart, an equation*
- ***History***: *letters, diaries, oral stories, maps, a globe, a book*
- ***Music***: *a song, an instrument, a musical note, a chord*
- ***Athletics***: *mitts, gloves, balls, ropes, mats*

Reflecting

After students complete their memory chains, consider the following questions for reflection and discussion:

1. What did you discover about yourself from the memory association exercise?
2. What did you discover or learn about writing from the memory association exercise?
3. What did you discover or learn about our discipline from the exercise?
4. Did you learn any discipline-related creative or writing skills?

For Your Students: "Returning to a Place" Memory Writing

Teacher Instructions

1. After reading Steven Handel's model "Beginning at the End" and Ella Pfahler's student model "A Window in Time," ask your students to write their own memory piece "returning to a place" important to them. It's best for reflection if students put distance between the past and present.
2. For students no longer living in the place of their important memory, encourage them, if possible, to visit the location before they write. For students still living in the important memory location, encourage them to spend some time in the location before they write, or to write on site.
3. Once written, ask students to reflect upon the memory of their return. Ask them if they experienced self-discovery or realization. Did they learn something new about themselves or their past?
4. Ask students: Like Steven Handel's return, has your return suggested an interest, passion, or career path you may want to walk in the future?

Chapter 11 Note

1 "The Bell of Atri" was originally a narrative poem by Henry Wadsworth Longfellow, one I only read in the process of writing this book. (The poem is in the public domain and available on the website of poets.org.) As a child, I knew the story from my grandfather. On October 16, 1920, the American Humane Education Society popularized the legendary story by producing a film to promote the humane treatment of animals (bekindexhibit.org). As an educator, I can imagine now how my grandfather would have been acquainted with Longfellow's poem as well as its message: October 16, 1920 marked an important day in the visual history of Humane Education. This was the first public screening of *The Bell of Atri*, a film produced by the American Humane Education Society (AHES). The film was shown at the Exeter Theater in Boston, and in attendance were a large number of school children and their teachers. The film advocated kindness to animals and was popular at the time.

Chapter 11 References

Gorrell, Nancy (1993) "The River." *Footwork: Paterson Literary Review*, 23: 115. Paterson, NJ: Passaic County Community College.

Handel, Steven N. (2019) Beginning at the end. In Rovaldi, Antonio and Benedetto, Francesca *The Sound of the Woodpecker Bill: New York City*, 522–527. Milano, Italy: Humboldt Books.

Longfellow, Henry Wadsworth (1876–1879) "The Bell of Atri." https://poets.org/poem/bell-atri

Rilke, Rainer Maria (1875/2000) *Letters to a Young Poet* (10th edition). Novato, CA: New World Library.

Chapter 12

Discovering the Poet Within

A piece of art is good if it is born of necessity. This, its source, is its criterion; there is no other.

– Rainer Maria Rilke, *Letters to a Young Poet*
(Rilke, 2000: 12)

PART ONE: BORN OF NECESSITY

How I Wrote My First Poem: "Born of Necessity"

It began in the form of a phone call in early March from my mother. "Grandma has cancer. She's coming home from Florida for an operation." Shock. My beloved grandmother who had never been sick a day in her life, who danced at parties, who never spoke about dying because it was too sad would be dead within two months.

Shortly before that phone call, I was preparing a dinner party for friends. I remembered from childhood how beautifully my grandmother garnished platters with black olives, parsley, celery hearts, and radishes in the shape of rose-like flowers. I attempted to make my own flowers out of the radishes by cutting slivers along the edges. I put them on greens and set them aside. The next day they rolled around on the serving plates looking more like plain radishes than roses. This puzzled me to no end; they just didn't look like Grandma's, and I couldn't figure out why. For months thereafter, the images of my radishes, unopened and unrealized, and grandma's beautiful radishes in full bloom, kept surfacing at odd moments – when I was waking up in the morning, driving to school, or going to sleep at night. As a teacher, I was aware of such "recurring images" as powerful centers for poetry. I had been teaching a lesson on using recurring images to write memory poems. In fact, that lesson produced the award-winning poem written by Debbie Busch (Chapter 5), but I never experienced a recurring image until that moment when necessity presented itself.

It was one week before my grandmother's 83rd birthday. She lay in her hospital bed two states away. I was in the last month of my second pregnancy, and my doctor refused to let me travel. I wanted to communicate to my grandmother, but she was not the kind of person to talk about anything unpleasant, and I just couldn't broach the subject over the telephone. The last thing she ever wanted was to cause her grandchildren any pain. She would always say that when it was her "time," she would go off to a Greek Island, and then she would hum the song "Never on a Sunday," dance her silly little dance, and we, as children, would laugh alongside her.

My poem was born from the need to speak the unspeakable, and only poetry could do that. As I lay in my bed one early April morning, a "hidden" image resurfaced. I saw the radishes. But they weren't sitting on serving platters; they were on the counter, floating in cups of water. *That was it!* They bloomed as they swelled from the water. That's how grandma did it. As I reclaimed the hidden image of the blooming radishes, I was able to write the poem which I sent to her on her birthday, one month to the day before she died.

To Grandma
by Nancy Gorrell

only you
taught me how
to make roses
out of radishes

each year
we'd clean
and carve
blood-red
we'd watch
them bloom
in cups of water
for Thanksgiving

even now,
in your 83rd year,
you still make roses

I receive
the secret blossoms,
so bitter and so beautiful

I read that poem at my grandmother's funeral. When I teach this poem, I tell my students that "real" poetry is saying something you can't say in any other way. At that moment, there was no other way I could express my love and my anguish. She received the poem, I know, although we did not speak about its meaning. The experience helped me realize that poetry from within doesn't come from thinking about writing a poem. It comes from necessity, presenting itself to you, the writer, to "*go within and scale the depths of your being*."

To me, there is something miraculous about such moments. Why the hidden image finally surfaced when it did is rationally explainable, but to me, it is also unexplainable. Unlike "To Grandpa," I know this poem came from a different place. It was not the direct result of a warm-up exercise freeing my flow of memories and pointing me to self-discovery. There was something more than an occasion that prompted its creation. There was something else surrounding the moment of my grandmother's dying.

Days later, Elizabeth, my second child, was born. The day was my grandmother's birthday, April 19th. My grandmother passed away one month later, on the same numerical date, May 19th. Life and death, beauty and tragedy, love and loss, all converged to produce not only the birth a child, but the birth of a poet, myself. From that moment on, I had the courage to write poems, however simple they might be. I had seized the moment, and I discovered the poet within.

What I Learned: Discovering the Poet Within

I knew my poem "To Grandma," born in the moment of necessity, would not have been voiced if it were not for years of teaching and reading poetry. That context – what I like to think of as the fertile soil "seeding" the creative process – entered my poem as much as the moment of miracle. As a teacher, I can be objective and see this entering after the fact. Yes, my poem is my own voice, from my own moment of necessity, and yet I know that the poetic influence was also the poetry of Williams Carlos Williams. Having not written much poetry before, Williams gave me the model for the clean, concise, understated poem. The ending somehow echoes his poem "This Is Just to Say" (Williams,1938), which, as a brief note as well, ends "so bitter and so sweet." Although I was not ever consciously thinking of Williams when I wrote the poem, nevertheless, by the time I finished, I could sense Williams. Perhaps you did too when you read my poem. He ended his poem with a matter-of-fact statement, and somehow "so bitter and beautiful" came to me like that, surfacing in the flow of my writing. If I wanted to imagine a prompt for my own poem, I could use "This Is Just to Say." But it would not have produced the poem I wrote, and that is because "To Grandma" is an authentic poem, not a classroom exercise. It goes beyond technique, *saying something I couldn't say in any other way.*

For Your Teacher Journal: Discovering the Poet Within, Part 1

Reflecting: "Born of Necessity"

Recall from you past a brief moment "born of necessity." Reflect on that brief moment. Recall the images of that moment: sights, sounds, smells, tastes, and senses of touch. Replay those images in your mind until they become clear to you.

Responding: Writing Prompts

1. After reading the model poem "To Grandma," think of a person you associate with a moment of necessity or a moment important to you.
2. Write a poem or prose poem addressing that person. Say something to that person you couldn't say in any other way.

PART TWO: RECLAIMING A HIDDEN OR RECURRING IMAGE

Model Student Poems Reclaiming Hidden or Recurring Images

The following student models illustrate reclaiming recurring or hidden images with increasing time frames, complexity, and scale. First, Marni Rothman's notes from creative writing class presents a *recurring image* of less than 30 seconds. Second, Debbie Busch's poem presents a longer time frame that ends on a powerful recurring image – *a smell.* Third, Sheila Gorman's class notes present a *single recurring image* of an indefinite period of time.

"30 Second Memory" by Marni Rothman

30 Second Memory
by Marni Rothman

my face looked down
my hair fell down

I only saw
the soft black
of my tiny boots
I only heard
the relentless drone
of his voice
telling me
I should look this way.

(Marni Rothman, 1990)

"Christmas (Portland Oregon, 1969)" by Debbie Busch

Christmas (Portland Oregon, 1969)
by Debbie Busch

My silly Christmas bell
Came off the top of a bakery cake.
It was plastic and covered with cheap glitter.
But it smelled like icing,
And Grandma had given it to me.
And I loved it.
But so did Maria Lisa.
I only let her hold it
Because she promised
Not to throw it in the fireplace.

I could smell it even as it burned.

(Debbie Busch, 1990)

"Untitled" by Sheila Gorman, Single Recurring Image, Indefinite Time Frame

Untitled
by Sheila Gorman

I never knew him.
Only that he was
tall and dark,
your Italian lover.
He would come

to our tiny apartment
at night
when we were in bed,
but I knew.
I saw him
when he left your room.
He walked out grandly
and stood, naked
in a patch of light
flaunting his beauty
to my wondering eyes.
I never knew him.
Only that he was
tall and dark,
your Italian lover.
(Sheila Gorman, 1990)

For Your Teacher Journal: Discovering the Poet Within, Part 2

Reflecting: Reclaiming a Hidden or Recurring Image

1. Pick a brief moment or event in your life, 30 seconds or less; one you will never forget.
2. Close your eyes. See the moment.
3. Think of all your senses at the moment. What are you seeing, hearing, smelling, tasting, and touching?
4. See the moment again, in slow motion, step by step. Replay the moment in your mind.

Responding: Writing Prompt

1. Then open your eyes, and write down the all the images, step by step.
2. Write a poem or prose poem, beginning or ending your poem or prose poem with an image or images.

For Your Students: Discovering the Poet Within

Student Instructions: Writing Prompts

1. Choose to "Reclaim a Hidden or Recurring Image," in a poem or prose poem. Like "Christmas, Portland, Oregon, 1969," center your poem or prose poem on a recurring image that keeps coming back to you. Use all of your senses. End your poem or prose poem with that image.
2. Choose to "Recall a Moment of Necessity." Like "To Grandma," write your own poem or prose poem to a person important to you. Say something to that person you can't say in any other way.

PART THREE: INTERDISCIPLINARY APPLICATIONS

The *Discovering the Poet Within* exercises in this chapter are applicable for students and teachers in both the arts and the sciences. (See Chapter 18 for an in-depth discussion of science poetry as an interdisciplinary literacy tool enabling students to "discover the poet within" while expressing their knowledge and passion for science.) This chapter's exercises will engage students across the curriculum to use their creativity and imagination in original and discipline-related ways.

Model Contributor Poem: "Dipping into Infinity" by Amy Uyematsu, Mathematics Teacher

Dipping into Infinity One More Time: "Born of Necessity"

Amy Uyematsu has "dipped" into infinity more than once (Chapter 9); but this poem, "Dipping into Infinity," is different – one "born of necessity." Here the poet Uyematsu expresses her deeply personal experience of illness with poetic and mathematical eyes.

Dipping into Infinity
By Amy Uyematsu

One more dip—

my eye swimming
in this unseasonably
clear February sky.

The phone call was brief—

not "not I'm sorry, the news isn't good."
Simply,
"You have cancer."

One moment I woke up
and the horizon shifted
at least sixty-two degrees.

The rest of the world didn't notice
the laws of pull and release
will never be
the same.

No one but me knows I've grown
another set of eyes—

as if I'm watching

The part of me that is dying,
that has always been dying
but wasn't convinced
until now.

It comes down to a conjunction.
Talking with Luis, I say "if" I get through this.
What are you talking about, he replies,
your only choice is "when."

Take the left breast too if that will help.
    Just let the cancer stop there—

    let me be flat and unpretty
        and old, very old.

Through the thin shutter slat—

    between the dark grey cloud cover
    and the sloping roofs just across the street,

Rests a narrow opening of blue,
    swirls of white clouds
    illuminated from behind—

        my heart leaps in.

Scientists keep trying to defy
    the finite—hoping
    to simulate a black hole.

From what little I know of
    infinity—it's as close as
    that silence between
        inhale, exhale.

(Uyematsu, 2016)

On Self Discovery and the Poet Within: Email correspondence with Amy Uyematsu

Q: How has the act of writing, and writing poetry in particular, been an experience of self-discovery for you?

I am thankful that this writing path has allowed me to know more about myself and has provided an enjoyable, stimulating, challenging, and satisfying means for me to better understand myself and the world. I've often thought of poetry as a way of creating deeper and deeper connections – both within and outside myself. It's been my good fortune to have been mentored for 15 years by the Zen poet Peter Levitt. Peter's teaching was about both poetry and Zen spirituality; so much of how I approach my writing and view the world evolved during those years. Writing and the discoveries I make while writing are constant reminders of how interconnected all life is.

(Uyematsu, 2019)

For Your Students: Interdisciplinary Writing Prompts

Through the Eyes of Your Subject

Like Uyematsu in "Dipping into Infinity," try expressing personal experience through the "eyes" of your subject or discipline. For example, with mathematical eyes, scientific eyes, or artistic eyes.

- ***History students***: Imagine you are a person from history at a significant moment of "necessity," moral choice, or historical imperative. In the voice of the historical person, write a poem or prose poem "born of necessity." Show your historical literacy in your poem. Note: the person does not have to be "famous" or privileged, such as presidents and generals. Think: slaves, rebels, native peoples, abolitionists, suffragettes, astronauts, doctors, scientists, engineers, inventors, social workers, laborers, farmers, educators.
- ***Math students***: Write your own poem or prose poem "born of necessity" with an eye to mathematical concepts, principles, equations, terminology, numbers, shapes, or theories. Make your poem "count." Show your mathematical literacy.
- ***Science students*:** Write your own science poem or prose poem "born of necessity" with an eye to scientific concepts, principles, terminology, or theories. Show your scientific literacy.
- ***Language students*:** Use the "eyes" of another language in a poem or prose poem "born of necessity," or write a poem, prose poem or memoir with "eyes" to one or more languages.
- ***For all students:*** Write an ode honoring a person in your field of study or discipline. It may be someone you admire,

someone you wish you could meet, or someone you have a compelling question to ask.

Teachers of other subjects are encouraged to adapt similar writing prompts based on their subjects, courses, or disciplines.

Chapter 12 References

Busch, Debbie (1990) "Christmas (Portland Oregon, 1969)." Qtd in Gorrell (1990: 29).

Gorman, Sheila (1990) "Untitled." Qtd in Gorrell (1990: 29).

Gorrell, Nancy (1990) Taking off the mask: Teaching the recurring image in poetry writing. *English Journal*, 79 (7): 27–29. https://doi.org/10.2307/818712

Rilke, Rainer Maria (1875/2000) *Letters to a Young Poet* (10th edition). Novato, CA: New World Library.

Rothman, Marni (1990) "30 Second Memory." Qtd in Gorrell (1990: 29). https://doi.org/10.1049/ee.1990.0013

Uyematsu, Amy (2016) "Dipping into Infinity." *Basic Vocabulary*, 90–92. Pasadena, CA: Red Hen Press.

Uyematsu, Amy (August 6, 2019) Email correspondence with Nancy S. Gorrell.

Williams, William Carlos (1938) "This Is Just to Say." https://www.poetryfoundation.org/poems/56159/this-is-just-to-say

Chapter 13

Discovering the Professional Writer Within

If you do not express your own original ideas, if you do not listen to your own being, you will have betrayed yourself.

– Rollo May, *The Courage to Create*
(May, 1975: 12)

PART ONE: THE PROFESSIONAL WRITER WITHIN

A Teaching Story

"Have you ever published anything?" The eyes were expressive and probing.

"No, I really haven't," was all I could reply. The question was natural. I had just given a pep talk to my creative writing class about the value of publication. I had posted on the bulletin board state and national writing competitions and literary magazines for high school students.

"Why, Mrs. Gorrell? Why?"

"Well, I guess I haven't tried." My response startled even me. I felt a sudden sense of shame and hypocrisy as the "practice what you preach" adage quickly came to mind.

"But your writings are so good," the student persisted.

For well over a decade, I had been writing along with students in my creative writing classes. They had always been an appreciative audience. I knew they liked my childhood memories, especially when eighth-period students would beg me to read what third period had heard "about the time you wrecked the garden with Herbie." But I had never recognized my own ability as a writer. They were my students, so naturally I assumed they enjoyed hearing my work. Would they have said otherwise?

Shortly after that unsettling episode, I was sitting in the department office gazing over a colleague's desk when I noticed a xeroxed poem I had distributed to my classes the week before. Curious, I asked, "Mary, where did you get that poem?"

"Oh," she exclaimed with enthusiasm, "this is a fantastic poem. We just spent a whole period talking about it!" When I mentioned that this poem was central to a lesson I taught the week before, she was surprised. Apparently, a rather unassuming student, one we both taught, brought it into Mary's class to share. Mary was impressed and wondered where the student had found it. I explained that the "Parents" was "found poetry," and that for years I had been using it to introduce poetry to my English classes. As I explained the lesson, I could see by Mary's expression that I was talking about something important. "You know," she said as she got out of her seat to go to class, "you really ought to write that up."

And so the seed was planted. Yes, I thought to myself, maybe I should. I had never considered professional writing before. Full-time teaching while raising two small children had occupied all of my time. But this was 1987, and I realized my children were at the time older and more independent. Perhaps I could find the time. But when and how? Thus, I began walking the path of becoming a writer, a path of personal renewal and self-discovery, and ultimately, a path that would enable me to "enter the professional conversation."

How I Wrote My First Article

Although I was a beginning writer full of insecurities and self-doubts, of one thing, I was sure. I knew I was going to send my article, if written, to the *English Journal* for possible publication (Gorrell, 1992a)[1]. I had been an avid reader of *EJ* for nearly a decade and had used many ideas from other teachers that I found there. I felt inspired at the thought that I might be able to contribute an article, but I wasn't sure of the best approach. Should I just write up my lesson and submit it? Or would it be better to respond to a specific *EJ* call for manuscripts? With that thought in mind, I looked at the 1987 calls and noticed a category involving "Responding to Literature." My lesson certainly taught how students could respond to poetry, but it was through a special kind of poetry, *found poetry*. Should I focus on reader response or the genre approach of found poetry? This dilemma troubled me, and I wrestled with it. But I also felt I had to be practical and seize the moment. Why not write for the call?

But I did not begin right away. After all, I was teaching 125 students, buried perennially under all those papers I had to read and respond to. Looking back, I realize the wait-time was critical in my evolution as a writer: strange things started to happen to me while driving to work in the morning. My article, an embryo of an idea, started to grow in my consciousness. It developed a life of its own, coming to me at unexpected moments, and I began what I felt was a dialogue with myself. It was not until mid-June, when I was on a trip, that I actually took some notes during one of those dead moments while traveling. I began to jot down bits of text on the plane and in the hotel room. For the entire trip, my article was with me, and I felt the coming together of ideas in a way that I knew was preparing me to write.

When I returned home, I realized I had to hurry if I was to make *EJ's* August deadline. Early one evening, I wrote. It was an odd, comforting feeling, working until 3 AM with the sounds of my family asleep around me. I relished the solitude, the privacy, the uninterrupted moments of thought. I was where I wanted to be, at my typewriter (no computer yet) writing, and I felt at once a sense of productivity and inner peace. When I was finished, I had written the introduction, and drafted the first lesson, a comparison of the found poem "Parents" with the news article it was based upon. I did not realize at the time the importance of the step I had taken. I only knew I had begun, and I felt a growing confidence.

By mid-July I had completed a fifty-page manuscript titled "Found Poetry: An Approach to Developing Poetic Response." The introduction presented a reader response approach to poetry, and the value of beginning such an approach with a particular found poem, "Parents," by Julius Lester (Lester, 1969: 3–4). The lesson answered the question "What is poetry?" through a comparison of "Parents" with the news article it was based upon. I concluded the lesson with a found poetry writing assignment for the students. For a follow-up response, I compared the "not-so-poetic" found poem "Parents" to Robert Frost's highly poetic poem "Out, Out –" (Frost, 1916). I suggested students paraphrase Frost's poem to imagine the news article it was based upon. The manuscript concluded with a final note on the issue of response, in addition to several pages of student found poems.

I had written more than I had ever anticipated. Suddenly, I had the strangest apprehension. I hadn't done my homework. My entire manuscript was based on one poem, "Parents." Had anyone ever written about that poem before? The word "research" now took on new meaning. I needed to know. The August deadline was rapidly approaching as I found myself at the reference desk of the Somerset County Public Library. "I'm writing an article on found poetry, and I need to know everything that's been written on that poem in the last thirty years." Those words were startling for me: I was a writer, and the librarian took my request seriously.

Soon I had a twenty-page computer printout of all the articles written on the found poetry going back to the early 1960s. Through interlibrary loan, I had the most important monographs and manuscripts in my hands. Although there were several pertinent articles, not one addressed the use of found poetry as a starting point for poetic understanding and response. Most importantly, no one seemed to mention the poem "Parents."

At this juncture, a solution presented itself in a way that still amazes me. I had read somewhere that acceptance of an article might be expedited if all the information regarding serial rights were included for the editors. I knew "Parents" would require such rights. Perhaps I could get the information? After several phone calls, I discovered the original publisher no longer existed, and the rights had been taken over by a new press. I immediately called and was referred to the person in charge of serial rights. "My," she exclaimed, "we haven't had such a request in over ten years!" Those were the words I wanted to hear. I felt assured I would be bringing something new to the attention of the *EJ* audience. I mailed the completed manuscript on August 1, 1987.

That fall my mailbox (no email yet) became an overwhelming preoccupation. Coming home from school was exciting, since I poured through the heap of mail hoping to find a letter of acceptance from *EJ*. But no letter came. Now I knew how writers felt. By the end of October (*EJ* had indicated decisions would be reached within three months), I could no longer contain myself. I picked up the phone and called. I simply asked the female voice on the other end if she knew the status of my submission. "Hmm," she said, "I think it's in some committee." Shortly thereafter, the phone rang. It was Ben Nelms, the editor. Although my article was not accepted for the "Responding to Literature" issue, he wanted me to know that "everyone on the committee thought very highly of your work." Those words were the confirmation I needed to feel I had written well. "But," he continued, "your article might be better for our February 1989 issue focusing on literary genres." I was so delighted to still be under consideration that the thought of publication a year and a half away didn't faze me. I barely heard his final comment about "the Frost poem being very costly to publish." I was soaring.

If the manuscript was going to be accepted for a genre approach, I knew I had to revise it. I also knew it was way too long. I kept reading over the February 1989 call for manuscripts on "Writing in

Literary Forms," realizing that anyone else could submit an article as well. I had no guarantees.

That summer I learned a lot about revision. I retitled the manuscript "Let Found Poetry Help Your Students Find Poetry," and I wrote a new introduction focusing exclusively on the poem "Parents." I also cut the manuscript in half, omitted the Frost poem and the follow-up lesson, which seemed to trouble Ben Nelms, and I wrote a new conclusion stressing the enduring value of found poetry:

> The enduring quality of found poetry lies in its ability to forever change students' attitudes, values, and sensibilities. Because it challenges them to find poetry in all the "wrong" places, it continues to thrill them with those rare and elusive encounters. One year after engaging in the "Parents" lesson, a student of mine surprised me with his own found poem discovered while reading the *Wall Street Journal*. Just the thought that he would continue to think poetically outside the strictures of teacher and classroom attests to the enlightenment and sheer fun of found poetry.
>
> (Gorrell, 1989: 34)

I could not have written those words the summer before. In the interim, a former student of mine, Geoff Klingsporn, "found" and wrote one of the most exemplary found poems I had seen. I knew it would be the best way to end the article. I wrote, "I believe Julius Lester would enjoy the following result," and I concluded with only one sample of student work, Geoff's found poem "Veteran."[2]

When I was finished, I knew it was practical. The cutting, however severe, was necessary, refocusing the article from a reader response thesis to a genre approach. By early August, I mailed the revised manuscript and waited. This time I didn't wait long. In a few weeks *EJ* accepted my revised article, and I received my first consent-to-publish form for what was published as "Let Found Poetry Help Your Students Find Poetry" (Gorrell, 1989).

What I Learned: Entering the Professional Conversation

The two years it took me to write my first article proved to be a major turning point in my professional life. In the process I discovered writing for the profession. Such joy is its own reward, and I felt at the time an overwhelming sense of renewal. Ultimately, I began to recognize that I had changed. I realized that writing was a natural consequence of my teaching lessons and life, and that I could teach and write, all at the same time. Publication helped me realize I had a voice to be heard, and there were audiences beyond my students and colleagues at Morristown High that wanted to hear it. Much of my feeling of renewal came from that emerging recognition, a new identity, that of *writer entering the professional conversation.*

PART TWO: WHY PUBLISH?

To Enter the Professional Conversation

At the time, I only thought of the meaning of publishing within the context of my classroom and students. I was completely unprepared for the larger context of a wider audience reading my work. But that is where the professional conversation begins. Part of renewal stems from the simple action of stepping out, seeking wider audiences for your work, your student's work, and in collaboration, your colleagues' work as well.

Shortly after publication, I received a letter from a college professor who said:

> I enjoyed and was intrigued by your article on found poetry and I decided to use the Lester poem and your ideas with a large group of freshman and sophomores. Hope you enjoy the enclosed two responses. Thanks for your article. This has been a pleasure.

For the first time, I had a taste of what it feels like to reach a wider audience. Teachers "out there" were reading my article and doing my lesson! My writing had a life of its own. Over the next several months, I received responses from teachers nationwide as well as editors asking me to write for academic and educational book publications.

Yet it was not until the arrival of the September 1989 issue of *EJ* that I experienced the full scope of the professional conversation. I remember sitting at the kitchen table, skimming the table of contents, when I noticed an article titled "Let Found Poetry Help Your Students Study Literature." I remember my sudden confusion. Someone was using my title? It never occurred to me that this was an article in response to mine. When I read Don Phillips's first paragraph, I was astonished: "Among the many articles in recent issues of the *English Journal* which have tempted me to try something new, Nancy Gorrell's 'Let Found Poetry Help Your Students Find Poetry' proved irresistible" (Phillips, 1989). Don Phillips, an instructor from Lambton Vocational Institute, Ontario, Canada, had adapted the concept of found poetry to literature. He mailed me a note of thanks: "Until I read your article, I was not really aware of it [found poetry] as a genre," along with more samples of his students' found poems.

Words seem to fall short in trying to describe how I felt, knowing my lesson had helped other teachers and students internationally. I can only say I was no longer the same person or same teacher that began two years before trying to write my first article. I was transformed. I was teacher, I was writer, and I was coming to recognize my teaching life and my writing life converging as one creative act. That convergence would enable me to walk the path of a new self – the *teacher-writer* self.

To Contribute to Your Community

After publication, I did not seek audiences or future publication. From that moment on, teacher-writers, poets, academics in the field, editors, and educational publishers approached me to participate in their book projects, anthologies, and educational textbooks.

I was now writing for editors who knew what they wanted and asked me to write for specific purposes. As a consequence, I made contributions to books by Patricia Phelan (Gorrell, 1990), Karin Dahl (Gorrell, 1992a), and the poets Steven Dunning and William Stafford (Gorrell, 1992b). I was fortunate. The 1990s was the beginning of a decade of professional publishing that confirmed my identity as a teacher-writer.

But most importantly, I didn't do it alone. My students were with me on my teacher-writer path. Their writing was integral to my writing. Many of them became published as I wrote about and published our class lessons and projects like "Poem Pals" (Chapter 10). Such was the case with Geoff Klingsporn's found poem "The Veteran" (Note 2). But getting published was not Geoff's motivation for writing the poem. Nor was it my motivation for teaching the found poetry lesson. Publication was part of the writing process, affirming for myself and my students the identity of professional writer.

To Publish with Your Students

Getting the Knack Book Project

As a result of "entering the professional conversation," my students and I were invited by poets Stephen Dunning and William Stafford to participate in *Getting the Knack: 20 Poetry Writing Exercises* (Dunning and Stafford, 1992), commissioned by the National Council of Teachers of English. My students were excited to participate. They tackled the exercises with enthusiasm as we all became co-learners and writers together exercising our craft. The project confirmed to my students their identities as writers: their engagement with the teacher-artists, their engagement with poetry writing, and their engagement with acceptance and rejection. Several of my students' poems were published, but not all. That is the life of the writer: some works make it into print, some don't. I could tell them from my own experience because I was a writer, too.[3]

To Self-Publish Books with Your Students

Publishing the Poetry Chapbook

From the moment I began teaching creative writing to middle school students in 1970, I "published" collections of students' poetry at the conclusion of the school year. The first was in 1971 and was printed on purple mimeograph paper with a few student illustrations. The impact on the school community far exceeded any expectations I might have had. The students were proud; they felt like writers. But the reaction of the parents and the headmaster (this was a private day school) confirmed to me that I wanted to be a creative writing teacher.

As a high school teacher, I expanded the concept to culminate a year of creative writing with each student self-publishing their own poetry chapbook. The chapbook, meaning simply "cheap book," is an ideal first book publication for beginning writers. Most chapbooks are pamphlets of 30 pages or less. The form has historically been used by poets as an intermediary step between magazine and book publication (Gorrell, 1993). The chapbook is still used by poets in the digital age, especially at poetry festivals and readings. Creating, designing, and organizing a chapbook of one's work is the ultimate task for any poet, let alone an emerging one, but my students took on the task eagerly, ultimately producing books that reflected their authentic voices and selves. Deciding on an organizing principle or theme for the book, what poems to select, what order to put them in, and a title for the book caused students to write more poetry for the book itself than they otherwise might have produced. Peers edited and proofread books for each other as well as giving feedback during the entire process. Upon completion, each student had self-published a book of 15–20 original poems, some older works, and some new for the book. Several students chose to professionally print copies of their books and a select few chose the root of copyrighting their work. We held a chapbook reading for our school community and dedicated a copy of each book to the school library. A student commented to me after the chapbook reading: "This is the most awesome thing I've ever been to at the high school. It really makes me want to be a writer."

To Publish with Your Students: The Literary Magazine

Publication is an end and a beginning for students. Seeking publication actualizes students' identities as professional writers whether that publication is a self-published poetry chapbook, a high school literary magazine, newspaper, yearbook, or online blog or website. As advisor to Morristown High School's literary magazine from 1978–2008, I became from the outset a strong advocate for student publications. My goal was to make the magazine a school-wide extra-curricular activity, not just the providence of the AP English class. The *Tricorn* became a collaboration between the art and graphic arts departments where the magazine was initially published. Submissions came from all student writers, and writings were read and selected anonymously by an editorial board of 10 students. Student writers and artists felt honored to be published in the *Tricorn*, and the magazine won the highest awards from Columbia Press Association. (Gold Medalist: 1997, 2000) and National Council of Teachers of English (Highest Award: 1997; Superior Award for nine consecutive years, 1991–2002).

To Write "Opinion Shaper" Columns

In the fall of 1991, I was selected as New Jersey State Teacher of the Year. As a result, I was thrust onto the public stage as a speaker representing teachers at educational conventions and New Jersey schools. Suddenly, speech writing became another artform to be mastered. But most important to me was the request by my local newspaper, *The Daily Record*, to write ten Opinion Shaper columns on educational issues, one per month throughout the 1991–1992 academic year. No writing assignment I ever had in school prepared me for this "job," and no other task was more high stakes.

But my years as a creative writing teacher served me well, and I could speak from the heart and from experience while advocating for critical issues important to students, teachers, and education at the time. The assigned topics were controversial, and I was speaking not for myself, but all teachers. I held my breath each month as the *Record* would print letters to the editor in reaction to my column. Fortunately, the letters from teachers and the general public were so positive, I wrote 10 columns that year to my amazement.

So why do we teachers publish? In sum:

- *To renew ourselves personally*
- *To transform ourselves creatively*
- *To enter the professional conversation of our disciplines*
- *To seek and teach multiple audiences across the disciplines*
- *To create, innovate, and break boundaries across the disciplines*

You have original ideas to express; you have an inner voice waiting to be heard. All you have to do now is take that first courageous step: write what's in your heart and mind and enter the professional conversation of your discipline.

PART THREE: INTERDISCIPLINARY APPLICATIONS

Model Contributor Opinion Editorial: "Seed Op-Ed" by Steven Handel, Plant Ecologist

Steven Handel's "Seed Op-Ed" (Handel, 2021), excerpted below, is a model of creative writing across the curriculum. Here he gives voice to the overlooked "seed" who speaks to the restoration scientists of his "plight." Handel personifies the seed with humor as well as scientific knowledge to make his case for advancing ecological issues. This boundary-breaking model should be shared with students to illustrate how scientific writing can be accessible and engaging to both the lay public and the scientific community.

As Handel notes:

> Restoration scientists and practitioners are always talking about the plants and methods they are using to initiate populations. A posting to the Editorial Office of *Ecological Restoration* was received wanting, we suppose, respect for a seed. (p. 1)

Handel opens his editorial reply by giving the Seed voice.

> **To the Restorationist:**
>
> WHAT ARE YOU DOING? DON'T YOU KNOW?
>
> I'm hauled and slung around like I was inert, some small pebble! I'm alive; I'm complex; I have needs; I want a future. Look at me, Buster! Do you know what I've gone through to be ready for planting?
>
> Even getting fertilized and maturing were terrors. So, if plant populations are restored with no thought to the availability of required pollinators and their breeding and feeding niches, you know how many flowers in the fields never get visited? It's a pollination desert out there. As if some green leaves and pretty posies will create a sustainable population without our beloved mutualists, and that's just the beginning! Growing up on the maternal plant is the next horror. A huge number of seed herbivores are the norm. Where's the availability of parasitoids or other trophic specialists that attack my enemies on restored lands? I'm on my own half the time, dependent on my bracts and toxins and rapid maturation to get out of here before being found. Oh, for a happy childhood; it's not to be for us seeds. Just when maturation is almost complete, in comes some restoration crew to cut down the stalks so the plant community looks neat during the dormant season. Can you wait 'til my development is complete? Can you wait 'til I disperse by the wind or some animal? Mowers are a nightmare for so many seeds in the pasture. We spend all this time evolving fleshy fruit, or parachutes and pappus for wind dispersal, or floating bracts to get us away

> from home. The number of restoration projects that pay no attention to dispersal agents is a crime, a crime against demography. How about some surrounding habitat to facilitate populations of animal dispersers or some connected waterways to allow floating seeds to flow and reach favorable sites? Without dispersal, a seed drops next to the mother plant and its shade, shade, and more shade. "I'm outta here" is a cry for survival, not of rebellion, so let's have some help!
>
> (Handel, 2021: 1)

Handel then concludes his Op-Ed quoting an Emily Dickinson poem that begins: "Longing is like the Seed / That wrestles in the Ground/Believing if it intercede / It shall at length be found" (Dickinson, 1873).

Handel's Commentary on "Seed Op–Ed"

Why did I write it?
Often people think of plants as passive and dull, because they don't move or talk or have complex behavior patterns as animals do. I hate this; plants are complex, fascinating, and alive, in so many senses of the word. I wanted to write about seeds, small, silent, seemingly dormant, to show the complex biology that they contain that allows them to persist and then grow.

For what audience?
I wrote in the journal which is read by restoration ecology practitioners, people who actually try to improve habitats. Many of them are volunteers and are unaware of the complexity of plant biology. I wrote the article from the point of view of the seed, giving agency to something which is usually considered inert.

Reaction of people?
Some people, academics, told me they liked the piece because it was so *different* from the normal science writing that is around, just factual, albeit nicely written. People still tell me it is fun to read because it is so oddball. The *best* reaction: I got an email from an environmental group in Illinois (I had never heard of

> them). They wrote: each fall they have a meeting where people collect seeds of native prairie plants, for use in restoration actions the next spring. After the day of collecting, they have a pot luck dinner. That year, at the dinner, they passed around the Seed Op-Ed article and different people each read a paragraph out loud to the group. Isn't that something?
>
> (Handel, 2019)

For Your Teacher Journal: Discovering the Professional Writer Within

Reflecting

1. Reflect upon your teaching lessons. Which ones do you think impacted your students the most? Which ones opened windows of learning for you and your students? Which ones were transformational for you and your students? Reflect upon writing an article for publication for your discipline.
2. Have you shared a teaching lesson with a colleague? Has a colleague ever taught one of your lessons? Reflect upon presenting a lesson for professional development or at a professional convention.
3. Reflect on innovative projects you may have engaged in across the curriculum: in WAC, STEM, or STEAM, for example, or in summer writing or science institutes.
4. Reflect on joining professional organizations and subscribe to their publications. Watch for calls for publication and submit appropriate discipline related-writing. Become part of the professional conversation in print, online or your own blog.

Responding

1. Write for your discipline your most important lesson – the one that transformed not only your students, but you as a teacher. In doing so, you will have much to say to your colleagues and the profession. Whether the article is in print, online, or in your own blog, you will be entering the professional conversation.

2. Write up your innovative projects (STEM, STEAM) and lessons for one of the many across-the-curriculum publications and/or online sites.
3. Start your own blog or website for not only students and parents, but for disseminating your own educational messaging, lessons, and projects.

For Your Students: Discovering the Professional Writer Within

1. ***Self-Publishing a Class Book***
   Afford students the opportunity to publish a collection of discipline-related creative writing from selected topics or a focused topic of study. Such focused topics could come from particular units of study in history, science, languages, and the humanities. For example, the oral history of your town or scientific research on local ecological or environmental issues.

2. ***Self-Publishing a Poetry Chapbook***
   Afford students the opportunity to publish a collection or book of their poetry at the end of a unit, class, or school year. Conclude with a program of readings to debut student books or poetry chapbooks. Encourage the student-authors to invite family and friends to hear them read a selection from their books. I have used such occasions as moments when the students donate duplicate copies of their books to the school library or writing centers.

3. ***Writing Letters to the Editor***
   Encourage students from all subjects and disciplines, to write their own discipline-related letters to the editor on local issues or issues that matter to them. Often local newspapers and magazines have student sections or columns.

4. ***Suggestions for All Students***
Take an object, number, concept, theory, or principle from a subject area or discipline and give it voice: personify it to make a persuasive point of advocacy about a subject, current or local issue, or education in general. (See Handel's "Seed Op-Ed" as an example of personification.)

5. ***School Publications***
Encourage students to submit their writing to school-related publications such as the school's newspaper, literary magazine, and yearbook. This will require helping students to select appropriate pieces and preparing them for submission. Submitting for publication enables students to act like writers, entering the "writerly" life. This solidifies their identities as writers, whether they get published or not.

6. ***Online Formats***
Encourage individual students to seek publication online in various formats: their own YouTube videos of performance poems; their own podcasts or blogs.

7. ***Contests and Competitions***
Encourage students who are interested to enter state, national, and professional poetry, and discipline-related writing contests and festivals, especially those with publication or reading (performance) opportunities.

Chapter 13 Notes

1 Refer to "A Teacher's Story of Renewal" (Gorrell, 1992a). I am indebted to the National Council of Teachers of English and editors and colleagues who mentored me in my formative years of becoming a writer in the professional conversation: Ben Nelms, Patricia Phelan, Karin Dahl, and Leila Christenbury.

2 **Found Poem "Veteran" by Geoff Klingsporn**

Veteran
by Geoff Kingsporn

(Wall Street Journal, October 27, 1987)

when the shooting comes
he (instinctively) dives
    for cover.
    as young men with machine guns
    run over his territory,
he scurries back
    to safety.
    (he has lived (so far))
he is wise
he feels no pain
he is hard
he is not unscathed, he suffers
        "what psychologists call
        post-traumatic stress
            disorders."
he has seen three young men die.
but that is what happens in war
and in life,
in the housing projects of Chicago.
        for this veteran is
        twelve years old.
(Geoff Kingsporn, 1989)

3 Two students, Arielle Siebert and Krista Wark, along with myself, were published in *Getting the Knack: 20 Poetry Writing Exercises* by Stephen Dunning and William Stafford (Dunning and Stafford, 1992). Each of us had two poems accepted, for a total of six to represent Morristown High School in the anthology: Arielle, "Dear Queen Anne Boleyn" (Siebert, 1992a) and "Memory" (Siebert, 1992b); Krista, "Finnegan's Alley" (Wark, 1992a) and "There" (Wark, 1992b); and myself, "Dear Dolphin" (Gorrell, 1992b) and "To See" (Gorrell, 1992).

Chapter 13 References

Dickinson, Emily (1873) "Longing is like the Seed." https://www.poetry-verse.com/emily-dickinson-poems/longing-is-like-the-seed

Dunning, Stephen and Stafford, William (eds.) (1992) *Getting the Knack: 20 Poetry Writing Exercises*. Urbana, IL: National Council of Teachers of English.

Frost, Robert (1916) "Out, Out–." *Mountain Interval*, 65. Rahway, NJ: Henry Holt.

Gorrell, Nancy (1989) Let found poetry help your students find poetry. *English Journal*, 78 (2): 30–34. https://doi.org/10.2307/819126

Gorrell, Nancy (1990) Poetry to engage the person. In Phelan, Patricia (ed.) *Literature and Life: Making Connections in the Classroom*, 35–43. Urbana, IL: National Council of Teachers of English.

Gorrell, Nancy (1992a) A teacher's story of renewal. In Dahl, Karin (ed.) *Teacher as Writer: Entering the Professional Conversation*, 19–33. Urbana, IL: National Council of Teachers of English.

Gorrell, Nancy (1992b) "Dear Dolphin." In Dunning, Stephen and Stafford, William (eds.) *Getting the Knack: 20 Poetry Writing Exercises*, 32. Urbana, IL: National Council of Teachers of English.

Gorrell, Nancy (1992c) "To See." In Dunning, Stephen and Stafford, William (eds.) *Getting the Knack: 20 Poetry Writing Exercises*, 130. Urbana, IL: National Council of Teachers of English.

Gorrell, Nancy (1993) Publishing the poetry chapbook: Defining a public self. *English Journal*, 82 (2): 42–46. https://doi.org/10.2307/819702

Handel, Steven N. (2011) A seed op-ed. *Ecological Restoration*, 29 (4): 320–321. https://www.academia.edu/49390765/A_Seed_Op_Ed. https://doi.org/10.3368/er.29.4.320

Handel, Steven N. (2019) Email correspondence with Nancy S. Gorrell.

Kingsporn, Geoff. "Veteran." Qtd in Gorrell (1989: 34).

Lester, Julius (1969) *Search for the New Land: History as Subjective Experience*. New York, NY: Dial Press.

May, Rollo (1975) *The Courage to Create*. New York: W.W. Norton.

Phillips, Don (1989) Let found poetry help your students study literature. *English Journal*, 78 (5): 68–70. https://doi.org/10.2307/819207

Siebert, Arielle (1992a) "Dear Queen Anne Boleyn." In Dunning, Stephen and Stafford, William (eds.) *Getting the Knack: 20 Poetry Writing Exercises*, 150. Urbana, IL: National Council of Teachers of English.

Siebert, Arielle (1992b) "Memory." In Dunning, Stephen and Stafford, William (eds.) *Getting the Knack: 20 Poetry Writing Exercises*, 150. Urbana, IL: National Council of Teachers of English.

Wark, Krista (1992a) "Finnegan's Alley." In Dunning, Stephen and Stafford, William (eds.) *Getting the Knack: 20 Poetry Writing Exercises*, 152. Urbana, IL: National Council of Teachers of English.

Wark, Krista (1992b) "There." In Dunning, Stephen and Stafford, William (eds.) *Getting the Knack: 20 Poetry Writing Exercises*, 103. Urbana, IL: National Council of Teachers of English.

Chapter 14

Discovering the Power of Audience

For a poem is not the end, but the beginning of an excursion.
– William Stafford, *Writing the Australian Crawl*
(Stafford, 1978: 5)

PART ONE: THE STORY OF A POEM IN TWO VOICES

"Blueberry Pie" by Nancy Gorrell

Poet: My grandmother died. Seven years passed. Seven years of writing one grieving poem after another. And then early one morning when I awoke, something inside me said: *stop writing those grieving poems! You can't go on this way.* I was still in bed when I grabbed my journal and pen. Then, I heard an inner voice, and it said: "It was blueberry pie," and from there came a flow of memories about baking with my grandmother, so clear, so fast, I began to write with an ease I can only compare to riding on the crest of a high wave:

Blueberry Pie
by Nancy Gorrell

It was blueberry pie
and the crust was rolled
and folded and flaked and baked

and the heat of the summer day
blended with the heat of the oven
and grandma as pink as a sunset
kissed my cheek with her soft wet
cheeks and the pie splattered blue ooze
on the oven floor and there was only
blueberry air and she peeked in the oven
and it was cooking and grandma said "good"
"it will be ready soon" and she took a spoon
in one hand and me in the other and we opened
the oven door once more and the hot winds slapped
my face and grandma scraped the viscous blue and handed
me the spoon and the burning blue kissed my lips
and we smiled blue all day.

When it was over, I knew it was right. It came as a rare gift and spoke in a voice I had not heard before. I reveled in the joy of it and the hope that "it" would happen again and again.

Poem: *She listened; she heard; she wrote. She did not scratch, cross out, erase or rephrase. She believed in herself. She believed in me. She let me be. Now, she and I talk. She remembers me. Often her soft eyes gaze upon me. I am her poem. Her poem alone but not for long.*

Poet: I am feeling a new feeling – a feeling of light, a feeling of peace, a feeling of connection with myself. I listen to myself all the time now, and I hear. Poems seem to flow off the tip of my pen. One day I decide to take "Blueberry Pie" out of my journal and type it up. I type it up for Newark Public Library's call for poems.

***Poem**: Out of the dark and into the light. . . Suddenly, I am words on a white page. Neat. Typed. I feel her eyes upon me, urgent, expectant. I am on a voyage somewhere. . . out of the dark, into the light. I am posted on a wall with other poems. More eyes gaze upon my words. Now she is carrying me. I am in darkness again, somewhere among the pages of her journal.*

I like it here. It's safe. It's quiet. I am hers. But she is not happy. She is frightened and nervous. She is listening, but not to me. She is hearing the words of other poems. Lots of them. And they are angry and strong. Now she is walking, walking a long walk, down an aisle, up to a podium. Light breaks upon me. She is speaking, speaking my words, shaking, shaking, louder, louder. Then "ah." Silence. Crack, clap, crack, clap. Her heart pulses to the beat. She walks to her seat and sits down. She closes her journal. Darkness falls. I am her poem, but not her poem alone. I have a life of my own.

Poet: "Blueberry Pie" is chosen by the Newark Public Library not only for exhibition, which is why I sent it, but for public reading. Surprise. I have never read a poem to an audience before let alone a poem I have written. I am not prepared, but I am honored. I go with my family. The audience is filled with artists and poets from the Newark arts community. Many are dressed in African garb. The poet before me reads an angry poem to shouts of "Right on, brother!" *How can I go up there and read "Blueberry Pie?"* I am more than frightened. I almost freeze. But I have to go. My poem is announced. I walk quickly. I read slowly, very slowly, putting every word out there. When it is over, I hear the "ah" of delight. Surprise again. I did not know I wrote an "ah" poem. There are smiles and lots of clapping. My poem is a feel-good poem. I feel good, too.

Poem: *She is very proud of me. I am happiest in her heart. She smiles now when she thinks of grandma, and I smile when I think of her eyes upon me. I am never alone. Every day more poems embrace me in her journal. Every day I go from darkness to the light. One day, I hear the typing of keys. Again, I am on a voyage. This time many eyes gaze upon me. I am in darkness a long time. Then the light is so bright I feel hundreds of eyes upon me. I am black words on shiny paper. . . Once again, I have a life of my own.*

Poet: I get up the courage to type up "Blueberry Pie" and send it, along with other poems, to the *English Journal* poetry editor,

Paul Janezco. I wait. While I am waiting, I attend the National Council of Teachers of English convention in Seattle. My friends convince me to read my poem at the "Fountain of the Muse," a late evening reading by teachers and poets. A strong, male poet reads from his work. This poet is none other than a noted teacher-writer from Hawaii. He reads an inspiring poem about his manhood with a plethora of vegetables as metaphors. Oh no, I think, I cannot follow this poem with "Blueberry Pie." But it is my turn, my name is called, and my friends push me up from the table. I hear myself reading at the microphone. I am slightly embarrassed, thinking my poem is too sentimental. I hear polite clapping. Afterward, the poet comes over to me to shake my hand. "Keep writing those sensuous poems," he says with enthusiasm. I am overwhelmed. I did not know I wrote a "sensuous" poem. I think, just maybe I really am a poet.

Poem: *Out of the dark. . . into the light. She is on a voyage, too. Like me, she is discovering who she is and what she means. She has been in the dark a long, long time, but now, she is learning. . . learning that eyes speak a thousand words, sounds speak a thousand words, faces speak a thousand words, and she has spoken just a few. And the words still say, go within. She is learning. . . learning it takes many eyes and many years to get to know me. . . many eyes and many years to go out of the dark, into the light.*

Poet: I am teaching "Blueberry Pie" to my English class. I say to my students, "Every poem is a window into the poet self." I draw on the board a window with four panes marked: *open*, *hidden*, *blind*, and *dark.* I tell my students, "The *open* part is known to you and the poet; the *hidden* part is known only to the poet; the *blind* part is unknown to the poet but known only to you; and the *dark* part is unknown to both you and the poet."

Poem: *She doesn't tell them I have a life of my own and I have been voyaging. Out of the dark into the light. . . onto the pages of poetry books like Reflections on the Gift of a Watermelon Pickle (Gorrell, 1995) and onto the tips of the tongues of Japanese school children learning English. I have traveled to places she* *has never been. I will travel to places she has never known. She is my creator but I am the creation. I will be born again and again, out of the darkness, into the light for as long as the eyes can see.*

PART TWO: ENTERING THE POETIC CONVERSATION

What I Learned: The Power of Audience

> *As the reader seeks to know a poem [...] the reader can return again and again to the poem.*
>
> – David Swanger, *The Poem as Process*
>
> (Swanger, 1974: ix)

I think it is fitting that Poem has the last word, *see*. See, no poem is an island unto itself. Every poem has a creator. That creator is the poem's first audience. That is why I wrote this chapter as a dialogue between myself (creator) and my poem (creation) to give voice to those two selves. That process of "entering," conversing and going "within" produces self-discovery. Step one of "entering the poetic conversation" that should not be underestimated or overlooked is *writing for oneself*, the private inner work that gets drafted and then at times put back in the dark of waiting only to resurface years later when the creator takes on the identity of poet. Such a writer is a poet and should take on the identity of a poet. But taking on that identity is not so simple. (I remind you of the discussion about discarding baggage in Chapter 5.)

Nevertheless, if that creator were the only audience, that poem would live in darkness. Every poem must have a life of its own. That life comes from the moment the poem is seen by other eyes. For such sight brings the poem to light. That light gives the poem a life of its own. After "Blueberry Pie" was exhibited in Newark Public Library and given public voice, I read the poem in multiple poetry venues and submitted it to literary magazines and journals. It gives me joy to think "Blueberry Pie" traveled to Japan, where young children were reciting it. How do I know? Shortly after its publication in *English Journal* (Gorrell, 1990), a teacher from Hawaii emailed me a request for rights to use “Blueberry Pie” on a CD he was preparing for teaching Japanese children English. He told me how the children “loved it so.”

What have I learned entering the poetic conversation? I learned from the path of “Blueberry Pie” the power of audience. Without readers, writers are blind to the mystery of their poems. I was blind to the accessibility and appeal of my poem. I thought of it only as a private, healing poem. I thought of it as my poem. In the process of “entering the poetic conversation with my students, and then the wider audiences of poetry and my discipline, I learned the power of audience to create and re-create meaning in poetry. In the process, I learned I am a poet.

PART THREE: TEACHING “BLUEBERRY PIE” AS WINDOW

> *A poem is never finished, although it can be abandoned. As this is true for the working poet, so it is true for the reader [...]. [T] he poem is a dynamic form for both the poet and the reader.*
>
> – David Swanger, *The Poem as Process*
>
> (Swanger, 1974: ix)

Teaching “Blueberry Pie” and the Johari Window[1]

The Johari Window (Luft and Ingham, 1955) is a psychological model that I have adapted for poetic analysis. In the Johari window model, the window has four quadrants that represent four combinations:

- *Open Space: Known to you – Known to others*
- *Blind Spot: Unknown to yourself – Known to others*
- *Hidden Area: Known to yourself – Unknown to others*

- *Unknown Area: Unknown to yourself – Unknown to others.* I prefer to call the "unknown area" the "Dark" area.

Applying the Johari Window to the teaching of "Blueberry Pie" in creative writing and English classes taught me the power of audience. When I ask students what they think is hidden in the poem, students seem puzzled. I prompt discussion by asking students if they think "Blueberry Pie" is a happy or sad poem. Students seem to divide here in their reactions. Some see happiness in the poem. They say the child loves the grandmother and enjoys tasting the pie. They point out *kiss* and *smile*. Others sense underlying pain, pointing out *slapped*, *viscous*, and *smiled blue.* An astute student says, "I think the grandmother is dead." I ask, "How did you know this?" The student says, "The word *sunset.*" I am pleased. I mention to the class that theoretically, the reader cannot know the hidden part, that once it is known, it becomes *open.* But then I praise my students. I tell them that they have truly found the hidden part of my poem. I tell them my grandmother died a long time ago, and that the poem "Blueberry Pie" was written as a concerted effort to end my grieving and reclaim a happy memory. To me, the poem was born in pain but grew to become an experience to share and savor. "Blueberry Pie" and the Johari Window has become central to my creative writing pedagogy when teaching memory writing.

When I am teaching poetry in English classes, I am tempted to use the "Blueberry Pie" lesson to introduce the concepts of diction and tone. In fact, "Blueberry Pie" is a useful resource for teaching tone, diction, and ambiguity. What words are well-chosen? What is the tone? Happy? Sad? Nostalgic? Bittersweet? When I do this, I also speak like a writer, and in this case, the poet. I tell my students that I did not write "Blueberry Pie" with diction in mind. Nor did I consciously select certain words over others. I explain that the poem was written from within; the images came quickly and subliminally, and there was no editing involved.

Then why, my students often wonder, should they learn to analyze diction and tone? The answer I tell them is two-fold. First, these are the tools readers have to discover the hidden parts of every poem. These hidden parts may or may not be known to the poet, but they are still there, waiting to be discovered. Second, many poets upon revision apply the tools of the craft – precise word choice, concreteness, imagery – to further elucidate, clarify, or enhance meaning. Knowing these tools may help in the process of creating meaning and appreciation of poetry as an art form. But these tools can never define the "truth" of a poem or replace the power of audience in discovering *poetry as window*[2] – on the self, on others, and on the world.

For Your Teacher Journal: "Recalling a Moment Shared"

Reflecting

1. Travel back in your memory to early childhood. Reflect and recall a moment shared with a parent, close relative, or friend.
2. Picture yourself in that moment. What are you doing? Sense all the details of the moment – sights, sounds, smells, tastes, and senses of touch.

Responding

1. Write a memory poem, or prose poem, or memoir of that shared moment.
2. Write a memory poem, prose poem, or memoir inspired by your reading of "Blueberry Pie." It may be a poem when you had mixed or complex feelings about the moment or shared experience.
3. Share your poem with your class using the window lesson framework. Explore with your class the *open, hidden, blind, and dark* parts of your poem. Did you learn something new about your poem or yourself?
4. Reflect upon the power of audience to act as a window into your poem. Enter the poetic conversation with your students.

For Your Students: Teaching "Poetry as Window"

1. Teach your students "poetry as window" by sharing with them the "Blueberry Pie" model or your own response to the "Recalling a Moment Shared" exercise.
2. Have students write their own poems, prose poems, or memoirs to the "Recalling a Moment Shared" writing prompts.
3. If appropriate, have student peers or small groups share results and apply the window framework to their poems.

Model Student Poems: "Moments Shared"

"Daddy's Shoulders" by Sarah Beth Kaufman, Creative Writing, Senior

Daddy's Shoulders
by Sarah Beth Kaufman

I rode on my daddy's shoulders
for seven miles
after I got tired of walking so far.
He said I was so little
He didn't mind too much.
Before we got there
He made me repeat
My name my address my phone number
And daddy's grown-up name too
Because he said there would be
Lots of people there.
He was right.
Everybody was pretty happy.
We sang songs and held up posters:
"No nukes"
Daddy said nukes were big bombs
That could make us all dead.
He said everybody was walking in Washington
To make the nukes disappear.
I wasn't sure what "dead" was yet,

But I sure was proud to be
Riding high on Daddy's shoulders.
I told Daddy that
I was going to carry my kids on my shoulders
When we walked in Washington
Someday too.
He said he hoped I didn't have to.

"Grandpa" by Elise Rosenberg, Creative Writing, Senior

Grandpa
by Elise Rosenberg

He just sat there.
wrinkled, colorless eyes
distant,
lost in the New York humidity.

Nobody said a word.
my hushed, saddened family
stood around
rubbing his shoulders, patting his knee
as loud cars
and the busy traffic of 34th Street
cut the silence
of the crammed third floor apartment.

Perhaps there was a tear
or soft whispers
but as minutes passed like hours
I couldn't bear to look
at my weakened grandfather
covered in his pain.

So, I just stared out the window
at the noisy street below
counting yellow taxi cabs
and wondering how long
I would have to wait
for my grandfather to play with me.

PART FOUR: INTERDISCIPLINARY APPLICATIONS

Discovering the Power of Audience: The Signature Poem

Model Contributor Poem: Arthur J. Stewart, "Ladoga Lake and Nyos," Nominated for a Pushcart Prize

Poets may write many poems. But there comes a time in the life of the poet when a singular poem becomes important to the evolution of the poetic self. Such was the writing of "Ladoga Lake and Nyos" for Arthur J. Stewart. The poem didn't come easily. Rather, it was a long work in progress. Completed and published after 11 years, it took on a life of its own and was nominated for a Pushcart prize, distinguishing Stewart among his science colleagues. What makes this poem an important one rests not only in its passion, heart, and authenticity, but the fact that it is a teaching poem, one that speaks to the moment, to fellow scientists, and to generations of science students: "this is your duty—listen/to each technical thought with the heart: feel it/tremble like water."

Lagoda Lake and Nyos
by Arthur J. Stewart

1.
Ladoga Lake is cold
six months a year,
two hundred thirty
meters deep, all black water
trembling and running loose under waves
and back in autumn of 1942 at night

nothing howled: just the wind
working around basaltic rock on shore.
Leningrad lay in siege
under the German thumb

nine hundred bitter days
and nights and when Ladoga
that winter froze
under the hard glitter of ice
deep enough, it bore trucks
and souls

starving for freedom
and a crust of bread.

Women stood in chill houses overlooking
the lake, breathing frost, thin
trickles of smoke rising, burning the last
sticks of furniture to cook
leather shoes and wall-paper paste
to a weak soup
trying to sustain life.

At night
Ladoga became the lake of life,
ice moaning and snapping like shots.
A truck or two, fed petrol from a brittle can
wrapped in a rag
enough to muffle it
in darkness, everyone listening
for the stuttering drone of German planes
drawing closer.

2.
Forty-four and a half years later,
far to the south, in Cameroon –
Lake Nyos: tropical, sullen
creature like a chameleon
motionless but feeding nonetheless
in silence on volcanic gases
deep in its basin, with the water
trembling as though it knew

just the right time, the perfect thing
for death, before breathing out
a flood of carbon dioxide, killing

one thousand seven hundred
souls sleeping
or walking about in villages
dreaming in life.

3.
A lake
giving life to the dying by freezing –
a lake
breathing death to the living –

nothing in the classical limnology course
I took years ago prepared me for this.
Now my devotion
to life and to lakes in these times
of neither good nor evil, I say

to my students,
this is your duty – listen
to each technical thought with the heart: feel it
tremble like water
(Stewart, 2010)

Stewart's Commentary on "Lagoda Lake and Nyos"

> I like to think this is one of my best poems to date. After being published in final form, "Ladoga Lake and Nyos" was nominated for a Pushcart Prize but did not win. My first draft of this poem was written in January, 1999. It remained an electronic rough-draft file for 11 years before being edited and published first in Circle, Turtle, Ashes in 2010.
>
> (Stewart, 2017)

(See Chapter 15, "Discovering the Creative Process," for drafts of Stewart's "Ladoga Lake and Nyos" in progress.)

For Your Students: "Poetry as Window" Writing Prompts

1. "Listen to each technical thought with the heart." After reading Stewart's science poem, respond to his message in a poem of your own. It could be a memory poem, science poem, or prose poem.
2. Find an aspect of science or a scientific issue that touches your heart as deeply as "lakes" touched Stewart's heart. Write that science poem inspired by what inspires you to wonder and question.
3. Write your own poem of address to science or math or any other subject. What is its "duty?" This could also be a poem addressing the scientist, the mathematician, the environmentalist, the naturalist, the historian, the artist and so forth. Title the poem "To the Scientist," for example.
4. What makes you "tremble?" Write a poem, science poem, nature poem, or prose poem in which one word, or the word "tremble" reverberates and has several meanings for you.

Chapter 14 Notes

1 The Johari Window was developed in 1955 by Joseph Luft and Harrington Ingham that talks about the relationship and mutual understanding between group members (Luft and Ingham, 1955). The term, *Johari*, was coined by Luft and Harrington by joining their two first names. The Johari Window is primarily used in communication theory (https://www.communicationtheory.org/the-johari-window-model/), but I find it useful for "entering" poetic understanding and literary criticism. I've found it especially useful when using a reader response approach.

2 "Poetry as Window into Self" is the title of a workshop I have facilitated for professional development to Morris School District teachers and also for adult poetry groups. The use of "Blueberry Pie" through the lens of the Johari window serves as the central starting point of the pedagogy of the workshop.

Chapter 14 References

Gorrell, Nancy (1990) "Blueberry Pie." *English Journal*, 79 (8): 88. https://doi.org/10.2307/818838

Gorrell, Nancy (1995) "Blueberry Pie." In Dunning, Stephen and Stafford, William (eds.) *Reflections on a Gift of a Watermelon Pickle and Other Modern Verse* (2nd edition), 10. Glenview, IL: Scott Foresman.

Luft, Joseph and Ingham, Harrington (1955) The Johari window, a graphic model of interpersonal awareness. *Proceedings of the Western Training Laboratory in Group Development*. Los Angeles: University of California at Los Angeles.

Stafford, William (1978) *Writing the Australian Crawl: Views on the Writer's Vocation*. Ann Arbor, MI: University of Michigan Press.

Stewart, Arthur J (1999) On the need for poetry by scientists. *Bulletin of the Ecological Society of America*, 80 (2): 133–134.

Stewart, Arthur J. (2010) "Ladoga Lake and Nyos." *Circle, Turtle, Ashes*, 39–41. Knoxville, TN: Celtic Cat.

Swanger, David (1974) Preface. *The Poem as Process*, ix–xi. New York, NY: Harcourt Brace Jovanovich.

Chapter 15

Discovering the Creative Process

To make something well is to give yourself to it, to seek wholeness, to follow spirit. To learn to make something well can take your whole life. It's worth it.

– Ursula Le Guin, *Steering the Craft*
(Le Guin, 1998: xi)

PART ONE: A TEACHING STORY

It Came without Warning

Nearly three decades ago, while driving to do errands in my hometown, I passed the local supermarket. I looked up at the sign. The next thing I knew, I heard the words that came from within – *when grandma came down*. I quickly pulled over, grabbed a pencil and a scrap of paper. I let the words flow. . . *when grandma came down. . . from the porch step by step. . . black shoes marking the path to where I was sitting. . . she took off her apron. . . brushed the hair from her windswept eyes and sat in the grass. . . she didn't say "feh" when I ate the dandelion weed, and the stockings rolled at her ankles sparkled in the sun when she took off her shoes. . . and we walked down the path to the water's edge. . . my hands waving the breeze . . . her hands waving goodbye. . . our feet touching, touching, the earth and then the water. . . and when she took off her dress and placed it ever so gently on a rock. . . our hands fished for fish in the water. . . and nothing said 'thou shall not' when grandma came down.*

I had no idea why these words came to me when they did, or how they did. I just knew it was a "gift" from grandma, and that I had to write it down. I also knew it felt good. I smiled to myself, started the motor, and drove home. Once there, I went to my computer and typed up the words without editing to shape a poem. Still reveling in the mystery of its presence, I titled it "Grandma Came Down."

Grandma Came Down
by Nancy Gorrell

when grandma came down
from the porch
step by step
black shoes marking
time on the path
to where I was sitting
she took off her apron
brushed the hair from
her windswept eyes
and sat in the grass

she didn't say 'feh'
when I ate the puff
of dandelion weed
and the stockings
rolled at her ankles
sparkled in the sun
when she took off
her shoes

and we walked
down the path
to the water's edge
my hands waving the breeze
her hands waving goodbye
our feet touching

touching the earth
and then the water

and when she
took off her dress
and placed it
ever so gently
on a rock
our hands fished
for fish in the water

and nothing said,
'thou shall not'
when grandma came down.

(Gorrell, 1993)

I looked on the screen. At the time I wasn't thinking of craft. I was thinking of how it made me feel as I wrote it. It felt right; it felt true. I was in awe of the wonder of its coming. I only knew that it came *without warning*. Even to this day, I do not know why it came.

One possible answer: faith. At the time of writing, I felt grandma was somehow talking to me. The poem was her way of saying *I'm here; I'll always be with you*. I am a child in the poem, and she is coming back down to me from the porch steps. I am happy; she is happy. The words seemed to come to me and through me. I was the conduit writing it down.

In the years that followed, I have re-read "Grandma Came Down" many times. I have never edited it. I have let the mystery be the mystery, but I have reflected upon its truth. There are images in the poem that puzzled me from its creation. Some images are true. Others are not. True: there is a picture in an album of grandma standing on the porch in the Adirondacks. She has her hand over her eyes to shade the sun. She's wearing an apron over a long summer dress. It looks as if she has just stepped out from a hot day cooking. Her stockings are rolled at the ankles. I always remember her stockings rolled at the ankles. She did say "feh" whenever I did messy things like eat rocks and snails. Not true: grandma never fished; she never swam; she never touched anything "dirty;" and she never would take off her dress and swim partially naked. Most importantly, what happened did not literally, happen.

Another possible answer. This poem came from another place – my unconscious self – the place that writers tap to let it flow. "The unconscious creates, the ego edits."[1] I recall hearing Stanley Kunitz express it this way at one of his readings at the Geraldine R. Dodge Poetry Festival at Waterloo Village in Stanhope, New Jersey, which I attended over the years with my students. It was my unconscious that created the poem "When Grandma Came Down." My ego, or conscious self, not only edits, but thinks, reflects, and searches for meaning. What is the truth of my poem? Every poem is a window into self through the lenses defining what is *open*, *hidden*, *blind*, and *dark* (recall Chapter 14). "Grandma Came Down" is the darkest poem I have written to date.

Much time has passed since the writing of "Grandma Came Down" and the writing of this chapter. In the process, I now realize something I could not have realized before. "Grandma Came Down" was the last poem that I wrote about grandma. Why? Perhaps because my wish for her "to come down" came true. She's down here with me in memory. As I remember, I pass on her legacy to my children and my children's children.

PART TWO: HOW WRITERS WRITE

Joyce Carol Oates: On her Writing Process

> *Writing, for me is primarily remembering. Which means that "writing" isn't specifically verbal for me, as it must be for most poets: it's as likely to be cinematic, dramatic, emotional, auditory, and shimmeringly unformed before it becomes actual language, transformed into words on a page [...]. I need to imagine first, purely without language; and then remember.*
>
> – Joyce Carol Oates, *The Faith of a Writer: Life, Craft, Art* (Oates, 2003: 140–141)

That "Precious Little Area of Confusion"

William Stafford puzzles about the process of writing held by "what others say." As a poet, it suggests a problem for him:

> They talk about "skills" in writing. Without denying that I do have experience [. . .] I must insist that I am often baffled about what "skill" has to do with the precious little area of confusion when I do not know what I am going to say and then I find out what I am going to say. That precious interval I am unable to bridge by skill. What can I witness about it?
>
> (Stafford,1978: 19)

For Stafford, the problem "remains mysterious." How do you resolve that "precious little area of confusion" when you do not know what you want to say and then you find out what you are going to say? Is it (a) intuition, (b) imagination, (c) faith, or (d) skill? All of the above? None of the above? E. M. Forster answers the question with a question: "*How do I know what I think until I see what I say?*" (Forster, 1927/2005: 99; cited from Swedberg, 2020: 1, 3, 14; emphasis added).[2] That question rings so true that it has become an axiom or aphorism for the writing to learn and process writing movements for nearly a century. (See Part Three below for further discussion of the Forster aphorism.)

William Stafford's puzzlement says more about how to write than many texts on craft. He faces the undeniable fact that most writers cannot explain the mystery, the "how" of the artist self. Why? Because the artist self, the part that creates, comes from the unconscious self, the realm of mystery. Yet Stafford encourages us all by showing how simple it is to write from within:

> All of us must feel puzzled about how we are so inventive as to be able to talk along through complexities with our friends, not needing to plan what we are going to say, but never stalled for long in our confident forward progress. Skill? If so, it is a skill we all have, something we must have learned before the age of three or four.
>
> (Stafford, 1978: 19)

The Dual Nature of the Writer: Artist and Artisan

Early in the 20th century, Dorothea Brande in *Becoming a Writer* (Brande, 1934/1981) sheds light on the how writers write by explaining what she identifies as the dual nature of the writer. She encourages writers to first think of themselves as "two-persons-in-one." Person #1 is the "artist" self – the creator, the child within, the "emotional" side that is the unconscious self. Person #2 is the artisan self – the workman, the critic, the adult within; the discriminating, temperate, and just side that is the conscious self (Brande, 1934/1981: 38–39). "It [the artist side] must work continually with and through the emotional and childlike side, or we have no work of art" (p. 39). Brande concludes: "The writer's first task is to get these two elements of his nature into balance, to combine their aspects into one integrated character" (p. 39). But paradox prevails because "the first step toward that happy result is to split them apart for consideration and training!" (p. 39). (You may wish to refer back to Chapter 9 on "Balancing Freedom and Structure.")

In writing "Grandma Came Down," I certainly can see how it emerged from "the child within," the unconscious "creator self." But what "skill" was involved? I did almost no editing. Was there any adult, conscious self? I think the answer is "yes," in the sense of both conscious receptivity and conscious action. No work of art would exist if I were not receptive to the voice I was hearing. In that receptivity, I took a risk, pulled over the car, and took some notes. That would have ended it all if the disciplined, adult, artisan hadn't taken over. Then I went home, typed up the notes, shaping a poem. No work of art would exist if I were not practiced in writing it down; that is, practiced in writing from the flow of my unconscious self and practiced in composing poems. The skill to write it down in poem form enabled the final work of art to be.

Ursula Le Guin in the introduction to *Steering the Craft* guides us further: "Skill in writing frees you to write what you want to write. It may also show you what you want to write. Craft enables art" (Le Guin, 1998: xi). Le Guin distinguishes between art, which she considers a "gift," and skill, which can be learned and earned. "There's luck in art. There's the gift. You can't earn that [...]. But you can learn skill, you can earn it. You can learn to deserve your gift" (p. xi).

How do writers write? To fully answer the question, we must consider the writer's nature, the dual personality of artist and artisan within, as well as the dual sources of the writer's craft – the unconscious and conscious realms. The former houses our creativity, the latter our skills of craft. That is why writers need to develop two practices – a *creative practice* to develop the creator within the unconscious realm and a *writer's practice* to develop the artisan within the conscious realm. Both Stafford and Le Guin inform us about the dual nature of the creative writer and the creative writing process. Clearly, we need to integrate the two selves by nurturing the creative powers of the unconscious realm while honing the skills of the conscious realm. When the "creative juices" run dry, the writer needs to *recharge* with the challenges of craft; when the creative juices run too fast, the writer needs to *restrain* with the art of craft. In the process of practicing craft, the writer hopes inspiration will emerge. Conversely, if a writer dwells too much in the realm of craft, with conscious technique and imitation, vision and voice may be lost. The aim, according to Le Guin, is to use practice until "we don't have to think about them consciously at all because they have become skills" (p. xi). At such a point, the artist and artisan have become one – the *writer self.*

Write from Your Heart, Edit with Your Head

So how do you write? You write from your heart, from your unconscious self, from your spirit, if you will, listening to the inner voices that are there to be heard, always being receptive and open to flow. Then afterwards, you re-read, rewrite, revise, write some more, re-read, rewrite, revise, and write some more. You keep going back, then move forward, then going back, over and over the material, until at last, you think you have discovered what you want to say, and at least for the moment, the best way to say it. It's not a linear process but a recursive one, looping back and forth, never quite sure of its conclusion. But somehow you know, through instinct, intuition, exhaustion, heart and head, and all of the above that it is "finished." The poem "Grandma Came Down" concluded itself. I could not write another line. Not from exhaustion or frustration but because what was to be said was, in fact, said.

The Critic Within: Separate the Creator and the Editor

> *It is important to separate the creator and the editor or internal censor when you practice writing so that the creator has free space to breathe, explore and express.*
>
> – Natalie Goldberg, *Writing Down the Bones: Freeing the Writer Within*
>
> (Goldberg, 1986: 26)

There was one part of my writing self that was absent during and after composing "Grandma Came Down," and that was the critic. The critic comes from the head, not the heart. The critic, all head, brings intellect to bear. The critic analyzes, separates, dissects. Dorothea Brande gives us guidance:

> There is no arrogance like that of the intellect [...]. The reason is confirmed in its delusion of being the more important member of the writing team. It is not. Its duties are indispensable but secondary; they come before and after the period of intensive writing.
>
> (Brande, 1934/1981: 57)

If we heed Brande's wisdom, we will keep the critic at bay.

What Writers Tell Us About the Writing Process

> *There is no logical A-to-B-to-C way to become a good writer. One neat truth about writing cannot answer it all. There are many truths*
>
> – Natalie Goldberg, *Writing Down the Bones: Freeing the Writer Within*
>
> (Goldberg, 1986: 3)

As for writing the wrong way, there is almost no wrong way to write fiction; there are only ways that, for a given writer, are more efficient or less. Any approach will do.

– John Gardner, *On Becoming a Novelist*
(Gardner, 1983/1999: 137–138)

A writer is not so much someone who has something to say as he is someone who has found a process that will bring about new things he would not have thought of if he had not started to say them.

– William Stafford, *Writing the Australian Crawl: Views on the Writer's Vocation*
(Stafford, 1978: 17)

William Stafford gets it right when he says writers "engage in a process." Stafford calls this "process-rather-than-substance" view of writing. His final reflection is an affirmation to all who want to be writers:

> Writers may not be special, sensitive, or talented in any unusual sense. They are simply engaged in sustained use of a language skill we all have. Their "creations" come about through confident reliance on stray impulses that will, with trust, find occasional patterns that are satisfying.
>
> (Stafford, 1978: 20)

The Creative Process: What Research Says

Five-Step Creative Process: Recursive not Linear

If there are "many truths," "no one way," and "any approach will do," what commonalities exist in the creative process? According to Csikszentmihalyi (1996), the creative process proceeds in five steps:

- a period of *preparation*, becoming immersed, consciously or not, in a set of problematic issues;

- a period of *incubation*, during which ideas churn around below the threshold of consciousness;
- a period of *insight* called the "Aha!" moment, when pieces of the puzzle fall together;
- a period of *evaluation*, when the creator must decide whether the insight is valuable and worth pursuing;
- a period of *elaboration*, which takes the most time and the hardest work.

(pp. 79–80)

Implications for Our Teaching: Emphasize Becoming

Awareness of how writers write informs our teaching in critical ways. Clearly, we must teach for both the artist and the artisan within ourselves and our students. Note that major references for this chapter emphasize becoming, more specifically, *Becoming a Writer* (Brande, 1934/1981) and *Becoming a Novelist* (Gardner, 1983/1999). Our teaching must focus on becoming as well for ourselves and our students. Our activities and the models, exercises, and prompts we use to teach; our classroom norms, feedback and evaluation methods, and the grading systems we apply; together with the overall objectives and goals of a course – all must focus on nurturing and developing the creative heart as well as the skillful head. Equal time and space should be allotted for creativity, intuitive "daydreaming" activities, and reflection that free the unconscious self, as well as lessons in craft, modeling, revising, rewriting, reorganizing, and editing. Most importantly, we must empower ourselves and our students to find our/their own voices and styles of writing. Knowing there is no one way to write, knowing there is no absolute answer to the "how to" question, and knowing that the teacher-writer takes on multiple roles in the classroom frees us all to become our own writer selves and then to teach according to that expanded *teacher-writer self*.

PART THREE: INTERDISCIPLINARY APPLICATIONS

How do I know what I think until I see what I say?
– E. M. Forster, *Aspects of the Novel*
(Forster, 1927/2005: 99)

Richard Swedberg, a social scientist from Cornell University, uses E. M. Forster's aphorism – *How do I know what I think until I see what I say?* – as a point of departure for his groundbreaking discussion on creative theorizing (Swedberg, 2020): "It's literal meaning is that through the very act of speaking you get to know what you think; but the aphorism also has a suggestive quality to it" (p. 1). Swedberg's article confirms the aphorism's significance for science, social science, and creativity:

> It takes a few moments of reflection to figure out what is meant, namely that it is first *after* you have spoken that you are in a position to know what you are thinking. What a person is trying to say is in other words inseparable from the very act of speaking. At first this may seem paradoxical, then commonsensical. Don't we all we begin to speak without knowing exactly what we are going to say? This is no doubt true for everyday conversation. But it is also true – and this is where it gets interesting – for moments of creativity. A writer, a painter and so on will often start to work on something, without knowing exactly what the result will be. It is probably this vague but suggestive link to creativity that explains why the aphorism has been so popular with writers and scientists.
>
> (Swedberg, 2020: 1)

Implications of the Forster Aphorism for Creativity

Swedberg notes the "suggestive link" to creativity of the Forster aphorism while confirming its popularity with writers and scientists alike. This book supports the relevance of the aphorism for writers, teachers, and students by noting that there is no one way to write creatively, by advocating process writing, and by the concept of teachers, students, and their writing as works in progress (see Chapter 1). The significance of the aphorism is central to this book's discussion of creativity (see Chapter 2), the creative process itself, and our teaching as co-learners and co-writers in the classroom (see Chapters 6 and 7).

Implications of the Forster Aphorism for the Creative Process: "Court Your Subconscious"

Swedberg describes the creative process, which he particularly references to theorizing, as a more general process involving a first stage of staying in, or "courting" your subconscious, followed by a more intentional stage:

> [Y]ou need to court your subconscious, approach it hat in hand, so to speak. You need to court it and spend time with it, hoping in this way that something interesting will happen. And when it does, you need to be ready to switch gears because the next step is to explicate the idea and build it out. At this latter stage analytical thought must replace intuitive thinking. Switching back and forth between these different types of thinking, over a period of time, is what will allow that first little fish of intuition to grow into one that is bigger […].
>
> (Swedberg, 2020: 12)

This book's pedagogy supports the idea of "courting your subconscious" through the use of stream-of-consciousness writing, non-stop writing, freewriting, recalling hidden images, visualization, relaxation, and brainstorming activities. As a poet, I have experienced writing poetry from my subconscious self. Recall the model of my poem, "Grandma Came Down" in this chapter. I describe my creative process as "coming without warning" while I was driving to the supermarket. I didn't know why "grandma came down" at that moment. I just know that it happened and that it came somewhere from my subconscious. The why of it remains a mystery.

What I do know is that the creative process from Brande's "artist self" or Kunitz's "heart" or Swedberg's intuitive self is ongoing and without end. Perhaps "grandma will come down" again someday.

Implications of the Forster Aphorism for Science and Scientists

> *Very importantly, according to Merton, the Forster aphorism may help to explain what scientists actually do when they do their research, which is something that differs from the way that scientific research is usually portrayed in textbooks.*
>
> (Swedberg, 2020: 10)

Swedberg sees the aphorism as applying to science and social science. In his discussion of this point, he reproduces a passage which Robert K. Merton, drawing from his earlier work *Social Theory and Social Structure* (Merton, 1949/1968), quoted in a letter to the Nobel Laureate Gerald Edelman (Merton, 1978b) discussing the Forster aphorism in its application to science. The passage characterizes:

> […] a rock-bound difference between the finished versions of scientific work as they appear in print and the actual course of inquiry followed by the inquirer. The difference is a little like that between textbooks of 'scientific method' and the ways in which scientists actually think, feel, and go about their work. The books on method present ideal patterns: how one ought to think, feel and act, but these tidy normative patterns, as everyone who has engaged in inquiry knows, do not reproduce the typically untidy, opportunistic adaptations that scientists make in the course of their inquiries. Typically, the scientific paper or monograph […] reproduces little or nothing of the intuitive leaps, false starts, mistakes, loose ends and happy accidents that actually clutter up the inquiry. (Merton, 1949/1968: 6; 1978b: 8; qtd in Swedberg: 5).

This book's pedagogy encourages a creative process that allows for "the intuitive leaps, false starts, mistakes, loose ends and happy accidents" that may not be reflected in the finished product. It also encourages interdisciplinary initiatives in the curriculum and specifically in writing that bring science and social science together with English language arts. It further supports an interdisciplinary approach to scientific inquiry, method, and teaching whereby students are encouraged to express how they feel about science, scientific inquiry, and discovery through the use of on-site field work, field journals, laboratory journals, and additionally, the writing of science poetry. This author advocates that students act as professional scientists and science writers through STEM and STEAM projects and through Writing Across the Curriculum (WAC) and Creative Writing Across the Curriculum (CWAC) projects.[3]

Serendipity, Creative Cognition, and Thinking

> *Serendipity: "the discovery, by chance or sagacity, of valid results which were not sought for"*
>
> "Sociological theory"
> (Merton, 1945: 50; qtd in Swedberg, 2020: 15, note 3)

Merton connected the Forster aphorism to serendipity and other significant facts about thinking:

> - Creative cognition is an ongoing process. It's very different from having a routinized, carefully scripted, linear mode of analysis.
> - When one is thinking anew, the essential is to discover what one is thinking as it moves along. It's a process not a conclusion.
> - Thinking is not a thought; it is an activity giving rise to thoughts […].
> - The creative thought is registered by one's being surprised by what one says. (Merton, 1984: 360; qtd in Swedberg, 2020: 3)

Much that can be said about creative cognition and theorizing for science and scientists applies as well to writers and writing. What writers and poets say about their creative process in this chapter confirms critical commonalities. Writing creatively is much more a recursive, ongoing process than a linear one. For teacher-writers and student-writers, chance and serendipity play critical roles in discovery and surprise. So does "writing to learn" (Emig, 1977). As pointed out in the Introduction, this author encourages teacher-readers to journal while reading this book. Such journaling while teaching will provide not only raw material for writing, but will provide the "activity giving rise to thoughts" that will inspire and transform teachers becoming writers while they teach.

Implications of the Forster Aphorism for Creative Theorizing: Speaking and "That Moment in the Classroom"

Richard Swedberg's first major point about "creative theorizing with the help of speaking and writing is that this will take different forms depending on who is being addressed" (Swedberg, 2020: 10). He identifies "at least three potential audiences for the theorizer: yourself, other social scientists, and students" (p. 10). He offers considerable discussion of Merton's capacity to come up with new ideas while lecturing to his students. For example, he cites the following reflection by Merton:

> No matter how carefully prepared the lecture, I have always derived the greatest satisfaction from hearing something said, even hearing myself say something, that was wholly unanticipated and interesting. The kind of observation that grew out of the sheer experience of pursuing a thought or problem that had been formulated to the point that it was in my notes, but which I hadn't been about to carry any further until that moment in the classroom.
>
> (Merton, 1978a; qtd in Swedberg, 2020: 5)

As teachers, we have all had "that moment in the classroom" while speaking or lecturing, when a new idea miraculously occurs. It confirms at once the aphorism's significance for the act of speaking as well as for teaching and learning, and the role our students play as audience and co-learners in the process. Most importantly, such moments in the classroom are often surprising, eureka moments to be shared by teachers and students with appreciation and understanding as co-learners.

"Speaking to Enlighten Oneself": "The Effect of a Muse"

Swedberg (2020: 8) relates an important anecdote by Kleist (1951), who wrote about the way in which ideas can be triggered by speech. Kleist described how he had sometimes spoken to his sister when he could not solve a mathematical problem. Although his sister knew nothing of algebra, "lo and behold, if I mention it to my sister, who is sitting behind me and working, I discover facts which whole hours of brooding, perhaps, would not have revealed" (Kleist, 1951: 42; qtd in Swedberg: 8). Swedberg (2020: 11) suggests that Kleist's sister was like a *muse* who inspired him. Swedberg suggests that Kleist's sister inspired him to see a solution to the algebraic problem while he was speaking. In his view, the inspiration for Kleist was certainly his sister, his muse, but also the act of "speaking to enlighten oneself" (Swedberg, 2020: 11).

"Writing to Enlighten Oneself": Private Writing

Attention to audience is central to the core beliefs, thesis, and pedagogy of this author as demonstrated throughout this book (see Chapter 14). Writing for oneself is an experience encouraged for teacher-readers (see Introduction) and student-writers (see Chapter 6). Writing for oneself is encouraged when teacher-readers journal and student writers keep private journals and engage in multiple personal writing activities (for example: non-stop writing, freewriting, subconscious writing, memory association technique, imaging, recalling hidden images). Writing for others is encouraged for student writers in the creative writing and composition classrooms when students choose to share or voice their writings (see Chapter 6). Such moments clarify thinking, new ideas, and creativity. Students and teachers are encouraged to act as professionals by seeking wider audiences beyond the classroom by entering contests or the professional conversation through publication (see Chapters 10 and 13).

Swedberg describes his process of private writing as occurring over a period of time in short notetaking spurts, "proceeding every day for two to three weeks; and by the end of the period, I have often made progress" (p. 11). This author uses private writing for student journals in creative writing and composition classrooms as well as English literature classrooms, privileging the privacy of students' writing in journal, electronic, and digital forms.

"Speaking to Enlighten Others": The Context of Justification

> *When the audience changes from being yourself to that of other social scientists, the whole dynamic of speaking and writing changes. You now typically find yourself in that part of the research process that is known as the context of justification.*
>
> (Swedberg, 2020: 11)

Swedberg (2020), in agreement with Merton (1978b: 9–10, 13), maintains that "speaking to enlighten others" or reporting what you already know, is not part of the creative process, and in fact, obscures the process of discovery. Yet Swedberg notes that scientists and social scientists both write and speak with others in mind (pp. 11–12). He therefore wonders whether "a whole group of [scientists or social scientists] could operate as a collective muse for one another (p. 11). He speculates that under "the right circumstances," speaking can be an occasion for enlightening oneself, clarifying thinking, and finding inspiration to be creative – though he believes this is not common (p. 11).

The Forster Aphorism and the "Heart of Theorizing"

Swedberg's final message is heartening for teachers across the disciplines seeking to engage in the exciting, at times messy and mysterious, creative process. This chapter I hope will inspire and empower you to engage in the process of "court[ing] your subconscious" (Swedberg, 2020: 12), which is summed up below:

> The process […] stands at the very heart of theorizing: spending time with yourself, gently coaxing your subconscious into saying something interesting, perhaps by taking notes of what you think, by speaking to yourself, or just by doing nothing except being attentive to yourself. If this process is repeated day after day for some period of time (say, 2–3 weeks), the original idea may grow into something that can become a theory with propositions and testable hypotheses – a nice big fish. This is how you will get to know what you think – and also to create something that you could not have figured out in advance.
>
> (Swedberg, 2020: 12)

Implications for Our Teaching: Let Teaching be Your Muse

The Forster aphorism presents to teachers across the disciplines critical questions for consideration about speaking, writing, and teaching:

- *Is not the act of teaching also "speaking to enlighten oneself"?*
- *Have you ever taught a class where your speaking began with one idea or point but ended with a new idea or realization?*
- *Have you ever taught a class where your speaking/lecturing began in one place and ended in another place of realization?*
- *How can we facilitate speaking and writing to learn (WTL) activities within our subject classrooms?*
- *How can we facilitate speaking and writing to learn (WTL) activities across the curriculum?*

These open-ended questions are best answered by teacher-readers becoming teachers who write. If you are reading this chapter, you have already experienced the activities in the Writer Self chapters of this book (Chapters 11,12, 13, and 14), and you are most likely to be able to view teaching as a creative process and an as an art form. Whether you are an English teacher, a science or math teacher, or a teacher in any other discipline, you also most likely have experienced the creative process. It is this author's hope that at this point you have also experienced the joy of teaching as creative muse.

Model Contributor Poem: "Ladoga Lake and Nyos" – Arthur J. Stewart Shares His Creative Process

> *Every science thing has a history and has factual facets that can and should be understood emotionally as well as technically.*
>
> – Arthur J. Stewart (February 12, 2017)

Arthur Stewart, in "On the Need for Poetry by Scientists" (Stewart, 1999), discloses to his colleagues:

> At a professional (technical) meeting several months ago, I was bold enough to tell an audience of scientists that a national award I had recently earned for one poem was 'logistically, about ten times more difficult to achieve than National Science Foundation funding." The statement generated a good laugh, yet it is true. (p. 133)

The poem Stewart was referring to, "Ladoga Lake and Nyos" (Stewart, 2010), did not ultimately receive the award. Yet it is a signature poem for Stewart, one dearest to his heart, inextricably tied to the essence of his field of science, aquatic ecology, and his teaching of limnology. For the last two decades, Stewart has published numerous technical papers, but he has also published seven books of science poetry. He remains a tireless advocate for the "need for poetry by scientists." Conversely, he's a model for the arts on the need for science in arts and humanities education as well.

"Ladoga Lake and Nyos" in Draft Form

The poem "Ladoga Lake and Nyos" is a study in the creative process. A poem in progress for 11 years (1999–2010), it demonstrates Arthur Stewart's sustained commitment and artful skill. Addressed to his students, the poem embraces both head and heart. As Stewart shares with us his *poem in progress* and his commentary on his process, we see the artist and artisan at work. In his email interview, I asked him the question: Can you share with us your 11-year process in writing "Ladoga Lake and Nyos?"

Arthur J. Stewart's Commentary on Drafts and Process

> **"Ladoga Lake and Nyos"**
> My first draft of this poem was written in January, 1999. It remained an electronic rough-draft file for 11 years before being edited and published first in *Circle, Turtle, Ashes* in 2010. The early draft version of this poem, like the final published version, contained three parts, in the same sequence. However, the poem's final version was quite different than the draft, with respect to line breaks and word choices. In particular, the third part of the poem, in the final version, became student-focused and much more intentional.

Original Draft (The third portion of Ladoga Lake and Nyos)

I am confused
today about a frozen lake
giving life, a tropical lake
capable of breathing out death.
I tell you in these times
of neither good nor evil
more than the water trembles.

Final Version

The final version, in comparison, turned out like this:

A lake
giving life to the dying by freezing—

a lake
breathing death to the living—

nothing in the classical limnology course
I took years ago prepared me for this.
Now my devotion

to life and to lakes in these times
of neither good nor evil, I say

to my students,
this is your duty—listen

to each technical thought with the heart: feel it
tremble like water.

> The section became longer, and led with the lakes, rather than with "I am confused." This change was important because it directs the reader to the technical question, rather than to the author. Then the final version of the poem alludes gently to the idea that I might be confused ("nothing … prepared me for this") before expressing, in a strongly worded statement, the singular important message "this is your duty—listen / to each technical thought with the heart: feel it / tremble like water."
>
> (Stewart, 2017)

In his email correspondence with me, Stewart further comments:

> Note that trembling/tremble is used once in each portion of the poem, which I think reinforces its importance and value in the poem's singular message to limnology students.
>
> (Stewart, 2017)

(See Chapter 14 for Stewart's complete poem.)

Stewart then states:

> I would definitely include this poem as a teaching tool in a limnology course, if I ever have the opportunity to so. I would

use it on the first day of class, to "set the stage" for the idea that every lake is different from every other lake, and that scientists – regardless of discipline area – should lead their students to understand "every science thing has a history, and has factual facets that can and should be understood emotionally as well as technically."

(Stewart, 2017)

For Your Teacher Journal: Artist and Artisan

Interdisciplinary Exercises

1. Choose any work in progress you have written from your Teacher's Journal or the exercises from Section Two, the Writer Self. Choose a piece of writing important to you or close to your heart. Find a key word or image in your poem, prose poem, or memoir, one that represents the "heart" of your writing. Like Stewart, consider repeating a key word; that is, using repetition in different contexts in various verses or lines.
2. Choose from your Teacher's Journal or exercises from Section Two, the Writer's Self, what you consider a finished piece of writing. Re-read your writing like an artist. Does the writing have heart? Is there an underlying emotional side? Now re-read your writing like an artisan (with head or intellect). Does your writing make sense? What could make it stronger? More meaningful? Cut out 5–10 words, phrases, or lines that you now see as unnecessary verbiage. Tighten your writing. Make every word count in your poem, prose poem, or memoir.
3. Choose any poem, prose poem, or memoir from the exercises in Sections One and Two. Start a new piece of writing from the first or last lines of the writing. Expand your imagination, flow, and fluency. Create a new piece of writing from the original.

For Your Students: Discovering the Creative Process

1. Introduce your students to "discovering the creative process" through the exercises in this chapter suggested for teachers practicing the dual nature of the writer – artisan and artist, head and heart. Share or model for your students your own experience with the "head" and "heart" exercises.
2. Have students practice using "head" to tighten or cut out unnecessary words, lines, or passages in a piece of writing from their journals, or any practice exercise from Sections One or Two. Challenge them to make every word count in a poem, prose poem, or memoir by cutting 5–10 words.

Chapter 15 Notes

1 Although this quote is attributed in many online sites to Stanley Kunitz, neither my editor, Martha Pennington, nor myself could find a published source for it.

2 Richard Swedberg (Swedberg, 2020: 3) confirms the literary origin of Forster's aphorism as *Aspects of the Novel* (Forster, 1927/2005: 99), crediting the research to Robert K. Merton's letters (Merton, 1978a, b) and meetings with Gerald Edelman. According to Swedberg (2020), "Merton suggested that Forster had emphasized the whimsical nature of the aphorism by placing it in the mouth of an older woman, known by her acquaintances as being not very logical" (p. 3). Contextualized in this woman's dialogue, the Forster aphorism expresses a defiance of logic: "'Logic! Good gracious! What rubbish!' she exclaimed. '*How can I tell what I think till I see what I say?*'" (Forster, 1927/2005: 99; qtd in Swedberg, 2020: 3, 14; emphasis added).

3 See this author's work *Writing Poetry through the Eyes of Science: Scientific Literacy and Poetic Response* (Gorrell with Colfax, 2012) and Chapter 18 on Curious Science (cSw) Writers; Anne Osbourn's Art and Writing Initiative (SAW); and Youth Birding Alaska (YBA).

Chapter 15 References

Brande, Dorothea (1934/1981) *Becoming a Writer*. New York, NY: Tarcher/Putnam. Originally published by Harcourt, Brace.

Csikszentmihalyi, Mihaly (1996) *Creativity: Flow and the Psychology of Discovery and Invention.* New York, NY: Harper Perennial.

Emig, Janet (1977) Writing as a mode of learning. *College Composition and Communication*, 28 (2): 122–128. https://doi.org/10.2307/356095

Forster, E. M. (1927/2005) *Aspects of the Novel*. London: Penguin Classics. Originally published by Edward Arnold. Cited from Swedberg (2020: 1, 3, 14).

Gardner, John (1983/1999) *On Becoming a Novelist*. New York, NY: W. W. Norton.

Goldberg, Natalie (1986) *Writing Down the Bones: Freeing the Writer Within.* Boston, MA: Shambhala Publications, Inc.

Gorrell, Nancy (1993) "Grandma Came Down." *Footwork: Paterson Literary Review*, 23: 114. Paterson, NJ: Passaic County Community College.

Kleist, Heinrich von (1951) On the gradual construction of thoughts during speech (tr. Michael Hamburger). *German Life and Letters*, 5 (1): 8–9, 42–46. Cited from Swedberg (2020: 8, 11). https://doi.org/10.1111/j.1468-0483.1951.tb01029.x

Le Guin, Ursula K. (1998) *Steering the Craft*. Portland, OR: Eighth Mountain Press.

Merton, Robert K. (1945) Sociological theory. *American Journal of Sociology*, 50 (6): 462–473. https://doi.org/10.1086/219686

Merton, Robert K. (1949/1968) *Social Theory and Social Structure* (3rd edition). New York, NY: Free Press. Cited from Swedberg (2020: 5).

Merton, Robert K. (1978a) Letter to Gerald Edelman on the Forster aphorism, November 12. Robert K. Merton Papers, Rare Book & Manuscript Library, Columbia University in the City of New York. Cited from Swedberg (2020: 5).

Merton, Robert K. (1978b) Letter to Gerald Edelman on the Forster aphorism, November 23. Robert K. Merton Papers, Rare Book & Manuscript Library, Columbia University in the City of New York. Cited from Swedberg (2020: 5).

Merton, Robert K. (1984) An interview with Robert K. Merton by Caroline Persell. *Teaching Sociology*, 11 (4): 355–386. Cited from Swedberg (2020: 3). https://doi.org/10.2307/1317796

Oates, Joyce Carol (2003) *The Faith of a Writer: Life, Craft, Art*. New York, NY: Harper Collins.

Stafford, William (1978) *Writing the Australian Crawl: Views on the Writer's Vocation*. Ann Arbor, MI: University of Michigan Press.

Stewart, Arthur J. (1999) On the need for poetry by scientists. *Bulletin of the Ecological Society of America*, 80 (2): 133–134.

Stewart, Arthur J. (2010) "Ladoga Lake and Nyos." *Circle, Turtle, Ashes*, 39–41. Knoxville, TN: Celtic Cat.

Stewart, Arthur J. (February 12, 2017) Email correspondence with Nancy S. Gorrell.

Swedberg, Richard (2020) '*How do I know what I think till I see what I say*?' An aphorism and its implications for creative theorizing. *Distinktion: Journal of Social Theory*, 21 (1): 1–18. https://doi.org/10.1080/16009 10X.2019.1630846

SECTION THREE:
THE TEACHER-WRITER SELF

Chapter 16

Discovering the Teacher-Writer Within

In a sense, as we are creative beings, our lives become our works of art.

– Julia Cameron, *The Artist's Way: A Spiritual Path to Higher Creativity*
(Cameron, 1992: xvi)

THIS IS HOW IT HAPPENED

Imagine this. You are a teacher. You are teaching writing. In the process of teaching writing, you become a writer yourself. Now you are a teacher and a writer. As you teach, as you write, something else seems to happen. Without knowing it, your teaching life and your writing life start to flow together into one – that of *teacher-writer*. You find yourself writing *with* your students, *to* your students, and *for* your students. You know it because you can feel it, inside the world of yourself. And you can see it, outside the world of yourself, in your classroom as you teach. You have acted, you have written, you have created. Now your students ask not, "Have you published anything?" But how? (1) "How did you write that poem?" and (2) "How did you get that poem published?" and (3) "How can I get my poem published, too?" Somewhere, somehow, in your path of becoming, the world begins to whisper to you a new name; a name that seems strange at first, but then makes sense to you. The name confirms your new self: *teacher-writer*.

PART ONE: WRITING *WITH* YOUR STUDENTS

A Teaching Story: Poem Challenges

This is the "joy" at the moment of creating that Rollo May refers to when work becomes play. (May, 1975: 45) You look forward to it because you know you are going to write. No longer do you struggle to find time to write; your work time and your writing time are one in your classroom. You say to your class, "Today as a warm-up we are going to take the challenge, the 'poem challenge.' Think of any three, random words; challenge the person next to you with those three words to write a poem. We'll share our poems in our circle at the end of class."

Then Scott smiles, "Ms. Gorrell, I want you to write a poem. Write a poem with blue goo in it; you know, the kind they put combs in." He laughs. Then says, "Add a vibrating egg."

"Ok," and I find myself asking, "What exactly are the three words?" The class responds: "Blue goo, comb, and a vibrating egg."

"Ok," I say again taking up the challenge, "Now let's begin."

Students exchange words in rapid succession. The room hums with imagination and the energy of expectation. I begin to write. I wonder how I'm going to work with Scott's absurd combination. I think *blue goo.* Nothing comes but the image of blue. I think of *comb.* Suddenly I see my daughter Sara, her golden curly locks spilling over in my hand. I have a comb in my hand and I'm combing my daughter's hair. I begin by writing the obvious. He said, "Write me a poem but first start with blue goo the kind you put the combs in and end with a vibrating egg." The instruction. Next, what did I think? "I thought of you," and then the words start to flow and spill as the image rises to the surface, "your hair spun gold, and your eyes. . ." And suddenly I'm back into the thick of it: "and your eyes, pools of blue. . ." And then one word rubs against another, and new meaning emerges, and I am "combing a memory."

The rest of the poem surges in a wave and ends on the shore of logic with subliminal ease: *He said write me a poem but first start with blue goo the kind you put the combs in and end with a vibrating egg and I thought of you, your hair spun gold, and your eyes, pools of blue and I was combing my memory of you first with the part and then with the brush and then with the braids and then with your neck, soft and white and then with the kisses in the nape of your neck and then with the breeze of your breath and your laugh and the blacks tights and sneakers and the laces all tangled and the waiting, bent down, tying and tying your shoes, and the strings of my heart tied to the strings of yours and I remembered when you were just an egg, vibrating inside me.* How I arrived at that conclusion is the intensive process of flow. I certainly never thought of it when I began writing. But I know I am there – and I stop.

At the end of class, students can't wait to share. Scott reads the three challenge words he got from his partner. Then he reads his poem as his partner delights in surprise. The challenge strategy never fails to produce fresh and unexpected results and a lot of laughter. I am always the last one to share in the circle. I do this for several reasons: first, if time runs out, I want all my students to have the opportunity to read. I can always share the next day; second, it gives me an opportunity to sense the results of the class and determine if my result is or is not appropriate to read; and third, it gives me the opportunity to comment on the process and results of the class as a whole. I do not want to be the "star," but rather, I use my results to comment on the process. When I read my notes, Scott bounces in his seat, "Yes!" he says. I smile and thank Scott for giving me blue goo, comb, and a vibrating egg.

That night, I return to my journal notes. I know I am committed to this poem. I want to type it up and include it in my poetry portfolio. As Robert Scholes says in *Textual Power,* "many a text begun in school has finished in the world. The 'real' and the 'academic' deeply interpenetrate on another" (Scholes, 1985: 10). As I enter and reenter my creation, again and again, I shape the words to fit the moment of surge:

Combing a Memory
by Nancy Gorrell

He said,
write me a poem
but first start with blue goo
the kind you put the combs in
and end with a vibrating egg and
I thought of you, your hair spun gold,
and your eyes, pools of blue
and I was combing a memory of you first
with the part and then with the brush
and then with the braids and then with your neck,
soft and white and then with the kisses in the nape of
your neck and then with the breeze of your breath and
your laugh and the black tights
and sneakers and the laces all tangled
and the waiting, bent down, tying and tying
your shoes, and the strings of my heart tied
to the strings of yours and I remembered
when you were just
an egg, vibrating
inside me.

I call this poem "Combing a Memory." Now I know I have written an authentic poem, not just an exercise, because this poem seems to matter, and more poems seem to want to "leap" off the page. I am intrigued by the metaphor of combing. I write some more poems. This one I call "Combing":

Combing
by Nancy Gorrell

her hair fell in golden
strands, long ringlets
of fine gossamer curls
whirling around in ethereal
bliss, down, down, past

blue pools of eyes glimmering
in the mirror, past the whiteness
of neck, the curve of shoulders,
the arch of back, down, down,
almost to her waist, floating,
falling, weightless into my waiting
fingers, hands, comb, brush
and then up, up, grasping
the thick essence of her self,
I rake a wake, parting
the twisted waters,
strand by strand, we stand,
mother, young daughter,
combing our way home.

The following day I begin class by telling my students I have written another poem from the previous day's challenge. Then I ask, "Has anyone else done the same?" Two students volunteer that they were able to write additional poems from their challenges. Holly was inspired by blue goo, comb, and vibrating egg, and tried her own version of the combination. I call their attention to the two versions of my challenge poem. I tell my students I like to call such poems, *leaping* poetry, or "arcs of association" when one poem seems to leap out of another (Bly, 1975: 4). I point out that a leaping poem is a not a revision, but a new poem based on an image, association, or metaphor from the original. I then ask students to look in their portfolios for a poem they have written which they feel inspired by. Then I ask them to "leap" into the poem and continue writing, or "leaping" into a new poem or association.[1]

Model Student Leaping Poem: "Poetry on a Plane" by Elise Rosenberg

"Poetry on a Plane" (Rosenberg, 1997), inspired by the "window" prompt in Chapter 2, also serves as a model student leaping poem illustrating Robert Bly's "arcs of association" (Bly, 1975: 4).

Poetry on a Plane
by Elise Rosenberg

If I were to write a verse
sitting on a plane
in my cramped seat with my stiff legs
I would probably produce
a terribly contrived
stanza
with as many beats per line
as there are seats in my row
and words as small and mechanical
as the tiny overhead compartments.
And it would be about as satisfying
as the honey roasted peanuts
that you nibble on
for the same reason
you would read this poem
. . . because it's there.

But
if I were to climb out
the little window
next to me
and sit on the wing of the plane
I would feel the air and the clouds
against my skin
and I would pound out
the most liberated poem in the sky
with no rhyme, no meter, no reason,
no walls.
But then gusts and breezes
would snatch my paper away
to blow in all directions
and feed my letters
to the birds and the rain.

And
perhaps my new poem
would have been even more satisfying
than any peanut on any airline
with its carefree thoughts
and unsalted lines,
but now
it will go unread. . .
unless
you climb out your own little window
away from all walls
and have the wind recite my words.
Then
like my poem
you can fly away.

(Rosenberg, 1997)

Elise's poem moves from "If I were to write a verse" in the first stanza, to a series of leaps in subsequent stanzas (indicated by my underlines): "But / if I were to climb out" in the second stanza, to "But / then gusts and breezes" in third stanza, to "And / perhaps my new poem" in the fourth stanza to "but / now / it will go unread," pausing. . . and then, leaping once more to "unless / you climb out," to "Then / like my poem / you can fly away."

What I Learned: Writing with My Students

What I learned and what I keep learning is the value of challenges, the value of exercises, and the value of process to flush out the unexpected. Most importantly, I learned the value of the community of writers to inspire and generate not only new writing but new teaching ideas as well. For here's the truth: "Combing a Memory," written in class with my students, enabled me to conceive of the leaping poetry lesson. In essence, the process of being a teacher-writer enabled me to produce a pedagogy that I continue to use in the teaching of creative writing. *To teach is to learn, to learn is to teach.* Writing *with* my students generates for me not only authentic writing that matters, but new, immediate and fresh teaching lessons as well. In the process, I have woven together the threads of my teaching and my writing. For me, they remain one, inseparable, creative act.

PART TWO: WRITING *TO* YOUR STUDENTS

Poems of Address

Writing poems of address to our students is a natural consequence of process writing and teaching as co-learning. As such, the poem of address often serves as a teaching poem, a message to the student addressee as well as the wider audience which both poet and student share in the "learning." Arthur Stewart's poem "Learning" is worth revisiting in this context of the core thesis of this book.

Model Contributor Poem: "Learning" by Arthur J. Stewart Revisited

Learning
by Arthur J. Stewart

My nine and duckling students dear –
I cannot teach you how iron-weed
by slamming purple softens
wild hills in autumn.

So on this bold day I say just
iron-weed blooms, and dig in stitching
raw data with statistics,
explaining the need to round
to whole near numbers, values
that have clear meaning.

But when I look up at last
I must stop and lean forward, learning
in your young eyes

how beautifully these tumbling
fragments of knowledge adorn you.
(Stewart, 1999a)

As Stewart, picking up on the last stanza of the poem, reflects:

> I realize, in that jumbled precious instant, that one or more of the students also realizes that the facts are naught but tools: the bond is created. I see then, in that instant, that *I* have learned from the students I am trying to teach.
>
> (Stewart, 1999b)

Writing to Your Students: Modeling Poetry

Carpe diem! When the occasion arises, teacher-writers seize the moment and write to their students. In doing so, they model for their students, what writers do – that is, respond to the moment, the world, and others by writing.

Moments of tragedy unfortunately present themselves far too often inside and outside of our classrooms. As colleagues, we have all taught students who have attempted suicide, suffered from debilitating mental illnesses or disease and succumbed to violence in one form or another. One such student, Chris, remains close to my heart. I can still see his bright blue eyes shining under the shock of his curly blonde hair. Chris was one of the most gentle and spiritual of all the students I have ever known. He was a seeker in the truest sense of the word. In his senior year of high school, he divested himself of material possessions and donned a monk's garb, cloak, hood, and sash. In our annual, evening poetry reading program, he sat on the floor, played a drum, and mouthed poetry in the form of a mantra: "om, om." After graduation, Chris wandered the world. Then, tragedy struck. In the Pacific Islands, he was hit by a truck in a near fatal accident. He remained in a coma for many long months. While in this state, I wrote a poem to him in the hope that someday he would be able to read it. After many months of waiting, I shared the poem with his mother, who later shared it with Chris upon his awakening. Fortunately, Chris has recovered.

To Chris, Gentle Spirit of the Earth
by Nancy Gorrell

where are you now
my blue eye son
where are you now
my darling young one
are you off to find, silent
blue waters?
I've gone off to find. . .
Chris crossed oceans of love,
oceans of fear, oceans of tears
even now I hear his words
sung deep from somber sleep
as the caterpillar creeps over
my watering can, as the trees
bend and blow in the breeze
as the waters of my heart
ebb and flow. . .
I know I hear your rising
like the cicadas, I know I hear
your rising
like the cicadas. . .
rising like –
you are resting now
in the white space of thought
on the edge of letters
curled in the fetal
position of vowels,
embedded. . .
coma, comma, caesura, merely
a pause in the breath of life, only
to rise again, like the cicadas, to
sing the song of the earth,
om, om, om
I'm home.

What I Learned: Writing to Students

I learned that writing to my students is a powerful teaching tool for both my students and myself. Whether in poetry, letter, or email form, the writing is personal, immediate, and instructive. I am able to model what writers do in terms of both process and product. But most importantly, such writing is authentic, building the relationship of teacher-writer to student-writer. By writing to your students, you have the opportunity to be at once authentic and professional. As a result, the community of writers grows and, as Stewart poetically expresses it, "the bond is created."

For Your Teacher Journal: Writing to Your Students

Reflecting

1. After reading the poem "Learning," have you experienced a similar moment of learning in your student's young eyes?"
2. Reflect on a moment when you felt you and your students were co-learners, learning together.

After reading the poem "To Chris, Gentle Spirit of the Earth," have you experienced a moment of occasion or *extremis* causing you to want to say something to that student? Reflect upon that student and moment.

Responding: Writing Prompts

1. After reflecting on "Learning," write a poem, prose poem, or letter of address to the student's "young eyes," "the moment of connection," or the knowledge of co-learners and co-learning. You can choose to model from Stewart's poem if you are so inspired.
2. After reading "To Chris, Gentle Spirit of the Earth," write your own poem of address seizing the moment of an important occasion or the moment of *extremis* or urgency.

PART THREE: WRITING FOR YOUR STUDENTS

Writing Models for Instruction

Writing your own models for instruction provides limitless creative and cross-curricular and discipline-related teaching opportunities. In doing so, you can use your creativity to select appropriate textual readings from your subject course, model your own writings based on those readings, and inspire your students to respond in kind. Such modeling enables students to see you as a teacher-writer, struggling with the same problems they may struggle with. In sharing your results, you will foster not only the literacy goals of the discipline you are teaching, but the ethos of being co-learners.

Guidelines for Modeling as a Teacher-Writer

- *Be the teacher-writer not the star of the class. Being the star might discourage students from feeling that they can write at all. I want to encourage my students to think – I can do that – after reading or hearing my work. So make your model simple, clear, and instructive.*
- *Show "writing in progress" not "writing in perfection." The former encourages while the latter discourages writers. Don't worry about showing an unfinished or unedited model. Let the students correct it. Show your process.*
- *Model the role of teacher as co-learner in the spirit that we are all apprentices, rather than teacher as master.*
- *Model your use of writerly tools and techniques of craft for your students; And that means taking risks. Only when you share your risk-taking will you learn whether your writing is as you imagined it to be.*

Fortunately, when I began teaching creative writing, I took one such risk. In the process, I learned how effective the *if-I-can-do-it-you-can-do-it* modeling attitude is as a motivator for student writing. I also learned much about myself both as a person and as a writer.

The narrative piece of writing that produced these realizations I titled at the time "Shame."

Writing for Your Students: Modeling Narrative Structure

My effort in modeling emerged in the process of teaching my English III classes an introductory lesson on narrative structure. I had been using an excerpt in Chapter 1 from Richard Wright's autobiography, *Black Boy*, which I will refer to as "The Kitten" incident (Wright, 1945/1966: 16–21). This excerpt encompasses an early childhood incident in which Richard killed a kitten to get back at his father, and as a consequence, was severely punished for his actions by his mother. Wright's incident was written in linear fashion: exposition (background information), action (the incident), aftermath (consequences of the action) – in other words, beginning, middle, and end.

Reading as writers, we would discuss non-linear ways Wright might have introduced his story, beginning with dramatic action, or the aftermath (flashback) method. We would discuss why writers begin with exposition and its linear value, and why writers might choose non-linear action or flashback openings. After the discussion, I would suggest to my students to write their own early childhood narratives about a time when they, like Richard, did something "bad." This lesson remains a mainstay of my introduction to non-fiction writing in my English courses. Students respond to the prompt with ease – Who hasn't done something "bad" in their childhood?

One evening after teaching the Wright lesson, I felt compelled to write my own story of when I did something bad as a child. The image of my mother reprimanding me flashed in my mind. I started with that image and wrote quickly from there in flashback form. It took great risk on my part because the incident for me was the most traumatic of my early childhood. In fact, at the time of writing as an adult, I was still suffering from the guilt.

Non-Fiction Model Narrative: "Shame" by Nancy Gorrell

Shame

by Nancy Gorrell

The first time I ever heard the word "reputation" I was six years old. The word thundered from my mother's tight, red lips – her jugular swollen and exposed in the dense humidity of the backyard. I remember very little else of that moment. Mostly, the sickening feeling of humiliation, the blur of it all. *I'm not here… this isn't happening to me*. Reputation. I had gotten one – a bad one at that – an affliction. I remember my mother instructing: "A bad reputation is hard to live down; people always remember the bad things you do." I walked away from the catechism feeling like a leper, rotten, contaminated, exposed, unable to show my face to anyone.

It was all Herbie's fault, or so I used to like to think. Herbie was the kind of kid any devilish little six-year-old girl would love to play with. Bully on the block, he was big, tough and always getting into trouble. Herbie already had a reputation, a bad one, which made playing with him all the more exciting and mysterious. His world was filled with the forbidden: Herbie was the one who introduced me to cap guns (outlawed in my house); "four letter words" (the first one I remember was *whore)*; and what it really meant to be "bad." He was also the one who introduced me to Judy.

Judy was a new kid on the block, and I hated her from the start. She was everything I was not and could not be – thin, dainty and coy. She would come out to play in ruffled dresses and patent leather shoes always carrying a doll or a purse. Judy came from a snobby sounding place, Levittown, which she pronounced with great pride. That summer I was a ninety-pound tomboy – hair in pigtails, corduroy pants, plaid shirt, and ragged and always muddy sneakers. I spent my time in the woods, the brooks and with Herbie, my best and most notorious friend.

I can't remember whose idea it was, but that summer, while Judy's family was away on vacation, Herbie and I took it upon ourselves to seek vengeance. It was only a few weeks before that Judy told me in front of all the others that I was too old to play in the summer time without a shirt. Herbie and I tore into her father's prize garden. Systematically, we uprooted every vegetable – carrots, radishes, cucumbers, tomatoes – and threw them all into an old plastic swimming pool in the garage. I remember so clearly the smell of the earth under my fingernails, the mixed odors of the pungent vegetables, and the damp, mildew of the dark garage. But most of all I remember the tremendous feeling of excitement. We were flushed with elation as we proceeded with our destruction. We attacked the fruit on the surrounding trees and crushed them against the house. I was too short to break the cornstalks, so Herbie stood on the old fence and methodically ripped off the tops of each. When we were finished, the garage was piled high. Once again, I can't remember whose idea it was, or which one of us went first. But I do know that both of us had a final surge of primitive defiance. Herbie and I urinated over the whole mess in the pool.

To this day, I don't know how my mother found out so quickly, but when I came home, she knew. I can't remember if she spanked me, or what she said first. But whatever she did, it must have been good because to this day I still feel the incredible shame. I do remember that Herbie, my mother and I spent the remainder of the day trying to restore the garden. I remember my mother's disgust when she saw the cornstalks and tried the impossible task of uprighting them. But most of all, I remember the utter humiliation when she looked into the garage and saw the pool. By then the odors were building in the summer heat, and I remember my mother's despair as she looked at us and then back at the pool again.

After that, I wasn't allowed to watch TV or play with Herbie for a month. But the immediate punishments were small compare to the guilt I was to live with for years to come.

Commentary: On "Shame"

I carried that guilt for two decades before I read "Shame" in class as a model for instruction. Little did I know that by reading that model to my students, I would also experience the ultimate value of writing – writing as self-discovery. The discovery was my realization that I had been only a child, and that perhaps what I did was not so horrific. In the eyes of the child at the time, I only felt overwhelming shame, but in the eyes of the adult looking back, I could place the incident in context, bringing understanding to bear. My students seemed to understand and empathize. It was after all the first and last really "bad" thing I ever did in my life. Perhaps, over the years, my guilt grew more from the secret my mother kept from my grandfather than the actual incident itself. Decades later, I can share "Shame" with my students with little guilt at all. It's not that time has healed old wounds, but rather that the story is out – for good – and there is no secret anymore.

What I Learned: "Our Lives Become our Works of Art"

For teacher-writers, our lives most certainly become, our works of art. (Cameron, 1992: xvi) We write *with, to,* and *for* our students. We write daily, living the writer's life, in our classrooms with our students. For us, not only does our profession, *teaching,* engage, inform, and inspire our writing, but our writing engages, informs, and inspires our teaching. The relationship of the two selves is symbiotic, each benefiting the other to the extent that the whole – *teacher-writer* – is richer than the separate parts – teacher and writer.

As you walk your path of becoming, from teacher, to writer, to teacher-writer, you too will experience the power of writing not only as process and product, but as discovery. You will come to know writing from the inside, enabling you to teach writing as a teacher-writer.

For Your Teacher Journal

Reflecting

1. Think back to your childhood. What important subject-related learning lessons could you model for your students?
2. Consider perhaps how you learned the subject you are teaching when you were in grade school, middle school, or high school. Reflect.

3. What models for instruction could you write based on the textual materials from your subject course? Reflect.

Responding: Writing Prompts

1. After reading "Shame," write any discipline-related narrative or memoir for instruction that involves learning an important lesson.
2. Choose to write a model of a non-fiction, narrative text from your student's literature readings. Teach your model to the class comparing the original text and your model. Then have your students respond in kind.

PART FOUR: INTERDISCIPLINARY APPLICATIONS

Discipline-Related Models for Instruction

As teacher-writers across the disciplines, we "do" our disciplines with our students in the classroom. For example, this chapter opens with myself, the author, doing writing or "poem challenges" with my students. When we "do" with our students what professionals in our disciplines do, we are modeling our discipline. This section encourages teachers in any subject area to write discipline-related models of instruction for their students. One such model is "Rat Dissection" by Arthur J. Stewart. His poem shows us a teacher "doing" science with the "rapt" attention of "twenty-eight students." What lesson is learned?

Model Contributor Poem: "Rat Dissection" by Arthur J. Stewart, Aquatic Ecologist and Ecotoxicologist

Rat Dissection
By Arthur J. Stewart

For lab this week, the white rat—
Rattus norwiegicus: this was life,

respect it. Outside
on the female white rat find
twelve nipples, six by two. They grow
to produce milk to feed the young and shrink
when she's not pregnant. Lager the vestibule—the space
between the teeth and cheek but note now
vibrissae on each side of the head above
the mouth on masticular pads; and pink eyes
plus eyelids, nictating membrane,
pinnae, the external part of the ear. A quick look
inside: see, teeth on the top and bottom,
four incisors for gnawing, twelve molars
for grinding. The uvula
hangs in the back of the throat like a little pink
punching bag: it goes up to block off
the nasal cavity during,
for example, vomiting. Don't confuse it
with vulva or the car. Opening
the jaws wide later you will cut back
from the angle of the jaw
with the blunt-tipped blades of the scissors
inside the mouth, through bone.
Find the epiglottis, covering the glottis, the opening
of the trachea, cartilaginous rings—
the larynx, structure
housing vocal cords. You'll work then
just anterior of the urogenital orifice. Cut
a small hole through the skin, the abdominal muscles,
carefully
past the diaphragm, letting
the abdominal cavity see light (some
preservative may leak out here). Find the liver—
it's the largest organ, wrapped
around the esophagus; count the lobes. Locate
the purplish spleen, the creamy pancreas
nestling the stomach. You will be responsible
tomorrow for knowing this

and much more. You will be graded
not just for knowing structure but for
neatness of dissection. The twenty-eight
students are rapt: they stare
at the dripping rat held up by the gloved hand.

(Stewart, 2005)

For Your Teacher Journal: Writing Models for Instruction

1. After reading "Rat Dissection," write your own subject-related poem or prose poem for instruction. Think of this as a creative or alternate way to teach a challenging concept, principle, or theory to arts-minded students in your class if you are a science or math teacher.
2. After reading "Rat Dissection," write your own "how to" model of instruction for any subject-related lesson you may want to teach. Consider your voice and tone. Do you want to be the dominant voice of the "teacher/lecturer?" Do you want to try humor? You might even try writing the model from the point of view or voice of a questioning student or a personified subject like the rat.

Writing with Your Students: Poem Challenges and Leaping Poetry

Write with your students, teaching them the "Poem Challenge" lesson introduced in "A Teaching Story" (see Part Two of this chapter).

- ***For language teachers***: Try the poem challenge lesson with your students choosing three words from English and three words from the language they are studying with you.
- ***For science and mathematics teachers***: Try poem challenges with scientific and mathematical concepts, principles, terms, and expressions. Adapt poem challenge prompts to your discipline.

- ***For all teachers***: If appropriate, write your own "leaping" poem. Then suggest to your students, discipline-related models for "leaping" poems within your subject or course.

For Your Students: Writing Prompts

1. After reading the science poem "Learning," write any poem, prose poem, or memory piece on a learning experience with your teacher when a "bond was created," or you felt like a co-learner.
2. Like Stewart, if you could write a poem "on learning" to your teacher, what would you say? Write that poem.
3. Write a discipline-related poem, prose poem, or memoir "On Learning," or on "A Learning Experience" inspired by your reading of Stewart's poem.
4. After reading the model "Shame" from this chapter, write your own memoir of early childhood (or fictional narrative). You can begin with the following prompt: *"I'll never forget the time when. . ."*
5. After reading Stewart's science poem "Rat Dissection," write your own poem, prose poem, or memoir about a moment of learning when you felt "rapt" attention or a sense of wonder or awe. This could be in any subject area, one perhaps, you are interested in, or passionate about, or one when you were amazed by the lesson or teacher.
6. Choose to write about a moment of learning outside the classroom in which a special "bond was created." You may follow the instructions in #1.

Chapter 16 Note

1 I credit the poet Robert Bly with the term *leaping poetry*. He defines "leaping" in poetry as an "arc of association" (Bly, 1975: 4). Bly explains:

> My idea is that a great work of art often has at its center a long floating leap [...] but the work [also] can have many leaps, perhaps shorter. A poet who is leaping makes a jump from an object soaked in unconscious substance to an object or idea soaked in conscious substance.
>
> (p. 4)

In terms of language, Bly defines leaping as "the ability to associate fast [...]. In a great ancient or modern poem [...] the speed of the association increases the excitement of the poetry" (p. 4).

Chapter 16 References

Bly, Robert (1975) *Leaping Poetry: An Idea with Poems and Translations Chosen by Robert Bly*. Boston, MA: Beacon Press.

Cameron, Julia (1992) *The Artist's Way: A Spiritual Path to Higher Creativity*. New York, NY: Tarcher/Putnam.

May, Rollo (1975) *The Courage to Create*. New York, NY: W.W. Norton.

Rosenberg, Elise (1997) "Poetry on a Plane." *Tricorn Literary Magazine*, 32: 8–9. Morristown, NJ: Morristown High School.

Scholes, Robert (1985) *Textual Power: Literary Theory and the Teaching of English*. New Haven, CT: Yale University Press.

Stewart, Arthur J. (1999a) "Learning." On the need for poetry by scientists. *Bulletin of the Ecological Society of America*, 80 (2): 133.

Stewart, Arthur J. (1999b) On the need for poetry by scientists. *Bulletin of the Ecological Society of America*, 80 (2): 133–134.

Stewart, Arthur J (2005) "Rat Dissection." *Bushido: The Virtues of Rei and Makoto*, 80. Knoxville, TN: Celtic Cat.

Wright, Richard (1945/1966) *Black Boy* (2nd edition). New York, NY: Harper & Row.

Chapter 17

Writing About Your Students and Your Discipline

Joey can't explain why/but circles make him feel happy.
– Amy Uyematsu, "When Geometry Gets Mixed Up with God and the Alphabet" (Uyematsu, 2005b: 29)

PART ONE: THIS IS HOW IT HAPPENED

Imagine the Possibility of a 10th Muse – Teaching

Imagine the possibility of a 10th muse, that of teaching itself. As teacher-writers, we have listened to and heard our muse, teaching. And we have wrestled with the beauty and complexity of her close companion, learning. For teaching and learning are inextricably bound. This we know. That is why as teacher-writers we are inspired to write about our students and our disciplines. The major contributors to this book, myself included, have written about their students: the basic students (Chapter 1), the creatively gifted (Chapter 8), and the reluctant writers (Chapter 7). More often than not, this writing is about the marginal students, those who are not considered a "success" by their schools or the educational system. This book hopes to reach and teach the "others" with its ethos of creativity, creative writing, literacy, and cross-curricular learning.

PART TWO: WRITING *ABOUT* YOUR STUDENTS

A Teaching Poem: "To the Quiet One"

To the Quiet One
by Nancy Gorrell

she would not
raise her hand
lift her head
open her mouth
answer any question
even when asked
all year and all
year all I wanted
to do was say –
say something –
and then I heard
the echo of a prayer
lookie here girl
with the big brown eyes
in the first row, second seat,
when they gave out quiet
you got a whole lot of nuthin'
like the space between the clouds
like the space between the leaves
like the space between your fingers
like the space between your breath
and mine – a whole lot of nuthin' –
like the space within my heart

Commentary: On "The Quiet One"

"The Quiet One" was a student of mine in Creative Writing I. She was one of the few students in my classes that I truly felt I had "failed." She never spoke, raised her hand, or asked a question. I treated her with the utmost tenderness and care, using every teacherly strategy I had to bring her out of her shell. She was "on the margins" in every sense. She did not interact with peers in the class, and she wrote the minimum for every exercise. I tried to encourage her by using praise whenever possible, but I also tried to "do no harm." She would not share her writings in the sharing circle or in private exchange with a peer in class or in anonymous exchanges. I sat her in the front of the room so she could be close to me. I will never forget her or her big brown eyes that stared at me all semester. I tried patience, openness, and unspoken empathy. And I waited, to no avail. I never shared this poem with her.

What I Learned

Utmost humility. To teach is to learn, to learn is to be. Clearly, "The Quiet One" had set up boundaries, and I did not want to break them. I learned I could be patient and wait. But the question still haunts me: Did I wait too long?

For Your Teacher Journal

Reflecting and Responding

1. Reflect on the "marginal" student or students "on the margins" you have taught or struggled with. This may be students who are in some sense "outsiders" in your class, school, or extracurricular activity. Does one particular student come to mind? Write a poem, prose poem, or memoir about that student.
2. Reflect on your reading of "The Quiet One." Have you ever taught a "quiet" student? Write a poem, prose poem, or memoir about teaching that "quiet one."
3. Have you ever felt unable to "reach" a marginal student, or a student that is an "outsider?" Write a poem, prose poem, or memoir about that student.
4. Compare and contrast your reading of "The Quiet One" with your reading in Chapter 1 of "A Most Unlikely Creative Writing Class." In the latter case, the students were "reached" while in the former, the "quiet" student was most likely not.

Write a poem, prose poem, or memoir about teaching a basic or remedial student or class.

Model Contributor Poem: "When Geometry Gets Mixed Up with God and the Alphabet" by Amy Uyematsu, High School Mathematics Teacher

When Geometry Gets Mixed Up with God and the Alphabet
by Amy Uyematsu

Every time he writes "angel" she puts a big red circle
around it, not round like a halo but cranky
and shrill in her thick felt-tip pen,
just for misspelling "angle" again,
as she takes a point off here, another point there,
until he's down to a lousy C-plus.

She's gotta be the pickiest teacher Joey's ever had
'cuz she makes them spell the words
like it's some dumb English class
and a sin to write slop" for "slope"
or "rumbas" for "rhombus." She expects
him to give reasons and claims "just because
it looks that way" doesn't make it true.
It's usually Joey who blurts out,
"What's the point
if I can figure it out in my head?" –
but she'll throw him that look
that makes the whole room quiet
without saying one word.

Joey will never admit it to his best friend Andrew,
who sits in the corner and counts
the number of tiny holes in the ceiling tiles,
once up to 2,407 when the bell rang,
that geometry is his favorite class
even though he hates the homework.
Sometimes he'll figure out all the problems she assigns

but will never hold up his hand to answer
because Andrew and he can't stand
those show-offs who always wave their arms
like they want everyone
to know who's smartest.

Some days she puts on that crazy smile of hers
and starts asking questions like *How do we know*
a line is straight or *Do we believe that*
between any two points there's always one more?
Joey doesn't doubt that numbers can get bigger
and never stop, but he's fascinated
by the idea of infinity shrinking, too.
Once she asked if his class ever stops to wonder
why Egyptians chose triangles for their pyramids,
even believed these three-sided shapes held
secret powers. Joey joins in
as the kids laugh and roll their eyes
with that oh-no-here-she-goes-again sigh,
but lately he wishes they'd shut up a minute
so he can let his mind zoom
to a space he can't see,
where ocean meets sky and lines can curve.

Joey might even break his rule
about homework and answer her question –
"What geometric shape pleases you most?" –
because there's no doubt in Joey's mind
that circles are the best thing ever invented.
He even wishes he could meet the first genius
who drew a circle in the sand;
though the more Joey thinks about it
circles didn't have to be invented –
from the moon and the sun
to eyeballs, round stones, oranges,
humans have always seen circles –
from the minute they wake up
to when they go to sleep, circles.

And Joey can't explain
why circles make him feel happy –
but he's glad she's taught him
about "concentric" circles,
pondering one inside another
inside another without end.

(Uyematsu, 2005b)

Commentary on "When Geometry Gets Mixed Up with God and the Alphabet" : Paying Homage to Our Muse – Teaching

Uyematsu's poem pays homage to our muse, teaching, in all its complexity. Joey, the student who "can't explain why circles make him feel happy," just might break his rule, raise his hand and answer a question "because there's no doubt in Joey's mind/ that circles are the best thing ever invented." Uyematsu explains in her email correspondence: "My poem was based on many years of teaching high school geometry. Joey represents so many of the students I had. I really did ask my students those questions. Occasionally, I'd assign a writing response (prose or poetry) to the question, 'What is your favorite geometric shape?'" (Uyematsu, 2019).

In contrast to Joey, a student inspired by geometry, Uyematsu has also written "many poems about Latino students who were in gangs" (Uyematsu, 2019). For example, the poem "Florentino Diaz" (Uyematsu, 1998) is about "a student with that name who was alienated from the predominantly white school culture he was bused into" (Uyematsu, 2019). She also wrote a poem, "His Name was Marlon Gutierrez" (Uyematsu, 2016a) that was inspired by Marlon being shot and killed. "The poem talks about our gun-crazed culture back in the 80s when the piece was written" (Uyematsu, 2019).

"Juan's Numbers" (Uyematsu, 2016b) is about a gang member whom Uyematsu taught in one of her remedial classes. She explains: "The second section of the poem criticizes how the state 'tests' basic students for math competence" (Uyematsu, 2019).

Model Contributor Poem: "Juan's Numbers" by Amy Uyematsu, High School Mathematics Teacher

Juan's Numbers
by Amy Uyematsu

1. Thirteen

As in Culver City 13, Venice 13,
Playboy and Echo Park and Sotel 13,
Juan and his allies grin if the answer
falls on their favorite number
13 as in "m" the thirteenth letter
"m" as in "la Eme" for Mexican Mafia

Juan keeps changing schools
kicked out for fighting
or getting jumped by rivals
he has to ride a downtown bus
can't even hang out
on his own front sidewalk

For all his noisy bravado
he's still not hardcore
math sucks! he complains
but he never cuts class
lucky for Juan it's his mom
who still makes him fear for his life

2. Four Hundred Fifty

Less than 10 points separate Juan
from walking the stage
diploma in hand
he needs a score of 450
to prove to state bureaucrats
he knows enough math

But Juan knows no one cares
if he got pushed up to high school
barely knowing how to add
how in hell can he show them now
that he can calculate
the slope of a line

This is his last year to pass the test
and Juan knows his numbers
inside school and out
just don't add up
I'll be lucky if I live to be 30
a statistic no teacher can deny

(Uyematsu, 2016b)

For Your Teacher Journal: Writing about Your Students

Reflecting

1. After reading "When Geometry Gets Mixed Up with God and the Alphabet," reflect on whether you have ever taught a student like Joey, one inspired by your subject, but reticent to answer questions or to "raise his hand?"
2. After reading "Juan's Numbers," reflect on whether you have ever taught a student like Juan.

Responding: Writing Prompts

1. If you have ever taught a student like Joey, write a poem, prose poem, or memoir about teaching such a student. This may be a student who is interested in your discipline but is reluctant to show that interest.
2. If you have ever taught a student like Juan, write a poem, prose poem, or memoir about teaching such a student in the context of your school and subject. This may be a marginal student or one not "succeeding" by the school's standards.
3. Write any poem, prose poem, math or science poem, or discipline-related memoir about a student who is marginal or a "statistic no teacher can deny."

PART THREE: INTERDISCIPLINARY APPLICATIONS

Whether you are a math or science teacher, or a teacher in the arts or humanities, the major contributor poems below serve as portable models for writing about any discipline or subject. The models are followed by student writing prompts to further creativity, creative literacy, and discipline-related literacy.

Writing about Your Discipline

> *A man who is not somewhat of a poet can never be a mathematician.*
>
> – Karl Weierstrass, German mathematics teacher
> (Uyematsu, 2005a: 30)

Amy Uyematsu wrote her poem "The Invention of Mathematics" shortly after reading Karl Weierstrass' quote: "A man who is not somewhat of a poet, can never be a mathematician." Uyematsu said in her email correspondence that she "doesn't know why she selected numbers 1, 2, and 7, irrational and imaginary" though she "used to enjoy describing irrational and imaginary numbers to her Algebra II students, finding them much more fascinating" than her students did. Uyematsu confirms that "7 has long been my favorite number." (Uyematsu, 2020)

Model Contributor Poem: "The Invention of Mathematics" by Amy Uyematsu, High School Mathematics Teacher

The Invention of Mathematics
by Amy Uyematsu

A man who is not somewhat of a poet
can never be a mathematician.
Karl Weierstrass, German mathematics teacher

/ one

one is the only true number
the I in the eye
each baby the god
in a mother's sigh

/ two

after the number two there was no stopping
troubles blossoming
in geometric progression
two to tango
and two required for murder and war
Doris Day singing
love me or leave me
and the tragic lob
of my nervous girlheart
th-thump, th-thump
she already knew
that deafening silence
when the call goes unanswered
th-thump, th-thump
she already knew
that deafening silence
when the call goes unanswered
th-thump, th-thump
with its inevitable
downbeat on two

/ seven

how could 7 not be lucky for me
with four 7's in my phone number
the year I was born 47 reversing perfectly
to 74 when I gave birth to my son
whose sign is in July, the 7th month,
like my mother and father,
two stubborn Leo's in their vigorous 70's.

I'm thankful to be
a Saturday matinee kid
raised somewhere between
Snow White and the 7 Dwarfs,
7 Brides for 7 Brothers,
and Kurosawa's heroic
7 Samurai

Japan has 7 gods of fortune
with the only woman
being the goddess Benten,
ruler of the sea,
a lute-shaped biwa in her arms
she's the guardian
of literature and song

and 7 syllables, a gift of blood
the lines of a tanka swinging
to 5-7-5-7-7 rhythms
the tradition of haiku parties
jamming long into night
only natural I'd arrive
with a poem in my hand

/ irrational

how fitting there are even eccentrics
among the legions of numbers
so stubborn they defy
any notion of orderly arrangement
numbers like pi or the square root of two
whose decimal translations
burst all reasonable boundaries
the ever-erratic digits
never repeating
no end in sight to their
unwinding names

and I have to admit
I wave the banner
of every so-called irrational woman
who can juggle five things in each hand
a skill little girls learn by nine or ten
while our somewhat dazed
and mystified mates
stand by in hopeless wonder

/ the imaginary number i

my students don't get the joke
after all, every number is imaginary
even those we count out
as beads and stones and miles to the sun

I tell them about some nameless
mathematicians who nobody paid
much attention to
always gazing at stars

these early oddballs and nerds
locked in their rooms
pondering pages of silly calculations
as if all life depended on them

until someone yelled i
let's make up a new number
defined as the square root
of negative one

blasting open the infinite
which no one can see
able to chart arrow to bull's-eye
through windstorm and breeze

(Uyematsu, 2005a)

Model Contributor Poems: "Professor Thermocline" and "Limnology Quiz" by Arthur J. Stewart, Aquatic Ecologist and Ecotoxicologist

Arthur J. Stewart has written numerous science poems about his discipline, and in particular, his sub-specialty, limnology. (See Stewart's previously referenced science poems "Lagoda Lake and Nyos," Chapters 14 and 15, and "Rat Dissection," Chapter 16.) In the following poem, "Professor Thermocline," Stewart writes about his discipline with technical, "factual facets," yet never losing sight of his poetic, emotional understanding. In contrast, consider the poem below, "Limnology Quiz," also by Stewart but penned in a different tone. Which "professor" do you prefer?

Professor Thermocline[1]
by Arthur J. Stewart

Look—the lake
is emerald today and slick as glass.
On the boat two students together slip
the thermistor through bubbles down, the metered line
uncoiling from the spool and sliding
gray over the bow, four eyes peering
first to where it disappears
into the green before

goodness!

remembering to look
at the output: twenty-three point three
degrees Celsius but
declining now a little with depth, three, four, five
readings taken
at one-meter intervals until
wham! She drops

zero point eight degrees Celsius somewhere between
meters ten and eleven. Then they slow

the downward move of the probe to fish out
the thermal structure
ten centimeters at a time, searching

for Professor Thermocline: he knows
this lake from the bottom up.
The diel rise and sink of zooplankton
tickles his beard; he misses nothing; he counts
each slow fin-stroke of each bass,
he tallies
photons from above, he tabulates
the daily flux of elements through his gate.

(Stewart, 2010b)

Limnology Quiz
by Arthur J. Stewart

Show, on the graph below, where oxygen
exceeds ten milligrams per liter and indicate,
by shading, where and when anoxia prevails.
To the best of your ability, draw a horizontal line to represent
the time and depth of maximum thermal stability and note
the time when you would expect
manganese to diffuse upwards
from sediment to the overlying water. So much
can be summarized in a simple graph

if you work at it: make sure
the axes are labeled, and designate key things
by text and arrows. Make it clear
as a filtered sample; make it as pure a blue
as that which correlates
to the concentration
of molybdate-reactive phosphorus.

(Stewart, 2010a)

For Your Teacher Journal: Writing about Your Discipline

Reflecting

1. After reading Uyematsu's "The Invention of Mathematics," reflect upon the "invention" of your own discipline. Do you have a favorite or "lucky" number? Think of as many associations as possible with your favorite number, mathematical and scientific as well as poetic and personal. Write a poem, prose poem or memoir about your discipline and/or your favorite number.
2. After reading Uyematsu's poem "When Geometry Gets Mixed Up with God and the Alphabet," reflect upon geometric shape or shapes. Do you have a favorite shape? Favorite shapes may be associated not only with geometry, but with art, design, architecture, nature and the natural world. Write a poem, prose poem, or memoir about your favorite shape.
3. Write any poem, prose poem, or memoir about your discipline in praise of that subject or discipline. This could be in the form of a poetic ode: "Ode to mathematics," "Ode to Science," "Ode to Art," or "Ode to Music" or "In Praise of Language, Art, or English"
4. After reading Stewart's poems "Professor Thermocline" and "Limnology Quiz," compare and contrast and reflect upon the science teaching in each poem. What does each poem say literally and poetically about science teaching?

Responding: Writing Prompts

1. After reading Uyematsu's "Invention of Mathematics," write your own discipline-related poem.
2. After reading Stewart's "Limnology Quiz," write your own discipline-related quiz in poetic form. This quiz could be used for alternate assessment. For example, "Biology Quiz," "Chemistry Quiz," "Algebra Quiz," "Geometry Quiz," or "Physics Quiz."

For Your Students: Writing Prompts

Instructions

1. After reading "The Invention of Mathematics," reflect upon your "favorite" number or numbers. "Favorite numbers" may be associated with an important date, place, event, person, or ta number may have numeric or symbolic importance. You may have "lucky" numbers. Think of as many associations as possible with your favorite numbers – mathematical and scientific as well as poetic and personal.
2. After reading "When Geometry Gets Mixed Up with God and the Alphabet," reflect upon your favorite geometric shape or shapes. Favorite shapes may be associated not only with geometry, but with art, design, architecture, and nature and the natural world. Is the subject you are taking related to geometric shapes, principles, concepts, and theories in any way? Reflect and discuss with your teacher and class.
3. Write a poem, prose poem, or memoir about your favorite shape. Shapes relate not only to geometry, mathematics, and science but also to nature, the natural world, the physical world, art, and the humanities. From the figures of basic geometry to optical illusions, geographical formations, snowflakes, crystals, clouds, everything has a shape. What is your favorite shape?
4. After reading any of the models from this chapter, write a poem, prose poem, or memoir about your "favorite" subject or about a discipline you are passionate about.
5. Write a poem in the form of an ode to your favorite subject. For example, "Ode to Math," "Ode to Science," "Ode to Art," or "In Praise of Music."

Chapter 17 Note

1 Thermocline: a steep temperature gradient in a body of water such as a lake, marked by a layer above which and below which the water is at different temperatures. This prevents mixing between surface waters

and those beneath the thermocline. Thermistor: an electrical resistor whose resistance is greatly reduced by heating, used for measurement and control.

Chapter 17 References

Stewart, Arthur J. (2010a) "Limnology Quiz." *Circle, Turtle, Ashes*, 37. Knoxville, TN: Celtic Cat.

Stewart, Arthur J. (2010b) "Professor Thermocline." *Circle, Turtle, Ashes*, 36. Knoxville, TN: Celtic Cat.

Stewart, Arthur J. (February 12, 2017) Email correspondence with Nancy S. Gorrell.

Uyematsu, Amy (1998) "Florentino Diaz." *Nights of Fire, Nights of Rain*, 6. Brownsville, OR: Story Line Press.

Uyematsu, Amy (2005a) "The Invention of Mathematics." *Stone, Bow, Prayer*, 30–33. Port Townsend, WA: Copper Canyon Press.

Uyematsu, Amy (2005b) "When Geometry Gets Mixed Up with God and the Alphabet." *Stone, Bow, Prayer*, 27–29. Port Townsend, WA: Copper Canyon Press.

Uyematsu, Amy (2016a) "His Name was Marlon Gutierrez." *Basic Vocabulary*, 34. Pasadena, CA: Red Hen Press.

Uyematsu, Amy (2016b) "Juan's Numbers." In *Basic Vocabulary*, 32–33. Pasadena, CA: Red Hen Press.

Uyematsu, Amy (August 6, 2019) Email correspondence with Nancy S. Gorrell.

SECTION FOUR:
THE TEACHER-ARTIST SELF

Chapter 18

Discovering the Teacher-Artist Within

Now near the end of the middle stretch of road
What have I learned? Some earthly wiles. An art. . .

– Robert Pinsky, "Jersey Rain"
(Pinsky, 2000)

As writers, what we do is remember. And to remember this world is to create it.

– Toni Morrison, *New York Times Sunday Magazine*
(Morrison, 2019: cover)

PART ONE: THIS IS HOW IT HAPPENED

Your students are urging you on. Your colleagues are asking questions. They want to join you. The outside world beckons. Your windows are open. You anticipate a grasshopper landing on your classroom windowsill. You seize the moment with joy and teach the spontaneous lesson. You daydream about creating. Your imagination soars. Creating what? You've felt this feeling before and channeled it into teaching and writing. You know "as we are creative beings, our lives become our works of art" (Cameron, 1992: xvi). But now it's something else. It's something more. You know you are creative. But you wonder: Am I an artist? You have yet to name yourself. But then necessity calls.

PART TWO: A TEACHER-ARTIST STORY

A phoenix of creative hope arising from the ashes
– B. J. Adler, ARTifacts: Kids Respond to a World in Crisis
(Adler, 2002: 2)

September 11, 2001

Those of us teaching in classrooms on September 11, 2001, will always remember the moment. It was second period in Morristown High School, close to 9:00 am, when my creative writing students started getting messages from their parents. Announcements followed and we were in lockdown for most of the day. Lockdown meant "locked doors" classes not changing, windows shut indefinitely. The students, fear and confusion in their eyes, faced me, the teacher, writer, teacher-writer soon to be teacher-artist, though I did not know it – not yet. My first thoughts were for my students, many of whom had parents working in New York City, downtown. For the first half hour, everyone was allowed to contact home and loved ones if possible. Then a sadness set in and a restless anxiety. My students wanted out. No one knew if our country was being attacked. I knew I had to act, at least to react to the moment.

First, we talked about the moment, the unknown, the uncertainty about "being attacked." Were we at war? Nobody knew. Then I said, "Take out your journals. Writers *remember*. So start writing down everything you want to remember about this moment. It's going to be important." They wrote seriously: 30 minutes, then 60 minutes. Afterwards, I went to my resource cabinet and pulled out Carolyn Forche's *Against Forgetting: 20th Century Poetry of Witness* (Forche, 1993). I read with my students poems produced *in extremis*: on death marches, in prisons, and concentration camps.

When school re-opened, my class asked to mount a blank roll of canvas paper, all along the hallway outside our room for students passing by to write comments, reflections, and poems. Within a day, students from all walks of life were spontaneously collaborating in a mural that contained art and poetry in the aftermath of the 9/11 attacks. The mural was a conversation in progress that lasted until the end of the school year.

Then, necessity presented itself once again. The week before Christmas break, I received a holiday card from the Alliance for Young Artists & Writers. It contained images of award-winning student artwork lost in the attacks on the World Trade Center. Apparently, these "lost works," 14 in all, were on national exhibition on the 21st floor. When I showed the holiday card to my students and shared the story, they were deeply moved. We decided as a class to write poems to the "lost works of art." Students studied the images on the card, chose one image that moved them the most, and wrote a poem to that work. B. J. Adler, editor of the publication, *ARTifacts: Kids Respond to a World in Crisis* (Adler, 2002) explained in the Preface that the purpose was to commemorate 9/11 with student responses from the New York metropolitan area. The editors were particularly moved by the response of the students to the "lost works" because they wanted to conclude the publication "with some rays of hope." As a consequence, the editors chose to feature five "lost works of art" accompanied by five ecphrastic poems by Morristown's creative writing students. Adler explains further in the *ARTifacts* publication:

> After learning that works from the Scholastic Art and Writing Awards were destroyed in the attacks, they [Morristown's students] worried that this minor story might be forgotten among the thousands of bigger stories of the day. To honor those works, they wrote poems to the "lost art" and asked us to forward them to the young artists whose works were destroyed – a phoenix of creative hope arising from the ashes.
>
> (Adler, 2002: 2)

Just knowing that the student artists received their poems pleased my creative writing students to no end. Finding out much later, that some of their poems were about to be published was an honor received with humility and some sadness. One of my students asked me, "Can the art bring back the lives?" Consider Toni Morrison's words which appeared on the front cover of the *New York Times Sunday Magazine* retrospective, published in the last issue of December 2019: "As writers, what we do is remember. And to remember this world is to create it" (Morrison, 2019). Morrison reminds us of the artist's purpose: "to remember, to bear witness, to create and pass on the legacy of those we honor and have lost." Can art bring back the lives? The images and the words live to teach our children and our children's children.

Model Student Response: Ecphrastic Poem, "Figure Drawing" by Danielle Cerny

Figure Drawing
by Danielle Cerny

To the 9/11 lost work of art by Erica Brenner, "Figure Drawing"
If people were a single shape
Would they be circles
Like the history teachers preach,
Everything a single path leading back where we began?
Would people be squares,
Jagged unforeseen turns
Mixed with spurts of calm?
Would people be straight lines,
Predictable,
Never changing,
Comfortingly familiar?
What about color?
Would people be brown
From mixing all the rainbow shades together?
Would people be blue
Like the water that keeps us alive?
What language would we speak if there could be but one?
French for its seductive beauty,
Sign language for its much needed silence?

What if buildings fell from the skies
And the earth turned red below us
Simply because no one could agree on a shape
A color
A voice?
Objects and lives should not crumble
Because our hatreds and fears make the world fragile
With uncertainty.
They should be constructed, expanded, displayed and
praised
In honor of the beauty that is difference,
And the lack of need for paint by numbers
In a world that no longer has an assigned color for skin
Or shape for a face
Yet is still struggling to mesh all the colors
The shapes and the faces
Into something that resembles
Tolerance
Equality
And Love.

What I Learned: The Power of Ecphrasis, the Poetry of Empathy

Ecphrasis, what I teach as the poetry of empathy, is a term used by classicists and art historians concerning a long tradition of poetic response to great works of art, sculpture, monuments, and artifacts. By definition, ecphrastic poetry requires the viewer/poet to "enter into" the spirit and feeling of the subject through a variety of poetic stances: describing, addressing, personifying, and reflecting or meditating upon the subject (Hollander, 1995: 12). As Hollander notes, modern ecphrastic poetry includes responses to photography and photo-journalism as well (p. 67).

Decades before 9/11, I had been teaching ecphrastic poetry in my English classes as part of a unit of study on Holocaust and Genocide Studies. Mandated by the Holocaust Commission of the State of New Jersey for all middle and high school students, I developed a lesson centered on an historic piece of photo-journalism, the Nazi liquidation of the Warsaw Ghetto of April 1943. The tool for this learning, *ecphrasis*, produced poetic responses through which students were able to speak to the unimaginable. I wrote up this lesson, "Teaching Empathy through Ecphrastic Poetry: Entering a Curriculum of Peace," and submitted it to the *English Journal* accompanied by student poetic responses. The lesson was first published in the *English Journal* (Gorrell, 2000) and then in several books about teaching peace and tolerance. My students were proud getting their works published, and I felt honored to be teaching empathy and social justice.[1]

But that wasn't enough for me to take on the identity of teacher-artist – not yet. Not until the 9/11 project and what occurred after. Simply put, after that, teacher-artists looking for creative writing teachers and students to collaborate with started to seek me out for inter-arts projects. Working with other teacher-artists gave me the insight to recognize my own self as a teacher-artist. I knew I was a writer, but I also learned I was a teacher-artist of limitless possibility and purpose.

Chapter 18 is devoted to taking on the identity of the *teacher-artist*. For me, the process was the entire path of my teaching and writing life, the realization actualized through creating inter-arts and interdisciplinary projects with colleagues, artists, and teacher-artists. In the process, my student writers have collaborated with students across the curriculum in a range of projects.

This chapter offers model projects embracing three or more subject areas, art forms, or disciplines. Each project may seem unique to this author's experience, but they are replicable in format and pedagogy for students of all levels and in school districts in diverse communities, both urban and rural. The interdisciplinary applications section of this chapter offers model writing projects and pedagogies uniting the arts and sciences in furthering emerging literacies – creative literacy, ecological literacy, and interdisciplinary literacy – utilizing the writing tools of science poetry, ecphrasis, and creative writing across the curriculum.

PART THREE: INTER-ARTS PROJECTS

At a Glance – Inter-Arts Projects

- ***Jersey Rain: Creative Writing, Poetry, Musical Composition, Choral Performance***
- ***Our Town Book Project: Poetry of Place, Ecphrasis, Photography, Self-Publishing***

"Jersey Rain" Inter-Arts Project: Creative Writing, Poetry, Musical Composition, and Choral Performance

As the millennium was upon us, a teacher-artist opportunity presented itself. Two noted artists, Robert Pinsky, who was at that time the poet laureate of the United States, and David Sampson, a local composer of renown, approached me with a question: Would I like to collaborate with them in an arts project funded by the National Endowment for the Arts and the Geraldine R. Dodge Foundation of Morristown. They were looking for a high school creative writing teacher and class of students to work with for a their proposed "Jersey Rain" project. As they outlined the scope of the proposal, I was in awe. It would take an academic year. My creative writing students would have poetry workshops with Robert Pinsky, a native of New Jersey, learning about poetry and his signature poem, "Jersey Rain" (Pinsky, 2000). Then my students would write poetry or prose in response to "Jersey Rain" and/or their own location or place, Morristown. Concomitantly, the music composition students would have music composition workshops with David Sampson. Afterwards, individual students from music class would read the poetry produced from creative writing students and select individual poems to inspire musical compositions.

These in-school collaborations were especially exciting for the creative writing students, who were thrilled to hear their words set to music. David Sampson facilitated the performances that were held in the creative writing and music classrooms for all the participating students to hear. The project (Pinsky and Sampson,

2000–2001) culminated in a professional choral concert for the public involving the Harmonium and Masterworks Choruses and the Colonial Symphony of Morristown. My writing students witnessed professional choirs performing words from their poems while David Sampson composed an original score, *Jersey Rain,* for baritone solo, mixed choir, and orchestra for the event (Sampson, 2001).

What I Learned: The Power of the Poetry of Place – Returning to My Roots

If you are a teacher-artist and your teaching life is your art, then your life and your art must happen somewhere. That somewhere is your place or space. What I learned from ARTifacts and "Jersey Rain" was not only that I was a teacher-artist, but that I had returned to my roots, Morristown, in a deeper more creative way than I had ever recognized before. As Janelle Adsit frames it in "Place-Based Pedagogy and Creative Writing and Fieldwork," "The question, then, for creative writing becomes, not 'can it be taught' but '*where* can it be taught?'" (Adsit, 2017: 154).

"Our Town" Inter-Arts Book Project: Poetry of Place, Ecphrasis, Photography, Self-Publishing

> *Walking is the basic discipline of science of belonging, for this science is based almost entirely upon field work. On foot, we are able to imagine an accord between poetry and ecology.*
>
> – John Burnside, "A Science of Belong: Poetry as Ecology"
> (Burnside, 2006: 105)

> *The creative writing class that takes a fieldwork approach provides an environment where the common conceptions of the writing process can be tested*
>
> – Janelle Adsit, "Place-based Pedagogy and Creative Writing as a Field Work Course."
> (Adsit, 2017: 149)

The outdoors or going outside became early on a signature activity of my creative writing course, one my students frequently requested. (Recall the anecdote in Chapter 2, "It Takes Creativity and Windows," when my students asked to go outside.) It wasn't long before I received a grant to provide my students with instamatic cameras to accompany them on our walks. Students not only took notes; they photographed people (with permission), places, objects, and scenes for poetic responses as well. This resulted in a wealth of photographs of place to inspire poetry. Students were encouraged to take artistic photos – micro and macro images, mirror images, angle shots, blurry photos, upside down images, cut-off faces and objects, and naturalistic photos (all this before the iphone). The ecphrastic books produced were a collaborative effort. Most importantly, each one was different in theme, poetry, and photographic images, but united by relative time and place. Together, they resulted in a powerful and inspiring vision of Morristown through the eyes of its students. The books were shared at a poetry reading for teachers, parents, and the community at the end of the school year.

Model Student "Walk" Poem: "The Morristown Cycle" by Nicole Fortier

The following student model poem of place was written in response to the ecphrastic poetry book project. Nicole wrote the poem viewing a number of her Morristown photos, and Madalyn Baldanzi created a collage of them to illustrate the poem for our high school literary magazine, the *Tricorn*. There were ongoing echoes of 9/11 in the artistic images and juxtaposition of the mundane as the reader "walks" through Morristown, "listens to that fountain," and watches "Morristown go by" (Adding to the echoes of 9/11, the World Trade Center towers was on the cover of the 2004 issue of the *Tricorn*.) Nicole's poem is an example of the "walk poem," characterized generally as "any poem involving a walk" (Padgett,

1987/2000: 200–201). There are four basic types of walk poems, of which there are a great many variations:

- *A poem about what the poet sees during a particular walk;*
- *A poem about a walk that produces a revelation of some kind;*
- *A poem whose length, style and shape mirror the length, style and shape of the walk;*
- *A poem that reflects the way the mind works during the walk.*

The Morristown Cycle
by Nicole Fortier

If you start with the Creamery
With its warm smells and shiny counter
And you exit and turn right
You head towards Morristown.

Past the old police headquarters
Beautiful, remote, sparkling white
But something you don't notice
Anymore.

The Community Theater
Trying valiantly to bring in culture
A musty hall where memories perform.

Continue up South Street
Past those shops on the right
Quaint and small
On and on
A town block

A familiar pink awning
Jersey Boys Bagels
Can you see it?
Can you see their murals on their walls?

Come to the corner of South Street
And the Green
Cross across by the island
Over to Epstein's
A quiet and fragrant maze
Always there.

Then come to the corporate corner
Starbucks, Gap, Godiva, GapKids
Taken for granted
Caffeine, clothes and chocolate.
On back across the street
Pass a friendly hot dog vendor
With a smile and a wave.

Have a seat on a wooden bench
Look across South Street
Listen to that fountain
Watch Morristown go by.

(Fortier, 2004)

What Does Recent Scholarship Say?

In recent scholarship, Adsit (2017) confirms that going outside or teaching in the field has a pedagogy of its own, with a scholarship supporting its value and efficacy: "Place-based pedagogy has seen growing interest in recent decades as this mode of instruction has been linked to increased retention and hands on learning" (p. 149). She notes that since 1991, when little was written about teaching outdoors, scholars have come to agree that "the outdoors may best support our students' engagement with what the poet Mark Doty calls 'the art of description,'" (Doty, 2010). Englehardt and Schraffenberger (2015) propose that through *ecological creative writing* "creative writing teachers and students will deepen their own engagement with the world around them while also cultivating creative writing itself as a site where meaningful interdisciplinary work can be done" (p. 274). Adsit concurs, maintaining that "creative writing and environmental studies are not separate; they face some of the same problems, wanting to change and transform the world in all of its complexity (p. 159). Moreover, Adsit goes one step further:

> Many of us feel compelled to take part in ecosocial justice advocacy [. . .]. We teach a practice that *matters* in both senses of the word. To truly grapple with this fact is to seek new directions for creative writing as it continues to find its place in – and out (doors) of – the academy.
>
> (pp. 158–159)

For Your Teacher Journals: Discovering the Teacher-Artist Self

Inter-Arts Projects

As a teacher-artist, there is no limit to the possibility of inter-arts projects you can create with your students and colleagues. They will emerge organically from the wellspring of your teacher-artist self. Sometimes they will come at the urging and questioning of your students. ("Can we go outside?") Your openness, receptivity and listening will hear it. Other times it will come from your colleagues. ("Let's. . .") Sometimes it may be a moment of necessity. But mostly, it's going to come from your imagination and creativity – knowing your space, place, subject, and what you are passionate about. The best projects are the ones that emerge from the process of creation itself, with you and your students working together as co-learners, co-creators, and partners. Such projects will be exciting, and challenging, and they will take time.

Not every school has broad art offerings and departments (art, graphic arts, photography, and film) or electives like creative writing, journalism, music composition, or social justice. Not every school is safe for going outside. Some schools are safer to be inside. And "fences may make good neighbors" in some areas. Field trips may not be allowed or in some schools permissible. Colleagues may be cooperative or disinterested. Technology, books, and materials may be limited. Nevertheless, you as a teacher-artist can imagine and create.

In light of Covid-19 and the experiences of students and teachers from March 2020 to the present post-pandemic years of sub-variant uncertainty, we need teacher-artists more than ever. The following questions are for your reflection. They will help you brainstorm inter-arts projects for your particular students, school, location, space, and classrooms.

Reflecting on Inter-Arts Projects

1. Reflect on the ARTifact Project and the teaching tool of ecphrastic poetry, the poetry of empathy. How might you use this tool in your teaching and discipline? Can you imagine your students writing poetry to historic photo-journalism, or student-produced photographs, or ancestor photographs?
2. Reflect as a writer and teacher-artist on teaching *in extremis*. How will you respond? Will you seize the "teachable moment?" Will you engage in a spontaneous lesson? Will creative writing or the arts be a tool for you?
3. Reflect on the possibility of creating an inter-arts project for your discipline, course, or subject area. Think of the demographics of your region. Are there subjects to interview? Oral histories to reclaim? Stories to unearth?
4. Reflect on your subject or discipline. Is there an art form you are inspired by or passionate about? Brainstorm an inter-arts project with creative writing, art, music, photography, film, photo-journalism, or investigative journalism within the arts and humanities or across-the-curriculum in your school.
5. Reflect on the power of your place or location. As a teacher artist, imagine creating with your students and/or colleagues an inter-arts project on your place or location. Incorporate multiple art forms – art, architecture, monuments, music or cross curricular disciplines such as historical research, oral histories, investigative interviews, and surveys.

Responding: Writing Prompts

1. If your town could talk, what would it say? What would its waters, rivers, mountains, parks, streets, or monuments say? Write that poem, prose poem, or prose text.
2. Find an ancestor photograph. Write an ecphrastic poem to that photograph. Either (1) describe what you see, (2) address a subject in the photo, or (3) take on the identity of the ancestor in the photo and imagine what that ancestor might be saying to you.

For Your Students: Inter-Arts Project Writing Prompts

Student Instructions

1. Find a piece of artwork that inspires you. It could be a great work of art from the past or the present, or a work of art that represents the subject you are studying. For example, it could be a painting or drawing that in some way depicts one of the following topics: learning, thinking, writing, studying, looking through a microscope, or performing an operation in science. It could also be a work of art depicting an artist, musician, doctor, or scientist. Use the work of art as a title for your writing.
2. Write an ecphrastic poem to the subject in the work of art (poem of address) or take on the identity of the subject and let it talk.
3. Create your own photographic essay and ecphrastic poetry book on "My School," "My Neighborhood," "My Town," or "My City." Either with your class and/or with photography students, take photographs of your town or city, or your school or neighborhood with a theme in mind. Your theme might be the people, monuments, certain areas, architecture, landscape, urban renewal, then and now, parks, town history, demographic history, or environmental history. Write ecphrastic poetry or short essays to accompany the photographs.

PART FOUR: INTERDISCIPLINARY APPLICATIONS

The only true voyage of discovery [...] [is] to see the universe through the eyes of another [...].

– Marcel Proust, "The Captive," in *Remembrance of Things Past*, Vol. III (Proust, 1982: 259–260)

New Literacies, Pedagogies, and Fields of Study

Imagine merging the knowledge and power of the arts and the sciences to advance creativity and literacy. Imagine teacher-writers and teacher-artists joining with scientists, botanists, ecologists, environmentalists, and physicians to teach, write, and communicate to students, colleagues and the lay public. What do you get from such collaborations? New literacies in the academy such as "creative literacy," "ecological literacy," and "interdisciplinary literacy." Adsit (2017) identifies some of these new fields of study: creative writing studies, ecological creative writing, and hybrid pedagogies such as ecosocial justice, ecological ecphrasis, autobiogeography, and autoethnography (Adsit, 2017: 157–158). Additionally, new pedagogies emerge from high school teacher-writers and teacher-artists bridging the divide with (CWAC) and STEAM projects.

At a Glance – Interdisciplinary Teacher-artist Projects

- ***Science Poetry: Interdisciplinary Literacy Tool***
- ***Science, Art, and Writing Initiative (SAW)***
- ***Creative Writing and the Medical Field***
- ***Curious Science Writers (cSw)***
- ***Curious Young Writers (cYw)***
- ***Youth Birding Alaska (YBA)***

Bridging the Arts and Sciences: Creative Writing's Role

> *Any good poet, in our age at least, must begin with the scientific view of the world; and any scientist worth listening to must be something of a poet, must possess the ability to communicate to the rest of us his sense of love and wonder at what his work discovers.*
>
> – Edward Abbey, *The Journey Home* (Abbey, 1991)

Interdisciplinary Applications in Part Four is devoted to bridging the arts and sciences with interdisciplinary pedagogies that "matter" in the sense suggested by Adsit. In support of creative writing's role as "host" to those interdisciplinary efforts, Arthur Stewart's *Converting STEM into STEAM Programs* offer for science educators innovative across-the-curriculum projects to reflect the critical concerns that he and his co-editors identify as the "wicked problems: "*global climate change*, *social injustice*, and *pandemic diseases*" (Stewart, Mueller, and Tippins, 2019: abstract) and (Roth, 2019: 65). The interdisciplinary projects, initiatives, and pedagogies that follow provide innovative models representing teacher-artists and teachers of students from middle and secondary schools world-wide. These models are suggestions to inspire your imagination to create your own teacher-artist projects. The need is ever present. The moment is now. The "wicked problems" call for a new generation of students, teachers, scientists and artists.

Science Poetry: Interdisciplinary Literacy Tool

If ecphrastic poetry is the tool for teaching empathy, then *science poetry*, a close companion, is the *interdisciplinary literacy tool* for bridging the arts and sciences. Science poetry, a genre unknown to me until I began teaching in Morristown High School's Science Academy in 2006, remains one of the most important interdisciplinary tools for English, creative writing, science, and mathematics teachers. Why is this so? Because in teaching science poetry, you are at once teaching creativity, literacy, imagination, and discovery – whether that discipline is English, creative writing, or any sub-subject of science or mathematics. Marcel Proust got it right when he said: “to see the universe through the eyes of another, of a hundred others” is the “true voyage of discovery” (Proust, 1982: 259–260). Science poetry is that voyage. It opens eyes, transforming students and teachers alike. Nothing is more exciting than seeing those eyes open in your classroom when students are truly learning something new – something that they can relate to their authentic selves.

In sum science poetry unites scientific knowledge with creative inspiration, writing, and discovery. It is thus a powerful model for expressing what writers know and love about their chosen disciplines. Previous models in this book have demonstrated that the best writing in all fields is highly creative (recall Chapter 10 on “Breaking Boundaries” and Steven Handel’s creative scientific editorials). Science poetry writing is a model for creative writing in any discipline. It will inspire, inform, and transform, both you and your students to higher levels of creativity, discovery, and knowledge.

What is Science Poetry?

Broadly speaking, science poetry can be defined as any poem inspired and informed by science – its facts, phenomena, principles, theories, questions, observations, and methods. In creating a science poem, the science poet “fuses” together emotional and authentic experience with factual, scientific knowledge, and inspiration. Although a science poem may appear by its title to be “about” a subject of science, a poem to be a poem must mean more than its literal sense; that is, the poem must mean more figuratively or metaphorically than the literal meaning of the words on the page. Therefore, for pedagogical purposes, my science co-teacher in the Science Academy, Erin Colfax, and I stipulated our own working definition of science poetry, one that was instructive for science-minded students and at the same time one that distinguished science poetry from nature poetry as a genre. The definition below is taken from *Writing Poetry through the Eyes of Science: A Teacher's Guide to Scientific Literacy and Poetic Response* (Gorrell with Colfax, 2012: 137).

Our Working Definition of Science Poetry[2]

Any poetry inspired and informed by scientific facts, phenomena, principles, theories, questions, observations, and experience may be considered science poetry if it includes all or most of the following elements:

- *Utilizes both quantitative and qualitative data in a poem;*
- *Utilizes scientific facts, information, or experience to prompt or begin the poem;*
- *Utilizes science, scientific theories, or phenomena as allusion in a poem;*
- *Utilizes science, scientific theories, or phenomena as metaphor in a poem;*
- *Utilizes science, scientific theories, or phenomena as imagery in a poem;*
- *Utilizes specific scientific or technical terms or vocabulary in a poem;*
- *Utilizes science as a subject or theme of a poem.*

The student model by Anne Schwartz that follows exemplifies the artful fusion of the wonder and awe of poetry with scientific knowledge, terminology, and concepts. Most importantly, the student connects her authentic self not only to the poetic process, but to the wider context of what "matters" to her – in particular, evolution, creation, and faith, in the poem, "Us." We hear her voice and feel her longing for humanity, connectivity, and respect for the evolutionary process.

Model Student Science Poem: "Us" by Anne Schwartz, English III Honors, Morristown High School

Us
by Anne Schwartz

There is something comforting about evolution.
The notion that I
did not begin to live a mere sixteen years ago,
but three or four billion,
with the shock of life into that first cell.

I like the idea of a continuum;
A cycle of creatures, of steps along the way,
And I like my part in it.

My skin is not mine, but ours;
of prokaryotes and eukaryotes,
vertebrates and invertebrates,
amphibians and fish,
mammals and primates and humans
and
me.

Think of it! All of us connected,
Ancestors, brothers, sisters, cousins,
All children of that one cell.
That makes you feel a little less lonely,
doesn't it?

The thing I like best, though, is
Natural selection.
The idea of someone, somewhere,
Who's on our side.
Who creates miracles
of camouflage and opposable thumbs
and wings and fingers
Who raised me up to walk on two legs,
And will continue to do so,

in order to watch the world
Unfold.

(Schwartz, 2012)

Commentary on "Who Raised Me Up to Walk on Two Legs"

In "Us," Anne Schwartz fuses awe and wonder of her place in the universe with her scientific knowledge of the "continuum" of evolution. From the "shock of life into that first cell," she traces the "unfolding' – "My skin is not mine, but ours;/of prokaryotes and eukaryotes" – ultimately ending with "and/me." She likes "her part in it" and finds comfort "in the notion of evolution." Nevertheless, this deeply empathetic poem turns in the last stanza to thought provoking questions: "The thing I like best though, is Natural selection/ The idea of someone, somewhere/Who's on our side/Who creates miracles/of camouflage and opposable thumbs/ and wings and fingers/Who raised me up to walk on two legs." Here one can't help but sense. – Who is that "someone" on "our side" who makes "miracles?" And who raised her up to walk on two legs? "And will continue to do so." A creator? Her parents? Evolution? Or, herself?

The poem's open ending provides possible answers. Although some readers may view science, creation, and faith as opposing beliefs, Anne finds "something comforting about evolution," and that is her own connection to the universe through which she can sense "miracles of camouflage." For "Us" and our student poet, the universe if filled with mystery and ambiguity as she stands in wonder "in order to watch the world unfold."

When you read Anne's model science poem, I hope you will also think of teachers and learning. Might teachers have played a role in raising "Anne to walk on two legs"?

Model Student Science Poem: "Redwood" by David Pitt, English III Honors, Morristown High School

Redwood
by David Pitt

Standing tall
I don't suppose you wonder.

No quickened heartbeat
pumping H_2O and glucose faster
through sclerenchyma tracheids
as you watch your brethren fall.
No.
You stand hard as lignin.

You grow
not aging,
cambium augmenting ageless pith.
No
I don't suppose you listen
to the axes.

Majestic greatness
pays no heed.
You've been here a while.
And you might stay.

Although it's getting warmer
adjust stomata
go on growing.

(David Pitt, 2012c)

Commentary on Science Poetry as Ecosocial Justice

David's poem was inspired by a personal experience he had in the California redwood forest. He used the notes from his 10th grade biology class to fuse the science with the poetry in "Redwood" (Pitt, 2012a). David's poem of address to "majestic greatness" reveals his empathetic understanding: "You stand hard as lignin / […] I don't suppose you listen to the axes." David (2012a) comments, "I was trying to capture the reverence I felt towards the tree's passivity as other trees are being chopped down." His protest on behalf of the redwood ends in hope, "adjust stomata/go on growing." "Redwood" exemplifies many of the science poems written by high school students reflective of environmental and eco-social justice concerns. For David Pitt, "my poem deals more immediately with feeling (poetry), alluding to the botany (science)" (*ibid*). Through science poetry, David was able to use his knowledge of science as well as expressing his feelings of awe, reverence, and empathy about the natural world and ecosocial justice. You can almost feel the strike of the axes and hear the "majestic greatness" fall. His poem is timeless, and in the context of 2020, prophetic, too, alluding to the ongoing destruction of the Amazon rainforest, the "wicked problem" of global climate change, and the ongoing ecological predictions planet Earth is faced with.

The SAW Project: Science, Art, and Writing Initiative by Anne Osbourn

> *While scientific terminology and concepts may be off putting for many, stunning scientific images are not. Scientific images intrigue, drawing in children and adults alike. They provide a meeting place, a starting point for scientific exploration. I learned this when trying to find different stimuli to trigger my own creative writing.*
>
> – Anne Osbourn, "Transgressing the Disciplines Using Science as a Meeting Place: The Science, Art, and Writing Initiative"
> (Osbourn, 2019: 150)

Using SAW to Explore a Major Societal Challenge: Control of Infectious Diseases

The Science, Art and Writing (SAW) initiative, by far one of the most successful and exemplary STEAM projects, was born in 2004 as a consequence of research scientist Anne Osbourn's "frustrations as a scientist" with rising specialization in her field and the resulting "inability to communicate with those outside" her field of expertise (Osbourn, 2019: 149). With a degree in botany and a doctorate in genetics, Osbourn was leading an internationally recognized research program on plant natural products. Osbourn "always enjoyed literature and creative writing" (pp. 149–150) but the "constraints of the school curriculum" in the UK did not allow her to pursue both science and the arts (*ibid.*) Then in 2004 she was afforded the opportunity of a fellowship from the UK-based National Endowment for Science, Technology and the Arts (NESTA). Osbourn became a NESTA fellow in the school of Literature, Drama and Creative Writing at the University of East Anglia. For her, "it was an interdisciplinary adventure. My only remit was to find ways of bringing science into everyday lives and language through creative writing" (p. 150).

As a consequence, she founded SAW, a science poetry writing initiative for middle school children, ages 8–12, exploring major societal challenges like controlling infectious diseases with antibiotics. She conducted eight one-day SAW projects in schools in the Norwich area on themes relating to control of infectious diseases. Fourteen scientists took part, working in teams with professional artists and writers, each of which drew on the scientific theme, supported by the images, as a starting point for exploration (pp. 152–154).

The Pedagogy of SAW: Ecphrasis and Intriguing Scientific Images

Remarkably, the central pedagogy of SAW is ecphrasis; that is, writing science poetry in response to viewing a visual image – in Osbourn's case, a scientific one. Osbourn (2019) explains the utility of ecphrasis for science: "intriguing scientific images are central in SAW projects. They make science accessible and help link the science, art and writing sessions in the classroom" (p. 152). Osbourn uses scientific images from partner organizations like the Norwich Research Park (NRP) image library and the John Innes Center.

The images selected for the project related to "different aspects of control of infectious diseases. These included 'bad' bacteria (e.g. *Escherichia coli* in the human intestine), microbes isolated from soil (the source of many antibiotic-producing bacteria), [and] structures of engineered enzymes" (p. 152). For models of student work from the SAW project refer to *SEE SAW: An Anthology of Poetry and Artwork around Science by Children from Rockland St. Mary Primary School and Framingham Earl High School.*[3]

Creative Writing and the Medical Field

What "We Need Now More Than Ever"

> *Physicians who lack a passion for language or who fail to see beauty will be at a loss to translate these wonders in the most meaningful terms for their lay patients and into the larger society around us. We need now more than ever to be able to conduct ourselves in the realm of imagination because what is science if not the dream of something new?*
>
> – Rafael Campo, "Why Should Medical Students be Writing Poems?"
> (Campo, 2006)

Creative Writing for Physicians and Medical Scientists

In the last two decades there has been a growing consensus in science education that writing with clarity in order to communicate with the lay public is not only a necessity for scientists and the public, but for the larger purpose of solving some of the most important problems of our age. To that end, creative writing, poetry writing, and discipline-related writing courses and programs have been offered in medical schools and universities throughout the United States.

One early and prominent example is worthy of attention: "Creative Writing for Physicians and Medical Scientists," an elective taught by Suzanne Klingenstein through the Harvard-M.I.T. Division of Health Sciences and Technology (HST). (According to Liza Weisstuch, who interviewed Klingenstein for the *Harvard*

Gazette, HST students engage in probing analyses of classic works of literature in the setting of an intense writing workshop (Weisstuch, 2001). As reported in the *Gazette* article, Klingenstein advocates writing and the humanities for medical students and scientists: "[Doctors] need a handle on language to think and communicate clearly. When you enter a life of medical research, you enter the life of a writer" (Klingenstein; qtd in Weisstuch, 2001). There could not be a more prophetic statement given the challenges to come.

Narrative Medicine: Empathizing and Humanizing

Rita Charon, MD, PhD, Executive Director of Columbia's Program in Narrative Medicine, is widely recognized as the originator of the field. As early as 2001 (Charon, 2001), she was advocating for this field of study to her colleagues in JAMA. In an August 22, 2022, letter to the editor of *The New Yorker* magazine, Charon (2022) thanked Jerome Groopman for his comprehensive account of the field of narrative medicine that was published in the July 25, 2022 issue (Groopman, 2022). In her letter to the editor, she defines the field as follows:

> Narrative medicine applies the skills that one acquires from analyzing literature to the practice of medicine; it not only makes room for the sharing of war stories, but also provides literary, philosophical, and psychological training that allows medical professionals to perceive and interpret what goes on in the care of the sick. Complex narrative abilities are needed to comprehend patients' experiences of illness, and to represent with fidelity what one has witnessed.
>
> (Charon, 2022)

Groopman, a hematologist-oncologist as well as a writer, enables us to bear witness in his *New Yorker* review, "The Scalpel and the Pen: What Medical Narratives Teach Us" (Groopman, 2022). Reviewing Jay Wellons' mid-career memoir *All that Moves Us* (Wellons, 2022), Groopman demonstrates the power of both the scalpel and the pen to humanize illness. How? He notes that before Wellon began his medical training, he was an English major at the University of Mississippi where he took writing classes with novelists and poets (p. 66) confirming what we as teacher-artists know; that interdisciplinary education, collaborations, and projects foster discovery, innovation, and creativity by bridging students, teachers and disciplines. Such education is transformational for our students who will most likely take on multiple majors in college crossing disciplines and subjects to solve the complex problems and issues for a new generation.[4]

Curious Science Writers

> *With growing medical, environmental, and social issues facing us, the next generation of communicators must be prepared to help people make sense of complex science that affects their health and well-being as well as the world around them. Whether scientists, journalists, or citizen scientists, they will require critical thinking and technical skills to fight science illiteracy that has reached historic levels.*
>
> *Curious Science Writers is the only independent program in the US addressing this critical need at the high school level.*
>
> – Jayne Mackta, Founder, CuriousSCIENCEwriters (Mackta, 2020)

Curious Science Writers (cSw) is a unique and remarkable high school student initiative embracing a CWAC pedagogy that addresses complex issues of scientific, creative, and interdisciplinary literacy. With a focus on training future scientist-writers, the project's stated mission is to advance the art of science communication and promote science literacy. Founded by Jayne Mackta, Curious Science Writers is an innovative STEAM initiative, training creative high school communicators to bring complex science to the general public through the power of story. Designed to expose participants to the real world of science writing, this innovative extra-curricular program offers mentoring by volunteer science communication professionals. The initiative's collaborative process, which involves teams of student writers, editors, and graphic designers, results in credible, engaging science stories disseminated through a variety of traditional and trending media outlets.

curiousSCIENCEwriters (cSw) 2013–2018

cSw operated under the auspices of States United for Biomedical Research from 2013 to 2018. The program is currently (2023) hosted by Americans for Medical Progress (AMP), which has expanded the initiative. In 2015 a professional science communicator, Merry Brennan, helped to refocus the program and its mission statement. The project's emphasis shifted to training high school student writers with an experience that mirrors the real world of science writing. To that end, Monmouth University School of Science hosted a High School Science Communications Forum, and the name of the program changed to curiousSCIENCEwriters (cSw), website http://curioussciencewriters.org.

At the same time, a new teaching process was adopted. Professionals in the field of science writing volunteered to serve as mentors. New Jersey biomedical researchers acted as "Science Stars" while student writers interviewed them. Five teams were created: three to four writers, an editor, a graphic designer, a Science Star, and the committee's Mentor. Going forward, professionals in the field of science writing volunteer to serve as mentors for the project. Students interview the Science Stars and write a story focused on the scientist and his or her research. The students write in three story formats: straight news story, blog, or Q&A.

Current Status: curiousSCIENCEwriters

Americans for Medical Progress (AMP) continued to run cSw both before and throughout the Covid-19 pandemic. The 2020 and 2021 summer Boot Camps were held virtually for safety reasons. Exceptional student science writers and interested science teachers are encouraged to apply at the cSw website http://curioussciencewriters.org.

Curious Young Writers

Curious Young Writers (cYw), grew out of a summer writing project in 2010 sponsored by the New Jersey Association for Biomedical Research. The goal was to promote public understanding of the role of appropriate animal models in biomedical research through the lens of articulate teens. Janyce Mackta recruited six creative high school students to write articles about non-traditional animal research models for a lay audience. The original articles were published in a collection called "Wild Science" and were illustrated by a professional graphic designer. Examples of the Curious Young Writers' "Wild Science" are available at https://curiousyoungwriters.wordpress.com and https://curioussciencewriters.org/articles/2013/08/15/casper-zebrafish/.

Then, in the fall of 2011, a focus group of students and faculty from Morristown High School and High Technology High Schools in New Jersey explored taking the project to the next level. The focus group established a website, a logo, created a Young Science Writers blog, and renamed the group, curiousYOUNGwriters. They also created a Facebook page with a closed group of 59 Curious Science Writers members. In addition, Jayne Mackta and the focus group formalized the organization to include: a faculty advisory board; a team of graphic designers; a program coordinator and paid student staff (an editor in chief, IT coordinator and social media coordinator). The Young Science Writers blog featured stories about uncommon animal models to help researchers find better answers to some age-old health questions. Student bloggers circulated a call for writers to New Jersey biology teachers and eventually selected nine writers from three schools to write science stories on medical topics. In October 2012 the first science story by a student science writer was published on the website: "Golden Retrievers: Man's Best Solution for Duchenne Muscular Dystrophy" (https://curiousyoungwriters.wordpress.com/2012/12/09/golden-retriever-dmd/).

As of this writing (2023), Curious Young Writers continues to maintain a blog of high school student stories featuring uncommon animals that are helping researchers find better answers to some age-old health questions.

Youth Birding Alaska

Youth Birding Alaska (YBA), a model STEAM project, emerged from a small village in rural Alaska where students, teachers, and 15 graduate students from the University of Alaska collaborated on developing a birding project, "Science, Youth, and Integration: The Quest for Mindfulness Through Birding," by Erin A. Ingle and Michael Mueller (Ingle and Mueller, 2019), at the Newhalen School. According to Ingle and Mueller, "Students and their teachers showed a great deal of interest in the project, and we connected with several teachers who wanted to write a grant for the project and build a habitat" (p. 119). The birding habitat would help engage students in science inquiry, as they designed and conducted science investigations. The grant was funded and the habitat was built in 2017.

Birding Project (2017): Quest for Mindfulness Through Birding

In the first phase of Youth Birding Alaska, teachers and graduate students worked with students making observations of birds that visited the habitat, using nature journals and recording date, weather, and bird watching data.

Birding Project (2018): "Mindfulness through Singing"

The next stage of the project involved Erin Ingle leading the students in learning mindfulness through singing. "Singing, like photography, is an arts-based practice that can be used for engaging people in mindfulness" (Ingle and Mueller, 2019: 121). As Ingle and Mueller describe it, "The Newhalen School build-a-bird-habitat project expanded to a network of schools participating in the project premised on the emerging ideas of citizen science as a heuristic for mindfulness" (p. 121).

Birding Project 2018–2019: Measuring Climate Change, Developing Partnerships, Creating Citizen Scientists

The second phase of the project involved a network of schools across the state investigating phenology – the study of cyclical and seasonal natural phenomena in relation to climate. Ingle and Mueller posed the question: "Could teachers and their students become part of a meaningful project for measuring climate-change effects around the world?" (p. 122). For them, the answer was "yes" for several reasons: (1) birds migrate from all over the world to Alaska for summer breeding; (2) Alaska is expected to change faster than most places on Earth under various climate-change scenarios; (3) Alaska is 1/5 the size of the entire United States and could provide a "wide-sweeping" data collection opportunity; (4) students and teachers could connect to one of the most successful citizen science projects organized around phenology, the National Phenology Network (p. 122).

In September 2018, Erin Ingle began developing partnerships with schools across Alaska "as the importance of maintaining partnerships and creating partnerships became paramount to YBA's success" (Ingle and Mueller, 2019: 124). Mueller, with funding from UAA Center for Community Engagement and Learning, established a Resilient Communities Initiative. One of the schools the team collaborated with is based entirely on the YBA philosophy. "This school is called the STrEaM Academy (r=research), and it offers a project-based, experiential education, integrated with STEM for grades 6–8" (p. 128).

For complete appreciation of this inspiring and successful project that brings us full circle from hawk watching in New Jersey in the 1980s (recall Chapter 2) to tracking climate change today in Alaska, see Ingle and Mueller's (2019) work in Stewart, Mueller, and Tippins' (2019) edited collection, *Converting STEM into STEAM Programs: Methods and Examples from and for Education*.[5]

For Your Teacher Journals: Discovering the Teacher-Artist Self

Interdisciplinary Projects

As a writer and teacher-artist engaged in the disciplines of science or mathematics, there is no limit to the possibilities of projects to create, questions to research and answer, and problems to solve in the world of science given the "wicked problems" Arthur Stewart and his co-editors frame in *Converting STEM to STEAM* (Stewart, Mueller, and Tippins, 2019). This chapter's "Interdisciplinary Applications" offer writing-across-the-curriculum literacy tools (science poetry, scientific images, ecphrasis), model science writing, and STEAM projects to adapt to your classroom, subject area, locale, and discipline. Ideas that follow are for your reflection and consideration.

Reflecting

1. Reflect as a teacher-artist, scientist, or mathematician on Rafael Campo's previous quote: What do you think we need now more than ever? What do you think science needs?
2. Reflect upon the "wicked problems" of "global climate change," "social injustice," and "pandemic diseases." Do any of these come to mind as urgent concerns? Does your subject area, pedagogy, or discipline address these questions? How might you as a teacher-artist respond?
3. Reflect how the tool of science or math poetry might inform your students and teaching? How might you use science poetry strategies in your subject area or classroom?
4. Reflect upon a model lesson or model student science poem to use as a writing prompt or starter for discussion.
5. Reflect upon the use of ecphrasis and scientific images for your subject or discipline. How might you use scientific images and ecphrastic poetry to teach a principle or concept? How might your students respond to those scientific images? With scientific poetry and/or artwork?

6. Reflect on the power of your place and location in the sense of place-based pedagogy. As a teacher-artist, imagine creating with your students and/or colleagues scientific research on the environment, geological history, ecology, and climate changes in your region.
7. Reflect on the pedagogy of your place or town. What can your place teach you and your students? How do you approach and address the issue of science denial and illiteracy as it pertains to science and science education?

Chapter 18 Notes

1 "Teaching Empathy through Ecphrastic Poetry: Entering a Curriculum of Peace," originally published in the *English Journal* (Gorrell, 2000), has been re-printed in collective works on teaching peace, empathy, and social justice by Monseau (2004) and Weber (2006): Gorrell (2004, 2006). The lesson plan centers on an ecphrastic poem written by Holocaust survivor, Peter Fischl, titled, "To the Little Polish Boy Standing with His Arms Up" (Fischl, 1994). Students view an historic photograph of the 1943 liquidation of the Warsaw Ghetto and then write their own poetic response. The lesson plan is available at https://www.jstor.org/stable/822293. I presently teach outreach workshops based on this pedagogy through the Holocaust Memorial and Education Center at the Sara and Shimon Birnbaum Jewish Community Center (SSBJCC) in Bridgewater, New Jersey. The outreach workshop is titled "To the Little Polish Boy: Developing Empathy through Ecphrastic Poetry." You can view the students' poetry on permanent exhibition at the SSBJCC website: sssbjcc.org/poetry-intro.

2 *Writing Poetry through the Eyes of Science: Scientific Literacy and Poetic Response* (Gorrell with Colfax, 2012) does not include the pedagogy of teaching math poetry as a separate topic. Therefore, Erin Colfax and I did not stipulate a working definition of math poetry in our book. Nevertheless, in our teaching, several of our students chose to write math inspired poems as well as science poems. For example, the math poem "O Asymptote" by David Pitt (Chapter 8). Our working definition for science poetry may be applied to mathematics with criteria and stipulations applicable to discipline-related terminology, concepts, and principles (e.g. numeracy, equations, formulas, measurements). Mathematics

teachers may want to consult the scholarship of Patrick Bahls, "Math and Metaphor: Using Poetry to Teach College Mathematics" (Bahls, 2009), and the model poems by mathematics teacher Amy Uyematsu throughout this book – in particular, "The Invention of Mathematics" (Chapter 17) and her math poems on Infinity (Chapters 9 and 12).

3 For student models of the project, see Anne Osbourn, Matthew Sweeney, and Jill Pirrie's collection *SEE SAW: An Anthology of Poetry and Artwork around Science by Children from Rockland St. Mary Primary School and Framingham Earl High School* (Osbourn, Sweeney, and Pirrie, 2005).

4 This author recommends the teaching of narrative medicine for secondary students in English, creative writing, or composition for non-fiction and memoir study and writing. Also highly recommended for biology, sociology, psychology, philosophy, history, and humanities courses and elective studies. Students planning medical careers should consider readings recommended by Jerome Groopman: Anton Chekhov, "A Doctor's Visit" (Chekhov, 1898); Perri Klass, *A Not Entirely Benign Procedure* (Klass, 1987/1994); Oliver Sachs, *The Man Who Mistook his Wife for a Hat: And Other Clinical Tales* (Sachs, 1985); John C. Wellons III, *All that Moves Us* (Wellons, 2022); and William Carlos Williams, "The Girl with the Pimply Face" (Williams, 1934).

5 For teachers interested in the pedagogy of the "going outside" and the "outside classroom," Hal Crimmel's (2003) edited collection, *Teaching in the Field: Working with Students in the Outdoor Classroom*, offers useful strategies.

Chapter 18 References

Abbey, Edward (1991) *The Journey Home: Some Words in Defense of the American West*. New York, NY: Penguin. Cited from Brown, Kurt (1998) *Verse and Universe: Poems about Science and Mathematics*, 1. Minneapolis, MN: Milkweed Editions.

Adler, Barbara J. (2002) *ARTifacts: Kids Respond to a World in Crisis*. New York, NY: Alliance for Young Writers & Artists.

Adsit, Janelle (2017) Place-based pedagogy and creative writing as a fieldwork course. In Clark, Michael Dean, Hergenrader, Trent and Rein, Joseph (eds.) *Creative Writing Innovations: Breaking Boundaries in the Classroom*, 149–161. London, UK: Bloomsbury.

Bahls, Patrick (2009) Math and metaphor: Using poetry to teach college mathematics. *WAC Journal*, 20: 75–90. https://doi.org/10.37514/WAC-J.2009.20.1.06

Burnside, John (2006) A science of belonging: Poetry as ecology. Robert Crawford (ed.) *Contemporary Poetry and Contemporary Science*, 91–106. Oxford, UK: Oxford University Press.

Campo, Rafael (2006) Why should medical students be writing poems? *The Journal of Medical Humanities*, 27: 253–254. https://doi.org/10.1007/s10912-006-9022-9

Charon, Rita (2001) Narrative medicine: A model for empathy reflection, profession and trust. *Journal of the American Medical Association*, 286 (15): 1897–1902. https://doi.org/10.1001/jama.286.15.1897

Charon, Rita (August 22, 2022) Letter to the Editor, Stories as medicine. *The New Yorker*, 3.

Chekhov, Anton (1898) "A Doctor's Visit." https://web.seducoahuila.gob.mx/biblioweb/upload/A%20DOCTOR.pdf

Crimmel, Hal (2003) *Teaching in the Field: Working with Students in the Outdoor Classroom*. Salt Lake City, UT: University of Utah Press.

Curious Science Writers (cSw) website http://curioussciencewriters.org

Doty, Mark (2010) *Art of Description.* Minneapolis, MN: Graywolf Press.

Englehardt, James and Schraffenberger, Jeremy (2015) Ecological creative writing. In Peary, Alexandria and Hunley, Tom C. (eds.) *Creative Writing Pedagogies for the Twenty-First Century*, 269–288. Carbondale, IL: Southern Illinois University Press.

Fischl, Peter (1994) "To the Little Polish Boy Standing with His Arms Up." Los Angeles, CA: Archives of Simon Wiesenthal Center.

Forche, Carolyn (1993) *Against Forgetting: 20th Century Poetry of Witness*. New York, NY: W.W. Norton.

Fortier, Nicole (2004) "The Morristown Cycle." *Tricorn Literary Magazine*, 39: 8. Morristown, NJ: Morristown High School.

Gorrell, Nancy (2000) Teaching empathy through ecphrastic poetry: Entering a curriculum of peace. *English Journal*, 89 (5): 32–41. https://doi.org/10.2307/822293

Gorrell, Nancy (2004) Teaching empathy through ecphrastic poetry: Entering a curriculum of peace. In Monseau (2004: 73–88).

Gorrell, Nancy (2006) Teaching empathy through ecphrastic poetry: Entering a curriculum of peace. In Weber (2006: 32–50).

Gorrell, Nancy S. with Erin Colfax (2012) *Writing Poetry through the Eyes of Science: Scientific Literacy and Poetic Response*. Sheffield, UK and Oakville, CT: Equinox.

Groopman, Jerome (July 25, 2002) The scalpel and the pen: What medical narratives teach us. *The New Yorker*, 66–68.

Hollander, John (1995) *The Gazer's Spirit: Poems Speaking to Silent Works of Art*. Chicago, IL: University of Chicago Press.

Ingle, Erin A. and Mueller, Michael (2019) Science, youth, and integration: The quest for mindfulness through birding. In Stewart, Arthur J., Mueller, Michael and Tippins, Deborah J. (eds.) *Converting STEM into STEAM Programs: Methods and Examples from and for Education*, 117–132. Cham, Switzerland: Springer.

Klass, Perri (1987/1994) *A Not Entirely Benign Procedure: Four Years as a Medical Student*. New York: Putnam.

Monseau, Virginia (ed.) *A Curriculum of Peace: Selected Essays from English Journal*. Urbana, IL: National Council of Teachers of English.

Morrison, Toni (December 29, 2019) *New York Times Sunday Magazine*: cover.

Osbourn, Anne (2019) Transgressing the disciplines using science as a meeting place: The science, art and writing initiative. In Stewart, Arthur J., Mueller, Michael and Tippins, Deborah (eds.) *Converting STEM into STEAM Programs: Methods and Examples from and for Education*, 149–167. Cham, Switzerland: Springer.

Osbourn, Anne, Sweeney, Matthew and Pirrie, Jill (eds.) (2005) *SEE SAW: An Anthology of Poetry and Artwork around Science by Children from Rockland St. Mary Primary School and Framingham Earl High School*. The SAW Trust. www.sawtrust.org

Padgett, Ron (ed.) (1987/2000) *The Teachers & Writers Handbook of Poetic Forms* (2nd edition). New York, NY: Teachers and Writer's Collaborative.

Pinsky, Robert (2000) "Jersey Rain." *Jersey Rain Poems*, 52. New York, NY: Farrar, Straus and Giroux.

Pinsky, Robert and Sampson, David (2000–2001) *Jersey Rain Project*. Commissioned by the NEA and the Gerald R. Dodge Foundation and premiered by Harmonium and Masterwork Choruses and the Colonial Symphony.

Pitt, David (2012a) David's commentary on "Redwood." Qtd in Gorrell with Colfax (2012: 274).

Pitt, David (2012b) "Redwood." Qtd in Gorrell with Colfax (2012: 273).

Proust, Marcel (1982) "The Captive." *In Remembrance of Things Past*, Vol. III, 259–260. New York, NY: Vintage Books.

Roth, Wolff-Michael (2019) We need more (than) STEAM: Let's go for life-wide and lifelong education. In Stewart, Arthur J., Mueller, Michael C. and Tippins, Deborah J. (eds.) *Converting STEM into STEAM Programs: Methods and Examples from and for Education*, 55–66. Cham, Switzerland: Springer.

Sachs, Oliver (1985) *The Man Who Mistook his Wife for a Hat: And Other Clinical Tales.* New York, NY: Summit Books.

Sampson, David (2001) *Jersey Rain for Baritone Solo, mixed choir, and orchestra*. https://en.wikipedia.org/wiki/David_Sampson_(composer)

Schwartz, Anne (2012) "Us." Qtd in Gorrell with Colfax (2012: 385–386).

Stewart, Arthur J., Mueller, Michael C. and Tippins, Deborah J. (eds.) (2019) *Converting STEM into STEAM Programs: Methods and Examples from and for Education*. Cham, Switzerland: Springer.

Weber, Chris (2006) *Nurturing the Peacemakers in our Students: A Guide to Speaking about Issues of War and Peace*. Portsmouth, NH: Heinemann.

Weisstuch, Liza (December 13, 2001) A prescription for creative writing. *The Harvard Gazette*. https://news.harvard.edu/gazette/story/2001/12/a-prescription-for-creative-writing/

Wellons, Jay (2022) *All that Moves Us: A Pediatric Neurosurgeon, His Young Patients, and their Stories of Grace and Resilience*. New York, NY: Random House.

Williams, William Carlos (1934). "The Girl with the Pimply Face." https://www.coursehero.com/file/120023638/The-Girl-With-a-Pimply-Face-ENG002/

Epilogue: "The Students in the Window"

The Pandemic Radically Changes Education

As I write the Epilogue to this book, the actual grasshopper in the window of the Prologue that begins this book no longer exists. If it did, it would more likely be a lantern fly *(Lycorma delicatula)*, another planthopper species, an invasive one that plagued much of New Jersey in September of 2021 – quite prophetic. Yet, in actuality, what "plagued" my students and colleagues the most was the pandemic and the "new normal" of virtual education it created. In early March of 2020, the United States shut down in response to Covid-19. What happened next varied state to state and district to district. In New Jersey, all district schools closed, Morristown High School included. But education didn't stop. It just changed – radically. For students at Morristown High, the spring of 2020 brought "Google Meets," virtual schoolwork, and zoom meetings. Students were isolated at home, and "going to school" by viewing computer screens. For far too many students, the radical change brought much more than virtual education. Amarie Orbeta, a creative writing student in Jennifer Furphey's class, for example, recalls: "2 am zoom funerals and zoom novenas as two family members succumbed to Covid-19 within the same week."

A New Window Metaphor: The Windows of Virtual Education

Virtual education brought radical educational change during the pandemic prompting my long-time creative writing colleague, Jennifer Furphey, and me to wonder how we were going to collaborate during the pandemic while our students were looking at computer screens. We often successfully taught the *Inside Looking Out/Outside Looking In* exercise to the creative writing students (recall Chapter 2). With virtual education in mind, the computer presented a view, in a sense, of "inside looking inside" – at a computer screen – and also inside looking at multiple screens and faces in a zoom sequence. The windows of virtual education presented a radical educational change – a computer-window metaphor for our students to see and focus upon. How would they respond?

Poetry and Prose from the Pandemic: September 2021

In the spring of 2020, the students of Morristown High became "The Students in the Window." Their "Poetry and Prose from the Pandemic," written in September, 2021, in Jennifer Furphey's creative writing classes, speak to the moment.

Let's listen to their voices.

"The Restricted Window" by Colleen Lavin, 12th Grade

The Restricted Window
by Colleen Lavin

2 windows reside on separate sides of my bedroom
1 sits at the foot of my full-sized bed

April 2020
I spent a lot of time with Her.

She sat with me through my darkest days
The days where I wasn't sure if I'd see tomorrow
She covered my face, neck, arms with cold kisses

She sang to me as I wept, wondering what my next move
would be

  the red Japanese oak swayed in the breeze
  I studied the patterns of the leaves and rhythm of wind

  the gray and black clouds swept across the sky
  I picked out patterns and shapes

She taught me how to focus on the beauty that resides right
outside my wall,
rather than the demons sitting inside of myself

Our family cars remain in the driveway
for weeks on end

Exact spots, have not moved in weeks
Nobody has come, nobody has gone.

May 2020
the leaves have increased their vibrancy
the cars have left; but returned

I have started to make friends with others,
not only Her
rabbits make their rounds,
squirrels now scaling the oak
but of course, She was still there

She will always be there.

"I Owe Hozier My Life's Savings, Sunlight Really Does Hit Different Bro" by Amarie Orbeta, 12th Grade

I Owe Hozier My Life's Savings, Sunlight Really Does Hit Different Bro

by Amarie Orbeta

I'm not scared of the dark, but I have to admit I'd *hate* to get curtains like the ones my brother has in his room. They're the thick, heavy type that are supposed to help you sleep better, the kind that keeps the room in a perpetual state of deep, dark quiet. When I got my own room, I insisted on sheer curtains so I could gaze easily through the faint pastel tint of the drapery, straight through to mama's gaggle of flowers that lived just below, so every possible ray of sunlight could shine through, unrestrained.

Hozier once sang of sunlight, repeating the word again and again – *sunlight, sunlight, sunlight* – in dearly devoted prayer. It's a sort of sentimentality that I connect with.

My world narrowed in a fishlike lens during the pandemic, all distorted and watery, until there was no world except for my room and the surrounding area of our condo unit. I looked through that window less and less and stared more at school Google Meets and virtual schoolwork and zoom meetings and a 2 am zoom funeral and two different zoom novenas as two family members succumbed to Covid within the same week.

I stared blankly at my screen more after that, having no excuse to skip on virtual school yet unable to focus.

Then there was a sunny day. There'd been several sunny days as the year trudged on, but they hadn't quite registered properly in my mind. But then there was a sunny day when I'd finally thought to glance out that window again. I saw the trees as they bent to the wild frenzy of the wind, and as I glanced down, I watched as our outdoor trash containers went rolling down the driveway, swept away in the gusts. I bolted outside to grab them, but just as I got a grip on one, the most forceful gust yet pushed its way through. The other container bumped me on the leg as I staggered forward, completely taken off guard by the wind.

As I managed to regain my bearings and maintain a firm grip on both containers, I turned to face the wind and that's when I saw that *sunlight, sunlight, sunlight*. I made sure to secure the garbage containers first, but afterwards I just stood there in the driveway, basking in the sunlight. The wind would die down and pick back up erratically and the clouds would occasionally hide the sun, but I kept standing there in a trance. I couldn't tell you how long I spent there, raising my arms up to catch wind and sun alike, my hair a mess and my face cold, laughing.

I look out the window more often now. The wind has never gotten that strong again yet, but the sunlight always comes back.

Sunlight, sunlight, sunlight.

"Glass Doors" by Alexandra Lysiak, 12th Grade

Glass Doors
by Alexandra Lysiak

The sun penetrated through the glass,
Outside he sat staring into abyss
Unaware of me or the nearby deer,
His warm embrace was all I missed.
But he was far from reach,
Each time I tried to get close,
The glass door shut a little more.
I would yell and scream
But his gaze was to the trees.
The sun got brighter,
Burning me as I touched the glass
I reached out to him with all my strength,
But I knew,
His fight was over.
He was at peace.
And at once
The glass door shut,
And he was gone.
All that left was the penetrating sun
And the closed glass doors.

A Teaching Collaboration: September, 2021 – Jennifer Furphey's Creative Writing Class, Morristown High School, Morristown, New Jersey

Given the global pandemic, my colleague, Jennifer Furphey, and I were wondering how students might respond to the *Inside Looking Out / Outside Looking In* exercise after having experienced the virtual education of the past spring (recall the exercise in Chapter

2). Jennifer was eager to collaborate in a poetry writing project. Her students, grades 9–12, had spent the spring of 2020 in class for a total of four hours each morning. They learned on a rotating schedule, their class split: Half the class would be present in school, wearing masks; the other half of the class would be home on Google Meets, looking through a computer screen. Under such a virtual system, Jennifer and I speculated:

- *Would the "windows" the students were looking through take on different meanings – literal, figurative, or poetic?*
- *Would the students choose to write "zooming" poems?*

The Context of the Return: September 2021

By the law of the State of New Jersey, all students returned to school in September 2021. Masks and social distancing were mandated. At Morristown High School, teachers were instructed by the administration to spend the first two weeks of classes in ice breaker and socialization activities given the peer isolation students had experienced during the past spring. Jennifer thought the window writing exercise – *Inside Looking Out / Outside Looking In* – would be a valuable activity to do with her creative writing students in the opening days. The idea for the collaboration and the poetry writing project was born.

The poetry and prose Jennifer and I received exceeded our expectations. The students spoke to the moment with the authenticity that only comes from engagement in extremity. Such engagement is above all else transformational – that is, life changing for the writer, and transformative – that is, affecting change in the reader. The poetry and prose from the pandemic challenged us as teachers and readers. The remainder of the Epilogue includes additional poetry and prose from September 2021 during the pandemic, with comments from the student writers.

Windows of Memory: Additional Poetry and Prose from the Pandemic, September 2021

The window in my colleague's classroom looks out over the exact football field where my creative writing students saw the science students hawk watching four decades ago (recall Chapter 2). To our surprise, not one student wrote about looking out that specific window. Why? Most likely that window held little importance to them. The large majority of students closed their eyes, turned inward, and recalled "windows of memory." Memories – whether those memories were painful or pleasant was the clear choice many students made over the isolation, loneliness, sadness, and loss that so many felt and suffered over the past school year.

Mary Wisloff, a 9th grade student, writes of memories that led to overwhelming feelings of sadness:

> When I first started doing this prompt, I thought I'd see some happiness and all rainbows and butterflies and the sugar-sweet stuff. But my head went down and I closed my eyes and pictured my best friend's house. I saw her bay window that's in her kitchen. We have so many memories there. But when I looked out the window, it was a rainy day. The rain was dripping from the trees very slowly, and you could hear the leaves falling, and you could smell autumn arriving. But I just had such a pit in my stomach when looking out this window. It just felt like I shouldn't be looking out of it, or that I am not meant to be looking. When I reached out of the window to touch and feel the outside air, it was crisp outside. I reached out to touch a tree that looked close by, but the closer I got to touch it, the farther away it would go. I felt confused, so I just picked my head up and wrote about it.

"Everything Makes You Want to Go Back": "2019" by Jocelyn Andrade Mancia, 9th Grade

2019

by Jocelyn Andrade Mancia

hear the leaves fall,
everyone laughing, buses creaking

the cold breeze, the smell of fall and winter
the taste of Takis Fuego and pizza from lunch,
from no masks to hanging out,
meeting new friends, the joy of tears
from hearing 2019, the dances of TikTok
everything makes you want to go back.

"Blue is the Color" by Kasey Lynch, 12th Grade

Blue is the Color
by Kasey Lynch

Blue is the color of the walls in the room,
Shared by two sisters who never got along.
Purple is the color of her new room,
All to herself, for better or worse.
Pink were the streaks of the sunset,
As she peered out the window of the blue room.
Peaceful was her big sister laying on the roof,
Which they had learned to climb onto a few years before.
Louder grew the music as she opened the window,
Her sister's favorite songs that she never really liked.
Warm was the spring turned summer air,
As she stepped through the window and laid next to her sister.
Familiar was the view,
The street and trees and yard they had looked upon for years.
Crisp is the fall wind that blows in the window now,
The rustling leaves a tell-tale sign of change.
Empty is the blue room,
With the older sister thousands of miles gone.
Longing is the little sister gazing out the closed window,
For just another sunset on the roof, listening to music she never really liked.

"Through the Window Pane" by Haven McGuinn, 10th Grade

Through the Window Pane
by Haven McGuinn

Hands touching the frostbitten glass
A deer patters by leaping with grace
Trapped in this wintery impasse
All other buildings previously defaced

The smell of Christmas, hot cocoa and pine
Peppermint, cinnamon and clove
Snowflakes mixing starting to combine
Tucked away shivering in my cove

New, fresh and luminous
The promise of daydreams
The pale owl watching all numinous
A neighbor's smoky fireplace letting off steam

Most things frozen in time
My snowman, denizen
The skies of hope in their prime
The world is the shade of benzine

Opening the window, hit with a blast
Leaning out immersed
Feeling the inside and outsides stark contrast
Winter goes on as if rehearsed.

Haven's Reflection on "Through the Window Pane"

"Through the Window Pane" is a memory of how I feel in the winter time and the serenity it brings. The gloomy benzine is meant to be a reference to our current global conditions of climate change. My poem displays the winter magic and how it feels to be looking out through the inside, and at the end, finally opening up the window.

"My Window, My Friend," by Shivani Vel, 12th Grade

My Window, My Friend
by Shivani Vel

Most mornings, she greets me with a bright, sunny smile, her cheerful, chirping laugh clearing my head of sleepiness. Her sweet perfume tickles my nostrils, filling my nose with notes of wildflowers and cut grass.

She catches me up on current affairs: the changing seasons, snippets of neighborhood chatter, and the concert happening at the local park. She is my view of the outside world.

Sometimes, I am greeted with a downpour of tears, a booming voice, and eyes flashing like lightning. Behind the glass, her emotions may change suddenly and strongly. But she always protects me from them. I have never once been wet by her tears.

She is my friend, but close enough to be family. She sees my most intimate moments. She cheers on my successes and consoles me through disappointments. She has seen me grow into who I am today. In fact, she has shaped who I am today. No matter where I go, I always come home to her. My bedroom window, my dearest friend.

"Bad News" by Shane Quinn, 12th Grade

Bad News
by Shane Quinn

From the highest of highs
to the lowest of lows.

The light inside dies,
but nobody knows.

The silence is loud,
a friend seems like a stranger.

You feel in the midst of a crowd,
but they mustn't see the anger.

The lights of the night become a blur,
the darkness is evermore grand.

What the future holds, it is unsure,
all you know is you'll need a hand.

Your ears begin to ring,
It's all you can hear.

The pain will sting,
but the truth remains,

We persevere.

"Like a Leaf" Prose Poem by Jordan Robinson, 12th Grade

Like a Leaf

by Jordan Robinson

Looking through the window, the breeze tickles my skin. . . I am light. The serenity of the morning sun glistens through the double-panes enveloping my soul. I feel free. . . like a weight has been lifted off of my shoulders allowing me to levitate to new heights. I am light like the sun's soft rays – light like a leaf. I stand on my tippy-toes, reaching up to the calming sky above only to lean over and be whisked away by the wind. I am free. . . floating through the sky, my fluidity taking me to new heights. At the peak of my journey through the air, I no longer hear the whistle in my ears. I began to fall. . . no, not fall. . . descend. Gradually. . . softly. . . peacefully I kiss the ground. The grass embraces me as my back conforms to the damp soil. I look up at the sky, out at the world, down at the green surrounding me, and I feel light.

I turn my head, meeting myself in the window's reflection. I stretch my neck and wiggle my toes, mimicking my inverse image. . . or perhaps she is mimicking me. Inhaling the morning dew, exhaling any negativity, I feel calm. Not the calm you experience before a storm, but the calming energy of true peace. Grateful for my life journey, accepting of my character, in tune with my emotions. I am at as much peace with my life as I am with myself. Going with the wind like a leaf. . . I am light. I am me.

Jordan's Reflection on "Like a Leaf"

The window I pictured in my piece, "Like a Leaf," is the window across from me when I'm in my favorite seat at the kitchen table. Out of this window I can see night lights of the town, stars when the sky is clear, trees swaying in the wind. . . just little things in life that bring me peace of mind. The scenery is ever-changing like the dynamicity we all experience in life, so as I sip my tea, and look out of the window, I feel grounded. I feel light as I gaze beyond the four walls of my kitchen, and humbled in my existence knowing that like the world I view through this window, I am constantly adapting.

An Ending – "The Students in the Window"

"The Students in the Window" collaboration of September 2021 is over, but my colleague's teaching, your teaching, and the endemic continue. I have shared with you in this Epilogue just a fraction of the responses we received. We were surprise, heartened, and inspired by the responses. It is our hope that you have been inspired as well.

To that end, I offer "Light / Refraction" by Stefanie DeFronzo as a concluding poem. Stefanie wrote "Light / Refraction" from her non-stop writing exercise (recall Chapter 6).

"Light / Refraction" by Stefanie DeFronzo, Biochemistry and Molecular Biology Major, Drew University

Light
by Stefanie DeFronzo

Sizzle
Stress
Not manageable
Without the lid

The vegetables simmer on the stove top
In oil
Sitting
Spitting
Squishing
Next to one another
Pieces in the pan
Children in the sandbox
Tan, grey, green, orange, red, black, brown
In one sauté
On one cast iron
Fire in the hole
Like a belly

Refraction

Tan, grey, green, orange, red, black, brown
Pieces in the pan
Children in the sandbox
Crayons in the box
Each unique
Respected
And equal
Colors
Vegetables
Human beings
For love
Is not blind
But bountiful
And colors are not dividers
But reasons to celebrate
The complexion of life

Stefanie's Reflection on "Light / Refraction"

The "light" of this work stems from emotions I found within myself on a given day during the COVID-19 crisis. I was sitting in the kitchen while my parents were cooking dinner when I decided to start the non-stop writing prompt. Crowded by so many diverging thoughts and feelings, my senses seemed to help my brain focus on the concrete things around me while still allowing it to wander to raw sentiments. . .

Stefanie's Reflection on June 2020

Being a college senior during the Coronavirus pandemic was not easy. Having the quintessential (and sentimental) traditions surrounding a final university semester and commencement ceremony surprisingly stripped away from me and my classmates is definitely not how I envisioned ending my time at Drew University. My heart is breaking for the world, but in particular, all seniors during this time.

Thrown into the spotlight most recently was the fight for racial justice and equality. It seems everyone is fighting something and fighting for something, and these battles are not being won easily. In the "refraction" of my "light," I decided to hone in on these thoughts, specifically of racial and social equality. To me, the thought that this specific fight has not yet been won in 2020 is preposterous. Society, art, culture, science. . . life (!) thrives on diversity, and I believe that it is our differences that should not only be celebrated, but should bring us together in respect.

When the mind roams, the poetry flows. Let's all keep our minds open then. . .

Conclusion

No book for teachers can be published in the 21st century without addressing the global pandemic and its ever-changing consequences for learning, literacy, creativity, and education. I wrote the first draft of this book's conclusion in December 2019. That was then – *before*. Before March 2020, when a global pandemic of historic import – a 100-year event; a once in a lifetime *teachable moment* of unknown duration, closed American schools. Now it is *after.* Will it be possible to read any work after Covid-19 without placing it in its historic and social context? Not likely. I use the word *after* cautiously. Will there be an after? What will the "new normal" be like?

I Wonder What Lone Wolf Would Say?

With that thought in mind, I re-read Lone Wolf's poem, "To Teach is to Learn" that begins the Introduction to this book.

to teach is to learn
to learn is to be
to be is to sing the earth's song
and walk in the path
to become whole people
let us touch, let us listen
let us be a gift to the other
let our gifts and our spirits ride

in our hearts and minds
and give us the strength
to complete the great circle
do not be afraid to be
differences teach
do not be afraid to sing
your heart's song
to the earth with honor and love
walk gently
sing loudly
teach

(Lone Wolf, 1976)

In rereading, I had a startling revelation. Prior to the pandemic, I had always read the poem as hopeful, with a strong pedagogical message – *to teach is to learn.* But in the context of the global pandemic, the poem, as all great poems do, speaks to the moment with new meaning. Never before had I focused so clearly on the words, "and give us the strength." The emphasis on needing "strength" to complete the "great circle," to save lives underscores the moment of extremity. So, too, do the words "do not be afraid to sing" that resonate so powerfully when we must socially distance and when many are "afraid to be," to "touch," or to "sing the earth's song," masked from the breath of life of others.

In the context the pandemic, Lone Wolf's poem becomes a prayer –"let us touch / let us listen / let us be a gift to the other" – one that resonates for our time, and for our muse, *teaching,* itself, with courage and hope for humanity: "do not be afraid to be / differences teach / do not be afraid to sing / your heart's song.

Given the "wicked problems" identified in Arthur J. Stewart and his co-editor's work – the global pandemic, climate change, and social injustice – Lone Wolf's poem raises timely and urgent questions:

- *Can we "walk in the path / to become whole people?"*
- *Do we have "the strength / to complete the great circle?"*

- *Can we sing our "heart's song / to the earth with honor and love?"*

His answer, one that supports the thesis and ethos of this book, lies in his last three lines:

> We can but we must. . .
> walk gently,
> sing loudly
> teach

What We Need Now More Than Ever

> *We need now more than ever to be able to conduct ourselves in the realm of imagination because what is science if not the dream of something new?*
>
> – Rafael Campo, "Why Should Medical Students be Writing Poems?"
> (Campo, 2006)

> We need broad-thinking, courageous, highly interdisciplinary students – many of them!
>
> – Arthur J. Stewart, *Converting STEM into STEAM Programs*
> (Stewart, 2019)

We Need Teachers Who Are Becoming to Teach Students Who Are Becoming

Rafael Campo and Arthur Stewart get it right, but I might also add, we need teachers who are *becoming* to teach those students who are becoming, too. If you have been teaching and writing all along, you have undoubtedly been learning. Wherever you are has been your entry point. On the way, you have come to trust the process, have faith in yourself and your students, and you have found the center of your creative spirit. You have discarded baggage, reframed the myths of your professional life, and forged a new understanding of what it is to be a teacher, a writer, and a teacher-writer.

You have walked the path not alone, but with your many selves, and with your students, and colleagues. You have become a teacher who writes while you teach your students to write whether you are an English teacher, language arts teacher, or a teacher of another subject or discipline. By walking your path, you have redefined the space of your classroom to include the worlds inside and outside, local and global, and cyber. You have opened the literal and poetic windows of your life and the life of your students. You not only notice the "grasshoppers" on the window sills of your classroom, you anticipate their coming. And when they come, you are ready to teach the spontaneous lesson.

In your creative courage, you are patient. You wait for the moment and you know it when it appears whether it be a 9/11 moment, or on the tip of the tongue of a student or colleague. You seize the moment when it happens, and you teach, create, and write.

As a creative being, you know it as well. You feel it. Your life has become a work of art. You are a teacher-artist. You teach, write, and collaborate with your colleagues in your discipline or theirs. For the joy that it is to create, for the joy that it is to feel the identity of all selves – *teacher, writer, teacher-writer, teacher-artist* – you are grateful. Grateful for what you feel for the many gifts you receive from your muse, *teaching*. And now you are prepared, prepared to face whatever teaching situation may come, be it education, miseducation, or a global pandemic that no one could ever predict.

Our School Kids Are Not Alright: Effects of Remote Learning

What we need now more than ever are students to teach and teachers to teach them. But during the pandemic academic years of 2020–2021, that simple instruction was not so simple. An August 21, 2021 *New York Times* Editorial "The School Kids are not Alright" called to the public's attention "the worst disruption of public schooling in modern history":

> Virtually every school in the nation closed in March 2020 replacing face-to-face schooling with thrown-together online education or programs that used a disruptive scheduling process to combine the two. Only a small portion of the student body returned to fully opened schools the following fall. The resulting learning setbacks range from grave for all groups of students to catastrophic for poor children.
>
> (*New York Times* Editorial Board, 2021)

Most importantly, *The Times* reports that remote instruction was clearly a factor in driving what researchers call disenrollment. "Thomas Dee and his associates found that schools that went strictly remote experienced a 42 percent increase in disenrollment compared to those that offered full-time in-person learning (*New York Times* Editorial Board, 2021). "One thing everyone agrees on: The pandemic has left American public education in crisis" (Goldberg, 2021: 4).

> "We are now well into the third school year that has been deformed by the virus. In large districts around the country, enrollment is down. Many students are far behind academically and floundering emotionally.
>
> (p. 4)

Goldberg documents cases from parents recounting the depression experienced by their children, attempts of suicide, and the dropping of students' grades from "A's," to "D's," and "F's" (p. 4). Furthermore, *The Times* Editorial reported more than a million children who had been expected to enroll in local schools did not show up, either in person or online: "The missing students were concentrated in the younger grades, with the steepest drop in kindergarten – more than 340,000 students" (*New York Times* Editorial Board, 2021). If the pandemic were an experiment on the need for in-school, face-to-face education for students and teachers, there is no question the case has been proven.

Teaching in Endemicity and Uncertainty[1]

With the outbreak of Omicron, the latest variant of SARS-CoV-2 virus, it has become increasing evident that the "new normal" will be education during a *pandemic*, *epidemic*, or an *endemic* for an indefinite period of time. Science journalist Eleanor Cummins explains: "Every wave of the pandemic has posed its challenges, but Omicron offers the vaccinated a preview of one of the more frustrating aspects of *endemicity:* regular breakthroughs (Cummins, 2021: 7). Bioethicist Nancy Jecker explains further in identifying the crux of the problem: "We will continue to have variants of concern emerging as long as we have large swaths of the human population that are unprotected" (Nancy Jecker; qtd in Cummins, 2021: 7).

What is our best hope for teaching in endemicity? Cummins (2021) describes it this way:

> With the eradication of Covid-19 off the table, the hope has been that one variant – in the best-case scenario, an innocuous one – would finally push the United States toward endemicity, a consistent but relatively contained level of infection [...]. Ideally, people would be both vaccinated and regularly boosted so they have protection against disease when they are exposed to any variant.
>
> (p. 7)

How This Book Can Help

If you are teaching in the uncertain future, consider this: you are a first responder. Why? Because you may be the first "face" of the day your students will see in real time. And because there are so many variables you cannot possibly predict or plan for – too much educational loss, too much social and emotional loss, and too much uncertainty – you will have to both plan and be spontaneous. You, alone in your classroom, will have to decide: Where and how to begin? Do you greet your students by testing, assessing, and measuring? Or, do you greet your students with activities to affirm a sense of community, of belonging, and of the power of learning together? The pedagogy, the philosophy, and the ethos of this book encourage the latter – greeting your students with affirming activities to get them excited about learning your discipline. You could think of the activities as ice-breakers to introduce your students to each other or to your course.

Teaching in Uncertainty: Teach Creativity and Literacy

The underlying fundamentals that unite all teachers and all disciplines are creativity and literacy. By literacy we mean reading and writing which go hand in hand. Now more than ever, our students, our teachers, and our schools, need creativity, literacy, reading and writing as defined and explored in this book. We need now more than ever creativity – as process, as discovery, as collaboration across the disciplines. And we need now more than ever critical and divergent thinking – "How do I know what I think till I see what I say?" – teaching reading, writing, and speaking (see Chapter 15, "Discovering the Creative Process"). Furthermore, we need scientific literacy to "cut the communication fog" so that students – our future scientists – can read and write scientific information for themselves, and for the lay public.

You have read this book. *Teaching is your muse*. You are prepared with a host of activities, lessons, strategies, pedagogies, and ideas for inter-arts projects, and interdisciplinary collaborations. You can find the joy in teaching even in an age of uncertainty. Remember: *to teach is to learn.*

The following is a review of the pedagogies offered by this book, with particular attention to teaching exigencies during uncertain or pandemic and endemic times.

Teaching Pedagogies in Review

Works in Progress (Chapter 1)

A teaching philosophy of Works in Progress encourages risk-taking and creativity. It is an ideal pandemic pedagogy given global academic loss, social isolation, mental health issues, and the need for self-affirmation. The pedagogy holds that all writing is a work in progress as well as the writer is a work in progress. This pedagogy works best with portfolio assessment and a contract grading system. See Chapter 1, "A Most Unlikely Creative Writing Class" of basic students.

(CWAC) Creative Writing Across the Curriculum (Chapter 6)

Creative writing is a transferable skill that improves writing as well as close reading and critical thinking (Peary, 2015: 196). Creative Writing Across the Curriculum enhances WAC practice and is appropriate as a pandemic pedagogy in light of global academic loss and the need to teach creativity and literacy across the disciplines. This pedagogy supports the writing as process movements. See the related chapters on CWAC, including Chapter 7, "Knowing Your Students: Times of Transition and Transformation," and Chapter 8, "Knowing the Creatively 'Gifted' Student."

It Takes Creativity (Chapters 2 and Chapter 15)

Teaching creatively, teaching about creativity, teaching the creative process, and encouraging creative thinking and creative courage remain the foundational pedagogy of this book. This pedagogical orientation is also an excellent antidote for the pandemic. The activities below will encourage students to find the self-affirming creativity within themselves as they collaborate with their peers. See the related Chapter 8, "Knowing the Creatively 'Gifted' Student."

It Takes "Windows" (Prologue, Chapter 2, Chapter 14, and Epilogue)

The "Windows" pedagogy is a literal, figurative, and poetic theme throughout the book. A "Windows" orientation is moreover an ideal pandemic pedagogy given the isolation and social distancing as well as academic loss. See Chapter 2 regarding the pre-pandemic use of the window writing activity "inside looking out / outside looking in" and the Epilogue for pandemic poems: "The Students in the Window." See the Prologue for the "The Grasshopper in the Window or What Keeps Me Teaching." See the related Chapter 14, "Discovering the Power of Audience," and the Johari Window activity as a method to teach "what is poetry?" and human communication.

"Going Outside" Pedagogy (Chapters 2 and 18)

"Going outside" was a core creative writing pedagogy in pre-pandemic days linked to environmental and ecological studies (Chapter 2). "Going outside" is also a useful pandemic pedagogy to combat social isolation and social distancing as well as a strategy to further a healthier teaching environment – teaching outside in the open air whenever possible. See Chapter 18 for new ecological pedagogies and for the related genre of the walk poem, "The Morristown Cycle," and the Youth Birding Alaska (YBA) project.

Science Poetry Writing: Interdisciplinary Literacy Tool (Chapter 18)

Science poetry is an interdisciplinary tool for writing in which students can use language creatively and demonstrate scientific or mathematical literacy in a poetic form. Science Poetry Writing can function as a pandemic pedagogy to address the academic loss experienced by both arts and science-minded students in English, writing, science, and mathematics classes. See the related chapters of student reflections and model poems in Chapters 6, "The Second Law of Thermodynamics" by Alex Davis, and in Chapter 8, "O Asymptote" by David Pitt.

Inter-Arts Projects (Chapter 18)

Inter-Arts Projects foster creativity, student engagement, discovery, and critical thinking. In providing resources in different media for responding to academic loss, social isolation, and social distancing, inter-arts projects serve well as pandemic pedagogies. Create your own inter-arts projects that relate to your school, locale, and colleagues. See Chapter 18 for models.

STEM or STEAM Projects (Chapter 18)

STEM and especially STEAM Projects can function as interdisciplinary pedagogies to foster creativity, student engagement, discovery, and critical thinking. They have a valuable role as pandemic pedagogies in the face of academic loss and social isolation in the arts and sciences. See the project-based learning (PBL) models from Chapter 18, including The SAW Project: Science, Art and Writing Initiative; CuriousSCIENCEwriters (cSw): Model Science Writing Project; and Youth Birding Alaska (YBA): A Model STEAM project.

Ecphrasis, The Poetry of Empathy (Chapter 18)

Ecphrastic response inspires creativity by asking the viewer/poet to respond empathically to works of art or, more generally nowadays, to all kinds of visual images. Given its empathic basis, ecphrastic poetry can be an effective interdisciplinary pandemic pedagogy for combatting social isolation and social injustice. See the student model of an ecphrastic poem protesting social injustice by Danielle Cerny, "Figure Drawing" (Chapter 18). Also see Anne Osbourn's SAW project, which uses scientific images of bacteria for students' ecphrastic response (Chapter 18). You can refer as well to this author's use of ecphrasis to create empathy and social justice through poetic response to an historic photograph of the Warsaw Ghetto liquidation, 1943 (Gorrell, 2000).

Pedagogy of the "Power of Audience" (Chapter 14)

A pedagogy focused on the "Power of Audience" addresses communicative and collaborative teaching goals and can play an important part as a pandemic pedagogy in the context of social isolation and social distancing experienced by students. The Johari Window exercise in Chapter 14 explores four psychological dimensions of human communication that may serve as an ice breaker, discussion starter, creative writing exercise, or lesson in analyzing poetry or teaching "what is poetry?" See the related chapters addressing the power of audience in writing: for example, writing for oneself and writing for others (Chapter 15), writing for your students and discipline (Chapter 17), and writing for publication (Chapter 13).

Hope Arises. . . Open Your Windows and Listen to Your Students

I still believe in open windows. In the context of the global pandemic, now more than ever, we need them. We need air, we need open air, we need the outside, and going outside. Our students are saying this in their pandemic poems. They also are saying they want to "fly." I think of Jordan Robinson's pandemic prose poem, "Like a Leaf." This generation has hope. I think of the end of Amarie Orbeta's pandemic poem: "the sunlight always comes back. *Sunlight, sunlight, sunlight."* This generation is resilient. I think of the last words of Shane Quinn's poem: "the truth remains / We persevere." They are saying they are resilient and hopeful, too. My hope is that you will open your windows, literally if possible, and most definitely, poetically.

I offer for consideration a timeless, pre-pandemic poem written by Elise Rosenberg in creative writing class. Hope arises. . .

Poetry on a Plane
by Elise Rosenberg

If I were to write a verse
sitting on a plane
in my cramped seat with my stiff legs
I would probably produce
a terribly contrived
stanza
with as many beats per line
as there are seats in my row
and words as small and mechanical
as the tiny overhead compartments.
And it would be about as satisfying
as the honey roasted peanuts
that you nibble on

for the same reason
you would read this poem
. . .because it's there.

But
if I were to climb out
the little window
next to me
and sit on the wing of the plane
I would feel the air and the clouds
against my skin
and I would pound out
the most liberated poem in the sky
with no rhyme, no meter, no reason,
no walls.
But then gusts and breezes
would snatch my paper away
to blow in all directions
and feed my letters
to the birds and the rain.

And
perhaps my new poem
would have been even more satisfying
than any peanut on any airline
with its carefree thoughts
and unsalted lines,
but now
it will go unread. . .
unless
you climb out your own little window
away from all walls
and have the wind recite my words.
Then
like my poem
you can fly away.

(Rosenberg, 1997)

Conclusion Notes

1 An *epidemic* quickly and severely affects a large number of people and then subsides; an *endemic* is a disease that is continually present in an area and affects a relatively small number of people; a *pandemic* is a widespread epidemic that affects entire continents or the world. Examples: malaria is endemic to hot, moist climates; the pandemic of 1918 ushered in a period of frequent epidemics.

2 For analysis of "Poetry on a Plane" as a leaping poem, see Chapter 16 with reference to Robert Bly.

Conclusion References

Campo, Rafael (2006) Why should medical students be writing poems? *The Journal of Medical Humanities*, 27: 253–254. https://doi.org/10.1007/s10912-006-9022-9

Cummins, Eleanor (December 19, 2021) Most Covid infections may soon be breakthroughs, Opinion Guest Essay, *New York Times*, 7.

Goldberg, Michelle (December 19, 2021) The hardest school year, *Sunday Review*, *New York Times*, 4.

Gorrell, Nancy S. (2000) Teaching empathy through ecphrastic poetry: Entering a curriculum of peace. *English Journal*, 89 (5): 32–41. https://doi.org/10.2307/822293

Hollander, John (1995) *The Gazer's Spirit: Poems Speaking to Silent Works of Art*. Chicago, IL: University of Chicago Press.

Ingle, Erin A. and Mueller, Michael (2019) Science, youth, and integration: The quest for mindfulness through birding. In Stewart, Arthur J., Mueller, Michael and Tippins, Deborah J. (eds.) *Converting STEM into STEAM Programs: Methods and Examples from and for Education*, 117–132. Cham, Switzerland: Springer.

Leonhardt, David (May 6, 2022) Long school closures came with high costs, *New York Times*, A18.

New York Times Editorial Board (August 21, 2021) "The Kids Are Not Alright" *New York Times*, 7. https://www.nytimes.com/2021/08/21/opinion/covid-education-schools.html

Osbourn, Anne (2019) Transgressing the disciplines using science as a meeting place: The science, art and writing initiative. In Stewart, Arthur J., Mueller, Michael and Tippins, Deborah (eds.) *Converting STEM into*

STEAM Programs: Methods and Examples from and for Education, 149–167. Cham, Switzerland: Springer.

Peary, Alexandria (2015) The pedagogy of creative writing across the curriculum. In Peary, Alexandria and Hunley, Tom C. (eds.) *Creative Writing Pedagogies for Twenty-First Century*, 194–220. Carbondale, IL: Southern Illinois University Press.

Rosenberg, Elise (1997) "Poetry on a Plane." *Tricorn Literary Magazine*, 32: 8–9. Morristown, NJ: Morristown High School.

Stewart, Arthur J., Mueller, Michael C. and Tippins, Deborah J. (eds.) (2019) *Converting STEM into STEAM Programs: Methods and Examples from and for Education*. Abstract, xii. Cham, Switzerland: Springer.

Afterword: On Musings

What Comes Next?

I'm curious about you. What has happened to you as a teacher and a writer as you read this book? Were you left with a different image of the creative writing classroom, the interdisciplinary classroom, or your own classroom, subject, or discipline? What was your response to the "windows" theme and its applicability to teaching? Did any of the writing prompts, lessons, or pedagogies resonate with you? Were you able to write *with* your students, *to* your students, and *for* your students? Were you able to co-learn with your students and collaborate your colleagues? Did any particular poem, prose piece, or student model speak to you? Did the concepts of *works in progress* and *becoming* inform your understanding of your evolving self – *teacher self*, *writer self*, *teacher-writer self*, and *teacher-artist self?* Did any project spark your imagination?

What comes next is uncertain. But one thing is certain. What comes next is up to you. What inspired you, what transformed you, what writing prompts you tried, what teachable moments you seized, what spontaneous lessons you have taught. So I would like to hear from you. Why? Because I'm still teaching, writing, learning, and *becoming,* and I'd like you to be part of it.

Still Searching for Your Muse?

This author recognizes and honors the many muses possible in one's life, and that you, as a teacher, may still be searching for your muse. To searchers still searching, welcome! Know that searching is part of the process. In that spirit, I offer a "delicious" poem written by Randi Brookman Harris, a former creative writing student of mine.

A-Muse Yourself with This Delicious Poem

Muse Soup
by Randi Brookman Harris

it wasn't that i didn't have my muse.
i had many muses
    but i just didn't always use them.
i liked to let them
        simmer on low,
    on the rear burners,
until
they were flavorful and
boiling with energy,
waiting to inspire
    becoming a work of art
    sipped from a spoon.

(Brookman Harris, 1997)

Afterward Reference

Brookman Harris, Randi (1997) "Muse Soup." *Tricorn Literary Magazine*, 32: 9. Morristown, NJ: Morristown High School.

Notes on Contributors

Mark Gutkowski is a Global Academic Dean who joined Avenues: The World School in 2015. A leading practitioner in the field of Self-Determined Learning, Mark's work at Avenues has primarily focused on the development of the Mastery Program, a key learning experience for the school that reflects its commitment to "developing future world-wise leaders, uniquely equipped to understand and solve global-scale problems." Mastery supports and encourages students to develop and pursue their interests over a multiple-year journey. Prior to joining Avenues, Mark spent 18 years at Morristown High School, a public high school in New Jersey. While at Morristown, he built a number of innovative programs, including a self-paced environment for studying Latin and a multi-year academy experience for students interested in interdisciplinary learning. He has worked as a consultant and an instructional leader, and has acted in various capacities as a representative for teachers through the New Jersey Department of Education. An award-winning educator and program designer, recognized by Princeton University (2005), the New Jersey Department of Education (2015), and Avenues (2018), Mark consistently challenges the status quo in education. Thematically, his work focuses on empowering student autonomy in the classroom and on transforming traditional power relationships between students and teachers. You can hear about some of these ideas in his TEDx talk, *Let's Start Taking Genius Hour Seriously*, available on You Tube (https://youtube/G2n29DECje4).

Steven N. Handel is Distinguished Professor of Ecology and Evolution at Rutgers University and Visiting Professor of Landscape Architecture at Harvard University. He is a restoration ecologist studying habitats and biodiversity in urban and coastal areas. His background is in plant population ecology and he has collaborated broadly with landscape architects on urban park design. Handel was the lead ecologist for the restoration of Orange County Great Park in Irvine, California, and his other projects include Brooklyn Bridge Park and the landscape for the 2008 Summer Olympics in Beijing, China. A native of Brooklyn, Handel received a Bachelor of Arts in Biological Sciences from Columbia University and a Master's degree and PhD degree in Ecology and Evolutionary Biology from Cornell University. Handel began his professorial career as a biology professor at the University of South Carolina and then Yale University, where he also held the post of director of the Marsh Botanical Garden. Honors include being an Aldo Leopold Leadership Fellow of the Ecological Society of America and Honorary Membership to the American Society of Landscape Architects for "nationally or internationally significant achievements." In 2011, he received the Theodore Sperry Award from the Society for Ecological Restoration for "pioneering work in the restoration of urban areas." In 2023, he was awarded the American Society of Landscape Architecture La Gasse Medal, which recognizes "notable contributions by individuals to the management and conservancy of natural resources and/or public landscapes." Currently retired from the Academy, Handel continues to serve as Editor of the journal, *Ecological Restoration*.

Sarah Beth Kaufman is Associate Professor of Sociology and Anthropology at Trinity University, San Antonio, Texas, and author of *American Roulette: The Social Logic of Death Penalty Sentencing Trials* (University of California Press, 2020). She has also published in *Qualitative Sociology*, *Critical Criminology*, *Law and Social Inquiry*, and *Punishment and Society*. Kaufman graduated from Morristown High School, and in her senior year, she elected Creative Writing I and II with this book's author, who saved her portfolio of writing and has included three of her poems in this volume ("Here's to 18," p. 142; Humanitarian at Age Six," p. 154; and Daddy's Shoulders, p. 273).

Arthur J. Stewart of Lenoir City, Tennessee, is a scientist and science educator specializing in aquatic ecology, ecotoxicology, and effective science writing. His niche is "science flavored" poetry, and he has authored seven volumes of science poetry and a poetry chapbook. He earned his Ph.D. at Michigan State University in aquatic ecology, and he worked at Oak Ridge National Laboratory (Environmental Sciences Division) for 17 years as an ecologist and ecotoxicologist before becoming a science education program manager for Oak Ridge Associated Universities (ORAU). After 10 years at ORAU, he accepted a position at Pellissippi State Community College to help set up a new program in Environmental Technology, focusing on water and wastewater treatment. Stewart is currently retired from the aforementioned professional organizations. Stewart is a science educator who advocates converting STEM programs into STEAM. He is co-editor of a work in Environmental Discourses in Science Education titled *Converting STEM into STEAM programs: Methods and Examples from and for Education* (2019). In addition to publishing numerous scientific articles, book chapters, and technical reports, Stewart has had literary essays published in *Big Muddy*, *the Bulletin of the Ecological Society of America*, *Breathing the Same Air*, and elsewhere. His poetry has been published in many literary magazines and more than a dozen anthologies. Stewart is a 2013 inductee of the East Tennessee Writers' Hall of Fame. He has been described as a "good-hearted provocateur within the culture of science."

Amy Uyematsu is a third generation (*sansei*) Japanese-American poet and retired public school mathematics teacher. She was raised in southern California by parents and grandparents who had been interned in American camps during World War II. Her sansei background heavily influenced her poetry and her decision to become a public school mathematics teacher to please her father. Uyematsu earned a B.A. in mathematics from the University of California at Los Angeles. She taught Honors and basic mathematics to students for more than 25 years at Venice High School, Los Angeles before retiring. Upon graduation from UCLA, she became a founder of and advocate for Asian-American studies. Uyematsu was co-editor of *Roots: An Asian American Reader* (1971, UCLA Asian American Studies Press). *Roots* is credited as one of the earliest anthologies in Asian American Studies. Her own work has been included in the anthologies *Bear Flag Republic: Prose Poems and Poetics from California* (2008), edited by Christopher Buckley and Gary Young; *The Misread City: New Literary Los Angeles* (2003), edited by Scott Timberg and Dana Gioia; and *Sister Stew: Fiction and Poetry by Women* (1991), edited by Juliet Kono and Cathy Song. Uyematsu's poems consider the intersection of politics, mathematics, spirituality, the natural world, and Zen. She was mentored for 15 years by the Zen poet, Peter Levitt. Uyematsu is the author of five poetry collections: *Basic Vocabulary* (2016), *The Yellow Door* (2015), *Stone Bow Prayer* (2005), *Nights of Fire, Nights of Rain* (1997), and *30 Miles from J-Town* (1992), which won the Nicholas Roerich Poetry Prize.

Featured Student Contributor

Stefanie DeFronzo graduated in 2020 from Drew University in Madison, New Jersey, with a Bachelor of Science degree in Biochemistry and Molecular Biology. Upon graduation, she has been working as an associate researcher in a bioengineering laboratory at the Icahn School of Medicine at Mount Sinai Hospital in New York City. Growing up in Voorheesville, New York, Stefanie developed interests that span from science, to musical theatre, and to poetry – all of which she still passionately pursues day to day. She will forever let her creativity keep her on her toes – in life and in the lab.

References

Abbey, Edward (1991) *The Journey Home: Some Words in Defense of the American West*. New York, NY: Penguin. Cited from Brown, Kurt (1998) *Verse and Universe: Poems about Science and Mathematics*, 1. Minneapolis, MN: Milkweed Editions.

Adler, Barbara J. (2002) *ARTifacts: Kids Respond to a World in Crisis*. New York, NY: Alliance for Young Writers & Artists.

Adsit, Janelle (2017) Place-based pedagogy and creative writing as a fieldwork course. In Clark, Hergenrader, and Rein (2017: 149–161).

Arum, Richard and Roska, Josipa (2011) Academically adrift: Limited learning on college campuses. Arum, Richard and Roska, Josipa (2011) Academically adrift: Limited learning on college campuses. Cited from Peary (2015: 195).

Atwell, Nancie (1987/1998) *In the Middle: Writing, Reading and Learning with Adolescents* (2nd edition). Portsmouth, NH: Boyton/Cook Heinemann.

Bahls, Patrick (2009) Math and metaphor: Using poetry to teach college mathematics. *WAC Journal*, 20: 75–90. https://doi.org/10.37514/WAC-J.2009.20.1.06

Berke, Jacqueline (1972/1981) *Twenty Questions for the Writer* (3rd edition). New York, NY: Harcourt Brace Jovanovich.

Bishop, Wendy (1994a) Crossing the lines: On creative composition and composing creative writing. In Bishop, Wendy and Ostrom, Hans (eds.) *Colors of a Different Horse: Rethinking Creative Writing Theory and Pedagogy*, 181–197. Urbana, IL: National Council of Teachers of English. https://files.eric.ed.gov/fulltext/ED366967.pdf

Bishop, Wendy (1994b) Afterword – Colors of a different horse: On learning to like teaching creative writing. In Bishop, Wendy and Ostrom, Hans (eds.) *Colors of a Different Horse: Rethinking Creative Writing Theory and Pedagogy*, 280–295. Urbana, IL: National Council of Teachers of English. https://files.eric.ed.gov/fulltext/ED366967.pdf

Bishop, Wendy and Ostrom, Hans (eds.) (1994) *Colors of a Different Horse: Rethinking Creative Writing Theory and Pedagogy*. Urbana, IL: National Council of Teachers of English. https://files.eric.ed.gov/fulltext/ED366967.pdf

Bly, Robert (1975) *Leaping Poetry: An Idea with Poems and Translations Chosen by Robert Bly*. Boston, MA: Beacon Press.

Brande, Dorothea (1934/1981) *Becoming a Writer*. New York, NY: Tarcher/Putnam. Originally published by Harcourt, Brace.

Britton, James (1970) *Language and Learning.* Coral Gables, FL: University of Miami Press. Cited from Peary (2015: 201).

Britton, James (1982) Spectator role and the beginnings of writing. In Pradl, Gordon M. (ed.) Prospect and Retrospect: Selected Essays of James Britton, 46–67. Upper Montclair: Boynton. Cited from Peary (2015: 202).

Britton, James, Burgess, Tony, Martin, Nancy, McLeod, Alex and Rosen, Harold (1975) *The Development of Writing Abilities.* Basingstoke, Hampshire and London: Macmillan. Cited from Peary (2015: 201).

Brookman Harris, Randi (1997) "Muse Soup." *Tricorn Literary Magazine*, 32: 9. Morristown, NJ: Morristown High School.

Burnside, John (2006) A science of belonging: Poetry as ecology. Robert Crawford (ed.) *Contemporary Poetry and Contemporary Science*, 91–106. Oxford, UK: Oxford University Press.

Busch, Debbie (1990) "Christmas (Portland Oregon, 1969)." Qtd in Gorrell (1990c: 29).

Cameron, Julia (1992) *The Artist's Way: A Spiritual Path to Higher Creativity.* New York, NY: Penguin/Putnam.

Cameron, Julia (2002) *Walking in this World: The Practical Art of Creativity*. New York, NY: Tarcher/Putnam.

Campo, Rafael (2006) Why should medical students be writing poems? *The Journal of Medical Humanities*, 27: 253–254. https://doi.org/10.1007/s10912-006-9022-9

Charon, Rita (2001) Narrative medicine: A model for empathy reflection, profession and trust. *Journal of the American Medical Association*, 286 (15): 1897–1902. https://doi.org/10.1001/jama.286.15.1897

Charon, Rita (August 22, 2022) Letter to the Editor, Stories as medicine. *The New Yorker*, 3.

Chekhov, Anton (1898) "A Doctor's Visit." https://web.seducoahuila.gob.mx/biblioweb/upload/A%20DOCTOR.pdf

Chik, Alice, Costley, Tracey and Pennington, Martha C. (eds.) (2015) *Creativity and Discovery in the University Writing Class*. Sheffield, UK and Oakville, CT: Equinox.

Chomsky, Noam (1966) *Cartesian Linguistics: A Chapter in the History of Rationalist Thought*. New York, NY: Harper & Row.

Clark, Michael Dean, Hergenrader, Trent and Rein, Joseph (eds.) (2017) *Creative Writing Innovations: Breaking Boundaries in the Classroom*. London, UK: Bloomsbury.

Conroy, Pat (2003) *My Losing Season*. New York, NY: Bantam Dell Random House.

Crimmel, Hal (2003) *Teaching in the Field: Working with Students in the Outdoor Classroom*. Salt Lake City, UT: University of Utah Press.

Csikszentmihalyi, Mihaly (1996) *Creativity: Flow and the Psychology of Discovery and Invention*. New York, NY: Harper Perennial.

Curious Science Writers (cSw) website http://curioussciencewriters.org

Davis, Alex (2012a) Alex's commentary on "The Second Law of Thermodynamics." Qtd in Gorrell with Colfax (2012: 146).

Davis, Alex (2012b) Comment on first learning about science poetry. Qtd in Gorrell with Colfax (2012: 36).

Davis, Alex (2012c) "The Second Law of Thermodynamics." Qtd in Gorrell, with Colfax (2012: 145).

DeFronzo, Stefanie (2021) "Annemarie Hohensee." Copyright Stefanie DeFronzo.

Dewey, John (1938) *Experience and Education*. New York, NY: MacMillan.

Dickinson, Emily (1873) "Longing is like the Seed." https://www.poetryverse.com/emily-dickinson-poems/longing-is-like-the-seed

Doty, Mark (2010) *Art of Description*. Minneapolis, MN: Graywolf Press.

Dunne, Pete (November 5, 1989) In the natural state. *New York Times*. https://www.nytimes.com/1989/04/30/nyregion/in-the-natural-state.html

Dunn, Stephen (1991) The poet as teacher: Vices and virtues. In Schwartz, Mimi (ed.) *Writer's Craft, Teacher's Art*, 145–152. Portsmouth, NH: Boyton/Cook.

Dunning, Stephen and Stafford, William (eds.) (1992) *Getting the Knack: 20 Poetry Writing Exercises*. Urbana, IL: National Council of Teachers of English.

Elbow, Peter (1973/1998) *Writing without Teachers* (2nd edition). New York, NY and UK, Oxford: Oxford University Press.

Elbow, Peter (1990) *What is English?* New York, NY: Modern Language Association of America and Urbana, IL: National Council of Teachers of English.

Emmert, Mark A. (1997) Poets, painters, and the future of science. *Science*, 278: 1381. https://doi.org/10.1126/science.278.5342.1381

Emig, Janet (1977) Writing as a mode of learning. *College Composition and Communication*, 28 (2): 122–128. https://doi.org/10.2307/356095

Englehardt, James and Schraffenberger, Jeremy (2015) Ecological creative writing. In Peary, Alexandria and Hunley, Tom C. (eds.) *Creative Writing Pedagogies for the Twenty-First Century*, 269–288. Carbondale, IL: Southern Illinois University Press.

Fischl, Peter (1994) "To the Little Polish Boy Standing with His Arms Up." Los Angeles, CA: Archives of Simon Wiesenthal Center.

Fleischman, Paul (1988) *Joyful Noise.* New York, NY: Harper Row.

Fluck, Sandra (1973) *Experiential English*. New York, NY: Glencoe Press.

Forche, Carolyn (1993) *Against Forgetting: 20th Century Poetry of Witness*. New York, NY: W.W. Norton.

Forster, E. M. (1927/2005) *Aspects of the Novel*. London: Edward Arnold. Originally published by Edward Arnold. Cited from Swedberg (2020: 1, 3, 14).

Fortier, Nicole (2004) "The Morristown Cycle." *Tricorn Literary Magazine*, 39: 8. Morristown, NJ: Morristown High School.

Frost, Robert (1916) "Out, Out–." *Mountain Interval*, 65. Rahway, NJ: Henry Holt.

Gardner, John (1981) Forward. In Dorothea Brande, *Becoming a Writer*, 11–18. New York, NY: Tarcher/Putman.

Gardner, John (1983/1999) *On Becoming a Novelist*. New York, NY: W. W. Norton.

Giovanni, Nikki (1978) "Cotton Candy on a Rainy Day." *Poems by Nikki Giovanni*, 21–23. New York, NY: William Morrow.

Glanz, James (1997) Cut the communications fog, say physicists and editors. *Science*, 277: 895–896. https://doi.org/10.1126/science.277.5328.895

Goldberg, Natalie (1986) *Writing Down the Bones: Freeing the Writer Within*. Boston, MA: Shambhala.

Gorlewski, Julie and Gorlewski, David (eds.) (2014) From the editors. *English Journal*, 104 (2): 11–12. https://doi.org/10.58680/ej201424637

Gorman, Sheila (1990) "Untitled." Qtd in Gorrell (1990c: 29).

Gorrell, Nancy (1989a) "Kindergarten Creation." *The Rockford Review*, 8: 62. Rockford, IL: Rockford Writers' Guild.

Gorrell, Nancy (1989b) Let found poetry help your students find poetry. *English Journal*, 78 (2): 30–34. https://doi.org/10.2307/819126

Gorrell, Nancy (1990a) "Blueberry Pie." *English Journal*, 79 (8): 88. https://doi.org/10.2307/818838

Gorrell, Nancy (1990b) Poetry to engage the person. In Patricia Phelan (ed.) *Literature and Life: Making Connections in the Classroom*, 35–43. National Council of Teachers of English: Urbana, IL.

Gorrell, Nancy (1990c) Taking off the mask: Teaching the recurring image in poetry writing. *English Journal*, 79 (7): 27–29. https://doi.org/10.2307/818712

Gorrell, Nancy (1992a) A teacher's story of renewal. In Dahl, Karin (ed.) *Teacher as Writer: Entering the Professional Conversation*, 19–33. Urbana, IL: National Council of Teachers of English.

Gorrell, Nancy (1992b) "Dear Dolphin." In Dunning, Stephen and Stafford, William (eds.) *Getting the Knack: 20 Poetry Writing Exercises*, 32. Urbana, IL: National Council of Teachers of English.

Gorrell, Nancy (1992c) "To See." In Dunning, Stephen and Stafford, William (eds.) *Getting the Knack: 20 Poetry Writing Exercises*, 130. Urbana, IL: National Council of Teachers of English.

Gorrell, Nancy S. (1993a) "Grandma Came Down." *Footwork: Paterson Literary Review*, 23: 114. Paterson, NJ: Passaic County Community College.

Gorrell, Nancy (1993b) Publishing the poetry chapbook: Defining a public self. *English Journal*, 82 (2): 42–46. https://doi.org/10.2307/819702

Gorrell, Nancy (1993c) "The River." *Footwork: Paterson Literary Review*, 23: 115. Paterson, NJ: Passaic County Community College.

Gorrell, Nancy (1995) "Blueberry Pie." In Dunning, Stephen and Stafford, William (eds.) *Reflections on a Gift of a Watermelon Pickle and Other Modern Verse* (2nd edition), 10. Glenview, IL: Scott Foresman.

Gorrell, Nancy (1997) "Sometimes Poems Come." One person's opinion: What keeps me teaching. *English Journal*, 86 (5): 18–19. https://doi.org/10.2307/820437

Gorrell, Nancy (2000) Teaching empathy through ecphrastic poetry: Entering a curriculum of peace. *English Journal*, 89 (5): 32–41. https://doi.org/10.2307/822293

Gorrell, Nancy (2004) Teaching empathy through ecphrastic poetry: Entering a curriculum of peace. In Monseau (2004: 73–88).

Gorrell, Nancy (2006) Teaching empathy through ecphrastic poetry: Entering a curriculum of peace. In Weber (2006: 32–50).

Gorrell, Nancy S. with Erin Colfax (2012) *Writing Poetry through the Eyes of Science: Scientific Literacy and Poetic Response*. Sheffield, UK and Oakville, CT: Equinox.

Groopman, Jerome (July 25, 2002) The scalpel and the pen: What medical narratives teach us" *The New Yorker*, 66–68.

Handel, Steven N. (2011) A seed op-ed. *Ecological Restoration*, 29 (4): 320–321. https://www.academia.edu/49390765/A_Seed_Op_Ed. https://doi.org/10.3368/er.29.4.320

Handel, Steven N. (2019a) Beginning at the end. In Rovaldi, Antonio and Benedetto, Francesca *The Sound of the Woodpecker Bill: New York City*, 522–527. Milano, Italy: Humboldt Books.

Handel, Steven N. (2019b) Birnam Woods, moving closer, shadows our work. *Ecological Restoration*, 37: 1–2. https://doi.org/10.3368/er.37.1.1

Handel, Steven N. (2019c) Email correspondence with Nancy S. Gorrell.

Harper, Graeme (2017) The unworkshop. In Clark, Hergenrader, and Rein (2017: 21–31).

Higginson, William J. with Harper, Penny (1985) *The Haiku Handbook: How to Write, Share and Teach Haiku*. New York, NY: McGraw-Hill.

Hipple, Ted (1989) The tyranny of the Ts. *English Journal*, 78 (5): 19–22. https://doi.org/10.2307/819194

Hollander, John (1995) *The Gazer's Spirit: Poems Speaking to Silent Works of Art*. Chicago, IL: University of Chicago Press.

Hunley, Tom C. and Giles, Sandra (2015) Rhetorical pedagogy. In Peary, Alexandria and Hunley, Tom C. (eds.) *Creative Writing Pedagogies for the 21st Century*. Carbondale, IL: Southern Illinois University Press.

Ingle, Erin A. and Mueller, Michael (2019) Science, youth, and integration: The quest for mindfulness through birding. In Stewart, Arthur J., Mueller, Michael and Tippins, Deborah J. (eds.) *Converting STEM into STEAM Programs: Methods and Examples from and for Education*, 117–132. Cham, Switzerland: Springer.

Kim, Michelle (2004) Idiocy? What's love got to do with it. *Tricorn Literary Magazine*, 39: 26. Morristown, NJ: Morristown Public High School.

Kingsporn, Geoff. "Veteran." Qtd in Gorrell (1989b: 34).

Klass, Perri (1987/1994) *A Not Entirely Benign Procedure: Four Years as a Medical Student.* New York: Putnam.

Kleist, Heinrich von (1951) On the gradual construction of thoughts during speech (tr. Michael Hamburger). *German Life and Letters*, 5 (1): 8–9, 42–46. Cited from Swedberg (2020: 8, 11). https://doi.org/10.1111/j.1468-0483.1951.tb01029.x

Lasky, Dorothea (2014) Examining 'small c' creativity in the writing classroom. In Millan, Harriet Levin and Pennington, Martha C. (eds.) *Creativity and Writing Pedagogy: Linking Creative Writers, Researchers, and Teachers*, 117–136. Sheffield, UK and Bristol, CT: Equinox.

Le Guin, Ursula K. (1998) *Steering the Craft*. Portland, OR: Eighth Mountain Press.

Leonhardt, David (May 6, 2022) Long school closures came with high costs. *New York Times*, A18.

Lester, Julius (1969) *Search for the New Land: History as Subjective Experience*. New York, NY: Dial Press.

Lim, Shirley Geok-lin (2015) Highways and sinkholes: Incorporating creativity strategies in the writing classroom. In Chik, Alice, Costley, Tracey and Pennington, Martha C. (eds.) *Creativity and Discovery in the University Writing Class*, 252–276. Sheffield, UK and Oakville, CT: Equinox.

Longfellow, Henry Wadsworth (1876–1879) "The Bell of Atri." https://poets.org/poem/bell-atri

Luft, Joseph and Ingham, Harrington (1955) The Johari window, a graphic model of interpersonal awareness. *Proceedings of the Western Training Laboratory in Group Development*. Los Angeles: University of California at Los Angeles.

Macrorie, Ken (1968/1976) *Writing to Be Read* (2nd edition). Rochelle Park, NJ: Hayden.

Macrorie, Ken (1988) *The I-Search Paper* (revised edition of *Search Writing*). Portsmouth, NH: Heinemann.

Marsen, Sky (2014) Detecting the creative in written discourse. In Millan, Harriet Levin and Pennington, Martha C. (eds.) *Creativity and Writing Pedagogy: Linking Creative Writers, Researchers, and Teachers*, 89–118. Sheffield, UK and Bristol, CT: Equinox.

May, Rollo (1975) *The Courage to Create*. New York, NY: W.W. Norton.

Mayers, Tim (2015) Creative writing and process pedagogy. In Peary, Alexandria and Hunley, Tom C. (eds.) *Creative Writing Pedagogies for the Twenty-First Century*, 30–51. Carbondale: Southern Illinois University Press.

Menand, Louis (June 8, 2009) "Show and tell – Should creative writing be taught? *The New Yorker*, 106–112. Cited from Lim (2015: 252).

Merton, Robert K. (1945) Sociological theory. *American Journal of Sociology*, 50 (6): 462–473. https://doi.org/10.1086/219686

Merton, Robert K. (1949/1968) Social theory and social structure (3rd edition). New York, NY: Free Press. Cited from Swedberg (2020: 5).

Merton, Robert K. (1978a) Letter to Gerald Edelman on the Forster aphorism, November 12. Robert K. Merton Papers, Rare Book & Manuscript Library, Columbia University in the City of New York. Cited from Swedberg (2020: 5).

Merton, Robert K. (1978b) Letter to Gerald Edelman on the Forster aphorism, November 23. Robert K. Merton Papers, Rare Book & Manuscript Library, Columbia University in the City of New York. Cited from Swedberg (2020: 5).

Merton, Robert K. (1984) An interview with Robert K. Merton by Caroline Persell. *Teaching Sociology*, 11 (4): 355–86. Cited from Swedberg (2020: 3). https://doi.org/10.2307/1317796

Mervosh, Sarah (September 1, 2022) Pandemic set schools back two decades: Children's reading and math scores suffer. *New York Times*, 1.

Millan, Harriet Levin and Pennington, Martha C. (eds.) (2014) *Creativity and Writing Pedagogy: Linking Creative Writers, Researchers, and Teachers*. Sheffield, UK and Bristol, CT: Equinox.

Moffett, James (1973) *A Student-Centered Language Arts Curriculum Grades K–13: A Handbook for Teachers*. Boston, MA: Houghton Mifflin.

Moffett, James (1981/1992) *Active Voice* (2nd edition). Portsmouth, NH: Boyton/Cook Heinemann.

Moneyhun, Clyde (2015) A basic writing teacher teaches creative writing. In

Monseau, Virginia (ed.) *A Curriculum of Peace: Selected Essays from English Journal*. Urbana, IL: National Council of Teachers of English.

Moxley, Joseph (1989) *Creative Writing in America*. Urbana, IL: National Council of Teachers of English.

Moxley, Joseph (1989) *Creative Writing in America*. Urbana, IL: National Council of Teachers of English.

New York Times Editorial Board (August 21, 2021) "The Kids Are Not Alright" *New York Times*, 7. https://www.nytimes.com/2021/08/21/opinion/covid-education-schools.html

Oates, Joyce Carol. (2003) *The Faith of a Writer: Life, Craft, Art*. New York, NY: Harper Collins.

Osbourn, Anne (2019) Transgressing the disciplines using science as a meeting place: The science, art and writing initiative. In Stewart, Arthur J., Mueller, Michael and Tippins, Deborah (eds.) *Converting STEM into STEAM Programs: Methods and Examples from and for Education*, 149–167. Cham, Switzerland: Springer.

Osbourn, Anne, Sweeney, Matthew and Pirrie, Jill (eds.) (2005) *SEE SAW: An Anthology of Poetry and Artwork around Science by Children from Rockland St. Mary Primary School and Framingham Earl High School*. The SAW Trust. www.sawtrust.org

Padgett, Ron (ed.) (1987/2000) *The Teachers & Writers Handbook of Poetic Forms* (2nd edition). New York, NY: Teachers and Writer's Collaborative.

Palmer, Parker (1998) *The Courage to Teach*. San Francisco, CA: Jossey-Bass.

Peary, Alexandria (2015) The pedagogy of creative writing across the curriculum. In Peary, Alexandria and Hunley, Tom C. (eds.) *Creative Writing Pedagogies for the Twenty-First Century*, 194–220. Carbondale, IL: Southern Illinois University Press.

Peary, Alexandria and Hunley, Tom C. (eds.) (2015) *Creative Writing Pedagogies for the Twenty-First Century*. Carbondale, IL: Southern Illinois University Press.

Pennington, Martha (2014) Towards a creative writing pedagogy. In Millan, Harriet Levin and Pennington, Martha C. (eds.) *Creativity and Writing Pedagogy: Linking Creative Writers, Researchers, and Teachers*, 17–24. Sheffield, UK and Bristol, CT: Equinox.

Pennington, Martha C. (2015) Writing creativity and discovery: Process and pedagogy. In Chik, Alice, Costley, Tracey and Pennington, Martha C. (eds.) *Creativity and Discovery in the University Writing* Class, 61–92. Sheffield, UK and Oakville, CT: Equinox.

Phillips, Don (1989) Let found poetry help your students study literature. *English Journal*, 78 (5): 68–70. https://doi.org/10.2307/819207

Pinsky, Robert (2000) "Jersey Rain." *Jersey Rain Poems*, 52. New York, NY: Farrar, Straus and Giroux.

Pinsky, Robert and Sampson, David (2000–2001) *Jersey Rain Project*. Commissioned by the NEA and the Gerald R. Dodge Foundation and premiered by Harmonium and Masterwork Choruses and the Colonial Symphony.

Pitt, David (2012a) David's commentary on "Redwood." Qtd in Gorrell with Colfax (2012: 274).

Pitt, David (2012b) "O Asymptote." Qtd in Gorrell with Colfax (2012: 297).

Pitt, David (2012c) "Redwood." Qtd in Gorrell with Colfax (2012: 273).

Proust, Marcel (1982) "The Captive." *In Remembrance of Things Past*, Vol. III, 259–260. New York, NY: Vintage Books.

Rilke, Rainer Maria (1875/2000) *Letters to a Young Poet* (10th edition) Novato, CA: New World Library.

Rittel, Horst W. and Webber, Melvin M. (1973) Dilemmas in a general theory of planning. *Policy Sciences*, 4 (2): 155–169. https://doi.org/10.1007/BF01405730. https://www.cc.gatech.edu/fac/ellendo/rittel/rittel-dilemma.pdf

Robinson, Sir Ken (June 26, 2006) Do schools kill creativity? https://www.ted.com/talks/sir_ken_robinson_do_schools_kill_creativity

Robinson, Sir Ken (May 10, 2013) "How to escape education's death valley" https://www.ted.com/talks/sir_ken_robinson_how_to_escape_education_s_death_valley

Rosenberg, Elise (1997) "Poetry on a Plane." *Tricorn Literary Magazine*, 32: 8–9. Morristown, NJ: Morristown High School.

Roth, Wolff-Michael (2019) We need more (than) STEAM: Let's go for life-wide and lifelong education. In Stewart, Arthur J., Mueller, Michael C. and Tippins, Deborah J. (eds.) *Converting STEM into STEAM Programs: Methods and Examples from and for Education*, 55–66. Cham, Switzerland: Springer.

Rothman, Marni (1990) "30 Second Memory." Qtd in Gorrell (1990c: 29).

Sachs, Oliver (1985) *The Man Who Mistook his Wife for a Hat: And Other Clinical Tales.* New York, NY: Summit Books.

Sampson, David (2001) *Jersey Rain for Baritone Solo, mixed choir, and orchestra*. https://en.wikipedia.org/wiki/David_Sampson_(composer)

Scholes, Robert (1985) *Textual Power: Literary Theory and the Teaching of English*. New Haven, CT: Yale University Press.

Schwartz, Anne (2012) "Us." Qtd in Gorrell with Colfax (2012: 385–386.

Schwartz, Mimi (1991) *Writer's Craft, Teacher's Art*. Portsmouth, NH: Boyton/Cook.

Shelnutt, Eve (1989) *The Writing Room*. Atlanta, GA: Longstreet Press.

Siebert, Arielle (1992a) "Dear Queen Anne Boleyn." In Dunning, Stephen and Stafford, William (eds.) *Getting the Knack: 20 Poetry Writing Exercises*, 150. Urbana, IL: National Council of Teachers of English.

Siebert, Arielle (1992b) "Memory." In Dunning, Stephen and Stafford, William (eds.) *Getting the Knack: 20 Poetry Writing Exercises*, 150. Urbana, IL: National Council of Teachers of English.

Snow (1959/2007) *The Two Cultures* (10th edition). Cambridge, UK: Cambridge University Press.

Stafford, William (1978) *Writing the Australian Crawl: Views on the Writer's Vocation*. Ann Arbor, MI: University of Michigan Press.

Stewart, Arthur J. (1999a) "Learning." On the need for poetry by scientists. *Bulletin of the Ecological Society of America*, 80 (2): 133.

Stewart, Arthur J. (1999b) On the need for poetry by scientists. *Bulletin of the Ecological Society of America*, 80 (2): 133–134.

Stewart, Arthur J. (1999c) "What They Found." On the need for poetry by scientists. *Bulletin of the Ecological Society of America*, 80 (2): 133.

Stewart, Arthur J. (2003) "Weavers Needle." *Rough Ascensions and Other Poems of Science*, 10. Knoxville, TN: Celtic Cat.

Stewart, Arthur J (2005) "Rat Dissection." *Bushido: The Virtues of Rei and Makoto*, 80. Knoxville, TN: Celtic Cat.

Stewart, Arthur J. (2010a) "Getting it Right." *Circle, Turtle, Ashes*, 91. Knoxville, TN: Celtic Cat.

Stewart, Arthur J. (2010b) "Ladoga Lake and Nyos." *Circle, Turtle, Ashes*, 39–41. Knoxville, TN: Celtic Cat.

Stewart, Arthur J. (2010c) "Limnology Quiz." *Circle, Turtle, Ashes*, 37. Knoxville, TN: Celtic Cat.

Stewart, Arthur J. (2010d) "Professor Thermocline." *Circle, Turtle, Ashes*, 36. Knoxville, TN: Celtic Cat.

Stewart, Arthur J. (2017) "Edges." *Elements of Chance*, 51. Knoxville, TN: Celtic Cat.

Stewart, Arthur J. (February 12, 2017) Email correspondence with Nancy S. Gorrell.

Stewart, Arthur J. (2021a) "Blank Page." *Hallelujah Series and Other Poems*, 62. Nashville, TN: Periploi Press.

Stewart, Arthur J. (2021b) "Pathway." *The Hallelujah Series and Other Poems*, 3. Nashville, TN: Periploi Press.

Stewart, Arthur J. (2021c) *Uncoils a Snake*. Nashville, TN: Periploi Press.

Stewart, Arthur, Mueller, Michael and Tippins, Deborah (eds.) (2019) *Converting STEM into STEAM Programs: Methods and Examples from and for Education*. Cham, Switzerland: Springer.

Swanger, David (1974) Preface. *The Poem as Process*, ix–xi. *The Poem as Process*. New York, NY: Harcourt Brace Jovanovich.

Swedberg, Richard (2020)'*How do I know what I think till I see what I say*?' An aphorism and its implications for creative theorizing. *Distinktion: Journal of Social Theory*, 21 (1): 1–18. https://doi.org/10.1080/1600910X.2019.1630846

Swenson, May (2013) "Distance and a Certain Light." *Collected Poems* New York, NY: Literary Classics of the United States.

Ubben, Gary (2019) How to structure project-based learning to meet STEAM objectives. In Stewart, Arthur J., Mueller, Michael and Tippins, Deborah (eds.) *Converting STEM into STEAM Programs: Methods and Examples from and for Education*, 85–100. Cham, Switzerland: Springer.

Uyematsu, Amy (1998) "Florentino Diaz." *Nights of Fire, Nights of Rain*, 6. Brownsville, OR: Story Line Press.

Uyematsu, Amy (2005) "When Geometry Gets Mixed Up with God and the Alphabet." *Stone, Bow, Prayer*, 27–29. Port Townsend, WA: Copper Canyon Press.

Uyematsu, Amy (2005) "The Invention of Mathematics." *Stone, Bow, Prayer*, 30–33. Port Townsend, WA: Copper Canyon Press.

Uyematsu, Amy (2005) "Desert Camouflage." *Stone, Bow, Prayer*, 50. Port Townsend, WA: Copper Canyon Press.

Uyematsu, Amy (2005) "Simple Division." *Stone, Bow, Prayer*, 49. Port Townsend, WA: Copper Canyon Press.

Uyematsu, Amy (2005) "The Weight of Nothing." *Stone, Bow, Prayer*, 72–74. Port Townsend, WA: Copper Canyon Press.

Uyematsu, Amy (2016a) "His Name was Marlon Gutierrez." *Basic Vocabulary*, 34. Pasadena, CA: Red Hen Press.

Uyematsu, Amy (2016b) "Juan's Numbers." *Basic Vocabulary*, 32–33. Pasadena, CA: Red Hen Press.

Uyematsu, Amy (2016) "Dipping into Infinity." *Basic Vocabulary*, 90–92. Pasadena, CA: Red Hen Press.

Uyematsu, Amy (2016) "This Thing Called Infinity." *Basic Vocabulary*, 102. Pasadena, CA: Red Hen Press.

Uyematsu, Amy (2016) "A Handful of Knowing." *Basic Vocabulary*, 65–66. Pasadena, CA: Red Hen Press

Uyematsu, Amy (2016) "On Poets." *Basic Vocabulary*, 76. Pasadena, CA: Red Hen Press.

Uyematsu, Amy (2018) Five decades later: Reflections of a yellow power advocate turned poet. In Schlund-Vials, Cathy J. (ed.) *Flashpoints for Asian American Studies*, 21–35. New York, NY: Fordham University Press.

Uyematsu, Amy (August 6, 2019) Email correspondence with Nancy S. Gorrell.

Uyematsu, Amy (May 6, 2020) Email correspondence with Nancy S. Gorrell.

Wark, Krista (1992a) "Finnegan's Alley." In Dunning, Stephen and Stafford, William (eds.) *Getting the Knack: 20 Poetry Writing Exercises*, 152. Urbana, IL: National Council of Teachers of English.

Wark, Krista (1992b) "There." In Dunning, Stephen and Stafford, William (eds.) *Getting the Knack: 20 Poetry Writing Exercises*, 103. Urbana, IL: National Council of Teachers of English.

Warner, John (2018) *Why They Can't Write: Killing the Five-Paragraph Essay and Other Necessities*. Baltimore, MD: John Hopkins University Press.

Warriner, John E. (1977) *English Grammar and Composition: Complete Course* (Series). New York, NY: Harcourt Brace Jovanovich.

Weber, Chris (2006) *Nurturing the Peacemakers in our Students: A Guide to Speaking about Issues of War and Peace*. Portsmouth, NH: Heinemann.

Weisstuch, Liza (December 13, 2001) A prescription for creative writing. *The Harvard Gazette*. https://news.harvard.edu/gazette/story/2001/12/a-prescription-for-creative-writing/

Wellons, Jay (2022) *All that Moves Us: A Pediatric Neurosurgeon, His Young Patients, and their Stories of Grace and Resilience*. New York, NY: Random House.

Williams, William Carlos (1934) "The Girl with the Pimply Face." https://www.coursehero.com/file/120023638/The-Girl-With-a-Pimply-Face-ENG002/

Williams, William Carlos (1938a) "Between Walls." Available at https://www.poetryfoundation.org/poems/49849/between-walls

Williams, William Carlos (1938b) "This Is Just to Say." https://www.poetryfoundation.org/poems/56159/this-is-just-to-say

Wright, Richard (1945/1966) *Black Boy* (2nd edition). New York, NY: Harper & Row.

APPENDICES

Appendix A

Poetry Watch and Hawk Watch Resources (Chapter 2)

POETRY WATCH: SAMPLE STUDENT POEM

Marni Rothman, "On the School Steps"

On the School Steps
Marni Rothman

Morning
the sun is new
even on this
October day.
Sparkling light
on chestnut curls
and black shoes.
Bright dusty rays
penetrating library windows
are absorbed
by red geraniums.
On green grass,
a lone paper
caught in the breeze
cartwheels with orange leaves.
But no one chases—

They just sit.
Schoolwork is insignificant
under a clear blue sky.

THE ULTIMATE PLAN: HAWK WATCHING CLASS PROJECT

Barbara Nadolny's "Ultimate Plan" demanded ultimate commitment and responsibility from her students – five hours a week for 20 weeks before and after school as well as in class and on field trips. She shared with me a folder of her lesson plans and student handouts for the hawk watch project. The originals were written and distributed to her students in her own hand. I have typed them up for legibility.

Hawk Watch – How Does It Work?

Student Project Instructions

1. You will need training – regular indoor classes. This is a must.
   When? 2nd or 9th period
   Sunday afternoons
   After school
2. Barbara Nadolny will try to be available when you are.
   You will need to serve on the actual Hawk Watch.
   When? Two or three periods per week. More if you wish.
   40 min before 7:50 AM
   40 min after 2:30 PM
   Saturday, Sunday, or holiday mornings
   Where? On the football field looking North.
3. You will need to spend time in November and December evaluating the results. This will be preferably done during the classes with me but students who wish to do work on their own time will get credit.

4. You will get credit for any hours spent in this work – classes during school or after – minutes out on the bleachers – time on your own reading, researching or writing, artwork, field trips.
5. Trips – I would like to take each person once to Len Soucy's Raptor Hospital. This would be an afterschool 3–6 PM trip. You would see the birds at 3 feet.
6. Trips – Maybe? Great Swamp, *Montclair Hawk Watch, *Hawk Mt. Pennsylvania. If we get the buses, priority for students with most time invested.
7. Credit 2 1/2 on transcript is 5 hours/week for 20 weeks (That's 100 hours or 6,000 minutes).

Student Hawk Watch Instruction Handout

What Do You Do While on a Hawk Watch?

1. Every 5 minutes scan the W, N, E sky in a definite pattern. Use the binoculars. Then scan the tree top horizon over 360 degrees.
   N.B. You often focus on an airplane which you never realized was there.
2. Practice with binoculars on anything that moves. That's how you learn to "zero in" and "follow."
3. Especially practice on any other birds. Watch how they fly. Note the differences.
4. *One person should always be watching for hawks. Don't forget to look behind you!
5. Bird identification. Concentrate on just a few points – size, bigger or smaller than a robin? Color? Tail shape? You can add other fine points later.
6. Notice the rest of the world in this small area. How do the trees, birds, people change over our period of observation?
7. Keep your own private diary of observations, comments, poetry, sketches. We can work out some "minutes of credit" for it. And if you save this notebook for many years, it will

be fun to read and realize what kind of person you were "way back then."

8. *Don't forget to record the weather, etc.
9. Don't get so involved in watching the gym class games that you forget why you are there!
10. Help your friends find what you see. Say: "Blue sky over bleachers" or Trees – right of school."
11. Think of a clock. Set a 12:00 point. You are at 6:00 am all else in between.
12. **Start back to school at least 3 minutes <u>before</u> the bell rings to end class.

Appendix B

"The Weight of Nothing" by Amy Uyematsu (Chapters 3 and 8)

The Weight of Nothing
by Amy Uyematsu

to end with nothing is something
Suvan Geer
or to rephrase a popular Billy Preston song,
"somethin' from nothin' is somethin'"

I

everyone loves
the disappearing
coin. a bird pulled from
an empty hat. the comfort of
trusting a magician's hands.
when we know we'll get some-
thing from what
he takes away.

II

the student's assignment—
concentrate on nothing
for fifteen minutes a day.
she tries to empty her head

but can't figure out how.
after all, she doesn't know what
nothing sounds or looks like,
and the teacher won't give
the slightest clue. yet
she's got a good hunch
the exercise might quiet
all that shriek and clatter
trapped between her ears.
so like a good pupil,
she devotes an entire year
searching for nothing.
some days she's as still
as a stone, but can't
escape the distractions
of river and wind,
footsteps approaching,
birds calling in the trees
overhead. or closing
her eyes, she'll focus
on a cloudless blue sky.
pillows and planes and purple
sunsets keep interrupting.
she silently repeats words
like *ocean* or *why*,
chants sounds that dwell
low in her throat
like *maah* and *uhmm*.
at year's end her teacher
asks if she's found nothing.
she tells him she's found
everything but nothing.
he smiles, *you're closer*
than you think. now
try for twenty minutes.

III

we've all seen them—
looking at their empty
outstretched palms,
and we're fooled, thinking
about what isn't there.
sighing, they marvel
at all they've held in those hands,
their history revealed
in the thickened joints,
the full weight of their desire—
even now, incredible
hands still opening
and grasping
when there's nothing to keep.

IV

without my friend Nothing
on the page, I'd never have to write
another poem. but Nothing waits
here, waving me on, inviting me
to rap and rant, pray sing, testify
what is, was, could, and always will be.
I greet all that's coming,
contained as sheer breath
into word, born
to crave and engrave the emptiness
that Nothing can't stop giving.

(Uyematsu, Amy 2005 "The Weight of Nothing." *Stone, Bow, Prayer*, 72–74. Port Townsend, WA: Copper Canyon Press.)

Author Index

Abbey, Edward 362, 379, 417
Adler, Barbara J. 379, 417
Adsit, Janelle 354, 379, 417
Arum, Richard 140, 417
Atwell, Nancie 122, 140, 417

Bahls, Patrick 379–380, 417
Berke, Jacqueline 57, 66, 203, 213, 417
Bishop, Wendy 87–88, 97, 121, 124, 140, 200–201, 203 213, 417
Bly, Robert 311, 326–327, 409, 418
Brande, Dorothea 53, 66–67, 117, 158, 176, 181, 194, 285, 287, 302, 418, 420
Britton, James 121–122, 139–141, 418
Brookman Harris, Randi xii, 412, 418
Brown, Kurt 379, 417
Burnside, John 354, 380, 418
Busch, Debbie xii, 1, 117, 234, 237–238, 244, 418

Cameron, Julia 70, 80, 108, 117, 157, 181, 194, 197, 213, 307, 327, 418
Campo, Rafael 370, 377, 380, 399, 409, 418
Cerny, Danielle 350, 406
Chekhov, Anton 379–380, 418
Chik, Alice 66, 97, 419
Chomsky, Noam 55, 67, 419
Clark, Michael Dean 97, 379, 419
Colfax, Erin ix, xii, 21, 26, 45, 46, 97, 112, 117, 135, 141, 172, 176, 302, 363, 364, 378, 381, 422
Conroy, Pat 1, 31–32, 45, 109, 160, 176, 419
Costley, Tracey 66, 97, 419
Crimmel, Hal 379–380, 419
Csikszentmihalyi, Mihaly 54, 57, 67, 109, 117, 150, 155, 157, 160, 167, 171, 175–176, 194–196, 213, 288, 303, 419

Davis, Alex xii, 1, 135, 137, 141, 172, 405, 419
DeFronzo, Stefanie xi, xii, 23, 42, 76–77, 80, 90, 92, 107, 121, 138, 225, 394, 416, 419
Dewey, John 67, 419
Dickinson, Emily 123, 258, 263, 419
Doty, Mark 357, 380, 419
Dunn, Stephen 104, 106, 117, 419
Dunne, Pete 65, 67, 419
Dunning, Stephen 185, 194, 253, 262, 263, 419

Elbow, Peter 16, 65, 67, 123, 140–141, 181, 194, 419, 420
Emmert, Mark A. 213, 420
Emig, Janet 19, 26, 141, 303, 420
Englehardt, James 380, 420

Fischl, Peter 378, 380, 420
Fleischman, Paul 4, 7, 420
Fluck, Sandra 213, 420
Forche, Carolyn 348, 380, 420
Forster, E. M. 284, 290 – 294, 297, 302–303, 420, 424
Fortier, Nicole xiii, 355–356, 380, 420

Gardner, John 54, 67, 105, 117, 288, 303, 420
Giles, Sandra 185, 194, 422
Ginsberg, Allen 152, 166, 169
Giovanni, Nikki 35, 40, 45, 420
Glanville, Lauren (Palmer) 132–133, 177, 186
Glanz, James 207, 213, 420
Goldberg, Natalie 287, 303, 420
Gorlewski, Julie 110, 117, 420
Gorlewski, David 110, 117, 420
Gorman, Sheila xiii, 237–239, 244, 420
Gorrell, Nancy xiii–xiv, xvi, xvii, 4–7, 10, 17, 21, 45, 46, 49, 51, 65, 81–82, 97, 107, 112, 117, 141, 135, 141, 146–147, 172, 176, 197, 198, 212, 213, 220, 222–223, 232, 232, 234, 244, 245, 247, 250, 253, 254, 261, 262, 263, 265–270, 279, 281–282, 302, 303, 308, 310–311, 316, 320–321, 329–330, 352, 364, 378, 380–381, 406, 409, 420–422
Groopman, Jerome 371, 379, 381, 422
Gutkowski, Mark vii, x, 8–10, 21, 413

Handel, Steven N. x, xiv, 22, 55, 58, 202, 206–207, 213, 226–228, 231–232, 256–259, 263, 414, 422
Harper, Graeme 26, 422
Hauser, Judd 142, 145–147
Hemingway, Ernest 101
Hergenrader, Trent 97, 379, 419
Hess, Mark 93, 119–120, 187–188
Higginson, William J. 194, 422
Hipple, Ted 110, 112, 114, 117, 199, 213, 422
Hollander, John 381, 409, 422
Hunley, Tom C. 66, 97, 98, 141,185, 193, 422, 425

Ingham, Harrington 278–279, 423
Ingle, Erin A. 375–376, 381, 409, 422

Kaufman, Sarah Beth 142–143, 154–155, 273–274, 414–415, 422
Kim, Michelle xiv, 204–205, 213, 422
Kingsporn, Geoff 250, 262
Klass, Perri 379, 381, 422
Kleist, Heinrich von 303, 422
Kunitz, Stanley 283, 302

Lasky, Dorothea 67, 423
Lavin, Colleen x, 384–385
Le Guin, Ursula K. 2, 280, 303, 423
Leonhardt, David 113, 116–117, 409, 423
Lester, Julius 248, 250, 263, 423
Lim, Shirley Geok-lin 104, 118, 122, 141, 423

Longfellow, Henry Wadsworth 231–232, 423
Lowell, Robert 185
Luft, Joseph 278–279, 423
Lynch, Kasey x, 390
Lysiak, Alexandra x, 387

Macrorie, Ken 16, 181, 194, 202, 213, 423
Mancia, Jocelyn Andrade x, 389–390
Marsen, Sky 54, 67, 423
May, Rollo 47, 55, 67, 69–70, 80, 158, 176, 180, 185, 194, 245, 263, 308, 327, 423
Mayers, Tim 26, 27, 58, 66, 67, 97, 423
McGuinn, Haven x, 391
Menand, Louis 104, 118, 423
Merton, Robert K. 292, 302, 303, 423–424
Mervosh, Sarah 113, 118, 424
Millan, Harriet Levin 97, 424
Moffett, James 16, 122, 141, 424
Moneyhun, Clyde 39, 46, 424
Mueller, Michael 362, 375–376, 377, 381, 382, 409, 410, 422, 427
Moxley, Joseph 32, 57, 67, 103, 106, 118, 141, 424
Mueller, Michael 362, 375–376, 377, 381, 382, 409, 410, 422, 427

Nadolny, Barbara x, 49, 65, 434–436

Oates, Joyce Carol 283, 303, 424
Orbeta, Amarie x, 383, 385–387
Osbourn, Anne 302, 368–369, 379, 381, 406, 409, 424–425
Ostrom, Hans 88, 97, 418

Padgett, Ron 185, 194, 381, 425
Palmer, Parker 71, 80, 194, 425
Peary, Alexandria 20, 27, 46, 62, 67, 97–98, 122, 124,135,139, 141, 404, 410, 420, 425
Pennington, Martha C. xii, xviii, 24, 38, 46, 54, 66, 67, 97, 106–108, 118, 141, 302, 424
Pfahler, Ella x, 61, 229–231
Phillips, Don 252, 263, 425
Pinsky, Robert 347, 353–354, 381, 425
Pirrie, Jill 379, 381, 425
Pitt, David xiv, 107, 172–173, 176, 367–368, 378, 381, 405, 425
Proust, Marcel 361, 363, 382, 425

Quinn, Shane x, 392–393, 407

Rein, Joseph 97, 379, 419
Rilke, Rainer Maria 125, 141, 217, 232, 233, 244, 425
Robinson, Jordan x, 393–394, 407
Robinson, Sir Ken 4, 73, 80, 81, 98, 108, 112, 118
Rosenberg, Elise xiv, 61, 274, 311–113, 327, 407–408, 410, 426
Rothman, Marni xiv, 237–238, 244, 426, 433
Roska, Josipa 140, 417
Roth, Wolff-Michael 382, 426

Scholes, Robert 196, 213, 309, 327, 426
Schraffenberger, Jeremy 380, 420
Schwartz, Anne xv, 364–366, 382, 419, 426
Schwartz, Mimi 117, 118, 419, 426
Shelnutt, Eve 105, 118, 426

Siebert, Arielle 262, 263, 426
Stafford, William xiii, 185, 194, 253, 262, 263, 265, 279, 284, 286, 288, 303, 419, 426 4
Stewart, Arthur J. xi, xv, 22, 43–44, 46, 62–64, 66, 68, 90, 94–95, 96, 98, 99, 114–115, 118, 190–191, 194, 195, 209–212, 213–214, 275–278, 279, 298–301, 304, 314–315, 317, 323–327, 340–341, 344, 362, 376, 377, 382, 394, 398-399, 410, 415, 426–427
Swanger, David 197, 214, 269, 270, 279, 427
Swedberg, Richard 55, 68, 290, 294, 302, 304, 427
Sweeney, Matthew 379, 381, 425
Swenson, May 105, 118, 427

Tippins, Deborah J. 362, 376, 377, 382, 410, 427

Ubben, Gary 68, 427
Uyematsu, Amy xi, viii, xv, xvi, 22, 44, 74–75, 76, 79–80, 156–157, 173–176, 192–193, 194, 208–209, 214, 241–243, 244, 328, 331–333, 334–335, 336–339, 344, 379, 415–416, 428, 437–439

Vel, Shivani x, 393

Wark, Krista 262, 264, 428, 429
Warner, John 201, 212, 214, 429
Warriner, John E 199
Weisstuch, Liza 370, 382, 429
Wellons, Jay 371, 382, 429
Williams, William Carlos 186, 194, 236, 244, 379 382, 429
Wisloff, Mary x, 389
Wolf, Lone (Apache Shaman) 11–12, 56, 397–399
Wright, Richard 319, 327, 429

Subject Index

Academic essay 55, 201–202, 206, 212
Alliance for Young Artists & Writers 349
Apprentice 101–105, 126, 318
Apprenticeship 104–105
ARTifacts 348–349, 354
Assessment 111–112, 116, 127, 131, 173, 212, 342, 404
see also Contract grading, Portfolio
Attitude 34–38, 53, 69, 89–90, 96, 114, 121, 125–129, 148, 150–151, 168, 189, 250, 318
Audience 17, 130, 246, 249, 251–252, 256, 258, 265–279, 294–296, 298, 314, 374, 406
Authentic writing 37, 179, 314

Baggage 13–14, 74, 99–117, 199, 269, 399
Basic students 24, 38–39, 328, 333, 404
Belief 12, 16, 33–34, 101, 114, 125, 195, 205, 211, 295, 366

Closed form poetry 169, 186–187
Co-learner xvii, 16, 25, 70–71, 73–74, 102, 126–127, 211, 253, 291, 295, 317–318, 326, 358
Collaboration 21, 41, 251, 255, 353, 361, 372, 387–388, 394, 403
Community of writers 161, 102, 127–129, 148, 150, 313, 317
Contract grading 45, 136, 140, 404
see also Assessment, Portfolio
Courage
Creative 72–74, 76–80, 111, 400, 404
Moral 72, 74, 76–79
COVID-19 112, 117, 139, 359, 373, 383, 386, 395, 397, 402
see also Pandemic
Creative act vii, 16, 24, 55–59, 64, 72, 109, 158–159, 185, 221, 252
Creative literacy 97, 108, 111, 124, 336, 352, 361
Creative teaching 53, 55, 97, 159, 170
Creative theorizing 55, 290, 294
Creative Writing Across the Curriculum (CWAC) 19–20, 62, 256, 293, 352, 404
Creative writing elective 3, 26, 93, 111, 120, 124, 126, 129, 131, 133–134, 143, 168, 185
Creativity, definition of 53–56
Creativity, types of
High-/low-level 54
Large C/small c 54, 109
Species-specific 55

Creativity and literacy xvii, 16, 20, 40, 97, 361, 403–404
Creative personality 54, 167, 170–171, 179
Creative writing workshop 133
  see also Poetry writing workshop, Workshop, Workshop model, Workshopping, Writing workshop
Creativity workshop 108
Curious Science Writers / curiousSCIENCEwriters (cSw) ix, 302, 353, 361, 372, 374
  see also Young Science Writers
Curious Young Writers / curiousYOUNGwriters (cYw) ix, 361, 374–375
  see also Young Science Writers

"Diamond in the rough" 130, 132, 137
"Diamond" introduction 201–202, 206–207
Dual genre poem 188
Dual nature of the writer 285–286, 302

Ecological creative writing 357, 361
Ecological ecphrasis 361
Ecological pedagogies 405
Ecosocial justice 358, 361, 367–368
Ecphrasis 351–354, 369, 377, 406
  see also Ecological ecphrasis
Ecphrastic poetry 351–354, 369, 377, 406
Education, definition as *educere* 47–48
Empathy 107, 169, 330, 351–352, 359, 362, 368, 378, 406
Endemicity, teaching in 402
Exposition 203, 319
Expository writing 57, 62
Extremis
  Moment of 317
  Poems produced in 348
  Teaching in 359
Faith
  Of students and teachers 4, 6–7, 32, 34, 86, 110, 160, 399
  Of a writer 282–284
  Religious 364, 366
  see also Unshakeable faith
Feedback 26, 66, 127, 152, 254, 289
Fieldwork 14, 354
  see also Place-based pedagogy
Five-paragraph essay 199, 201–202, 212
Five-step creative process 288
Flow 54, 57, 59, 63, 148, 160, 170, 181–182, 191, 218, 223, 235–236, 258, 265–280, 283, 285–286, 301, 308–309
Forster aphorism 284, 290–294, 297, 302
Found poetry 246–248, 250–253
Freedom and structure, 170, 177–194, 285
Freewriting 127, 140, 148, 153, 180–183, 189, 291, 295
  see also Interrupted journal writing, Nonstop writing

Genre 20–21, 45, 54, 62, 91, 112, 134–135, 171, 188, 190, 249, 252, 362, 364, 405
  see also Dual genre poem
Genre approach 247, 249–250
Gifted student 24, 107, 155, 158–176, 328, 404

Grasshopper 3–6, 126, 203, 347, 383, 405
 see also Spontaneous lesson

Hawk watch x–xi, 56, 65, 180, 376, 389, 433–435
Hybrid pedagogies 361

Identities
 Of students 36, 127, 144–145, 149, 253, 255, 261, 360
 Of teacher 12–3, 17, 24, 251, 253, 269, 360, 400
Imitation 185, 193, 286
Imitation poem 185
Inter-arts project 352–36, 403, 405
 see also "Jersey Rain" project
Inter-arts students 150, 103
Interdisciplinary literacy 62, 135, 240, 352, 361–362, 372, 405
Interdisciplinary projects 352, 362, 377–378
Interrupted journal writing 183
 see also Freewriting, Nonstop writing

"Jersey Rain" project 353–354
Johari Window 270–271, 278, 405–408
Journal, definition for this book 23

Leaping poetry 311, 313, 305–327, 409

Math poetry 44, 74, 107, 172–173, 190, 378–379
Medical narrative 371
Memoir 22, 25, 31, 59, 76, 79, 96, 154, 159–160, 171, 224, 243, 272–273, 301–302, 323, 326, 330–331, 335, 342–343, 371, 379
Memory association 218, 222–225, 229–230, 295
Memory chain 220, 222–224, 229–230
Memory writing 218, 221–222, 231, 271
Muse, poetic 22, 185
Muse, teaching as ix, 7, 9–10, 12, 14–15, 17, 19, 37, 328, 333, 398, 400, 403
Muse, writing 166, 169, 185–186, 295–298, 412
Muses, the 8–10

Narrative 184, 189, 201, 231, 319–321, 323, 326, 371
Narrative medicine 371, 379
Nonstop writing 132, 190, 261
 see also Freewriting, Interrupted journal writing
Obstacles 13, 14, 58, 108
Openness 53, 169, 330, 358
Our Town Book Project 353–354

Pandemic x, xii, 14, 61, 66, 79, 112–113, 116, 229, 359, 362, 373, 377, 383–384, 386–389, 396–398, 400–407, 409
 see also COVID-19
Pandemic poem x, 404, 407
 see also Students in the window
Personification 256, 261, 325
Photo-journalism 351–352, 359
Photography 351, 353–354, 358–360, 375
Place-based pedagogy 354, 357, 378
 see also Fieldwork

Poem challenge 308, 323, 325
Poem pals project 197–198, 212, 253
Poetic stances 351
Poetry watch x, 50–52, 56, 65, 433–434
Poetry writing workshop 353
see also Creative writing workshop, Workshop, Workshop model, Workshopping, Writing workshop,
Portfolio 45, 73, 131, 145, 159, 163, 204, 309, 311, 404
see also Assessment, Grading
Post-pandemic 14, 359
Pre-pandemic 404, 407
Project-based learning (PBL) 65, 376, 406
Process writing 15, 26, 66, 123, 200, 283–284, 291, 314

Receptivity 53, 285, 358
Rhetorical approach 200, 203–204

Science, Art and Writing Initiative (SAW) 361, 368–370, 406
Science poetry ix, xii, 21–22, 45, 62, 65, 85, 107, 112, 135–137, 171–172, 240, 298, 352, 361, 364, 367–369, 377–378, 405, 415
Scientific literacy 172, 243, 403
Self-affirmation 36, 193, 404
Self-discovery xvii, 16, 145, 221, 224, 231, 235, 242, 246, 269, 321
Self-doubt 13–14, 378
Self-learning xvii, 16
Self-publishing 254, 260, 353–354
Serendipity 293–294
Sharing circle 26, 41, 51, 56, 65–66, 105, 116, 139, 147, 149
Sonnet 80, 169, 186–187, 194
Speaking, act of 80, 169, 186–187, 194
Spontaneous lesson 4, 13, 49–50, 52–53, 58, 112, 126, 347, 359, 400, 411
STEAM (science, technology, engineering, arts, and mathematics) xi, 64, 66, 77, 259–260, 361–362, 368, 375–377, 391, 406, 415
STEM (science, technology, engineering, and mathematics) xi, 64, 77, 259–260, 293, 362, 376–377, 406, 415
Stream of consciousness 140, 183, 193, 218, 223, 225–226, 291
Students in the window 383–394
Subconscious, the 222, 291, 297
see also Unconscious, the

Tchelitchew, Pavel 157
Teaching poetry 101, 172, 185, 197, 212, 271
Trust the process 15, 88, 399
Tyranny of the T's 110–112, 199

Unconscious, the 181, 283–286, 289, 327
see also Subconscious, the
Unshakeable faith 32–33

Villanelle 169, 187–188, 194
Voice
Authentic 254
Individual 126, 150, 172

Inner 33, 37, 120, 182, 256, 265, 286
Personal 59

Walk poem 188, 355–356, 405
Windows, defined for this book 53
Windows pedagogy 53, 404
Works in progress 12–13, 31–45, 74, 126, 132, 148, 150, 170, 291, 403, 411
Workshop 14, 16, 26, 66, 92, 99, 105, 116, 125–126, 128, 139, 278, 371, 378
see also Creative writing workshop, Workshop model, Workshopping, Writing workshop
Workshop model 122
Workshopping 66
Writing Across the Curriculum (WAC) xviii, 16, 19, 39, 54, 114, 122, 135, 204, 377
see also Creative Writing Across the Curriculum (CWAC)
Writing for your students 318–322, 407
Writing to your students 314–317, 322
Writing with your students 18, 307–314, 322, 325
Writing workshop 22–23, 92–93, 105, 133
see also Creative writing workshop, Poetry writing workshop, Workshop, Workshop model, Workshopping

Young Science Writers 374
Youth Birding Alaska (YBA) project 65, 302, 361, 375–376, 405–406